A

HITCH

IN

TIME

A YOUNG MAN'S COMING OF

AGE ON A JOURNEY

THROUGH

COLONIAL AFRICA

A HITCH IN TIME

A
HITCH
IN
TIME

IAIN FINLAY

HighAdventureProductions.com

Australia

Published in Australia
by
High Adventure Publishing
highadventureproductions.com
Tumbulgum, 2490 Australia

Copyright © Iain Finlay 2016
ISBN10:   0-9941793-0-8
ISBN13:   978-0-9941793-0-2

Cataloguing-in-Publishing data:
Finlay, Iain 1935 -

A Hitch in Time... a young man's coming of age on a journey
through colonial Africa

-1.Africa -travel.-2..Africa- Social life and customs – 3.history 20th century—4. Adult education

Maps: Our appreciation and gratitude to nationsonline.com for providing all but two of the maps used throughout the book.

DEDICATION

For Noel White and Shorty Bronkhorst
without whom I might not have made
the journeys....
and for my grandchildren
that their paths may be as rewarding

Also by Iain Finlay
THE AZANIAN ASSIGNMENT
SAVAGE JUNGLE

By Iain Finlay & Trish Clark
AFRICA OVERLAND
*SOUTH AMERICA OVERLAND
*ACROSS THE SOUTH PACIFIC
GOOD MORNING HANOI
THE SILK TRAIN

Titles marked with an asterisk were originally
published under Trish's previous name,
Trish Sheppard.

Notes on the text:

This book has been written in several stages. A forty-page draft...an overview of the two African journeys, was written in 1956 during the five-week voyage on board the Norwegian freighter MV Themis, on which I worked my passage from Norway home to Australia. Then the story languished, untouched for forty years until, around 1996, I resurrected it. Using scores of letters I had written to my parents and grandparents, telling of our adventures in the 1950s...which they had kept and passed on to me...I was able to recall many more of the events and people and flesh out the story almost to its current form.

Again, because events, as they do, change the course of our lives, the manuscript was put aside and forgotten. Now, a further twenty years down the track, its been resurrected again. This time, as I also mention in the Introduction, I felt there was a need, because of the vast differences in what Africa was like in those distant days, when compared to present-day Africa, to add some up-dating paragraphs in each chapter. These are intended to give some idea of what has happened in each of the fifteen countries I passed through...first with my Australian mate Noel White and then with Shorty Bronkhorst, from South Africa (its actually 16 countries now... counting the relatively new nation of South Sudan). These additional updating comments are written in *italics*.

Also, in the mid-1950s, at the time of our travels in Africa, we would normally have talked about distances in miles, feet and inches, having been brought up on the Imperial system of measurements. However, after a year in Europe, the decimal system did not seem so foreign to us, and, despite the fact that through most of eastern and southern Africa, the Imperial ystem still prevailed at the time, and as kilometres, metres and centimetres are now the universally accepted system...(with the exception of the United States), I have converted nearly all references to distance to the metric system.

AFRICA
Routes followed South and North
in 1955 and 1956
(map shows 2016 nations)

CONTENTS

Chapter	Title	Page

INTRODUCTION

I was not quite twenty years old at the time all this happened. Noel White, my best friend and companion through most of it, was 21. Although we haven't seen a great deal of each other over the sixty odd years that have passed since then...with him living in the United States and me in various parts of the world...he has remained a life-long good friend. Looking back on it, without him as a travelling companion, I may never have experienced the extraordinary adventure that he and I shared in Africa in 1955 and 1956. An adventure, as you'll see, that really began one night in Casablanca.

Lately I find I've been thinking quite a lot about those times. I'm sure, as everybody says, its just something that comes with advancing years... the acceptance of one's own mortality, a realisation that life doesn't go on for ever, coupled with a sort of yearning to be able to recapture the experiences of days gone by. Yet these recent thoughts have been far from morbid. Rather they've been highly pleasurable recollections, full of nostalgia and delight from the recalled memories of those great experiences as a young man, during the mid nineteen-fifties, in a Europe not yet fully recovered from the horrors of World War and an Africa that still consisted almost entirely of European colonies and possessions.

I had no idea when I hitch-hiked through Africa at that time that I was making the journeys at a crucial point in time; the last gasp before a period of momentous change for the whole continent. I was, as they say, a 'callow youth', with no other motives, or interests other than the adventure of the journeys and the fascination of Africa.

Its only with the benefit of these many years of hindsight and several subsequent journeys throughout Africa that I have been able to put it into some sort of perspective and recognise the amazing opportunity it presented and how lucky I was to have experienced it all at that time.

Obviously Africa was very different then from how it is today. Most of North Africa, for example, was either under French rule or, in the case of

Libya, run by the British. It was also possible to travel from Cairo all the way to Capetown and, for the whole distance, always be in a country that was either under direct rule from Britain, or at least some form of serious British influence.

A British company controlled the Suez Canal, for instance, and there were still British troops and air bases in Egypt on the Canal Zone. The Sudan was the Anglo-Egyptian Sudan, jointly ruled by Britain and Egypt. Kenya, Uganda and Tanganyika (Tanzania) were British colonies. Northern Rhodesia (Zambia) and Southern Rhodesia (Zimbabwe) were both colonies, joined in a Federation with a third British colonial territory, Nyasaland (Malawi)... and the status of the Union of South Africa, as a member of the British Commonwealth, was similar to that of Canada and Australia. Other European powers, Belgium, Portugal and France ruled the rest of central and southern Africa.

Trying to document all of the changes that have occurred over sixty odd years in fifteen or so countries, to try to bring things up to date, didn't quite seem to fit with the overall theme of the book. So I've confined that aspect to some relatively brief comments in each chapter, which I hope give some concept of the massive changes that have swept the continent since our journeys through it.

In general though, thinking back on it all, I suppose the fact of being European must have made things easier for us, that is, myself and Noel, on our way south through Africa in 1955 and then, with Shorty Bronkhorst, a South African, on the way north in 1956. But we were always almost broke and couldn't afford to do anything but sleep out and to hitch-hike, which in itself had a great levelling effect. One was automatically put in the position of a being a supplicant... of asking a favour. Of course, we were not right at the 'bottom of the ladder'... but a fair way down.

I think though, in retrospect, that all of the hitch-hiking I did in Europe and Africa and also in Australia, at different times, has been good for the soul. The need to get on with people at all levels during those two years in Africa and Europe more than likely had a greater impact on me than I would have generally realised.

I'm convinced now that the experiences I had on those journeys, before I had even turned twenty one, set me on a path and perhaps even shaped my life. In particular, the concept of risk-taking, of not being frightened to jump in at the deep end and then survive, in whatever circumstances... has been a part of my life ever since that time.

I also know that I tend to feel a little uncomfortable whenever I become too settled and I am never happier than when I'm on the road.

I suppose the whole experience also had a few negative impacts, although I can't think of many. I do know that the endless hassles we always seemed to be confronted with by immigration authorities in Africa, as we made our way across the continent, then down and up again, left me quite irrationally paranoid about crossing frontiers and passing through immigration posts. Its there even now. But overall, it was a wonderfully enlightening experience that set the scene for a lifetime in which I have found real enjoyment in travel, both rough and smooth, an interest in the world as a whole and in the wider community of peoples. At the end of the journeys I was not the same young man that had set out. But, perhaps best of all, I find it interesting to think that every individual is a part of history, however insignificant that part might be and that I and my two mates, hitching through Africa in the 'fifties were also a little part of history...well, at least as observers.

oooooo

MOROCCO

MOROCCO

1

THERE'S ONE BORN EVERY MINUTE

They say there's one born every minute and on that night in 1955...June 24th it was... when Noel and I staggered, blind drunk, off the Danish freighter *Tekla Torm* in Casablanca harbour, I fitted that quote to a tee. Not sure whether its a 'sucker' born every minute, or a 'fool', but I definitely matched that other quote: 'a fool and his money are soon parted'... as I was to find out, in a rather nasty way even before leaving the docks.

Noel and I had joined the *Tekla Torm* in Genoa as deckhands, simply to work our passage to Casablanca.In those days, it was easier than it is now to sign on for work on ships without a seaman's ticket. And we definitely weren't seamen. We'd spent the past year in Europe, hitch-hiking around and working in Norway as lumberjacks and in Britain in all sorts of jobs... from toy salesmen to lavatory cleaners. More of that in a moment, but, as this night could technically be seen as the beginning of a great adventure in Africa, I'd better fill in a few details.

The *Tekla Torm*, a vessel of some 7,000 or 8,000 tonnes, owned by the Torm Lines and registered in Copenhagen, sailed directly from Genoa to Casablanca, a journey of about three days. Noel and I had been taken on, on the understanding that we only wanted to go as far as North Africa and not on to its main destination, New York. We probably could have continued on there if we'd wanted to...I don't know, it may have been that they would have needed experienced seamen for that. Anyway, our work on board certainly required very little experience. We chipped rust and painted decks, railings and various items of the ship's superstructure, as well as doing whatever the bosun told us, the whole way. It was a breeze. The weather was fine, the food was good... and the company too.

Because we'd spent time, the previous autumn, working in a forest in Norway and later at a paper factory in Lillehammer, we both had a smattering of Norwegian which the Danish crew of the *Tekla Torm* seemed to be able to understand. But their English, like that of most Scandinavians, was excellent anyway, so we got on well together, particularly in the mess, over dinner and a Karlsberg or two.

'We went on the tour of the Tuborg Brewery, when we were in Copenhagen last year,' I told them. 'We didn't get around to doing the Karlsberg tour, but I believe it is just as good.'

They all laughed. Most of them had also been on either one, or both of the brewery visits at some stage. 'You should have,' one of them said. '...the Karlsberg tour is better. They give you more beer to drink at the end.'

That evening, around 7.30 PM, full of faith and confidence that we would shortly be on our way south, to the Belgian Congo and maybe the Rhodesian copper belt, we left the Casablanca Youth Hostel to walk down to the docks for our farewell dinner with the crew on board the *Tekla Torm*.

On board, we talked about Copenhagen...about Tivoli Gardens.. and other things we'd seen. We told them we had met some Danish girls who had taken us home and given us Danish open sandwiches.'

'Ha! Is that all they gave you...open sandwiches?' they laughed.

'There was no time,' Noel protested, almost apologetically. 'We had to move on,' and then, as if to compensate for an apparent lack of initiative on our part, went on to tell them that more recently, over the past few weeks, we'd been hitch-hiking with two beautiful girls from Oslo. 'We've been sleeping in barns and under hedges, as well as in youth hostels and little pensions all across France, Austria and Italy... almost right up until we joined the ship.'

'Oho,' they guffawed and chortled, 'Why didn't you bring them with you?'

'Well, they wanted to come with us...at least they said they did. But in the end they were too sensible. They went back to Oslo to their studies. They were at University there.'

In Casablanca, although we had signed off and left the ship on the morning of its arrival to look for the city's main youth hostel, we had planned to return to the ship on the following evening for...well, for want of a better word, a party. The crew, whom we'd got on so well with, wanted to give us dinner and something of a sendoff before they sailed. So, on leaving the ship and having located the hostel on a map, we made our way there, carrying our only possessions in two somewhat battered, but well-worn rucksacks.

Getting to the hostel was an experience in itself. It was not far from the Port...walking distance of only fifteen or twenty minutes, but it was right in the middle of the old Arab quarter of the city, the Medina, which we found teeming with life and such frenetic activity that it was initially a little unsettling, if not frightening, particularly in the light of the unrest and animosity that existed between the Arabs and the French at that time.

We had been in Middle Eastern towns like Aden, Port Said and Suez, as well as Colombo, in Ceylon on the sea voyage from Australia to Europe, just a year before. To some extent all that had been an introduction to the so-called sights, sounds and smells of the orient. But on those occasions, we had been stepping off a big, secure ship for a brief foray, with a group of others, into a foreign world to return to that same ship-board security a few hours later, carrying our carved souvenirs, postcards, cheap watches and lots of photographs, to then sail on to the next port.

Now we suddenly found ourselves in the midst of it all; a potentially hostile environment, on a semi-permanent basis, with no apparent support mechanism close at hand.

There was an uneasy air about the city...a sort of troubled and restive frustration because of a desired, but as yet unfulfilled independence for the country, the prospect of which Arab and French inhabitants of Casablanca and the rest of Morocco had been living with for several years. Although Moroccan separatists had not yet chosen the open confrontation of an armed revolution, like that launched only six months previously in neighbouring Algeria, an uncomfortable and anxious tenseness, with great potential for violence, permeated the whole country. Jeeps carrying white-capped Foreign Legionnaires back and forth along the boulevardes and on the outskirts of the Arab quarter had apparently become much more common in recent months.

Casablanca in those days had a population of about a million, with something like twelve to thirteen million people for the whole country... including about 650,000 French farmers, settlers and civil

'Noel and I had joined the Tekla Torm in Genoa as deckhands...'

'Broad avenues radiated out from the Place de Liberté...'

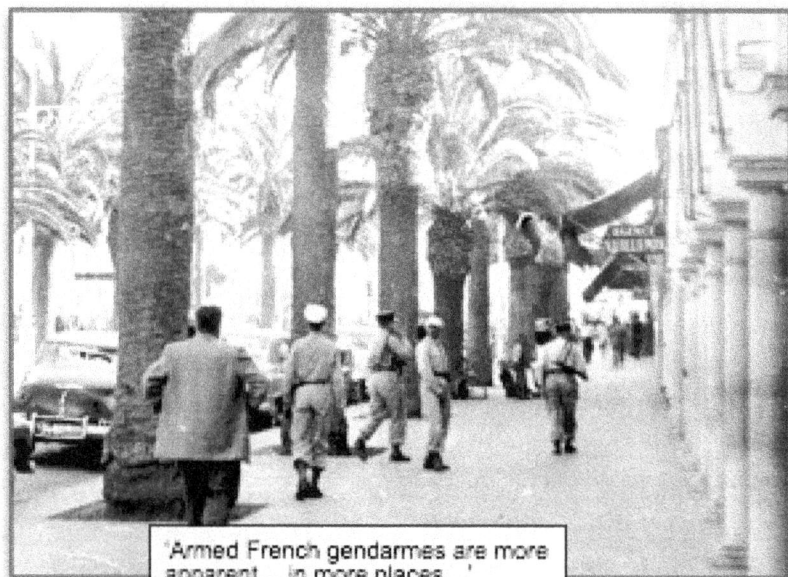

'Armed French gendarmes are more apparent... in more places...'

servants. Morocco had been occupied by the French in 1907 and administered since then as a French Protectorate. Although predominantly Arab in population and Muslim in religion... the impact of French and Western culture was widespread... particularly in Casablanca.

Beyond the confines of the Medina lay the main modern town of Casablanca, largely built by the French. Broad avenues radiated out from the Place de Liberté, intersected by ring roads that reached the coast on either side of the harbour. Tree-lined avenues with high-rise apartments sat close by to the business and administrative centres of the town, where the banks, hotels and large, modern shops were located. To the west of the central district, stretching to the coast, were the gardens and villas of the upper and middle-class residential districts. However, on the outskirts of the city, kilometres of shanty towns testified to the existence of a large under-class of much poorer, and disadvantaged people.

The Medina was what was left of the original Arab town called Anfa that was first settled in the 12th century. Still enclosed in part by ancient rampart walls, the area is a maze of narrow streets and whitewashed brick or stone houses. The aromas of sandalwood and saffron mingled with those of smoke and leather and of shish-kebabs cooking on charcoal fires. Dark Arab men with curly moustaches and wearing red fez's, or loose white turbans, brushed past. Beggars stood hunched over, or crouched on the ground, with their hands held out to us and other passers by. Women in long, all-concealing burkhas... the niqab veils pulled high over their noses, leaving only their dark eyes to be seen, as they hurried busily about their errands, shopping for vegetables and spices in the market stalls along the winding lanes, while ragged children ran and played, weaving their way, as we were also, through the crowd.

Our initial concerns quickly evaporated however, as we walked, with the realisation that we were hardly noticed and when we were, it was generally with a friendly acknowledgement or wave.

Then, before too long, we finally found the Auberge de la Jeunesse, where we showed the manager, an affable Frenchman in his late forties or early fifties, our hostel membership cards and booked in.

Like most houses in the older parts of Casablanca, whose exteriors faced onto narrow and busy lanes or streets, the outside was unprepossessing. It had only a big set of double wooden doors, with no windows facing onto the street. But inside, it opened onto a wide, stone-paved courtyard with whitewashed walls that was surrounded by a shaded cloister that ran completely around the courtyard, with a dining room, sitting room, dormitories, washing and toilet facilities and other rooms opening off. From the second floor, above the cloister, whitewashed steps led up to the roof, where the residents hung out their washing to dry.

We also quickly discovered, as in almost any other youth hostel, lots of people in similar circumstances and of like mind, that is: young, not much money, already done lots of interesting travelling and planning on doing much more. There were several young French men and women, as well as Dutch, Germans, Danes...and we two Australians, who were the object of initial amazement.

'Australia!?' one of the Germans, called Dieter, exclaimed. 'What the hell are you doing here?'

'Well, what the hell are you doing here?' I retorted... with a smile, although I thought his question a bit aggressive. 'We're just doing the same as you...' I went on. 'Well, almost. We're having a look around and then figuring out where to go next.'

'Yes, but... but, its different for us. We're from Europe. Australia is so far away.'

'No. Europe is so far away. It just depends on how you look at it.'

'Okay, Okay,' He shrugged. I guess its just a bit unusual to see Australians here.'

How long have you been here? I asked.

'Three months.'

'Three months!? what are you doing?' Noel asked.

'There are two of us. He gestured to his friend Max. We've been down to Marrakech and up into the Atlas. We get a little work here from a German travel agent...taking tourists around. What about you.? What are you guys planning to do?'

'We want to get to South Africa. Know anybody heading there?'

'South Africa!' he blurted. 'How...How the hell are you going to get there?'

We told him about working our way to Casablanca on a ship. and that we hoped to find another one heading south.

He nodded. 'Hell...' It seemed to be his favourite English expression. 'That's a hell of an idea. how are you going to do it?'

'Just keep trying the ships in the port.'

On the following morning we began trying. It was a relatively easy process in those days, at least in Casablanca. At the entrance to the Port, after showing our passports and the papers we'd received on signing off from the *Tekla Torm*, we could approach whatever ships we wanted to in search of jobs. And after three or four vessels, which were not going in the right direction, we suddenly seemed to have struck it lucky. There was a Belgian ship in port which was due to sail, in two days time, for Matadi, a port about 150 kilometres up the Congo River, on the border of the then Belgian Congo and the Portuguese territory of Angola.

'From there you go further south to Lobito, where you might be able to get on a coal train.'

Our informant was a Dutch crew member on the ship, whom we spoke to on the deck after our first brief meeting with the Captain. On the bridge deck we'd been told by the chain-smoking skipper, a sallow, sleazy, pock-marked man who looked as though he was around seventy, but was probably only fifty and as though he wouldn't last the voyage himself, that there was a possibility we could ship out on the Belgian ship as unpaid deckhands. We should come back the next day with our papers for him to check through and make up his mind.

'Where do the coal trains go?' I asked the Dutch crew member.

'Right across the Congo, almost into Northern Rhodesia,' he replied. 'To the Copperbelt.'

'The Copperbelt?'

'Uh huh' he nodded. 'The huge copper mines in the eastern part of the Congo... and into Rhodesia. If you're white, you can make a lot of money there. Its like South Africa. There's big money on the mines.'

The information was filed in both our memory banks for future recall.

That evening, around 7.30 pm, full of faith and confidence that we would shortly be on our way south, to the Belgian Congo and maybe the Rhodesian copper belt, we left the hostel to walk down to the docks once more for our farewell dinner with the crew on board the *Tekla Torm*. On the waterfront, the scene was superficially calm. Apart from a couple of ships being worked under floodlight, most of the Arab wharf labourers had gone home. The temperature, even at this time of night, was almost thirty degrees celsius and the windless air was like velvet. Patches of yellow electric light lay in small circles along the wharf beside where the *Tekla Torm* and two other ships were tied with long hawsers, one behind the other. Lights were glistening and music floated from these and other ships tied up on nearby wharves.

On board the *Tekla Torm* we were welcomed by the crew... the deck crew mind you...not the officers. We were all crammed in around a big table in the tiny mess room by the stern galley. In other words, beneath the poop deck, as far from the bridge and the officers' quarters as you could get.

Out came the Karlsberg... and Tuborg! Out came a bottle of Dutch Bols gin and Johnny Walker scotch. There was dinner in the middle somewhere. I can't remember what it was. Fish of some sort and cheese I think, and Danish roe. But the drinking and laughter continued from the start, until around 11.30 pm when things really began to get out of hand.

Noel, who has always been a fairly competitive spirit, must have said something about Australian swimmers being the best in the world.

'Bullshit,' one of the Danes scoffed good-naturedly. 'You might have a few good swimmers, but that doesn't mean everybody can win medals.'

Everybody was shouting. They all had something to say. They we're all trying to make themselves heard.

'Alright, alright,' Noel was also yelling, his voice slurred. 'But. I'll bet the average Aussie is a better swimmer than the average Dane.'

More raucous shouts and then Jan, a young man who'd worked on the deck with us during the past few days, was suddenly on his feet. 'So,' he said, pulling his shirt open with a hiccup, 'do I look like an average Dane?' His chest was slim and bony and pure white.

The room fell silent for a moment. Noel shook his a head a bit and laughed. 'I don't know. I haven't done much research, but I guess so....you could be.'

'Alright,' Jan said, peeling his shirt right off, then beginning to remove his pants and shoes. 'An average Dane...' He moved to the door and opened it onto the stern deck. Everybody followed, or began pushing to get out onto the deck. 'An average Dane...' he shouted again. ' Lets see what an average Australian can do.' Jan began climbing, in his jockey shorts, up onto the railing.

Noel & I looked at each other, and then over the railing. At least thirty feet below in the blackness was the water of Casablanca harbour. But there was no way you could see what was there. 'Jesus,' I muttered.

Jan dived out into the night.

The crew cheered.

Jan surfaced. The crew cheered again. Somebody ran to get a rope ladder.

Noel and I looked at each other again.

'Well, mate,' Noel said. 'This is what comes from having a big mouth.' He began to take off his clothes. I did the same.

Moments later Noel was standing in the same spot on the railing. 'Here goes nothing,' He yelled. 'Banzai' and dived into the blackness.

He surfaced, with a cry of triumph. Then I followed, jumping, instead of diving.

The water was surprisingly cold at first, but down there, our eyes becoming accustomed to the gloom, we could see more. A small boat was tied alongside the *Tekla Torm*, we'd missed it by only a few metres.

The rope ladder came flopping down the side of the ship and Jan started climbing up. The others at the top were all yelling out in Danish... Jan yelled back and pointed to where the dinghy was. Then suddenly everybody else started jumping, and screaming at the top of their lungs as they came down.

Eight or ten minutes of pure madness in the dark... climbing back up the rope ladder and leaping in again, each time trying to do something more outrageous. Then we were all back on the deck, drying off, putting our clothes back on and drinking hot tea, heavily spiked with rum, with one of the crew deciding to tell us now that large sharks have been seen in Casablanca harbour on many occasions!

Half an hour after that we were on the gangway, saying our goodbyes...with cartons of cigarettes that had been thrust on us, wrapped in a Danish flag that had been pulled from the aft flagpole and heading on our way back to the youth hostel. As we reached the bottom of the gangway, Jan called out and ran down after us. Noel, who had not heard him, kept on walking and singing to himself, while I waited for Jan.

'I have a secret,' he said. 'You can tell Noel later. I am not an average Danish swimmer. When I was a student, I was the champion diver for all the schools in Jutland.'

I laughed, shook his hand and wobbled off after Noel and to an unexpected and unwanted rendezvous with three Arab youths.

Noel had continued walking away, wobbling from side to side, laughing to himself and singing "...show me the way to go home, I'm tired and I wanna go to bed...'.

By the time I had turned away from the gangplank and set off after Noel, he was a hundred metres or more ahead of me... still singing. I followed after him at a somewhat shambling, irregular pace, also singing.

To one side and ahead of me, had I been sober and looking where I was going, I would have seen...between a row of large wooden packing cases... three shadows flit across the ground, moving in my direction. Instead, I yelled out to Noel to wait, but he didn't hear me and then, stopping, I put my armload of goods on the ground in order to relieve myself against one of the packing cases.

Suddenly, three Arab youths were beside me. Two of them, holding me by the arms and by my hair, pulling my head back and twisting me around to face the other, who raised his hand. The long blade of a knife flashed in the light of an overhead lamp. Their faces were hostile and angry. They spoke in French, in harsh and urgent whispers. My French, though rudimentary, was nevertheless sufficient to understand them implicitly. A rush of fear and adrenalin flooding through me somehow brought me to instant sobriety.

'Take it,' I said.' Take it all', pointing to the cartons of cigarettes and pieces of clothing on the ground.

'Votres poches,' the one with the knife snarled. At which, one of the youths released the grip on my hair and started going through my pockets.

'Not my passport! Please... not my passport.'
But, within seconds they had cleaned my pockets, gathered the various items from around my feet and, with a flourish of the knife and a

whispered threat, pushed me backwards to the ground, turned and vanished in the gloom and the maze of packing cases.

In the 2nd floor office of the Casablanca Port Police, Dominique Baldacci, the Special Commissar of the Maritime Port; Officer of the Judicial Police; Auxiliary to the Procurer and Government Commissar, sat behind a large wooden desk. At eleven in the morning the temperature outside was already uncomfortably hot...inside only marginally less so. An electric fan at one end of the desk rotated slowly, first lifting the corners of the papers piled on one side and then across Monsieur Baldacci's slim, tanned face. He picked up a blue packet of Citanes lying in front of him, tapped out a cigarette and lit it with a match. He was about forty-five years old, with dark hair, greying at the temples and a thin, curved gallic nose that dominated his face. He wore a white open-necked shirt with dark-blue epaulettes. Behind him, the shuttered windows were open to a small courtyard, beyond which I could see the cranes and derricks of the port.

Unfortunately the fan's arc did not swing far enough around for its cooling breeze to touch us, so Noel and I were both sweating. I was utterly dejected. I could not have felt worse. Here I was...with no money, no passport, stranded in one of the most notorious cities in the world, all through my own stupidity. At least that's how I saw it that morning. I cursed myself over and over for having allowed it to happen. Noel sat quietly beside me. At least there was one of us with a passport and some money. He had about five pounds left. At least it was something.

The two of us had been ushered in to Monsieur Baldacci's office after half an hour of nightmarish attempts in broken French and English to explain to gendarmes one floor below what had happened to me the night before.

'You say you are attacked?

Noel and I both breathed a sigh of relief that he spoke some English.

'Yes,' I said. 'By three men.'

'What time?'

'After midnight. I'm not sure. About 12.30'

'Where?'

'Near the Tekla Torm... about one or two ships along...there are some packing cases. I'm not sure exactly. I can show you.'

'These men. You can, how do you say... describe?'

The questioning continued. I had been worried that he would not believe me. We had discovered, even in the brief time available to us that morning, between waking up with terrible hangovers and finding our way to the office of the Maritime Police, that a thriving trade existed in stolen passports in Casablanca.

'You can get at least a hundred dollars for a European passport,' Marcel, one of the French boys at the youth hostel told us as we prepared to leave. 'American are more expensive. I don't know about Australian.'

A hundred dollars was a lot of money in those days. Some people, desperate enough, would sell their own passport and then say that it had been lost or stolen. I hoped Monsieur Baldacci didn't think that of me.

Fortunately not. After a further half hour of questioning in his office, he called an aide and dictated a letter to him.

'You can wait downstairs,' Monsieur Baldacci said.

After another half hour we were able to leave the office of the Maritime Police, with me carefully folding and putting away the paper Monsieur Baldacci had signed. A piece of paper headed 'Attestation de Perte' ...in reality nothing much more than a statement that I had lost my passport, but in effect, something that could possibly be used as a 'Laissez-Passer'. I began to feel a fraction... just a fraction... better.

ooooo

MOROCCO

2

'WE THOUGHT YOU LOOKED HUNGRY'

I visited Marrakech a few years ago and, though much had changed in the more than fifty years that had passed since Noel I first wandered in awe and amazement through the suq...the old bazaar, there, I still experienced something of the sense of wonder and amazement that I felt as young man.

Two hundred and fifty kilometres south of Casablanca in the desert, the oasis town sits in the centre of the uncommonly verdant Haouz plain, with a magnificent backdrop of the 4,000-metre, snow-capped Atlas Mountains looming some 30 kilometres away in the distance.

For much of the period of the French Protectorate (1912-56) Marrakech was administered, with French approval, by one family, the Glaoua... the last of whom, Haj Thami al-Glaoui, was instrumental in arranging for France to depose Mahummad Ben Yusuf (Later King Mohammed V) as the Sultan of Morocco in 1953. At the time of our visit, six months after the outbreak of the civil war in Algeria, the French were frantically trying to come to an arrangement with Moroccan leaders that would prevent a similar civil war in Morocco. Within a few weeks, they would introduce a complete change of policy as to the way Morocco was administered, that would lead to the return of Sultan Muhammad from exile in Madagascar and independence for the country within less than a year... by March, 1956.

Of course none of these things were apparent to Noel and I, who had come to Marrakech simply as tourists. And Marrakech, apart from its long history as a cultural crossroads, where city Arabs and mountain Berbers mixed with dark-skinned Senegalese and Nomads from the Sahara, has long been Morocco's prime tourist attraction. For many years it had been a popular winter watering hole for the French, both from within Morocco and from mainland France, as well as for foreign tourists. Winston Churchill returned many times to Morocco and Marrakech, in his later years, to paint.

The Medina, or the ancient Moorish town, which is also known as the Red City because of the colour of its buildings and ramparts of beaten clay, is surrounded by a vast grove of date palms. Within its crenelated walls, the heart of Marrakech is Jema al-Fna Square, a colourful marketplace which seethes with life, like a great circus... with snake-charmers, acrobats, dancers and fortune-tellers, all working their pitch in a Moroccan version of modern-day busking.

Noel and I wandered through the square, fascinated and entranced, before exploring the nearby 12th century Koutoubia Mosque, and climbing the vaulted rampways that wind upwards inside its 67-metre-tall minaret. Then we roamed through the suq, the ancient bazaar of Marrakech, under huge tent-like coverings that were strung across the narrow alleyways, providing shade and some respite from the super dry heat. The market was then, as it still is now, overflowing with every imaginable kind of oriental product; exotic foods, spices, teas, shoes and sandals, colourful materials and fabrics, rugs and carpets, wonderful brass and copperware...all hanging from shop fronts, so as to all but obscure the entrances.

Arab men wearing turbans or a fez... would emerge: 'Venez... Venez voir!'

And when we'd shake our heads and start to move on, they'd switch to German...then English, 'Come, come and look!'

But generally our appearance was sufficient to dissuade them from persevering too much. We couldn't have looked more different than the locals; the men, for the most part, were dressed in their baggy knee-length pants or long djalabeas, plus turbans and white leather slip-on sandals, with turned up toes. We, on the other hand, were dressed in shorts and tee-shirts that had seen better days...my tee-shirt had a hole in one shoulder and army boots that had done a lot of walking. I'm not sure what they made of us. There were very few other foreigners in the suq.. and those others that were there, were French... but probably also locals. In any case, I think it was clear to most of the shop-keepers that we had no money to spend, so they didn't spend too much of their own time trying to corral us. They could see we were simply window shopping... and enjoying it.

There was so much to look at; carved furniture and crafts, in sandalwood, ebony and ivory, bronze lanterns and tableware, wonderful Moroccan leather-ware in clothing, belts, handbags, and suitcases, as well as enamel-ware, ceramics and pottery. Jewelry stores overflowed with beautiful Moroccan silver belts, necklaces, rings and earrings.

But, when I think about it now...no electronics stores! Japanese products, other than cheap toys, were nowhere to be found and 'Japanese-made' meant pretty crappy stuff. This was way before Toyota or Honda. It was before television. Long before Walkmen, cassette-players, MP3s, iPhones, video games, ghetto-blasters, organizers or computers...let alone Facebook, Twitter, Pinterest and Linked-In. The electronic revolution was not even on the horizon. About the closest to hi-fi you could find then would have been a Grundig short-wave radio about the half the size of a kitchen oven.

Hard to relate the Marrakesh we were visiting then to a 2011 Al-Qaeda suicide bomb attack in a popular café, not far from the Medina, where 17 people, mainly foreign tourists were killed. Casablanca had previously experienced two similar bombings in 2007 and in 2003, when forty people were killed in a Spanish restaurant and a Jewish community centre.

Noel and I had hitch-hiked down from Casablanca firstly to see Marrakech, its market and the Atlas Mountains, but also to kill a little time. In the week after our disastrous first night in Casablanca, we had set about trying to get ourselves back on track again... only to find we had quite a bit of waiting around to do.

'The first thing is to try to get a new passport,' I'd said as we came away from the meeting with Monsieur Baldacci... only to discover shortly afterwards that there was no Australian Consul in Casablanca. Nor was there one anywhere in North Africa, apart from Cairo, where there was an Embassy. But Cairo was almost 5,000 kilometres away and we had no money.

'We've got to get some more dough somehow,' said Noel. 'Perhaps we could write to the guys in London.'

We'd shared a flat in South Kensington during the previous winter with five other Australians who were still working there.

'The Redback owes me some money,' I said. 'Maybe he and Ronnie or Grant could come good.'

'And the Iron Man isn't short of bob,' Noel added... 'Nor Bruce. They might be able to put together and lend us twenty quid each.'

'Its still a fair amount of money.'

'Yeah, but we might as well try.'

We had sat down in the hostel to write to our friends in London, telling them of our predicament.

I know it's a bit silly to make comparisons of a value then to a value now, sixty years later but, for what its worth...and its pretty hard to take on board, but £20 in 1955 would be around £450 in 2015...over US $600!

During those first few days I was fortunately able to locate the British consulate in Casablanca. It was fortunate, because, while I am now keen to see Australia become a Republic, at that stage in my life I hadn't given it a moment's thought and this was definitely one occasion when I felt very strongly appreciative of Australia's close links to Britain.

Australian passports in those days still carried the words on the outside cover: 'British Passport, Commonwealth of Australia' and on the inside: 'Australian Citizen and a British subject', with a request to all and sundry in the name of 'Her Britannic Majesty'... that 'the bearer be allowed to pass freely without let or hindrance'.

The bottom line here was simply that the British Consul in Casablanca said he could issue me with a new British passport, valid for six months, or until I could get to an Australian Consul... whichever was the sooner. There I could be issued with a new Australian passport. That was the good news. The bad news was that in order to issue the new British passport, the Consul needed a birth certificate. I did have one, but it had been in my wallet, which was now gone.

This meant that I had to write to my uncle, who worked for the Department of Statistics in Canberra, to ask him to get a copy of my birth certificate. The fact that I was born in Canberra did make it a little easier, but it still meant a long delay. There were no faxes or emails then. Telegrams yes. But they cost money which we couldn't really spare. I might have sent him a telegram. I can't recall, but the main thing was we would have to wait at least two or three weeks in Casablanca for it all to come through.

'The worst thing is that we've missed that ship going to Congo,' I said to Noel when we realised how long it would all take.

'Yeah, but we'll find another one. And anyway, that captain bloke was a real drongo. We're probably better off not going on that ship anyway.'

We spent about three days in Marrakech, living extremely cheaply in the Auberge de la Jeunesse, and making forays into the market and the foothills of the Atlas. I remember on one occasion, while in the markets in Marrakesh, something fantastic happened. We had spent about an hour meandering around, looking at everyone and everything and then stopped briefly for a cool drink... a citron pressé, which was cheaper... and better than the bottled soft drinks. Noel had asked an Arab man sitting at the soft drink stall, in a combination of English, French and sign language... if he would show him the curved, inlaid dagger that hung at his side.

The man, at first suspicious, then friendly, withdrew the dagger and showed it to us, emphasizing, in Arabic, how sharp the blade... and the point were. And how effective it could be. After a few minutes admiring the weapon, nodding knowingly and indicating our apparent respect for someone with such a weapon... something he seemed to appreciate...we thanked him and walked away, heading out of the bazaar.

Hardly more than twenty metres further on our way, in a crowded alleyway, lying on the ground, in the dust, with peoples' passing feet turning it over, was a 500 franc note. Noel picked it up in a flash, looking around immediately to see if anyone had dropped it. The alley was crowded with people coming and going, passing by. No one turned or looked like claiming it.

'Should we ask if it belongs to anyone? I said to Noel.

'Not bloody likely. What do you reckon they're going to say...whoever you ask?'

Five hundred francs in those days was worth about ten shillings in English money. It doesn't sound much now, but in 1955 in Morocco

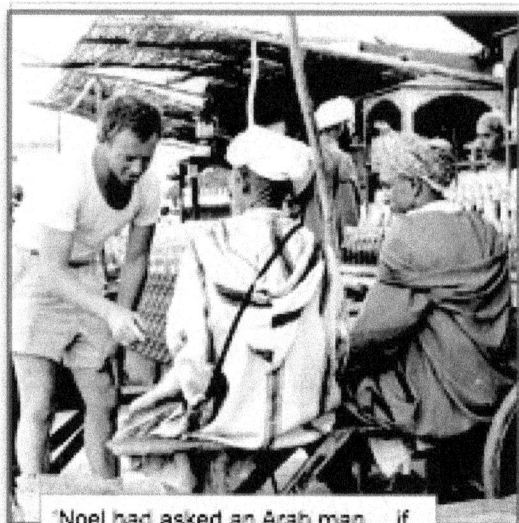

'Noel had asked an Arab man... if he would show him the curved, inlaid dagger that hung at his side.'

'...we roamed through the 'suq', the ancient bazar of Marrakech...'

With Michelle

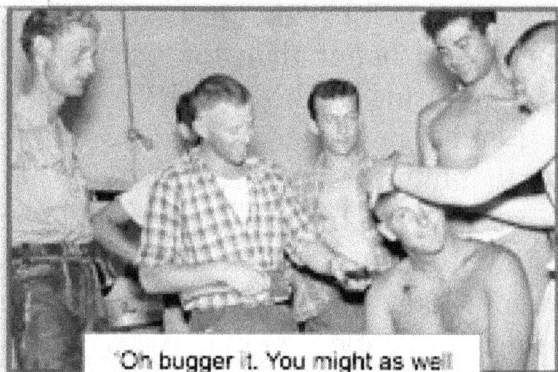

'Oh bugger it. You might as well take the whole lot off,' I said.

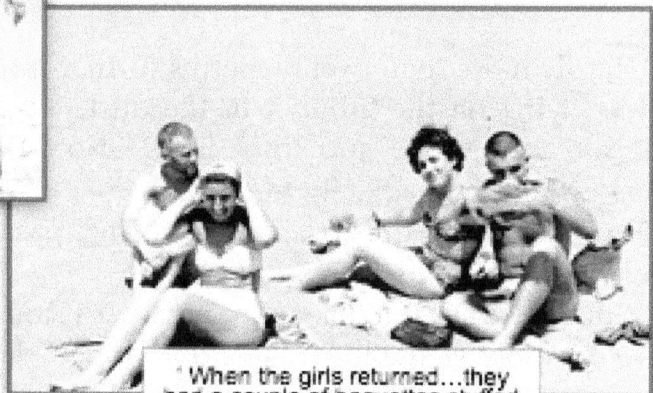

' When the girls returned...they had a couple of baguettes stuffed with ham and cheese for us...'

it represented accommodation, with meals and a litre of wine... for at least a couple of nights. And by this stage we needed every little bit we could get. To find that sort of money on the ground in the casbah at Marrakech was little short of providential.

The beaches around Casablanca left a bit to be desired. Not quite like Australian beaches. The sand was sand alright, but it was sort of a grey colour and, there was too much litter everywhere. Nevertheless, we were more than a little surprised on our first visit to one of the main beaches near the city, the Kon-tiki, to see a reasonable surf rolling in. It was a local, wind-driven surf... rough, irregular waves whipped up by a recent storm not far out in the Atlantic... not like the long, smooth swells that perpetually roll in along the eastern Australian coastline. Those swells, of course, are also born in storms and huge hurricanes, but it is weather that is generated for the most part hundreds, sometimes thousands of kilometres out in the Pacific Ocean. Nevertheless, it had been a long time since we'd seen anything resembling surf.

'Look at that,' Noel was already stripping his shirt off as we walked across the sand towards the water. 'Not a bad little swell running there. A few 'bodies', maybe even a decent one or two for a board. If we had 'em here,' he added ruefully.

As beaches go, most of the other elements also seemed to fit. It was hot. There were lots of people... mainly French... soaking up the sun. Arab merchants roamed up and down selling everything from soft-drinks to sunglasses and hats, people were frolicking in the water although, we noticed, only up to their waists, at most, in the shallows

'There's a few good 'sorts' too,' I noted, after a quick scan of the crowd on the beach. The local bikini talent was not too bad. We kept checking them out as we made our way across the wide beach, weaving a curving path, among the stretched out bodies, trying to find the hottest-looking girls, so that we could set our things down nearby.

Choosing three slim, attractive dark-haired girls who were sitting together, we dropped our towels and clothes a few metres away and with a friendly nod to them which, we were pleased to note, was reciprocated with a smile, we headed for the water.

'Wow, how about that one in the yellow,' Noel nudged me as we ran down to the water's edge. 'She's hot. Did you see the smile she gave me?'

Noting a reasonably strong rip to our right, we moved a little up the beach away from it and went in, past a couple of other bathers, to dive under the breaking waves and head further out. We swam past the shore break, probably no more than seventy or eighty metres or so out from the beach, to a point where the waves were building up to nice little crests, as they came in over the gradually shelving sandy sea floor. To help things along, there was a slight offshore breeze blowing, which tended to keep the crests from breaking until the last minute. They were a little tight...with not much space between each wave...as storm surf mostly is, but we could pick between them and quickly found some quite good body waves to ride in, where, after being dropped off, we turned and swam straight back out again.

We continued in this fashion for about ten or fifteen minutes, without noticing that we were the only ones so far out in the surf.

'Have a look at that crowd on the beach,' I said to Noel as we trod water, out the back, waiting for another wave. What are they doing?'

A large crowd had gathered down by the water's edge and were pointing out to sea.

'They're pointing out here. Are they pointing at us?'

'I think so... they're pointing right out here.'

'What do you reckon they're pointing at?' Noel said. 'Maybe there's a bloody shark out here or something. Do they have sharks here?'

'How the hell would I know. Look, there's someone running along the beach.' Two men were running along towards the crowd carrying a lifebouy. 'Maybe we should go in.'

We both caught the same wave...a good one which carried us about fifty metres or so into the shallower water, where we swam a little, then straightened up, in waist-deep water, to come out towards the crowd and the two men, who turned out to be life-guards and who started shouting at us in French. It took us a moment or so to realise that we were the object of all the fuss.

'Dangereux! Dangereux.... il est tres dangereux dans la mer.'

'Oh...okay, I see. You're worried about us. Sorry...sorry,' Noel and I were both speaking at once, trying to fit in a bit of French, here and there, at the same time: 'But its alright.... pas de problem... pas de problem. Nous sommes...er, lifesavers... from Australia.... Australie!'

There was a murmur in the crowd... 'Ah... Australie...' and some nodding.

But the two lifeguards were wagging their heads. 'Non. Non. C'est tres Dangereux.

'No,' I continued. 'Truly, we swim... er, that is... nager... nager, all the time in water like this...' I gestured at the waves... ' er, tout le temps, en Australie...like this...come ça. Yes that's right...come ça, en Australie. Pas de problem. We are professionals...like you...er, comme vous... professionale...lifeguards.'

Well the 'professional' might have been stretching things a bit... because there was virtually no paid life-saving on the beaches of Australia... certainly not then, anyway. Only voluntary lifeguards. But we were 'dinky-di' Aussie life-savers. We'd both gained our Bronze, Silver and Gold Medallions in Surf Life-Saving as members of Torquay Surf Life Saving Club on the south coast of Victoria and we'd both been out in much bigger seas than this. But we could also both see, that for the moment at least, discretion would be the better part of valour...and to back-peddle a bit. And anyway, the three girls who had smiled at us earlier were now standing in the crowd watching the proceedings with fascination. Noel and I spotted them at the same time and smiled at them again.

'Okay, okay,' I said to the lifeguards. 'No more swimming. Finis...finis. Now...we sit on the beach...sur le plage. Some sun, only sun... soleil. Okay?' The two men gave a little 'harrumph' and turned to walk away still mumbling 'dangereux... dangereux.' While we turned towards the young French girls... 'Hello,' I said to all three at once, 'Parlez vous Anglais.'

Two people trying to survive for three weeks on five pounds.... which was all the cash we had between us after my passport and wallet had been stolen...was admittedly pretty close to impossible. But we did our best. Leaving Genoa flat broke, we had been given our passage plus about five pounds each pocket money as we signed off from the *Tekla Torm*. In addition the crew had laden us up with four or five cartons of Lucky Strikes and Camels which we intended to sell in Casablanca. Fortunately it was only my cigarettes and money that had gone. Noel still had his intact. But the money from the sold cigarettes and his cash...

eventually ran out. Then we had nothing.

Although we had written to our friends in London to see if we could borrow money, that process, as well as the wait for my new birth certificate to come through, was taking time. In the meantime we had to eat and to pay for our stay at the youth hostel.

'We have no more money to pay for our beds, or food,' I explained to the manager after about ten days. 'But we do have some money coming through from England soon, to the bank here.'

The manager knew, from the start, of our predicament. He had witnessed my extreme distress on the morning after my passport had been stolen and had shown an almost fatherly concern and interest in developments from then on. In fact, everyone at the youth hostel knew about it and were all sympathetic. The problem for the manager, Jules, I think was his name, was that it was not his hostel. He was only an employee of the Moroccan Youth Hostel organization. He could hardly give us free accommodation and food just on our word that the money would be paid. But, to his credit and our endless gratitude, he did.

'I cannot give you every meal,' he told us. 'You can have petit dejeuner...that is, bread and coffee in the mornings. And a simple dinner at night. No wine, unfortunately,' he smiled. '....for another two weeks. Okay?'

'Okay?! You're dead right its okay!' Noel exclaimed. Our faces lit up, we grabbed his hand, shook it and practically hugged him. 'Fantastic.'

It was around this time that our spirits began to lift. We couldn't start looking for ships again...it was too early to start that until we were sure that the paperwork...the passports and money was all coming together. We did however, haunt the docks regularly in what turned out to be extremely successful searches for free lunches.

Casablanca harbour was a huge and busy port, even then, handling several thousand vessels a year. Cargo vessels were taking on sardines, cork, fresh oranges, olive oil, manganese and phosphates... Morocco's most important export...and offloading everything from grain and newsprint to farm machinery and automobiles.

Danish, Norwegian and Dutch ships we found offered the best chance for a feed. Strangely we didn't have much luck with British ships. We developed a certain technique that seemed to work: First, we would get on board as if we were looking for a job, striking up a conversation at an early stage, with a crew member on deck, that might go something like this:

'Where are you heading?'

'Singapore and Malaysia.'

'Oh that's too bad... we're trying to get to South America' (or if he'd said they were going to South America...we'd say we were heading for Singapore)

'Where are you from?' they'd invariably ask.

'Australia...'

'Australia! You're a hell of a way from home. How did you get here?'

'We came here on a Danish ship...the *Tekla Torm*.'

And if it happened to be a Danish or Norwegian ship we were visiting, the ice would be broken. We'd chat a bit more and then, if we'd timed it right, there'd be a whistle or some signal that it was lunchtime.

'What are you guys doing for lunch?' would be the natural question to us... and there we'd be shortly afterwards, sitting down to a hearty lunch on board ship. It didn't work all the time, but it was surprising how many times it did.

And then there were the three girls on the beach. After our first meeting, on the day we got into trouble with the lifeguards, we had seen them regularly there and a couple of the other Casablanca beaches, the Lido and the Miami and they had begun bringing us sandwiches every time we met. It started on the first day. After coming out of the surf, we'd returned to where our gear was on the and sand sat down beside them to talk. I noticed Sarah wore a gold Star of David around her neck.

'You're Jewish?' I asked.

'We all are,' she smiled.

Later I asked if there were any problems for Jews in Morocco.

'No, why should there be?' asked Michele... the buxom one with short curly hair, whom I fancied... and who seemed to take a shine to me.

'Well, I don't know...only that this is a Muslim country and there are problems now between Muslims and Jews... in Israel.'

This was a full year before the first Arab-Israeli war of 1956 when the relationship between most Arab countries and Israel deteriorated dramatically. But the signs of tension were already there... as they still are. But even back then, the problems between Israel and the Palestinians seemed to be constantly in the news.

'Yes, that's true,' Michele said. '...but this is also a French country and here in Morocco we are all French. France would not allow it.'

'Perhaps not now. But France may not always be in charge here. Look what is happening next door in Algeria...there's a civil war against France.'

'Ah, yes. But that will not happen here. France will not give up Morocco. It is like a part of France.'

She spoke with such authority and confidence, and yet, less than twelve months later, France handed Morocco its independence on a plate, fortuitously with virtually none of the fighting or widespread violence that Algeria would have to go through.

'And anyway,' Lotte, the third one, said. '...the Jewish people have a long history here. There have always been Jews here, even from Roman times. And 500 years ago, in 1492, they came here in huge numbers....tens of thousands, from Spain, when Queen Isabella expelled all the Moors, as well as the Jews from Spain. This is where they came. That is where my ancestors came from. But now I am French.'

'What about boyfriends,' Noel said, changing the subject abruptly, 'do you girls have any boyfriends.'

They laughed. 'Oh yes,' Michele said. 'We have plenty.... many....' and then, with a smile, 'But not right now. Not here.'

'Good... good,' Noel and I nodded sagely.

They laughed. 'We are going to have some lunch,' Sarah said, pointing to one of the cafés that lined the beach. 'Are you eating too?'

Noel and I looked at each other. 'No, we're not hungry,' I lied. 'We'll stay here.'

The three girls then left us to go to the café for their lunch.

'What did you say that for?' Noel muttered, as they left. 'Maybe they would have bought us something.'

'Yeah, I guess so. Lets see how things go.'

And...surprise, surprise. When the girls returned, twenty minutes later, they had a couple of baguettes stuffed with ham and cheese for us.

'We thought you looked hungry...even though you said you weren't,' Sarah laughed.

Thanking them, we both wolfed the sandwiches down, telling them at the same time about our situation. From that day on, whenever we met 'our Jewish girls'...as we called them...on the beach, they brought us baguettes... but also olives and fruit and sometimes even a bottle of wine.

We managed to organize it so that it wasn't too much of burden on them, by timing our visits to the ships in port, for lunch there... and to the beach on alternate days.

There was one unfortunate interruption to the program though. My hair was getting a bit too long... as was Noel's... and when, at the youth hostel one evening, we saw one of the French boys, Serge, cutting somebody else's hair, we decided to ask him to do ours also.

'I'll go first,' Noel said. Although if he'd looked more closely at the job Serge had just done on the bloke before him, he might not have been so keen. And then, shortly afterwards, when I saw the hatchet job Serge performed on Noel, I wasn't too keen either. But there didn't seem to be much choice.

'Just go easy on the sides,' I said to Serge. 'Not too much off the sides... not as much as you've done on Noel's.' Noel now had what looked like a half-finished Mohawk cut.

'Huh?' Serge muttered. He didn't speak much English.

'Un peu... un petit peu cort.... à coté,' I struggled to explain in fractured French. But Serge just laughed. He was into it with the electric clippers with a vengeance. Noel and at least four others were standing around giving advice and also laughing. That was the disconcerting bit... the laughter.

'Has this bloke ever done this before?' I asked Noel.

'Haven't a clue.'

'No, he hasn't...' Dieter, the German boy we'd met on the first night, shook his head. He was also laughing. 'Its his first time.'

'Oh Jesus....' I muttered, but it was too late to change now. At the end of it... or what Serge obviously felt was the end of it, as he stood back and looked at my head with pride, I was left with the left side practically shaved up to about an inch above my ear and the right side shaved to two inches above the ear. I looked at it in the mirror.

'You better even it up,' I said, trying to hide my displeasure...

gesturing with my hands beside my head. 'Make the two sides even.'

And he was back into it again. This time the left side was an inch higher than the right. Another try: right higher than left. And after one more attempt:

'Oh bugger it. You might as well take the whole lot off,' I said, waving my hand across the top.

I finally ended up with a haircut remarkably similar to the one I have now, some sixty years later, that is, practically no hair on top.

Anyway, I looked at myself in the mirror then and saw that, while the rest of my face and body were heavily suntanned, all of my head, where my hair had been, was white. It looked ridiculous...at least I thought so. And human vanity being what it is, I thought I'll have to do something about it... get a suntan on my head.

The result? After a full day of intense sun at the beach.... Sunstroke! For a day and half I lay in bed in the hostel, throwing up... vomiting bile.... blisters on my head.

Things progressed slowly with our Jewish girls... as far as sex was concerned. Firstly there was the difficulty of there being three of them and two of us. These situations always produce a little tension and jockeying, until everyone knows who's going to be with whom and who's going to miss out. So that took time. And the fact that we had no money at all didn't help. We couldn't go out anywhere at night with them... dancing, for example... because we were so broke. But then, not long after I'd recovered from the bout of sunstroke and we'd started to sort out the boy-girl mix, Lotte announced that her parents would soon be going away for a week and that maybe we could come to her place for dinner.

Noel and I looked at each other. Noel raised his eyebrows. I whistled softly.

'That sounds great,' I said. 'We'll be there. No risk.'

But unfortunately, our lustful dreams were not to be fulfilled, as, in the space of a few days, the whole scene changed, with everything else starting to come together for us. The money from our friends in London arrived as a bank draft drawn on the Royal Bank of Morocco. We had been pestering the Foreign Currency section at the head office every day for a week. But now at last it had finally come through just as my birth certificate arrived in the mail from Australia. I took it straight to the British Consulate, with the passport application forms that had been filled out, ready and waiting, for almost three weeks. My new British passport was issued the following day... and we were ready to go.

Go... yes. But go where? For the past couple of weeks we'd kept ourselves very up-to-date with what ships were in port and where they were going and there had been nothing heading to South Africa, or anywhere on the West African coast, other than one for Dakar, in French West Africa. From our enquiries at the port office it appeared nothing was likely for the next few days.

'Dakar'd be just the same as here,' Noel said. 'We'd be in the same position, waiting for boats that might not come.'

The fact that we were now free to go... coupled with the forced relative inactivity of past few weeks led us inevitably to the question that had been hovering in the background all the while.

'Its no good sitting around here waiting,' I said. 'We might as well head off across to Cairo and try to get down overland.'

'Yeah... spot on,' Noel had agreed. 'I want to get moving. We're okay with our French visa now...for Algeria, at least '

'....and Tunisia, I'm pretty sure. Anyway,' I said, 'I'm sure we can get them as we go along, if we need them.'

We were however, sensible enough to check on the visa requirements and learned that we could obtain a visa for Libya in Tunis and one for Egypt when we got to the Libyan capital, Tripoli.

The decision was made. We kissed the girls goodbye, after one last swim at the beach, paid our bill at the youth hostel, packed up our rucksacks and took a local bus to the outskirts of Casablanca on the road to Rabat.

As we set our packs down on the side of the road to start thumbing a ride, the dull roar produced by the ten engines (six propellers and four jets) of an American B-36 bomber filled the air, as the huge aircraft droned overhead. Well before the era of ballistic missiles, these giant aircraft, based at Kenitra, to the north of Rabat, were part of NATO's Cold War nuclear bomber fleet.

Our route heading east took us, in short order, through three of Morocco's major cities, Rabat, the capital, then Meknes and Fez... all grouped in a line within less than 300 kilometres of Casablanca. During different periods over the centuries, all three of these cities, plus Marrakech have served as the capital of Morocco. In 1912 the seat of government moved from Meknes to Rabat with the introduction of the French Colonial administration in Morocco.

After independence in 1956 it remained in Rabat and it is from there that King Mohammed V, on his return from exile, ruled for just five years until his death in 1961. Then, for 38 years, his successor, Hassan II presided over a sometimes restive nation, surviving an attempted coup and continuing political pressures towards the establishment of a republic, as well as a long-running mini-war with Algeria. Since Hassan's death in 1999, his son, Mohammed VI, who's been described as a cautious modernizer, has introduced a degree of economic and social liberalization, while Morocco remains one of the world's last absolute monarchies.

At the time of our passage through Morocco, independence, although only six months away, was entirely unanticipated by the public at large...no one believed the French president, Charles de Gaulle would grant Morocco independence while Algeria was in the midst of a civil war... but that's the way it went.

Rabat, on the coast, was once the home port of pirate corsairs who became the scourge of Christian fleets in the Mediterranean and off the Atlantic coasts of North Africa and Spain during the 1600's. Now much of the harbour, where the pirate fleets would anchor, is silted up. The old castle, surrounded by rust-coloured walls, looks out over the harbour, while the royal palace, numerous Embassies and luxurious villas line the fore shore and the broad green parks and tree-lined avenues of Rabat.

We unfortunately caught only glimpses of Rabat as we were dropped off in the centre and made our way, as quickly as possible across the Bou Regreg River to Rabat's sister town Salé on the other side, before picking up a couple of lifts taking us on the way to Meknes, about 120 kilometres on and then to Fez, a further sixty. We had made up our mind to head eastward as fast as possible, so when the driver of the truck in which we were travelling took a ring road around Meknes, we didn't complain...even though, under different circumstances, we would probably have spent some time there. In any event, by the time we reached Fez, in the early evening, we decided not to go further but to locate the local youth hostel in the old walled city of Fez el Bali... or Fez the Old....and stay the night before making an early start in the morning.

But whatever hopes we'd had for covering a long distance by starting early didn't quite work out. We found ourselves picking up a series of short lifts, punctuated by long waits in between, that took us through the small towns of Taza, Guercif and Taourirt, each separated by about fifty or sixty kilometres. By three in the afternoon, with the Algerian border still over a hundred kilometres away, we began to think we might be spending another night in Morocco. But before long an electrician on his way to repair a damaged transformer in the border town of Oujda picked us up.

ooooooo

ALGERIA

3

THIS IS A DANGEROUS REGION

Crossing the frontier at Oujda in the late afternoon, we noticed immediately, the increased number of French soldiers. Although Algeria and Morocco are geographically side by side with predominantly Arab populations, the situation inside Algeria then was strikingly different from that in Morocco. To begin with, although they were both French territories, their systems of administration were far apart. Morocco was a French Protectorate, while Algeria was governed along complicated lines, almost as if it were a Department of France. And now, for the past several months....since November 1954... French Algeria was at war with an unseen guerrilla army... the FLN, the Front de Libération National.

The FLN's aim was to bring about a 'Sovereign Algerian State' by guerrilla warfare at home and diplomacy abroad...which it did, in 1962, but at a huge cost to the country.

Between 350.000 and 1 million Algerians are estimated to have died during the war, and more than 2 million, out of a total Muslim population of 9 or 10 million, were made refugees. Much of the countryside and agriculture was devastated, along with the modern economy, which had been dominated by urban European settlers. Nearly a million people, of mostly French, Spanish and Italian descent were forced to flee the country at independence due to the chaos of the civil war as well as threats from the victorious FLN.

One of the movement's main architects was a young Algerian veteran of World War II called Ahmed Ben Bella, who had won France's highest military award, the Croix de Guerre, as well as the Médaille Militaire. Back in Algeria after the war, he pursued a range of nationalist activities and also formed a secret organization whose aim was to take up arms as quickly as possible. Ben Bella was jailed in

1950 for eight years after robbing a post office to obtain funds for his organization, but escaped after only two years and fled to Cairo.

There, with the aid of the revolutionary supporters of the future president, Gamal Abdel Nasser, he planned and prepared for the Algerian War....and ultimately, after its conclusion, became Algeria's Prime Minister and then its first President, until ousted in a military coup in 1965.

That coup leader, Houari Boumédienne, survived more failed coups and an assassination attempt to remain in power until his own death in 1978, since when, seven successive leaders have struggled to deal with a militant Islamic Party, The Islamic Salvation Front, with not much progress. However, the present (2015) leader, President Abdelaziz Bouteflika...in power since 1999...has had encouraging success in restoring security and stability to the strife-ridden country and reducing violence to 'manageable' levels.

'You must be very careful in Algerie,' the driver of a small Peugeot truck, informed us. It was our first lift, which we picked up after walking about a kilometre from the border crossing. Steering with his left hand, he reached across us with his right to open the glove compartment, revealing the grey metallic sheen of a pistol.

'I have this,' he said. 'It is necessary here. But you have nothing. You must take care.'

'But how?' I asked. 'how do we take care? What do we have to do?'

'You must stay by French people. You must be very careful of any Arab people. It is sad to say... but it is true. Many French... European people are being killed by FLN.

'Are there any FLN around here?' Noel asked.

He paused.'...Mais Oui, certainement. But not so many on this side of Algerie. There are many more to the East, near Constantine. There they attack vehicles on the road and there is sometimes fighting. But even here, I do not like to travel on this road at night.'

'Does everyone carry a pistol?'

'Yes. Yes. It is only sensible to do it.'

We travelled some forty or fifty kilometres with him, before he set us down on the outskirts of the town of Tlemcen, where we waited only a further twenty minutes or so by the side of the road before being picked up by a French civilian... an automobile engineer on his way to Ain Témouchent, another seventy kilometres or so along the road towards Oran. We continued on with him until, with daylight fading, we reached Ain Témouchent. Here, as our driver was turning south, we had to leave him.

'Where will you stay for the night?' He appeared worried.

His feelings were certainly shared by us, although I don't think we let it show. 'Oh, we're not sure,' Noel said. 'We'll probably camp beside the road.'

Now he was really shocked.

'No, I'm sure it'll be alright,' I continued. 'We'll probably be able to find some little place where we can sleep and not be noticed.'

'No, No. This is impossible. You come with me. I have some friends... a little further on. Only five kilometres. They are farmers. You can stay with them. I will tell them about you. They will look after you until tomorrow, then you can continue to Oran.'

Arriving at the farm... which was a large olive orchard, we were surprised to find that our driver's friends were not French farmers, but Italian. They were from near Foggia in Italy and had been in Algeria for more than twenty years, building a thriving business there supplying a local cooperative that shipped olive oil to metropolitan France, as well as to other European countries.

There was the farmer, Guilio, a deeply tanned man of about fifty years, his wife, Maria, equally tanned, but six or seven years younger, with a huge smile...and their two children; a boy of ten and a girl of seven. Now, because of the 'troubles', they were considering moving back to Italy. After explanations by our driver, we were given a warm welcome by them.

'Owstralia! Multo bene...nous avons relatives...friends... live in Sydney.'

He spoke an amazing mix of Italian, French and English, which somehow we managed to understand surprisingly well.

As we had arrived just as Maria was preparing dinner, she simply switched into another gear, put some more pasta on the boil, cut up some more tomatoes and salad, lay out more bread, wine and olives on the table and, within twenty minutes we were all... including our driver, who the farmer insisted should also stay for dinner....sitting down to a hearty meal. For almost two hours we were laughing and talking about everything, from our hitch-hiking experiences in Italy and France the previous year, to life in Australia, the war in Algeria, international politics...the meaning of life. We covered the waterfront... in three languages plus a bit.

Our driver friend, whose name was Jean-Eve, still had some thirty kilometres to go to his destination, so he said goodbye and left shortly after nine o'clock, despite strong efforts by the farmer to persuade him to stay and not to take the unnecessary risk of driving at night. But he insisted on leaving. He was needed on a job first thing the morning and wanted to make sure that he would be there. 'My colleagues are expecting me to arrive this evening,' he said.

The following morning, after a comfortable night in deep, soft-mattressed beds, and an early breakfast of home-baked bread and coffee, Noel & I prepared to get on our way again, continuing east along the main road to Algiers.

The farmer insisted on driving us the five kilometres or so back to the junction of the main road... where, as we alighted from his truck and pulled our packs from the back, he left the engine running and came around to shake our hands. As he shook mine, I felt something in his palm. I looked down to see a 1,000 Franc note (the equivalent of about one pound) in my hand.

'Oh please... No,' I said, moving to hand it back to him.

He grabbed my hand again in his big fist and closed it on the note. 'It is for both,' He smiled first at Noel and then back to me. 'Not much. But I know you have not much money. You will need it... I am sure. Keep it.'

We were taken completely by surprise. 'But, but you've already done so much...' I began.

In a moment, however, he was back in the cabin of his truck, waving goodbye to us, revving the engine and driving off. 'Good luck...Buon Viaggio,' he called.

A stream of military vehicles in convoy came past us, The young French soldiers waving and calling out to us. It was the third big road convoy we'd seen since entering Algeria. We waved back and waited.

In general, we never sat long, waiting by the side of the road, unless we were in really remote places, before we were picked up and carried on our way. Hitch-hiking in those days, wherever you were, didn't have the bad name that seems to attach to it now. It was almost universally a young person's activity and people with cars and trucks seemed... most of the time... willing to help a hitch-hiker on his or her way. A sort of camaraderie of the road. I have to say though that when I see some people hitching these days I don't feel inclined to pick them up when they just walk along the road, with their backs turned and one arm held limply out to the side. We would always stand facing the traffic, with a big smile on our faces and motion with our thumb in the traditional way.

And, by giving a better impression, I think we gave ourselves a better chance of a lift. Anyway, Algeria... despite the war situation... seemed to be no different from the rest of Europe, as far as getting lifts was concerned so from our point of view, that was good.

'The sooner we're through Algeria, the better,' Noel said, as we waited for our first lift. 'It doesn't sound too healthy a place to be if you're French and the trouble is, they can't tell that we're not French.'

We did have a big map of Australia and the letters AUSTRALIA painted across the top of each of our packs, plus a flag sewn on the side... all of which we'd done during the previous year, while travelling in Europe. And it had often been a help to us. But in a civil war situation these things don't count for much.

'Well, if we just keep going and don't stop in Algiers, or any of the big towns, we should be able to cut straight through in two or three days.' I said. We had a Michelin map of North Africa open in front of us. 'Its about 1,200 kilometres from one side to the other.'

When you're hitching, distances covered in a day can be quite unpredictable...very big or very small. You can get a ride with someone who is travelling a long way, very fast...or sit by the road-side for hours waiting and then get a series of short, slow rides in which you make hardly any progress.

Our first lift of the day came from an Arab truck driver, who stopped with a big smile on his face and motioned for us to put our packs in the back and hop into the cabin beside him. We both experienced a momentary pause, thinking of the advice given to us by the driver of our very first lift in Algeria...(stay with French people...be careful of Arabs). But with a quick glance at each other and a shrug of our shoulders, we ignored the advice and climbed aboard. As it happened there was no cause for any concern on our part. We chatted away amicably with our driver in a combination of broken French and sign language for almost all of the seventy kilometre run into Oran.

Oran is the second largest city and port in Algeria. Founded in the 10th century, it has a fascinating history, involving Barbary pirates and constant struggles for its control by various European powers, including the Spanish, the Turks and the French, who finally occupied the city and its port in 1831, retaining their influence in one form or another, right through the colonial era until Algeria's eventual independence in 1962.

The setting of old Oran is quite dramatic... on a point, with the curving coastline of steep hills to the East of the town coming down to the sea and forming a large open bay. The original port and the old Spanish town of La Blanca, on the plateau above it, are crowned by the citadel of Santa Cruz... a massive fortress built by the Turks, during their two occupations of the city, but later modified extensively by the Spanish and the French.

Beyond the old town, which still has its Turkish and Spanish quarters, are the newer parts of the city...La Marine, near the sea and La Ville Nouvelle, the modern centre of town on the terraces of the right bank of the Raz el-Ain ravine. Our lift took us into La Marine, near the modern port of Oran, which had been greatly enlarged and developed over the past hundred years or so, resulting in a huge artificial harbour, seven large shipping basins and a three-kilometre-long jetty.

Once again, however, we didn't hang around to give Oran the attention it deserved, but pressed on, with a series of short lifts along the road heading out of the city to the south, to a small town called Oued Tlelat. Here we were once more on the main road for Algiers... still some 450 kilometres to the east.

About twenty kilometres from Oued Tlelat, at another small town called Sig, the Algiers road begins to turn towards the northeast to run roughly parallel with the coast, but about fifty kilometres inland. It follows the Chelif Valley between two long mountain ranges that run east to west, the Dahra Massif which separates the valley from the Mediterranean coast and the Massif de l'Ouarsenis to the south. The road, as I remember it, passed through areas of intensive farming, one of the more fertile areas of Algeria, where crops included barley, wheat, market vegetables, dates and fruit, as well as olives and tobacco. From a tourist's point of view the landscape was wonderful: rugged, arid mountains rising on either side of a verdant, irrigated valley which was lined, for large stretches, with date palms and small settlements of mud brick Arab houses, sometimes whitewashed, sometimes left the colour of the earth.

White-robed Arab men atop camels or leading donkeys laden with firewood, plodded along the sides of the road as we trundled through the valley in three or four different vehicles that we picked up one after the other during the course of the day.

The rest of our lifts during that day were with French settlers, either farmers or business people. The population of French settlers in Algeria was quite substantial...close to 400,000...a large percentage of which had been born in Algeria and considered it their home, rather than France. They had no desire to give up Algeria to the indigenous Algerians, so when the revolutionary movement started, it was met with strong opposition, not just from the French police and military, but from the settlers themselves.

Towards the end of the civil war, in the early 1960's, when France's determination was waning and it looked as if independence was inevitable, the settlers even formed their own secret army called the OAS... L'Organization de l'Armée Secrète... which began to employ forms of terrorism often just as brutal as those used by the FLN rebels... even against the Government of France, as it moved closer to handing Algeria its independence.

From our point of view however, all that was yet to come. But, at the time of our trip through Algeria, a huge buildup of French military strength was underway. During 1955 and 1956 a French army of half a million men was sent to Algeria to try to counter the control that the rebels had managed to establish in the more remote parts of the country. In these areas they collected money for their cause and carried out reprisals on their own countrymen who did not cooperate.

The feeling of tension we had encountered on crossing the border was apparent in nearly all of the people we travelled with during that day, although there were a couple of drivers, who more or less dismissed it as a passing phase... something that was occurring in the more out-of-the-way parts of the country and which the French authorities would soon crush. There had however, been recent strikes and some riots in the capital Algiers and when the opportunity came during one of our last lifts for that day, at a place called Blida, about seventy kilometres southwest of Algiers, to continue on past the capital heading eastwards, we took it, telling ourselves pragmatically that we would visit Algiers 'some other day'.

So by the end of our second day in Algeria, we found ourselves some eighty kilometres southeast of the capital near Lakhdaria and passing through fertile country in which much of the farming was centred on the growing of citrus fruits. As luck would have it, we were able to spend the night once again on a farm, although this time with little of the comfort and none of the friendly companionship we'd experienced with Giullio and Maria on the previous night.

We'd noticed, as we entered the region, an even larger number of army trucks in evidence on the roads, as well as trucks parked in the yards of farms. Apparently, for some weeks now, most of the farms in this area, to the east of Algiers, were being patrolled by soldiers during the nights, as, in many parts a night curfew had been introduced. It was not uncommon for Europeans, who happened to be passing through the area, to spend the night at a farm, rather than travel on the roads at night. And many of the farms, like this one, charged a small amount to provide a meal and simple bed. An ad hoc B&B.

'I wonder how long they'll be able to keep this up,' Noel said, as he and I ate some bread, cheese and tomatoes which had been prepared for us in the kitchen.

'You mean the farmers?'

'No, the French army. The bloke by the barn told me that, on each of the farms around here, there are at least three soldiers on patrol during the night. I mean, I wonder how many farms they're doing it on. They can't possibly do it all over Algeria.'

'Well, they weren't doing it over in the west, where we were last night, so I guess its only on the ones where they feel there's a threat.'

'Like here... you mean?'

'Hope not,' I muttered.

'...at least we were on the main road to Tunisia.'

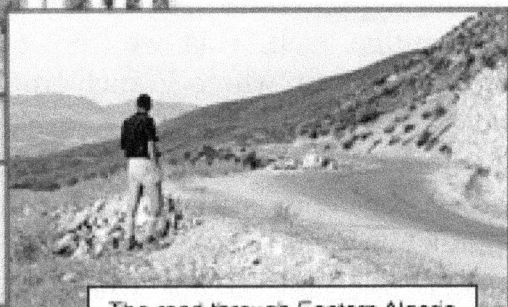

The road through Eastern Algeria

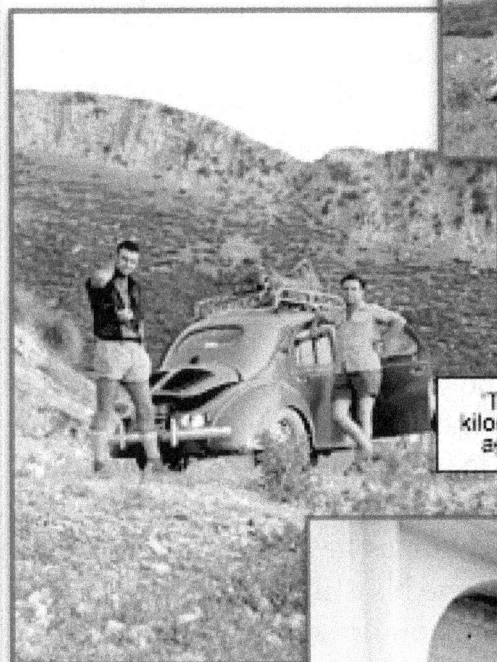

'There was an attack five kilometres from here a month ago. But I think its alright.

'...a soldier with an automatic rifle stood at the door.'

We slept in a small outbuilding that had been converted, in a rudimentary way, to provide some sleeping accommodation for up to six people and heard, on several occasions during the night, the conversations of people...presumably soldiers...outside. In the morning, after some croissants and coffee, we walked down the long tree-lined driveway of the farm and out onto the main road to start hitching.

The next part of our journey across Algeria was to take us through the dramatic landscape of the Constantine area and the city of Constantine itself. This, we were told, was one of the most dangerous parts of Algeria, where French troops were often in open conflict with the rebels. Now, our lifts were exclusively with French drivers... several of whom actually carried a pistol in a holster on their side... rather than in the glove compartment. One could sense the feeling of anxiety and apprehension in the way people drove their vehicles... in the way they looked from side to side when passing through roadside cuttings, or between buildings that were close by the road in the small towns and villages that we drove through on our way to Constantine. On one occasion, after we'd been picked up by a Frenchman driving one of those tiny, rear-engined Renault 4CVs, we found ourselves driving up a long winding road beneath the rugged escarpment of a mountain pass. The car was so small there was no room for both our packs inside. Fortunately the car had a small roof rack on which we tied one of the packs. I sat in the back seat beside the other, while Noel sat in the front.

Our driver, although not carrying a weapon, showed signs of unease, casting a wary eye around him as he drove. But half way up the long road, the call of nature overcame his caution.

'I must stop,' he said. 'I must...how do you say?.... make a pee.'

'Is it safe here?' Noel asked.

'I think so,' he smiled. 'There was an attack five kilometres from here one month ago. But I think it is alright.'

We all got out of the car to relieve ourselves, and took some pictures...looking somewhat nervously along the skyline, before driving on.

Constantine is a natural fortress. It occupies a rocky, diamond-shaped plateau about 650 metres high, surrounded on all sides, except to the southwest, by a precipitous gorge up to 300 metres deep. It is believed to have been founded more than 2,300 years ago by the Phoenicians, who had established the major western outpost of their empire nearby at Carthage, now modern Tunis. Constantine was then known as Cirta and was one of the most important towns in ancient Numidia. It became a Roman town during Julius Caesar's reign and later served as part of a confederation of four Roman colonies on the North African coast.

Driving through the town is an extraordinary experience as much of it is built right to the edge of the sheer cliffs of the gorge. The main crossing of the gorge by road is over the spectacular El Kantara bridge, a great stone arch, connected at either end to what looks like a huge Roman viaduct that runs for some distance along the vertical edge of the cliff face.

The plateau on which the city is built is divided into two parts: To one side, on the west, is the casbah... the old citadel, a mosque, converted by the French to a cathedral (now reconverted back to a mosque), a Moorish style palace (now occupied by the military), as well as administrative and commercial buildings set out by the French amidst wide squares and straight streets. On the other side, to the east, the buildings are of largely Islamic architecture with tortuous lanes forming a complex jig-saw puzzle where various trades all have their own quarter and entire streets are given over to one particular craft.

Having been dropped off from our lift near the centre of town, we stopped and bought a soft drink in a small cafe, as well as some supplies in a nearby grocery store. Then, after asking directions and locating a signpost pointing to 'Tunisie', we picked up a short lift, of about fifteen kilometres, which took us to a turnoff where our driver needed to continue south, while we wanted to go east. But at least we were now on the main road to Tunisia, with only a further 240 kilometres before we would reach the frontier. With a couple of good lifts we felt we could make it that day.

Before long we were picked up by a small utility truck driven by a diesel mechanic on his way to Guelma, about eighty five kilometres further east. There was only room for one of us in the front cabin. We tossed a coin and Noel won. I sat in the back... but I enjoyed the cooling breeze anyway.

Later in the afternoon we were travelling with a man and his wife, both French, for a stretch of the journey beyond Guelma. There was much less traffic on the roads than we'd found further west and its absence soon became even more noticeable. We were passing now through a section of arid countryside, lined on either side with barren mountains and rocky escarpments, which came down close to the road, first on one side and then the other.

Although, for the previous half-hour there'd been a lively interchange between us, in the back of their Citroen 15CV and them in the front seats....partly in our broken french, but mostly in their much better English... now the conversation lagged, drifting into an uneasy silence. Again there was a feeling of heightened anticipation as the driver seemed to focus his attention more on the road ahead, as well as scanning the escarpment to either side whenever possible. His wife also cast occasional anxious glances up into the rocky cliffs.

A sudden easing of the tension swept through the car as three French Army trucks and two jeeps came by in the opposite direction. There was a little laugh from our driver and his shoulders visibly relaxed, even though the trucks were past us in a matter of seconds. We too breathed a little more easily. I guess he figured and we also felt it... that, if the trucks had passed along it, the road ahead should be relatively safe. It wasn't really rational thinking because there could be no guarantee that this was the case, but we felt better anyway.

'It is very uncomfortable....this part of the country,' our driver said. 'There have been several attacks on Army vehicles, as well as cars... civilian cars... here. People have been killed.

'Are there many FLN here.'

'Yes. This country has many places for FLN commandos to hide. I do not like to pass through here.'

We continued along through similar territory for another hour, through the Mountains of the Medjerda, arriving eventually at Souk Ahras a small provincial town only 75 kilometres from the Tunisian border.

It was about 4.00 in the afternoon. With a good lift, we could still easily make the border, so, after thanking our driver and his wife, and saying goodbye, we shouldered our packs and began to walk through the town, making for the outskirts on the eastern side.

'What are they all staring at?' I muttered. As we walked along the road, passing shops and stalls. Everybody; mainly Arabs, but also an occasional European, was looking at us.

We waved and smiled... 'Salaam Ali Qum.' No response.

I guess there's not too many like us that come through here now.' As Noel spoke, three soldiers... two carrying automatic weapons, the other a junior officer... came towards us.'

'Vous allez ou?' the officer asked. ('Where are you going?')

'À Tunisie,' I replied. 'Nous sommes Australiens.'

'Comment voyagez? ('How are you traveling?')

'Auto-stop...' I gestured with my thumb... 'Hitch-hiking.'

He shook his head. 'Votre papiers s'ils vous plaît.' ('Your papers please')

We pulled out our passports and showed them to him. He looked at them for a couple of minutes, clearly not knowing what to do about us.

'Venez,' he said motioning us to follow him.

Passing the town's large market building, we noted that the entrance, reached by a short flight of steps, was sandbagged, and that a soldier with an automatic weapon stood at the door. A little further on we came to a small, white-washed two-storey building on the corner of two streets near the town's main square. It carried a blue and white sign, 'Gendarmerie' over the entrance, which was on the corner of the building. The whole building was surrounded, to roughly half-way up the height of the ground floor, by sandbags and barbed wire, with a makeshift pillbox near the entrance, which was manned by two more soldiers.

'You cannot go to Tunisie today.' The speaker now was the town's Chief of Police, or a Gendarme of similar standing...I can't remember his actual title. He spoke English fairly well, but more importantly, his manner was warm and friendly. He too had examined our passports, raised his eyebrows and asked us our plans.

'It is too dangerous. You must be aware that this is a difficult and dangerous region?'

'Yes, of course,' I said. 'But we must continue to the border... we are heading towards Libya and Egypt.' His eyebrows lifted a fraction more ... 'What about tomorrow...' I asked. '...could we go then?'

'Tomorrow might be possible,' he smiled. 'It is the evenings and nights that are most difficile. We do not allow travel to the border after 17 hours. Also we have a curfew in the town from 22 hours to 6 hours in the morning. But tomorrow...there are army vehicles travelling to the border post... and I know a man who is going to Tunis.'

'Wow,' Noel exclaimed. 'That'd be great. Can we meet him?'

'Maybe not tonight. Where will you sleep?'

'Is there a youth hostel... an Auberge de la Jeunesse... here?'

'Non... it is closed. There was one, but with the troubles here, there is no business.' He hesitated a moment... 'You can sleep here.' He gestured towards the outer office, near the entrance. 'There are chairs...or the floor. It is not very comfortable, but you will be safe.'

That's fine,' I said. 'We have sleeping bags. We can sleep on top of them.'

'Good. I will try to contact the man who is going to Tunis tomorrow.'

Although we managed to make ourselves slightly more comfortable than it would have been on a bare wooden floor... with our bags and a couple of cushions from some office chairs... we didn't manage a great deal of sleep during that night. We were positioned just inside the main entrance doorway to the building, in a big room that had been partitioned off to provide what would have been a sort of enquiries desk in calmer times. Now, the room had been opened up and largely cleared of furniture to provide freer access to and from the outer enclosure of sandbags and the manned pillbox.

When the 10.00 pm curfew came into effect, the town was in darkness and silence, except for our police station, which seemed to be the centre of reasonably continuous activity. The windows were all darkened with blinds and tape, so that as little light as possible was thrown from the building...possibly so the night vision of the men behind the sandbags outside was not affected. Several times during the night, patrols of three or four soldiers came and went from the station, each time passing us, trying to sleep, on the floor. From time to time, from another office we could hear static-filled two-way radio transmissions...presumably from a patrol...and twice we heard prolonged bursts of automatic weapon fire in some other part of the town. On both occasions we sat up from our positions on the floor, to listen. But the sounds did not last more than a few minutes and elicited no more than passing interest from anyone else in the building. From about three in the morning, I think, until six, we managed to get some sleep.

We breakfasted on the remains of a large baguette we had bought the previous afternoon and some coffee that had been offered us in a small kitchen by a couple of young gendarmes.

'This is Monsieur Garray...' The police officer who had questioned us the day before came into the room, followed by a man in his late thirties, dressed in a pair of slacks and an open-necked, short-sleeved business shirt. '...he will take you to Tunis this morning.'

We were naturally elated and shook his hand enthusiastically. 'What time will you leave?' I asked.

'In half an hour. Can you be ready?'

'Certainment,' I laughed.

OOOOOO

TUNISIA

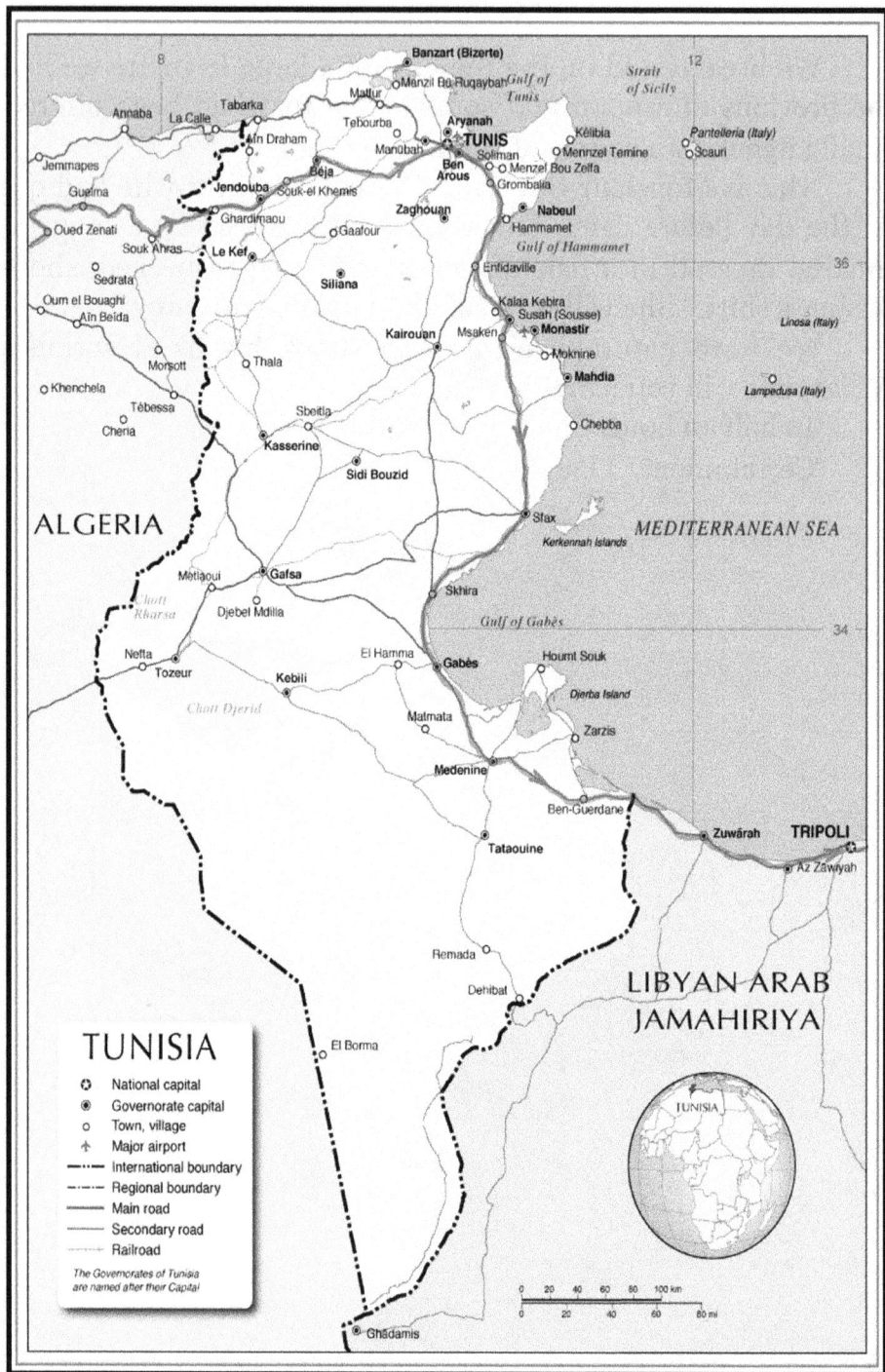

TUNISIA

4

TONIGHT...SOMETHING SPECIAL

The difference in atmosphere between Algeria and Tunisia was quite palpable. Although both countries were populated largely by Arabs and both had spent many years under French colonial administration, there appeared to be far fewer outward signs of animosity towards the French. This was something that had been of some concern to us, because Noel and I were often, quite naturally, but mistakenly taken by Arabs to be French. French by default... simply because we looked European and not Arab. We were always quick to try and let it be known that we were Australian, not French... particularly in Algeria, or in any situation where being French might prove to be a disadvantage.

We had crossed the border from Algeria at Ghardimaou after an uneventful drive through the remaining 75 kilometres of Algerian territory. We'd averaged just fifty kilometres an hour because we kept a position in the middle of four army trucks which were travelling in convoy to the border. But no-one was complaining. The feeling of security was worth much more than achieving a faster time.

The 260-kilometre run to Tunis from the border was also straightforward, with the traffic on the road gradually increasing as we approached the capital, passing through only three towns of any size...Jendouba, Beja and Medjez el-Bab on the way.

Tunisia is the smallest of the four Arab countries that make up what is known as the 'Maghrib', or the 'Arab West', consisting of Morocco, Algeria, Tunisia and Libya. Unlike its neighbours on either side, Algeria and Libya, Tunisia has comparatively meagre resources at its disposal. It had previously discovered petroleum deposits beneath the desert sands to the south, which though modest in size, compared to those of Algeria and Libya, had nevertheless become Tunisia's chief export.. In recent years the tens of thousands of tourists who are drawn annually to the sparkling beaches and clear blue waters along more than a thousand kilometres of Tunisian coastline, have also made a substantial contribution... almost the same amount as oil...to the country's economy.

But at the time Noel and I were there, there were no signs of these future contributions to the country's well-being. In the countryside the people were poor... existing basically as peasant farmers. French settlers were able to sustain a reasonable level of affluence as they still occupied large areas of the country, which were used for farming grapes, dates, olives and other fruits. They had begun coming to Tunisia in the late nineteenth and early twentieth centuries, after France invaded the country in 1881 and made it a French Protectorate. Although there was none of the wholesale confiscation of land and displacement of population that had occurred in Algeria, the most fertile portions of northern Tunisia had passed largely into the hands of Europeans.

However, in the years after World War II French influence had been waning, while moves towards independence had gained strength. In July 1954 the French premier, Pierre Mendès France, promised to grant complete autonomy to Tunisia, subject to a freely negotiated convention. One of the long-time leaders of the Neo-Destour independence party, Habib Bourguiba, who had been successively jailed, placed under house arrest or detained for one reason or another, over more than twenty years, was released and allowed to supervise the negotiations for a new convention.

In June 1955, while Noel and I were in Tunis, the preliminary document was signed, although it imposed limits to Tunisian autonomy in the fields of foreign policy, education, defence and finance.

However, nine months later, in March 1956 an accord was reached for full independence with Bourgiba as Prime Minister. Sixteen months after that, on July 25 1957, The Tunisian Republic was declared, and Habib Bourguiba became its first President. He remained President for 30 years, being ousted in 1987 by his own Prime Minister, Zine Abidene Ben Ali, who claimed that Bourguiba at 84 was to ill and too senile to govern. Bourguiba died in 2000 aged 97.

Ben Ali remained in power as leader of what became one of the most repressive regimes in the Arab World, for 23 years. Accused of corruption and of plundering the economy to benefit his family, he fled the country after being forced from office during the 2011 Tunisian revolution...the revolution which sparked the 'Arab Spring' uprisings across the entire Arab World.

In October of that year, the leader of the previously banned Ennahda Movement, an Islamist organisation, Moncef Marzouki, was named interim president.

Three years later, in December, 2014, in the country's first regular presidential election since the Tunisian Revolution, the moderate former foreign Minister and Prime Minister, 88-year-old Caid Essebsi won office to become Tunisia's first freely elected president.

But within months the country was in shock over the horrific murder, in March 2015, by Islamic State terrorists of 22 foreign tourists, including a young Australian, on the steps of the Bardo Museum in the centre of Tunis. Three months later 38 Western tourists, nearly all British, were mown down on a beach and in a hotel outside of the coastal city of Sousse.

These, as the world is coming to appreciate, are people with a very different and more horrifyingly brutal agenda than the rebels in Algeria at the time of our journey across North Africa. Murder is murder, I suppose, whichever way you look at it, but somehow, fighting for the independence of your country seems different than killing people en masse because they don't happen to adhere to your particular religious beliefs.

So, in those comparatively innocent times of 1955, events like that 2015 massacre would have been hard to believe and of course, naturally enough, when Noel and I arrived in Tunis, we knew nothing of the far more benign political convention that was being hammered out in the corridors of power to secure independence for the country.

What had occupied our minds... or rather, gave us a somewhat comforting feeling... prior to our arrival, was the knowledge that we had a place to stay, or at least the potential for it. We had the name of a Frenchman and his wife that had been given to us by friends of his... another French family... who had befriended us in Grenoble, while we'd been hitch-hiking through France, several months earlier.

We had been heading down through France towards the Riviera

and were picked up, in the middle of the afternoon, by a young businessman from Grenoble called Alain and his wife, Francoise, who were returning home after spending several days in Geneva..

'You are from Australia?!' he had said in surprise, and quite good English as we began a conversation in the car. It had become a little joke between Noel and I, whenever we got a lift, to watch the reactions after we'd given them the... 'we're from Australia' routine. We had a set of little faces we could pull later to mimic these reactions; raised eyebrows, a low whistle, shaking the right hand, with a limp wrist, back and forth (a universal gesture of amazement in France)... or a combination of all three.

'Yes,' Noel said. 'We have been in Europe for almost a year... travelling and working in different places. Now we are going to Africa.'

'We should give them the address of our friends in Tunis,' his wife interrupted.

'Are you going to North Africa?' Alain asked.

'No.... we are heading for South Africa.'

'Oh. It is a shame. We have good friends in Tunis. Are you not passing through Tunis?'

'I suppose there is a chance,' I said. 'But I think we will try to get to South Africa by ship.'

'You know, you may not plan to go there now....' Francoise persisted, turning to us in the back seat, '...but who knows, you may change your plans.'

And, as things turned out, it was some pretty good crystal-gazing on her part and we were extremely thankful to be able to turn up the contact in our address books, as we were dropped off by our driver in the centre of Tunis, that day in June, 1955.

When I think about it now, it seems amazing, how different things were then...that people would pick us up, as we thumbed a ride, from the side of the road and not only carry us along our way, but invite us into their homes, as Alain and Francoise did in Grenoble, feed us and put us up for the night. I'm sure it still does happen now... but far less frequently. People are too busy, too sophisticated, too affluent. Yet it was the sort of thing that happened to us quite often. I think it must have had something to do with the relative rarity of encounters with Australians... so far from home. We were something of an oddity. Of course there were plenty of other Australians travelling in Europe even in those days, ten years after the war, but in comparative terms, the numbers were small and for many people, we were the first Australians they had ever met. To them, at least, we seemed unusual...almost from another planet.

And of course, this was definitely the case when we turned up on Alain and Francoise's friends in Tunis. Marcel Juin was a lecturer at a Teacher's College, located in one of the outer suburbs of Tunis. At this time of year, the school was about to break for summer recess, and activities were generally winding down, but the students were still on campus and the lecturers, including Marcel, were not due to take off on their own vacation for another couple of weeks.

Marcel welcomed us warmly and said with a chuckle, as we introduced ourselves. 'You are very early.'

He told us that he had received a note from Alain in Grenoble warning him to expect a visit from two Australian hikers.

'But I did not expect it to be so soon,' he laughed. 'In fact, Alain was very vague. He said "sometime in the next twelve months!" And I only received that letter a month ago. How long will you stay?'

'Well,' Noel and I looked at each other. 'We'd like to try to organize our visas for Libya from here...' I said. '... and then move on. We are hoping to get across Libya to Egypt.'

'So, you will need a few days. You must stay here at the college. We have plenty of space. You can have one of the empty student rooms. Yes. Yes. It is perfectly all right.' He was talking to himself for a moment or two, as he sorted through the various possibilities in his mind. 'And of course, you can eat here, in the students' cafeteria.'

'But tonight...now, you will meet my wife and you must have dinner with us.'

'We are very dusty and dirty,' I said. 'In Algeria we did not have much opportunity to...'

'Of course, of course,' Marcel interrupted. 'You must wash. Certainly. There are douches... showers. I will show you where you will stay and you can wash there. Then you will come to meet my wife... and we shall eat.'

We were shown a small bedroom which contained four bunk beds, but which, Marcel explained, we could have to ourselves. He also introduced us to several of the young student teachers, who were all about the same age, give or take a year, as Noel and I. They were mostly French, although there were two or three young men who were clearly of Arab extraction, but who spoke in French all the time. On that first occasion, as we were being settled in, none of the students hid their fascination in us...two unexpected newcomers on the scene... nor their curiosity.

'Where do you come from?', 'What part of Australia?', 'What is Australia like?', 'Where are you going to?', 'Why are you travelling in Africa?', 'How did you come to Tunis?', 'What is Algeria like?', 'What is Morocco like?'....and so on.

We had plenty of opportunity to answer their questions later, but on that first evening, after scrubbing up and putting on clean shirts, we went straight to Marcel's small apartment in another part of the building, to meet his wife, Michele and to have dinner with them.

Michele was dark-haired and diminutive. But for her eyes, which were strikingly blue, she could perhaps have passed as an Arab... although I wouldn't have dared suggest it to her. The way things were at that stage between French and Arab... even in Tunisia, she would not have taken it well. Perhaps her origins were Jewish, or Lebanese... or perhaps Corsican. we never got around to asking her. Marcel, on the other hand, although dark haired, was fair-skinned and came, he said, from Brittany. The two of them had been in Tunis for three years. Michele worked in a bookstore in central Tunis.

'But you must tell us of Francoise and Alain.' Michele asked, as we sat at table. 'They are our good friends and we have not seen them for almost two years now.'

We told them of our meeting and of dinner with them in Grenoble and of the fact that we didn't really expect to ever be passing through Tunis.

'But now you are glad to have come, yes?' Marcel smiled. 'What do you think of Tunisia?'

'Well, we haven't really had a chance to tell,' Noel replied. 'But it seems much calmer than Algeria. It was often a little scary for us travelling there... with the civil war.'

'Yes. It is bad. We have had some disturbances here, but the tension here is not so great as in Algerie because the Tunisians have been promised independence by Mendes France... the Premier of France. They have just now signed a convention about it. Everybody is very happy.'

'Everybody?' I asked.

'He means the Tunisians,' Michele laughed. 'Many of the French settlers don't want it, of course.'

'And you?'

'Oh, we are French... but we are not settlers.' Marcel leant back in his chair and puffed on a pipe. 'We have come here to work... and we like it here, but we do not want to stay forever... to make it our home. So we think a little differently from the settlers. I can see that the country really belongs to the Tunisian people... not to the French. They should have it back.'

'Not a very popular view with other French people, I imagine?'

Now they both laughed. 'No. I must admit we are careful about expressing our opinions. But it is history... you cannot hold it back.'

Although it was a Monday, the students' exams had recently been concluded and, in the days leading up to their vacation, they had a certain amount of free time... at least that's what they told us. Several of the young men we had met on the evening of our arrival had joined our table at breakfast the following morning to renew the acquaintance.

'Would you like to see some of Tunis...and Carthage?' Jeanfois Lette, one of the group, asked us. Although all of the students were friendly, Jeanfois was perhaps the most extrovert of the four or five who seemed to attach themselves to us over the next couple of days. I think they saw us as some sudden light relief to the relative boredom of the last week or so at the college when nothing much was happening on the academic front.

Jeanfois had curly, sandy-coloured hair, with freckles on his face... and looked not unlike Noel, except that he was tall and slim. He spoke the best English of the group, but his most endearing features were a big grin and an infectious laugh.

'Carthage? Ancient Carthage. Is it far from here?' I asked.

'No, it is not far. We can go on the bus.'

'Okay, ' Noel said, 'that would be good, but first we must organise our visa for Libya. We can't leave Tunis until we get that.'

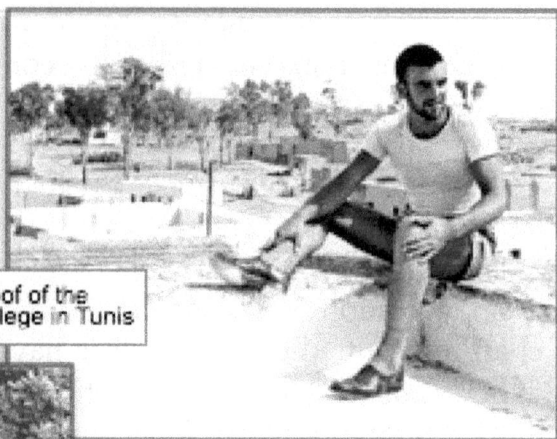

On the roof of the
Teachers College in Tunis

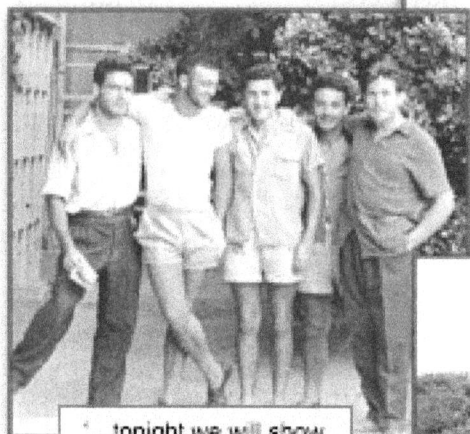

'...tonight we will show
you something special.'

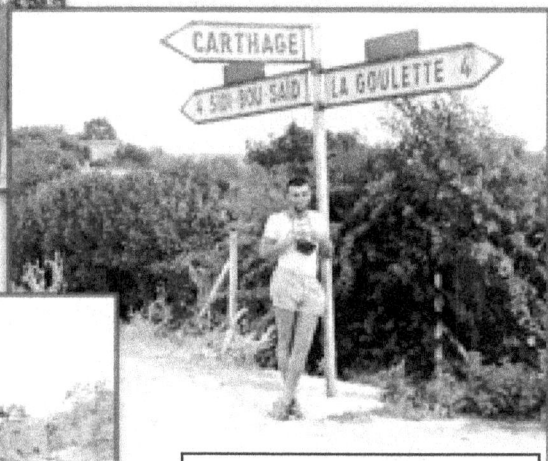

'Carthage? Ancient Carthage.
Is it far from here?'

'All of what is left now is
from Roman times...'

It sounds incredible now, but to Noel and I at the time, it seemed perfectly natural that a visa for Libya should be obtained from the British Consul in Tunis.

'We will find out where the consulate is,' Jeanfois said . 'So you can get your visa. Then we can go to Carthage.'

Our visit to the British Consulate was quick and efficient. It wasn't as if there were queues of people waiting for Libyan visas. And the political situation in Libya was vastly different from today. Since 1951 it had been a kingdom under the rule of a pro-British King, Idris I and in 1955, ten years after the end of World War II, both Britain and the United States still maintained military and air bases in Libya.

From the British Consulate, not far from the centre of Tunis, we went to the Post Office to send off some letters, which we'd written on the road, to our parents, to two Norwegian girls we'd met in France and to our friends in London. We then spent a hour in the famous Bardo Museum, to see the incredible collection of Carthaginian and Roman mosaics. (The same museum which, sixty years later was the scene of the horrific murders described above). Leaving it, we wandered under the trees on the main pedestrian thoroughfare of Tunis, through the hundreds of stalls along the centre of the avenue selling everything from ivory chess sets and mother-of-pearl chairs to monkeys and leather-bound books in ancient Arabic. Then we took a bus for the half-hour journey to the small township of Carthage.

The area is now a smart and wealthy suburb of Tunis that is sprinkled with expensive villas...and is also the site... adjacent to the ruins... of the modern Presidential Palace. Neither the palace nor the villas were there when we visited. They were well into the future.

According to tradition, Princess Elissa of Tyre led a band of Phoenicians to the northern coast of Tunisia in 814 BC and founded there the city of Carthage. In the following centuries Carthage grew in power and influence until it dominated much of the Mediterranean, including parts of Sicily and Sardinia, and vied with Rome for increasing control over a much wider area. Two Mediterranean superpowers became one too many and the Punic Wars between Carthage and Rome were the result.

When mighty Hannibal set out to conquer Rome, travelling in a wide loop, via Algeria, Morocco, Spain, France and the Swiss Alps, into northern Italy with an army of almost 60,000 men and 37 elephants... plus all the necessary equipment to support such an army, he set off from ancient Carthage (of course it wasn't ancient then). Its pretty hard to imagine...in fact its all but impossible, because all that remained of the once magnificent ancient Carthage when we came to see it, was a rather pathetic jumble of broken rock walls spread over a promontory that overlooks the sea.

Hannibal defeated Rome in three battles and would have changed the course of European history had he not lost the fourth. As a result of his last defeat, Rome descended on Carthage in 146 BC and utterly destroyed it, ceremonially ploughing the earth on which it stood and pronouncing a curse on the city, forbidding any human habitation. But a century later the Romans returned to rebuild and revitalize Carthage as the chief city of their North African province.

'All of what is left now is from Roman times,' André, one of the students told us. 'Virtually nothing from ancient Carthage remains.'

'They think though, that this was the site of the original Citadel,' Jeanfois added, sweeping his arm around the open area in which we were standing... which included the remnants of a couple of crumbling walls with large arches still intact, but only just. 'It was called the Byrsa. They have found some ancient Phoenician tombs here, but nothing of domestic or public buildings. The Romans, when they returned, put up a temple here to Juno and Jupiter and Minerva.'

'Its difficult to grasp,' Noel said, looking at the encroaching nearby buildings of the present day town. 'The ruins must spread underneath all these local buildings.'

'Of course,' André said. 'The city... I mean the Phoenician city, before the Romans... was very big. It is covered by all these houses. They...the archeologists, believe the walls were about thirty kilometres long and sometimes twelve or thirteen metres high and ten metres thick. They have traced the remains of them. And out here...' he pointed to the shoreline below and to the north of us, '...these two big lagoons were once the ancient harbour. In those times they think the harbour was divided into two... with one part for merchant ships and the other for warships.... over two hundred could be accommodated at a time.'

'Is anything being done at all to preserve it?' I asked. The ruins were falling down in many places and there seemed to be little in the way of restoration works underway.

'Yes, there are French archeologists who are still looking at it. But not very much work is being done now, I think.'

Fortunately, in the sixty years that have passed since that visit to ancient Carthage, much work has been done...firstly to prevent the encroachment of new buildings by modern developers and preserve what is left standing and secondly the extensive exploration by scores of international archeologists that have revealed more of what lies beneath the site. A West German team, for example has carefully removed some four metres of rubble, to discover an orderly grid of rectangular streets, as well as evidence of grand villas.

Carthage is now rightly recognized by the Tunisian government as a National Treasure that must be carefully managed and brought to light.

We spent the rest of the afternoon on the nearby beach... well it wasn't exactly a beach....but swimming off the rocks. The water, however, was crystal clear.

'What will you do tonight?' Jeanfois asked at one point, while we were sitting, watching some young Arab women entering the water.

'Tonight?' I said. 'Why...I don't know.' I looked at Noel. 'Nothing much, I suppose.'

'You have no engagement... with Monsieur and Madame Juin'

'No.'

The rest of students, who had crowded in around Jeanfois, were all smiling. 'Aha!' he said. '...then tonight we will show you something special.' At which all of the others broke into peels of laughter.

Noel and I looked at each other again... even more puzzled.

Before we reached where we were going that evening, both Noel and I knew what was happening, even though our student friends refused, with much laughter, to tell us. We had returned to the college, eaten a meal and, with Jeanfois and three others, left by bus for the centre of Tunis at about 9.00 pm. From near the centre, where we stopped in a small bar to drink some beer, they led us, through increasingly narrow, winding alleys, deeper into the old medina.

Long robed Arab men...and occasionally a woman in long dark robes with a veil across her face...thronged back and forth along the alleys. Tiny cafés and food stalls, crammed into what were hardly more than gaps in the walls and illuminated by dim lights hanging from fraying electrical cords, buzzed with activity....all men...drinking dark, black coffee and thick, sweet tea. Shops and stalls, like the suq in Marrakech, selling everything from safety pins to carpets. And over it all the smell of burning incense and the cacophonous sounds of Arab singing and music. As we walked by, the men in the cafés would eye us curiously.

'You wouldn't catch me coming in here on my own,' Noel said to me at one stage. I agreed. We both felt some security from the fact that there were six of us and that our friends knew their way around. They didn't seem in the least worried. In fact their laughter and merriment seemed to increase as we went along.

Soon we left the narrower alleyways of the bazaar and came out into slightly more open streets... only slightly. They would have been seven or eight feet wide, barely enough to take a vehicle. But there were no cars...only men walking back and forth. The buildings on either side of the dusty road were either of mud-brick or cement rendered. A few of them were single-storeyed, but more often they were of two floors in height and the streets were passably lit.

As if we hadn't known where we were going and the girls standing in the doorways, weren't evidence enough, Jeanfois let us know, with a flourish, 'This is...how do you say it in English? ... the Red Light area of Tunis.'

The fact that we'd guessed our destination did not, however, diminish our amazement. Neither of us had ever spent any time in a so-called Red Light district, let alone been in a brothel. As we walked up and down, among the milling crowd, our eyes must have been out on stalks. The fact that we were a group of young westerners, obviously out for fun...in the midst of a crowd of Arab men...seemed to make a difference, attracting the attention of the young women, several of whom called and waved to us. The majority of the other men walking by were, of course, all individuals, moving along the street on their own, looking at the women in the doorways... seeking to find one who appealed and with whom a price could be decided. Once that had been done, he would step into the room with her and the door would be closed behind them.

There must have been forty women and girls in the doorways of the houses we walked by on the three or four streets that make up the district. They ranged in age from probably fifteen to forty-five or fifty years old. They were predominantly Arab girls, although we also saw several pale-skinned women who could have been European. Many were slim and beautiful, others not quite so attractive.

'Hey, Joe... where you from?'

The shock of suddenly hearing English spoken took us completely by surprise. It was the last thing we'd expected here in the back streets of Tunis. Turning, we saw that it was one of the young European-looking women, with sandy hair, who had apparently heard the students speaking to us in English and called out...

'Hey, come over here. Where you from?'

Other Arab men in the passing crowd, stopped for a moment to stare, as we and our French friends moved across to talk to the young woman.

She looked be somewhere between twenty five and thirty years old... it was hard to tell, with so much makeup on. She could have been much less... twenty-one or so. And yet you could see that even without any makeup she would have been an attractive woman...probably more so than with it. She had high slavic cheekbones, blue eyes and relatively short-cut mousey-blonde hair. 'We're from Australia,' Noel said.

'And France...' put in Jeanfois, in English.

'What about you,' I asked. 'Where are you from?'

'Ah,' she smiled, and gave a little toss of her head, flashing a set of white teeth. Some of the other smiles we'd seen so far during the evening's tour had left quite a bit to be desired... particularly several of the Arab girls who were chewing betel nut, which had left their teeth stained a dark red. '...a long way from here... but not as far as Australia.'

'Europe?'

'Yes, of course.'

We began to guess... but she interrupted. 'No... No, it is Poland. I come from Poland.'

'Poland,' several of us said at once. 'But how did you come here? How long have you been here?'

Again she smiled... and was there something of a sigh? 'Ohh... that story is too long.' Then her professional gaze swept over us, as if time was a-wasting. 'Now...' she smiled and ran her hand over the stubble of my newly forming beard, '....who is to be first?'

I still remember the shock... and the excitement of that moment. It might seem hard to believe, but the idea of going with a prostitute had never seriously entered my head before. I mean in the past... in Australia, or in Europe, when we were hiking around. And even now, on this little tour with our French student teacher friends, we'd really only thought of it as a window-shopping exercise. We weren't going to actually do it. Now, suddenly it all seemed to be happening.

'Yes. Yes...' Jeanfois was laughing and pushing me forward. 'yes. You must go with her.'

'No... No... ' I also laughed, looking at Noel nervously. 'I... No... not now. You,' I grabbed Jeanfois, also with a laugh, 'You should go.'

'No. We can go any time we wish. But you are visitors. You must go now.'

I looked at the Polish girl. She was just standing there, listening to the conversation... and smiling. She looked more beautiful by the moment.

I felt my stomach tighten slightly with excitement. I turned to Noel... and then back to her. 'How much?'   Isn't that what you're supposed to say? I thought.

'Five hundred francs'.

'No... three hundred,' Jeanfois said. 'They do not have much money.'

Her face hardened a little. 'Four hundred... not less,' she said.

I did a quick calculation; seven shillings and sixpence... and turned to Noel again, 'What do you reckon...shall we have a go? There's that other girl we saw earlier, just down the road, who looked nice. Why don't you try her?... Or I could go there and you could take this one.'

The others were all shouting and laughing... urging us on. Noel thought for a bit and then also laughed... 'Okay,' he said, 'You go in here.'

I turned to the Polish girl and with a sweep of her arm, she pulled me past her, into a little bedroom, the door was closed and she was lifting her dress over her shoulders. Outside, the laughter and carrying on continued, but I didn't hear any of it.

After about ten or fifteen minutes, I emerged from the room to be met by raucous cheers from the others and was surprised to find Noel still with them.

'Didn't you go with the other one?' I asked.

'No way. I thought about it and decided that way one of us might get the clap. So I'm going to go with this one too. That way either we both get it... or we both don't get it. Was she any good?'

'Great,' I said, as Noel moved past me to be led by the Polish girl into her room.

oooooo

TUNISIA

5

JUST THE SOUND MADE BY OUR BOOTS

The main cities and towns of North Africa hug the coast. With good reason. All along the shores of Morocco, Algeria, Tunisia, Libya and Egypt, the waters of the Mediterranean create a climate in which moisture-laden air can provide some rainfall to coastal areas. But once you move inland from the sea, in any of the North African countries, you very quickly find yourself in desert... serious desert. They've all got their own deserts; the Moroccan Desert, the Algerian, the Tunisian, the Libyan etc. and as you continue south, in any of them, they all blend into the vast and seemingly limitless Sahara.

In Tunisia, as you leave the capital, heading towards Sousse, some 140 kilometres south on the coast, the countryside remains relatively fertile. There are rolling hills carrying vineyards, groves of olives and date palms. Travelling down a tarred highway, through this pleasant and verdant landscape, with the sea to our left, the desert seemed a long way away.

We had decided to leave Tunis that morning, on the day following our little escapade in the red light district. We had said goodbye, with many thanks, to Marcel and his wife, who fortunately had no idea of our activities of the previous evening...and to Jeanfois, André and their friends. They waved us off around noon and we had walked a few streets from the college towards the main road which would carry us south.

We quickly scored a short lift, of only a few kilometres, in a broken down truck carrying melons, to a small, dusty township on the southern outskirts of Tunis. There, after a half hour wait, we were picked up by an Arab driving one of those Citroen vans the gendarmes used to drive in French movies... the ones that looked as if they were made out of corrugated iron sheets. He was going all the way to Sousse.

Sousse... also founded by the Phoenicians and later used by the Romans, has, in more recent times, become an important trade centre where sardine canning, olive oil processing and textile milling, as well as fishing have been the major economic pursuits. An imposing monastery fortress, called the Ribat, with a tall, circular tower, dominates part of the city, which also has an impressive mosque and extensive marketplaces in the old walled town. But now, in addition to being the third largest Tunisian city... after the capital and Sfax, still some 130 kilometres further south... its become an important centre for tourism. Literally scores of resort hotels, casinos, apartments, restaurants and pizzerias line some twenty kilometres of beach, the so-called zone touristique, along the approach the city. You can swim, play tennis and golf, water ski, paraglide and spend plenty of money while you're doing it.

At least that was how things were until June 26, 2015 when a 23-year-old Tunisian, disguised as a tourist and carrying a beach umbrella on the beach outside the five-star Riu Imperial Marhaba hotel, just to the north of Sousse, suddenly revealed an AK-47 assault rifle and started shooting people. As mentioned in the previous chapter, he managed to kill 38 tourists, before he himself was shot by security forces. These ISIS attacks have understandably dealt the tourism industry in Tunisia a huge blow.

In 1955, of course, none of these problems existed. Nor did the tourst industry. The coastline nearing Sousse was almost completely empty. An occasional ruined mud-brick house... plenty of date palms, an Arab riding a camel or a donkey. But not much traffic at all on the roads then, as we trundled south in the corrugated van. Passing through the outskirts of Sousse, we asked our driver to drop us off at a crossroads in the western part the city, where we quickly picked up a lift to the next small town, Msaken, about ten kilometres on. There we found a good lift of a hundred kilometres or so, in another van, slightly more modern and larger than the previous one, carrying cartons of tinned milk to the town of El Djem.

We had been told of El Djem by Marcel. 'It was the ancient

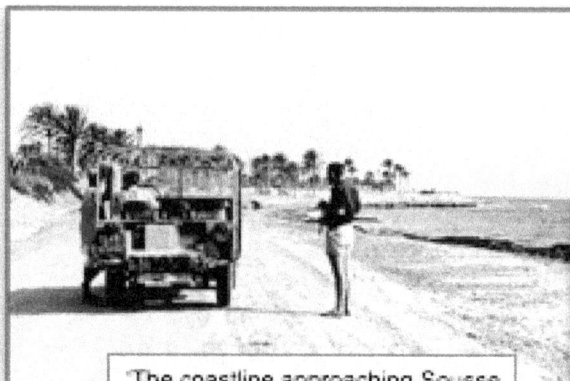

'The coastline approaching Sousse was almost completely empty.'

'El Djem...considered, even now, an engineering marvel.'

'...we asked out driver to drop us off at a crossroads in the western part of the city.'

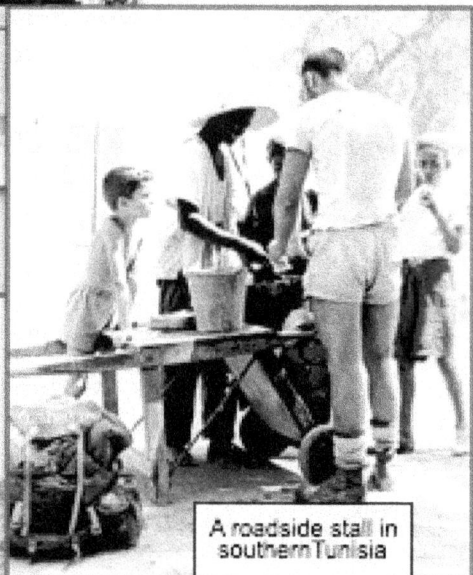

'We looked like a couple of bakers...or probably more like mental patients...'

A roadside stall in southern Tunisia

Roman town of Thysdrus,' he said. 'There is a great ruin there... a colosseum. One of the biggest in the world. You must try to see it.'

Once we mentioned our interest in the ruins to the driver of the van, he insisted on making a slight diversion, when we arrived in El Djem, to drop us right at the ruins.

And Marcel hadn't been exaggerating. The ruins were incredible. Apart from a section of it that had been blown away by explosives in the seventeenth century in efforts to evict squatters, much of the building is intact. Built between AD 230 and AD 238 and considered, even now, an engineering marvel, it could seat more than 30,000 people who came to see what the Romans of those days felt was sport and entertainment...men pitted against wild animals or other men, in a struggle to the death.

As we wandered around the ruins and reflected on those gruesome times, I wondered too at the absence of other people. There had been no entrance gate for us to pass through, no admittance charged, nor any evidence then of archeological work going on. There was nobody else there. No tourists. We just wandered in, took several photographs and then sat in different parts of the ruins for about half an hour, looking around in awe and talking about it.

'Amazing to think this place could have been being a centre of so much activity,' I said to Noel. '...to have supported such a large population. It must have been much bigger than it is now. Now it all seems so small-scale and low-key.' There was the present-day town of El Djem all around the great structure of course, but it was a hodgepodge sprawl of single-storey, white-washed mud-brick houses from amongst whose residents you couldn't have rustled up 10,000 people in a month of Sundays.

'The climate must have been quite different,' Noel noted. 'It must have been a good deal more temperate... more rainfall or something, otherwise why the hell would they stick around and go to such trouble as building things like this.'

In fact the area during the period of Roman rule had been quite prosperous, producing and exporting... to Rome and other parts of the empire... huge quantities of olive oil. And apparently the region still generates much of its income from olives and olive oil. Certainly, as we continued south, even though the landscape was becoming gradually more arid, we saw endless groves of olive trees.

From close by the ruins of El Djem, we had been picked up by an Arab driver and his cohort in an old truck that was obviously labouring heavily under a load of too many bags of cement. We could ride in the back, they said, with the cement bags, which they were delivering to a town called Djebiriana, about forty kilometres from El Djem, on the coast. We travelled with them on the main road south for about 25 kilometres before they turned off to head for the coast and we hopped down from the back of the truck to spend the next ten minutes trying to brush a fine powdery layer of cement from our skin, hair and clothes.

We were able to keep moving south after waiting for only a short while at the turnoff before getting two or three lifts that took us 120 kilometres or so further on to Tunisia's second largest city and port, Sfax. Once a stronghold of the Barbary pirates, it has a tenth century mosque and citadel which is surrounded by the high, original ramparts built in the 9th century. Driving through the city, we passed around the outside of the ramparts but didn't go inside.

In the outer southern suburbs of Sfax, we were once more on the main road south, hoping to press on and reach the southern town of Gabes, also a former Roman town that was in 1955 an important oasis and sponge-fishing port on the Gulf of Gabes, before night.

By the time we arrived in Gabes... whose main claim to fame now is that it is the site of two enormous chemical plants, converting phosphate, one of the few riches of the Tunisian soil, into fertilizers and other products... we found we still had a couple of hours of daylight remaining. So, although the chemical plants weren't in existence then, and Gabes would probably have been as good a place as any to stay, we decided to keep trying for a further lift at a fork in the road, by a sign pointing south to Medenine. If nothing came, we would walk through the town and camp somewhere near the sea.

We had not carried tents in all the time we had been travelling in Europe. Staying in youth hostels meant that a sleeping bag was quite sufficient. Now, in these parts of North Africa, we had basically run out of youth hostels. And, as we didn't want to spend any money, the only alternative was to camp out, which meant just sleeping by the side of the road, or wherever was more comfortable. Rain, or cold didn't come into it. The weather was hot and dry, throughout the night...and that was it. You didn't have to worry about a roof over your head.

As it happened, a Frenchman and his companion in a Jeep came by after about twenty minutes and picked us up.

'We can take you as far as Ben Guerdane, beyond Medenine,' he said when we told him we were heading for Libya. 'We are going further south, into the desert,' he continued, '...but it is not on your way.'

Ben Guerdane, we knew from our map, was the last town in Tunisia before the Libyan border... which was about 40 kilometres further on.

As we drove, the desert seemed to creep closer and closer to us... so that, while on our left we hardly ever lost sight of the deep blue Mediterranean, to our right...the west, the flat, barren countryside disappeared in haze of heat as the sun sank towards the straight line of the horizon which we knew was a formidable desert. And yet, a few kilometres out there to the west of the road we were travelling, in a place called Matmata, a group of troglodyte Berbers live permanently in the desert. They have created a settlement of unique underground homes. Because Noel and I didn't know about it, we didn't get to see Matmata on that occasion.

We did however eventually see it independently... about thirty years later, on the silver screen... when it was used by George Lucas as the desert setting for Luke Skywalker's home on the Planet Utapau in the film 'Star Wars'.

'Is there anything between Ben Guerdane and the border?' Noel asked our French driver. 'Any settlements?'

'No, nothing. You might get a lift to the frontier from Ben Guerdane, but it will be difficult. There is no traffic.'

The vehicle we were travelling in was clearly fitted out for desert travel. It carried sand mats and ladders lashed to the side and extra 25 litre water cans fitted on the back and one side. But there were no extra supplies or luggage, otherwise there would have been no room for Noel and I in the back. Even carrying no extras, a Jeep doesn't afford much room in the back seats and, with our packs, we were pretty cramped.

'Where are you going?' I asked, thinking there might be an

alternative route we could take with him.

'It has no name,' he said. 'It is just a couple of coordinates on the map.   We're part of an oil exploration group. We're surveying and looking for oil.   It is only about twenty or thirty kilometres from Ben Guerdane, but there is nothing there... only desert. Its of no use for you.'

In a way, we would have loved to have gone with them, to their isolated camp... just to see it, or perhaps even find some work there, but it wouldn't have made much sense. Our prime plan was to make as fast progress as possible towards Egypt, so, less than an hour later, we scrambled out of the Jeep on a dusty corner at the edge of the tiny village of Ben Guerdane and watched them head off into the desert.

Ben Guerdane might have been marked on the map, but there wasn't much there. For some reason in, the distant past, someone had decided this was the place for a town. It must have been water...that would have been the only reason...because there was nothing else that would have attracted anyone. And even water didn't seem in evidence at first glance. The landscape was totally flat all around us...full circle. A cluster of straggly date palms stood here and there, close by a collection of small buildings, some made of mud brick, of which half were whitewashed, the others left the colour of the soil. Others were made of stones collected from the surrounding desert,   which itself seemed to have been randomly strewn with countless millions of football-sized rocks. In the hot, dry and windless late evening air, two camels stood in the lengthening shadows of a building. Nearby, an Arab walking beside a donkey pulling a barrow full of onions moved towards us

Asking a few questions in French, we were told that there was virtually no traffic running from here to the border. He shook his head discouragingly and waggled a finger in the air, as if to say we would find it impossible to get there.

'Well, there's nothing much we can do but wait,' Noel said. 'We might as well find a place that we can sit and keep an eye on the road.'

'Right, but we shouldn't be too far away... in case anything comes along. They're not going to stop here, that's for sure.'

Looking around, we decided to dump our bags and sit in the long shadow of a small building not far from the road. It was quite a solid-looking building made of rocks, but was clearly empty, though its decaying wooden door was locked.

'I'll go and see if I can find some bread,' I said, leaving Noel to mind the packs and walking into the cluster of buildings that formed Ben Guerdane. Fortunately, there were a couple of tiny shops, one of which, for want of a better description, you would call a 'general store', which sold as many things as the people of Ben Guerdane needed, which wasn't much...plus quite a few they didn't need. I managed to buy some bread, a few tins of sardines and some surprisingly good tomatoes. We already had several tins of sardines, but I knew we'd be eating some tonight and they were always a good staple food, a standby to have with us whenever possible. I also asked a few more questions of the store owner and some of his Arab customers.

'They all say there's practically no traffic between here and the border,' I reported to Noel when I returned. 'But several of them told me that, once we get there... there's plenty of traffic going back and forth to Tripoli.'

Tripoli, the Libyan capital was a good 400 kilometres on from the border, over similar countryside to that of southern Tunisia. So we'd need some good lifts to cover the distance.

Noel nodded. 'Do they say there's any traffic at all on this side?'

'Yes. But its apparently pretty sparse. A few trucks... but they're few and far between.'

'So, there's still nothing we can do but wait.... I guess.'

As dusk fell, we settled down, a little gloomily, by the side of the building to prepare our sardines and tomatoes.

'Of course the shade'll be on the opposite side of the building tomorrow,' I commented. 'We'll have to move to somewhere else.'

'Maybe we wont have to wait that long,'

'Don't count on it.'

After two nights... that is, by the end of two full days in Ben Guerdane, most of the daylight hours of which we'd spent trying to find shade by the sides of buildings or... in the middle of the day, when the sun was directly overhead... beneath a nearby date palm, not a single vehicle had passed in the direction of the border. A total of five trucks, including two pickups, had arrived from the direction of Gabes; two on the first day, three on the second. But they'd just turned off the road to be swallowed in the jumble of small buildings that was Ben Guerdane.

Three of them did eventually emerge to return in the direction from which they'd come.

By about 4.00 in the afternoon of that second day, we were both feeling depressed and the need to do something. We'd tossed it around between us during the day, but now it required some action.

'I reckon we've got to make a move...walk to the border,' Noel said. 'If we wait an hour or so, it'll be starting to get a little cooler.'

'Okay,' I agreed. 'If we leave at five, we should be able to cover a good distance tonight. We'll take it slowly at first, until it gets dark... then we should be able to make better time, when its cooler.'

We'd decided to try walking during the night hours, sleeping during the following day... if we could find some shade... and then continue the walk the following night, if necessary. But with luck, we might be able to cover the 40 kilometres in one night.

We had filled our water cans and had bought an additional two large bottles of soft drink, which we'd stowed in our packs. And we'd told the keeper of the small general store that we planned to walk to the border. At first he was amazed. Then he shook his head and, like the man with the onions, wagged his finger, indicating he thought we were crazy, but left it at that.

The sun was setting at a little after seven-thirty in the evenings, so by five it was still pretty potent. Too hot to start walking.

'Let's give it another half-hour,' I said. 'We'll take off then.'

For some reason we didn't have hats... a pretty strange thing to have overlooked in that sort of heat. At least my hair had grown a bit in the short time since I'd been shorn almost bald, by Serge back in Casablanca, and both our beards were progressing, so there was some protection. But in addition, during the past couple of days, we'd each made makeshift hats by taking handkerchiefs, tying four knots in the corners and sitting them on our heads. We looked like a couple of bakers... or probably more like mental patients, which...when you think about what we were about to do, was probably closer to the mark.

'You know, if we walk five hours, at an average of, say five kilometres an hour tonight, we could probably stop around ten and have a sleep.' I said as we plodded off down the road towards a totally flat and featureless horizon. 'That'd be twenty five kilometres. Then, if we slept by the road for say another five hours and got up at three in the morning to walk for another five hours, we could cover another twenty five... or at least fifteen or so, before it got too hot to keep going and that'd do it.'

'I reckon we should keep going during the night for as long as we can,' Noel said. '...to make the most of the cool. Then, as it gets light tomorrow, we can keep an eye out for trees or any buildings so we can have some shade to sleep in tomorrow, if we don't get to the border.'

For a while, as the sun set slowly, almost directly behind us, our shadows became strange Humpty-Dumpty-like figures with long, spindly legs, topped by the big lumps made by our packs. They stretched along the empty road ahead and into the desert until the darkness came and they disappeared in the gloom.

Soon, it became so dark that we could hardly see the road, and could only tell when we were off the edge of it by the rocky, unmade feel of the verge. But as there were no distracting lights... anywhere... our eyes became gradually accustomed to the darkness. Soon there was just the starlight, which was quite incredible...so brilliant and clear was the sky above us that it was quite sufficient for us to make out the dim line of the road we were following.

For periods, as we walked, we would talk about all manner of things; the friends and good times we'd had back on the beach in Australia, the great parties we'd held during the cold London winter in our flat in South Kensington, the Norwegian girls we'd met in Cannes at the time of the Film Festival there. How, in those early days of the festival, it was relatively easy to meet the movie stars. How Doris Day and Peter Ustinov posed for photographs with us.. and how we swam, illegally, from the beach of the Carlton Hotel. Then there would be long periods of silence...twenty minutes, half an hour...when nothing was said and there was just the sound made by our boots as we walked.

By about ten, we were both ready to stop. But we went on for another half-hour...to make it five hours of walking. We'd paced it out quite well for the whole five hours, trying to ensure that we didn't go too fast and build up a sweat. Still, we felt reasonably confident that we'd covered almost 25 kilometres. And we'd only drank about half the water in our water cans. The soft drinks were still intact, but we both knew we would have to be careful.

'Just as well its bloody flat,' Noel commented as we cleared a few rocks to spread our sleeping bags down in the sand, between some low shrubs. 'I wouldn't have liked that if it was up and down hills.'

As we lay down, we both fell instantly into a deep sleep... not really a sleep of exhaustion, but the sort of satisfying sleep that comes when one feels...extended.   We had no alarm clock, but Noel's watch had luminous hands and during the early morning hours he checked it a couple of times before waking me at around three-thirty.

Rolling up our sleeping bags and shouldering our packs, we were on our way again, pausing only to eat a couple of biscuits and some dates, plus a mouthful of water. The stars were still brilliant against a totally black sky, with no sign yet of a lightening horizon in the east. And as we walked, we again experienced the weird sensation of hearing no other sound but that of our own walking. Somehow, it seemed different from the night before. The surrounding silence seemed more absolute. No human sound, other than our boots...no natural sound... not a bird, not an insect, no sound of wind or waves. Nothing. Just a huge globe of night all around us with the stars above. It was extraordinary...and quite wonderful.

After about an hour, around four-thirty, we started to see the first beginnings of dawn in the sky ahead of us and gradually, as we walked and watched, the desert began to emerge around us as a surface on which we were walking. Up until then, for all we knew, we could have been walking along a ridge, with bottomless pits on either side, it was so dark. Now we could make out the horizon encircling us in the eerie, almost greenish light of the half-dawn before the sun rose. The cool freshness of the morning made us feel as if we could walk forever. If only it could stay this way, I thought.

But before long a brilliant sliver of blood red broke the horizon ahead of us, growing and changing colour, to gold and then to a silver so bright we could no longer look at it.

And from the moment it appeared we could feel its heat.

Then, encouragingly, at a couple of places, on the landscape ahead of us, we could see a few date palms.

'At least there's a bit of shade ahead, if we need it,' I said.

About an hour later, I guess about 6.00 o'clock, Noel said, 'Have a look near those trees in the distance, a bit off to the left. There's somebody there.'

There were about three date palms clustered together. We could see movement near them and at least one person.

'There's a bloke there and...and some goats, it looks like.'

We kept walking towards him and, leaving the road went across to talk to him. This proved to be an impossibility, as he spoke only Arabic, but we managed perfectly good communication between us via sign language and laughter.

He was as surprised to see us as we had been to see him. He was a goats-herd with roughly twenty goats.

'Salaam Ali Qum...' Noel said, exhausting our Arabic in one moment.

'What the hell is he doing out here?' I said, making questioning gestures to him, and raising my eyebrows. I pointed to the goats, then at various points on the horizon and turned back to him, with more querying gestures and looks.

He smiled to indicate he understood, tapped his own chest, then, speaking in Arabic, pointed to the south.

'Kilometres?' Noel asked. 'How many ki-lo-metro?'

Kilometres he seemed to understand. He held both his hands up, fingers splayed.

'Ten kilometres. He comes from ten kilometres away down there. Or he's going there anyway.'

One goat, which he had on a lead, carried two bladders filled with goat's milk slung over its back. He untied one, held it in the air as if to show us, then tipped it so a thin stream of milk flowed into his mouth. Then he offered it to us. We each drank about half a pint of the thick, warm liquid before realising how awful it tasted, but recognised also that every bit of liquid in such situations is precious.

We opened our packs and each took a small tin of sardines out to give him. He laughed and waved his hands in refusal, but we insisted. He seemed very pleased and turning to a small sack on the ground, beneath one of the trees, he pulled out handfuls of dates, which he thrust on us.

'This could go on for quite a while,' I said, as we smiled and accepted the dates. 'What do we give him next?'

'Water,' Noel said to him next, showing him his water canteen.

'Water....l'eau... agua... where can we find water?' all accompanied by a further pantomime of ingenious hand signals and gestures around the horizon.

Again he understood perfectly and pointed East, along the road... in the direction we were walking.

'Yeah, but how far?' And as I spoke, he took Noel's arm and, lifting it up, looked closely at his watch. Then he pointed at the '9'.

'Nine o'clock,' Noel said. 'He says we'll get water at nine o'clock if we keep walking in that direction. At least that's what I think he means.'

'We hope he means.' I said. 'It could even be the border.'

We said goodbye to him, with handshakes and thankyous and more gestures, as he started leading the one goat away with the others following and we made our way back to the road to continue walking towards the sun.

Almost an hour before nine we saw where we were obviously supposed to be heading. A distant clump on the skyline that slowly revealed itself, as we walked the five or six kilometres between us and it, to be three low, mud brick buildings... and again a few date palms. We could also see, as we came nearer, two or three camels there. So there must be people, I thought.

Incredibly, we found the place to be a well, around which had been established a small trading post...a simple mud brick hut which carried the most basic of supplies; tinned food, tinned milk, some bags of pulses and rice, tobacco...not much more. Presumably its customers were the nomads who passed by and herdsmen whose flocks found some meagre sustenance in the parched earth of the region. There were only two people there when we arrived...Arab men, who though surprised to see us, were not particularly communicative or friendly. Very different, in fact, to our goatherd friend of a few hours earlier.

After hauling a bucket up from the bottom of the well, a stone lined, circular hole, that dropped about thirty feet into the ground, we drank some of the cool, but rather mineral-tasting water and refilled our water canteens. We carried no water-purifying tablets and, for the trip across North Africa so far, had trusted to luck where water was concerned, drinking whatever the locals drank.

As the sun was by now already oppressively warm... too hot for walking and this was clearly the safest and most sensible place to stay, we sought the shaded side of one of the three low buildings and settled

'The sun by now was already oppressively warm.... too hot for walking.'

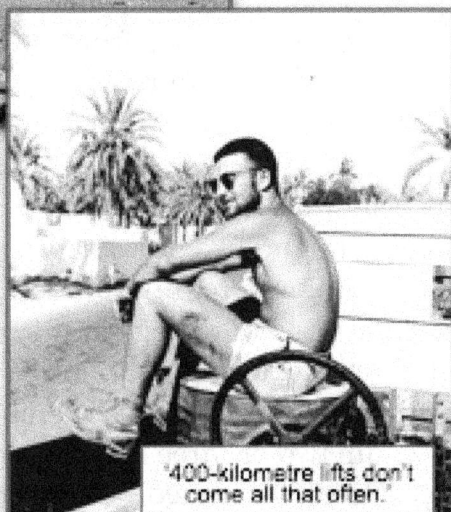

'400-kilometre lifts don't come all that often.'

Tripoli '...the ancient city, dominated by a 16th century Spanish castle...and a triumphal arch erected to the Roman Emperor Marcus Aurelius in AD 163.'

down on the dusty ground, close by the wall. There we could sleep and wait out the day until the cool of evening, before moving on.

But, about two hours later, as we dozed against our packs, a tiny sound began to grow and impinge on our consciousness. The distant rumble and roar of an approaching vehicle that finally had us both awake and upright, scanning the skyline.

'Its a bloody truck,' I shouted.

'Coming this way....from Medenine... or Gabes... or wherever.'

'Quick, lets get our packs by the road... he's not going to stop here.'

'We've got time. He's a good five or six kilometres away yet.'

The Arab driver of the truck, on seeing us standing and waving by the roadside, pulled over and stopped. He was completely dumbfounded to find two non-Arabs...and Australians at that...way out in the middle of nowhere, in southern Tunisia. He welcomed us aboard and after throwing our packs in the back of the truck, which was loaded up with crates carrying automobile parts, we climbed into the cabin and were on our way towards the border...which, to our amazement came up within two or three kilometres, as we caught sight of the coast.

'Gawd,' I moaned, 'We could have picked him up in Ben Guerdane and saved the walking.'

He explained to us in French that he had come down from Tunis the previous afternoon and had stayed in Gabes overnight.

'And where are you going,' I asked, as we pulled up to the small immigration post in the village of Ras Jedir.

He paused a moment. 'Tripoli,' and looked at us as if the question was completely redundant. Like, where else would he be going? Which probably made him even more surprised at our elation.

'Wow!' Noel had exclaimed. 'Great!'

400-kilometre lifts don't come all that often.

oooooo

LIBYA

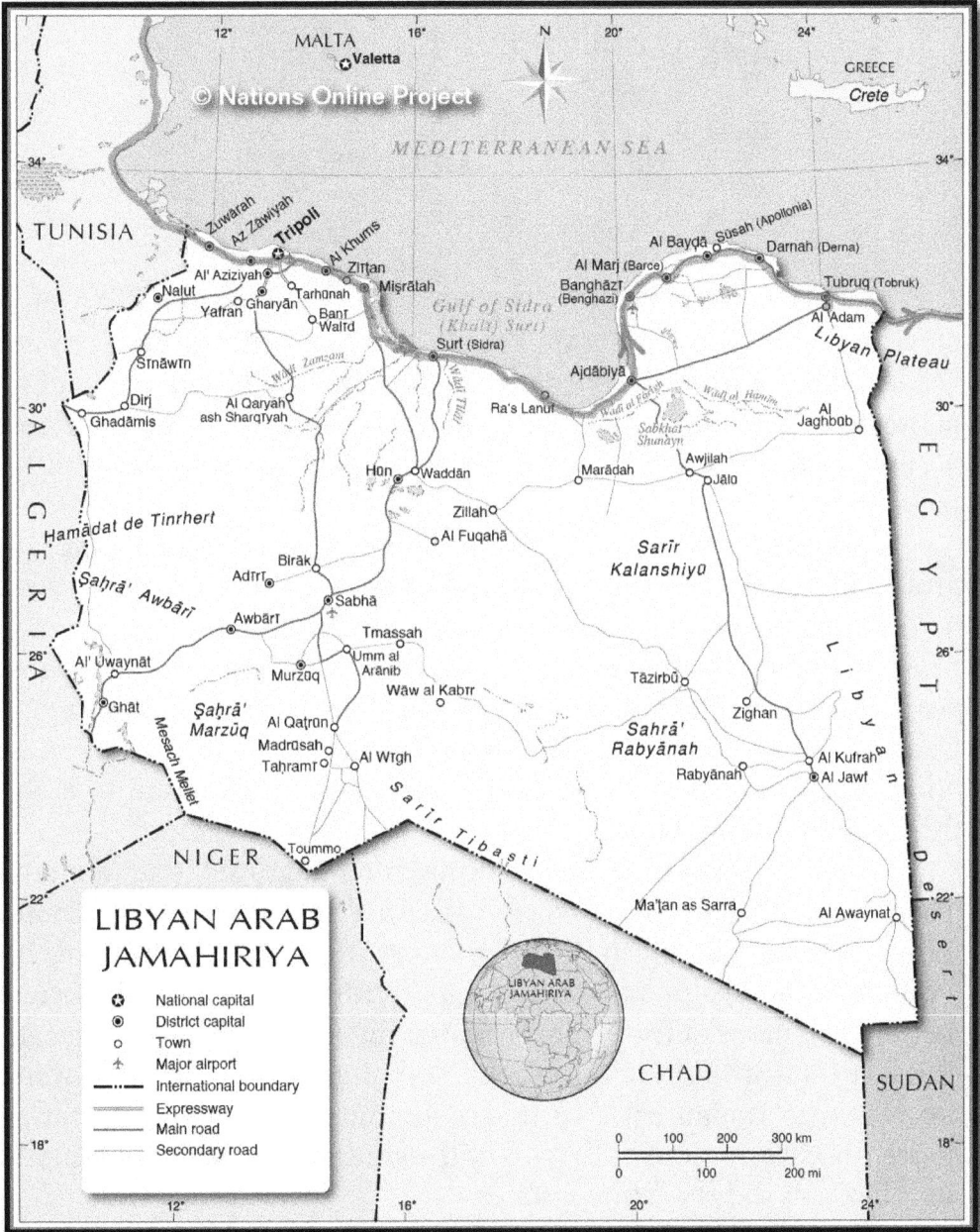

LIBYA

6

ITS A BLOODY HOME-MADE BOMB

I can't remember how the thought first came to us, but at some stage, either on the trip across French North Africa... or even during just the last stretch from the border in to Tripoli... we hit on a plan of future action which was to work greatly to our advantage for the rest of the trip across North Africa. And it was largely to do with the political situation in Libya at the time.

Following the World War II defeat of the German and Italian armies in the deserts of Libya, and Italy's loss of its colonial possessions in Africa, Libya had, since 1951 been an independent kingdom, with King Idris I as its monarch. The future of Libya had been debated for years in the United Nations...with suggestions including a United Nations Trusteeship, a Soviet Mandate for Tripolitania and various other compromises. The monarchy was finally decided on in a vote by the General Assembly.

Once in power, however, King Idris declared that all political parties should be prohibited and that his authority was fundamental. Libyans, who had been through more than thirty years of Italian occupation and colonization, and apparently felt that anything would be better than more of the same, accepted the monarchy largely because of the fact that Britain undertook the role of guaranteeing there would be no return to Italian rule. To this end... but more than likely for other, more obscure reasons... Britain still maintained several military bases in Libya... as did the United States.

Thinking about it now, as I write, it may have been the British Consul in Tunis who put the idea in our heads to approach the Army bases, as places where we might be able to stay for a night or two on our way across to Egypt.

'How do you think they'll react, when we just turn up?'

Noel and I were talking it through, as our truck barrelled along the desert road on the last twenty-five or thirty kilometres in to Tripoli. It was already four in the afternoon, so we'd decided that the first thing we'd do on arriving in the capital would be to find out where the British Army base was and head straight there.

'We'll have to play up our military service as much as possible,' Noel said.

Both of us had done National Service at home in Australia before coming to Europe... Noel in the Air Force, myself in the Army.

'We could say that we haven't completed our National Service obligation yet...' (This was partly true, as we did have an unfinished two-year part-time commitment in the Citizen Military Forces...a bit like the British Territorial Forces system, which we were still obliged to complete on our return to Australia) '...we'll tell them that we are making our way back to Australia to finish our obligation.'

'Australia via Libya?'

'Well, we could say we haven't got much money, which is true... and that we're hoping to get a ship to Australia from Port Said... something like that.'

Tripoli came as a pleasant surprise. It may have been the contrast from the sort of territory and towns we'd been passing through over the past few days, but it seemed to us to be relatively clean, with gleaming white buildings and plenty of greenery and tropical palms... the sort of classic North African beauty you associate with picture books. There were probably a few things affecting my judgment though because I have begun to realise, as a result of the travelling I've done over the years, that everything is relative... you tend to compare the place you're in to where you've just come from. The centre of the city was busy and full of activity as the shops and stores were opening again for the evening, following the afternoon's siesta. We had no trouble finding out where the British Army base was located. In fact, we were able to take a bus from the centre of town right to the front gate. And, as it happened, our concerns about acceptance there had been groundless.

'Could we speak to someone in the Base Commander's office? we said to one of the young soldiers manning the main gate.

'I'm sure you can,' he said. 'I'll check on it. Where are you from? What do you... I mean....what shall I say you... er want?'

'Tell them we're two Australian service personnel heading for Cairo,' I said. '...and that we'd like to see if it might be possible for us to spend the night at the camp.'

I really don't know what it was that made this sort of thing possible then, because I'm sure you couldn't just roll up to a military base nowadays and ask to stay. It may have been some sort of naiveté on the part of the military then, or the relative closeness to the end of the war...the isolation of the place...or the unusual aspect of two Australians being so far off the beaten track to ask the question in the first place... or a combination of them all.

Anyway, the result was that, after we'd gone through some preliminary enquiries from a young captain...who also made a brief phone call to a major for approval, we were welcomed into the camp.

'Yep,' he smiled. 'We can look after you for a few days... and help you on your way. Sergeant Thomson....' he called to the next room. 'Can you take Mr. Finlay and Mr. White and set them up with somewhere to sleep? And show them where the Mens' Mess is.'

Sergeant Thomson then led us across a parade ground into a hut which contained several rooms that were occupied by soldiers, but opened the door to one which held only six empty beds and six small upright cupboards.

'This room's not being used,' he said. 'You can take a couple of beds here.'

We dumped our packs on the beds. 'This is great,' Noel said enthusiastically. 'Really fantastic. Thanks a lot.'

The sergeant laughed. 'Well I wouldn't call it fantastic... but its probably better than some of the spots you might find in Tripoli. Now...' He looked out of the window. 'I suppose the first thing you'd like is something to eat. You've timed it right. Tea's on in about ten minutes...at the mess hut.' He pointed out the window to show us where it was. 'You could have a bit of a wash-up if you want... bathroom's at the end of the hut... and I'll see you there shortly.'

Tripoli, like Carthage, was founded by the Phoenicians several centuries BC and later ruled by the Romans. Built on a low rocky promontory overlooking the sea, the ancient town, originally known as Oea, grew into a walled city roughly in the shape of a pentagon, which hugged the small harbour. Invaded and successively occupied over the centuries by Vandals, Arab warriors, Sicilian Normans, Spanish and Turks, it was ruled by Italy from 1911 until 1943, then governed by Britain after the war, until independence in 1951.

The city now is divided into two parts...the old and the new, with the ancient city dominated by a 16th century Spanish castle, as well as many mosques and the beautiful triumphal arch erected to the Roman emperor Marcus Aurelius in AD 163. The new city, which stretches spaciously to the southwest, also fronts onto the vastly enlarged artificial harbour which is protected by a long curved breakwater with a single entrance to the east.

Our first job, in Tripoli on the morning after our arrival, was to make for the British Consulate to try to organize our visas for Egypt. Again, they were relatively straightforward to obtain... but expensive, we thought; 90 piastres (about 18 shillings) each. We could pick them up, we were told, with our passports, later in the afternoon. I remember as we walked out from the consulate hearing the sound of aircraft in the air and looking up to see three American fighter planes passing over the city to the south. These, we later discovered, were from the big U.S. Air Force Base at Wheelus Field, to the east of the city.

U.S. Airplanes operated from there, as part of NATO forces... for a further fifteen years, until the station was closed in 1970, not long after the military coup that brought Colonel Muammar al-Gaddafi to power in September 1969.

Figuring it out, I guess Gaddafi would have been just thirteen years old at the time Noel and I were in Libya. He was probably at school in Sirte, a town on the coast, some 500 kilometres east of Tripoli, which we would shortly pass through on our way across Libya. The son of itinerant Bedouin farmers, Gaddafi had been born in a tent in the Libyan desert, around 1942 in the midst of the Allied conflict with Rommel's Afrika Korps and the Italian armies.

After the war, he turned out to be quite a talented student. He graduated from the University of Libya and entered the Libyan Military Academy, from which he also graduated in 1965, aged twenty three. Within four years, as a young captain in the army, he had staged the military coup that overthrew the Libyan Monarchy of Idris I in 1969. He was named Commander in Chief of the Armed Forces and Chairman of the country's new governing body, the Revolutionary Command Council. He moved quickly to remove the British and American bases as well as expelling native Italian and Jewish communities from Libya.

He held power for some forty two years until he was captured and killed during Libya's NATO-supported Arab Spring uprising in October, 2011.

Since then Libya has descended into what has become known as the Second Libyan Civil War, involving a bewildering array of rival groups seeking control of the overall territory of Libya. These include: The Libyan National Army, The Government of National Accord, Libya Dawn, Islamic State of Iraq and the Levant, The Benghazi, Derna and Ajdabiya Shura Councils, Tuareg forces as well as a host of local forces spread across the northern coastline.

In other words...chaos.

During those pre-Gaddafi times when Noel and I passed through Libya, it was one of the poorest countries in Africa. The arid climate and the lack of any viable agricultural resources, apart from isolated grasslands for grazing sheep and goats, meant that the population outside the cities... and there were only two of any size; Tripoli and Benghazi, to the east... had few resources to rely on.

All that was due to alter though, within a few years. In 1959 Libya suddenly changed from being an impoverished state completely reliant on international aid and on the rent from British and American military bases, to a country with the potential for great wealth. The discovery of major oil deposits in several parts of Libya would assure it of income on a vast scale and transform the country into one of the wealthiest in Africa. So, when Gaddafi came to power, it had had ten years of enormous expansion of government services and construction projects, as well as a corresponding rise in standards of living.

Viewing it through 1955 eyes however, the country appeared to have little prospects ... particularly after we left the relatively clean and superficially prosperous orbit of the capital.

We stayed at the barracks in Tripoli for three days...or rather two nights, during which we made friends with several of the young soldiers there, most of them being National Service men, spending part of their two-year service in North Africa. From them we learnt that there were other British bases spread across the top of Africa to Egypt, from where the British Army, in addition to performing the role of preservers of the peace in the area, also trained its forces in desert warfare.

At the barracks we were able to prepare ourselves for the next part of the trip, which was a stunner...over a thousand kilometres, with not much but desert in between...from Tripoli to Benghazi. We were sitting down on steps of the hut, studying our map, when Sergeant Thomson walked up.

'You blokes are heading off tomorrow?'

'Yep, that's right. We're making for Benghazi.'

'I've been checking with transport...and we do have some vehicles going that way, but only for short distances. There are some going all the way to Benghazi, but not for a week. '

'Yes...we asked about it too,' I said. 'but its a bit long to wait. We may as well try our luck with the short distance ones for a start. I reckon we'd probably get there...to Benghazi by the time the other ones are leaving here'.

'What about your gear?   I noticed the boys gave you a couple of bush hats.' For walking around in Tripoli, we had borrowed a couple of army bush hats... and then been told to keep them when we tried to return them at the end of the day.

'Oh, we're okay,' Noel said. 'The hats make a difference. We've really needed something like that for a while. I don't know why we didn't get them before.'

'What about shorts and shirts,' the sergeant said. 'You're shorts don't look as though they'll last much longer.' (in fact they were almost falling apart) 'Listen... come with me. I've been talking to the QM. We'll get you blokes kitted out properly.'

Half an hour later we were the proud owners of a couple of new pairs of shorts, two shirts and a light-weight safari jacket each, plus two new army issue water bottles. We had to ditch some of our older stuff to make room for the new in our packs, but immediately felt much better prepared for the next part of the journey. Not that new shorts and shirts could really make any difference, but it was a very practical gesture, which gave us little lift.

'And all for free,' Noel chuckled as we repacked out rucksacks.

Our first lift when we took off from Tripoli was in a Land Rover, one of three from the Army barracks which were going to a place called Tarhuna, a desert outpost 160 kilometres to the south of the capital. Fortunately their planned route first took them some 50 kilometres or so to the east, along the coastal road, to a turnoff near a village called Gasr el-Garabulli. There, where they turned south, on a dirt road into the desert, we waved goodbye to the British Army.

It was a strange feeling. For the past few days, we'd enjoyed an unaccustomed, but very welcome sense of security within the friendly and protective realm of a similar culture. It had been quite a pleasant experience, brief though it was, being surrounded by what amounted to a sympathetic support mechanism... that also spoke English. Now, for the moment, we were back to relying on our own resources.

Our next lift...which came up pretty quickly, was for some 70 kilometres to the small town of Al Khums. There, right on the shoreline, a little to the east of the town, is an ancient harbour, behind which, amidst dry, shifting sands blowing in from the desert, are the great ruins of the Roman city of Leptis Magna. In size and scale, the ruins here are regarded as amongst the finest remains that have survived from classical antiquity.

I imagine that the arrangements for tourists and visitors generally, is better now than they were then, because once again, like the Forum at El Djem in Tunisia, we found them basically deserted. There were signs of some archeological work, but for most of the time, we were the only two people wandering around those superb ruins on that day.

Originally called Lpqi by the Carthaginians, who settled it around 600 BC, the city came under Roman rule after the Punic Wars, to eventually grow into one of the great cities of the Roman Empire. The Emperor Trajan made it a Colonia, a community with full rights of Roman citizenship, while the emperor Septimus Severus, who was born in Leptis Magna in 146 AD, conferred on the city's citizens

Leptis Magna. '…amongst the finest remains that have survived from classical antiquity.'

'Now this is what you'd call a really full-sized toilet block.'

'…we could look forward to basically empty territory over the next 600 kilometres…'

'…we dashed down to the water and swam for half an hour…'

permanent freedom from all property and land taxes.

Most of the outstanding monuments that remain today date from the time of Septimus Severus. They include a nineteen kilometre-long aqueduct, an ornate triumphal arch and the harbour. A huge basillica, near the harbour, measuring almost 300 square metres internally and some 30 metres from floor to ceiling, was built by Severus's son, Caracalla. There is also a monumental forum, a large ampitheatre, a 500-metre-long stadium, or circus, numerous arches and a large, finely preserved bath building that was erected in the time of the Emperor Hadrian, around 120 AD.

'And take a look at this,' Noel said. 'Now this is what you'd call a really full-sized toilet block.'

We were walking through the area that had once been that huge and luxurious bath facility, complete with cold baths...the Frigidarium, warm baths...the Tepidarium and hot baths in the Caldarium. Now here, along the sides of two walls of one of the rooms, were long white marble benches into which had been cut smooth holes for scores of toilets. I've since seen other Roman toilet facilities, in places like Pompeii and Ephesus, in Turkey and been somewhat fascinated by the fact that, in those ancient days, they would have had to...or perhaps they enjoyed... all sitting in a long row together, to go to the toilet.

As we walked in to the baths, we met two young English men, both soldiers from the base in Tripoli, who were spending a day off at the ruins. They introduced themselves as Mark and Geoff and we all walked up to the row of seats together.

'They must have been pretty chummy in those days,' Mark said, as we sat down on a couple of the ancient toilets. There were at least sixteen or so... all close together, around two sides of what was once a room. 'They probably sat here, side by side,' he laughed. '...chatting about the world's problems while they were having a crap.'

We looked down through the holes into the deep channel, about two or three metres beneath us, where once a sophisticated sewage and drainage system operated. Now, it was just filled with lush vegetation reaching up towards the light.

'Plenty of fertilizer down there, I suppose.' Noel said.

Fortunately, in the years following our experience there...even during Gaddafi's rule, the immense value of Leptis Magna was realised and extensive archeological restoration work was carried out. A substantial museum was established on the site and ongoing research and exploration has confirmed Leptis Magna as the site of some of the most impressive ruins remaining from the Roman Empire.

In the year 2000 archaeologists from the University of Hamburg, working along the shoreline of Leptis Magna, discovered a 10-metre length of colourful mosaics created during the 1st or 2nd century. The mosaics show with exceptional clarity, depictions of a warrior in combat with a deer, four young men wrestling a wild bull to the ground, and a gladiator resting in a state of exhaustion and staring at his slain opponent.

The mosaics decorated the walls of a frigidarium...a cold plunge pool in the bathhouse of a Roman villa. The gladiator mosaic is regarded by experts as one of the finest examples of representational mosaic art ever seen—a masterpiece, which is now on display in the Leptis Magna Museum.

Leaving the ruins at Leptis, we unfortunately found that, although Tripoli and Benghazi are the two largest towns in Libya, there was not a huge amount of traffic between them at the time and we found ourselves, when we came to try to move on from Leptis Magna, waiting for hours by the roadside with nothing coming by. The Road to Benghazi is even more desolate, in some ways, than the one we travelled in southern Tunisia...mainly because of the distances involved. There are only two towns of any size along the way, Misurata, with a population then of about 30,000, about ninety kilometres on from where we were and the much smaller town of Sirte, another 260 kilometres further on...both hugging the Mediterranean seashore on the edge of the desert. After that we could look forward to basically empty territory with not much more than a few tiny settlements sprinkled over the next 600 kilometres... plus long stretches of up to a hundred and fifty kilometres or so with virtually nothing in between.

We camped that first night near the road, almost within sight of the ruins of Leptis. By late morning of the following day, we'd only managed to reach Misurata, with so little traffic passing that we didn't think much of our prospects of moving on. Misurata is a coastal oasis that sits, amidst thousands of palm trees, above an underground water table. Its access to plentiful water has made it useful, from at least as far back as the seventh century AD, as a caravan supply centre and in recent times, through irrigation, it has become a centre for agricultural production.

We waited on the outskirts of the town for several hours with nothing happening...until finally, around three in the afternoon, a small and very old Fiat truck pulled up. The driver, an Arab of about fifty years, who was travelling with his wife and young son, told us in a fascinating mixture of English, Italian and Arabic, that he was going to somewhere called Buerat El Hsun. We couldn't see it on our map, so we asked him to show us where it was. He looked at it intently for half a minute or so, clearly not being able to read the English names.

'Misratha?' he mumbled, running his finger along the coast. 'Misratah?'

'Here,' Noel said, pointing to Misurata.

'Ah..Ah!' he nodded and then ran his finger along the coast towards Sirte to a point about half way along, then jabbed at it. 'Buerat... Buerat.' he smiled.

Noel and I looked at each other. There didn't appear to be anything there. 'At least its in the right direction.' I said. And then, smiling at him, 'Great! Thank you. Grazie...Shukran.' We threw our packs in the back of the truck and climbed up after them.

South of Misurata, the road moves inland from the sea for some distance, through arid seasonal grasslands and dried salt marshes with only the sparsest of vegetation. Returning to the coast after 170 kilometres or so, the landscape is totally flat and featureless, with the desert running virtually down to the seashore. An occasional dry wadi indicates where water might run off into the sea... if it ever rained. It was here, at a small settlement, presumably the fishing village of Buerat, that he dropped us off late in the afternoon.

Not holding out much hope for any more vehicles to be coming by, we had some hot sweet Arab tea in a small, dingy shop, bought some dates and walked along the road a way, to find a place to camp for the night. It wasn't as though there was much to chose from... or that there was anything in the way of shelter...or shade. We just put our ground sheets and sleeping bags down on the sand, lay down and went to sleep.

But at least we were close to the sea... and when we woke in the early morning, we dashed down to the water and swam for half an hour, keeping our eyes and ears tuned all the time, as we were mindful that at any moment a vehicle might come heading down the road from Misurata, on its way to Sirte, or beyond. We needn't have worried. We sat by our packs for three hours after our swim and some breakfast...from six until about nine in the morning, before a single vehicle came past. Fortunately, however, it was a good one for us.

It was a truck again, of course...carrying water melons to Sirte, but what was even better was the fact that, after offloading the water melons, the driver indicated he would be taking a load of grocery supplies to a small settlement called Wadi Ben G'auad, which shows on the maps as El Auegia, about 140 kilometres further on.

Waiting in Sirte for a couple of hours while the truck offloaded and loaded up again, we wandered down to the waterfront where we watched a bunch of young boys leaping into the water from a wharf. Strange to think that General Gaddafi might have been one of them.

The road, from Sirte along the coast was, somewhat surprisingly, in reasonably good condition. Fully tarred for most of the distance, with long, straight stretches of at least thirty and forty kilometres without a single bend, the highway was built by Mussolini... or rather, at his instigation, in the late 1930's. So at least we had a smooth ride as we travelled. Once out in the real emptiness that envelops the desert highway, away from any visible habitation, the first thing we noticed (it may still be the same even now) was the vast amount of abandoned and rusting military hardware, that lay in the sands along the roadside; old petrol tanks, ruined German scout cars, trucks...and an occasional tank...all becoming more common sights, the further East we went.

It took us more than three hours to cover the 136 kilometres from Sirte to El Auegia. The truck was pretty much overloaded and the moment the driver got it up to more than fifty kilometres an hour, it started swaying alarmingly, so he was forced to plod along at around forty, pulling in to the settlement at around five in the evening.

At El Auegia the road ran within less than a hundred metres of the shore. There, several small fishing dinghies were clustered next to a stone pier, which projected out for about twenty-five metres in the middle of the gentle curve of a half-moon-shaped bay. The settlement consisted of an Italian house, built of concrete, which was deserted, surprisingly...because it was by far the best looking structure in the settlement. It was surrounded by various forms of war time wreckage; including a couple of overturned and stripped German scout cars as well as numerous rusting petrol drums.

The other buildings nearby consisted of a collection of half a dozen mud-brick huts, one of which was a café...for want of a better word, that carried a sign on its roof saying 'RISTOBAR'. The walls of the building were painted, like an oversized signpost, with the distances from El Auegia (Wadi Ben G'auad) in either direction, to the rest of Libya. Tripoli, we noted was 620 kilometres to the West, while Benghazi still lay 412 to the East. A small general store stood next to the Ristobar to provide supplies for the population of El Auegia... which we learned later was about twenty.

We had no idea where they got their trade from.. other than the twenty locals, plus traffic passing to and fro between Tripoli and Benghazi. They must have been getting some, because we had been dropped off there by the truck, delivering supplies to the cafe and the general store, which turned around and went back to Tripoli. Somebody must have been buying the stuff.

We'd felt very lucky in getting our last lift in the grocery truck through to El Auegia...after all he had brought us over 200 Kilometres further on our way, but getting something to take us further along looked like it would be a bit of a problem. It was. We spent almost three days there.

Several vehicles came through, during that time, in the opposite direction, including a Land Rover that carried an Arab man...in a suit and tie! He was some sort of administration official from Benghazi, on his way to Tripoli for a conference and after showing some amazement that we should be waiting here, he insisted on having his photograph taken with us in the front of the Ristobar.

El Auegia did have one saving grace however. The water of the Mediterranean along this otherwise deserted stretch of coastline was absolutely pristine. It is also the warmest water in the Mediterranean... 31 degrees Celsius and the clearest and bluest I've ever seen. We swam in the crystal waters and waited, taking it in turns every so often to climb a few metres from the beach to a point where we could scan the highway to the West to see if there was anything coming. We had also befriended Aboud, the Arab proprietor of the small café, to the extent that, if any vehicle arrived while we happened to be swimming, without us knowing...he would alert us.

He also introduced us to a rather bizarre and thoroughly reprehensible practice that had been taken up by the Arab fishermen of the Libyan coast in the years since the war, which we observed during our wait there.

'We go fishing,' he said to us early in the morning of our third day. He spoke passable English, having spent time working at the British base in Tobruk, almost 700 kilometres further east... beyond Benghazi.

'Where are you going?' I asked.

'Here...' he pointed to the little bay. 'We go in boat. Plenty of sardines. Plenty.'

'Sardines? How do you catch them?' Noel had always been a keen fisherman. Even now, he still is... although now he concentrates on fly-fishing in the American northwest and in New Zealand.

Aboud smiled. 'With this.' He held up what looked like a small, rusted vegetable can. 'Bomb,' he said.

'Bomb? Explosives?!' I stepped back involuntarily as he nodded. 'Its a bloody home-made bomb,' I turned to Noel.

'I hope to Christ he knows what he'd doing,' Noel muttered...and then to him: 'Where did you get it?'

He looked amazed that the question should even be asked. He just swept his hand in an arc, gesturing to the surrounding desert. 'Out there. Everywhere... anywhere.'

'But how?'

'From bombs and... how you say...mines. We undo...' He made a twisting motion with his hands, as if it was the simplest procedure in the world. '...and we take out.'

Apparently the practice of delousing mines, and unexploded bombs, to obtain the explosives had become widespread amongst the desert Arabs in Libya and the explosives were widely available.

'We sell... we buy,' he laughed.

'How much?'

'Fifty piastres (about ten shillings) a kilo.'

We went with him in his boat out into the waters of the little bay. When the boat was still in about only three or four metres of water, he dropped the anchor and we waited. There were plenty of fish of all different sizes in the water anyway, but after only a few minutes we could see large schools of what were apparently sardines swimming nearby. He threw some bread or other food into the water to ensure they stayed around the boat and then, after activating a simple timing device, dropped his home-made bomb over the side. Within seconds there was the dull thud of an underwater explosion and an eruption of water to the side of the boat.

In the absolutely glass-like clarity of the water we could still see the sardines, thousands of them, but now they were a just a silver carpet, all lying dead on the white sand floor of the bay.

'There...' Aboud laughed triumphantly. 'Plenty of fish.' He picked up a mask and snorkel from the bottom of the boat, as well as some lead weights, which he tied around his waist. Then, with a small wire-mesh container in his hand, he was over the side to begin collecting the fish. In all, in about half a dozen dives, he brought up about 20 kilos of sardines. After he had finished, Noel and I took turns using his mask and weights to go down and shovel the fish into the basket and collected a further five or six kilos of the fish. But there must have been at least five times as many fish as we brought up left lying dead on the bottom. It may be a simple way to get lots of fish in the short term...but cruel...and stupid in the long run, because it would completely clean out fish and other sea life in that little bay.

'Its very wasteful,' I said. '....to leave so many fish there.'

'Huh... I do not understand,' Aboud said.

'Waste....wasteful. You leave plenty more fish down there.'

It took a while to get across the meaning of waste to him, but when he understood, he just scoffed and said, 'My friends will come here this afternoon and pick up some more.'

And on the idea that eventually there would be no more fish in the little bay, again a laugh, as if we didn't understand the vastness of the oceans: 'There are plenty fish out there,' he said. 'The sea is big. Allah will provide.'

oooooo

LIBYA

7

I CAN'T HOLD IT MUCH LONGER

A little before noon on that third day a truck came through from Sirte which stopped while the driver and his mate ate lunch at the Ristobar. After Aboud had spoken to them on our behalf, we arranged a lift with them...unfortunately only a further 150 kilometres along the coast, where they would be turning south to travel roughly the same distance again into the desert to an oasis called Marada. Once again it was a truck that was carrying supplies to small trading stores on the way. There was no room in the front cabin for us, so, as was often the case, we would be travelling in the back. Fortunately there was a canvas roof over the back, so we were protected from the sun.

Trundling off down the road as we left El Auegia, we waved goodbye from the back of the truck to Aboud and his friends who stood outside the Ristobar café waving and laughing and shouting to us. 'Come back again... Kan-gu-roos,' Aboud cried.

About an hour and a half after we'd left El Auegia, the road far ahead seemed suddenly to be lifting up into the sky.

'Look at that,' Noel said. 'Is that a mirage... or what?'

It was the middle of the day and the heat was intense. A shimmering haze rested on the skyline, creating what appeared to be a lake there. We'd seen the phenomena many times during the trip so far, but this was different.

'It looks as if the tarmac goes up beyond the level of the desert around it.'

'Like a tower... It... it is a tower,' Noel said. (He always had better long sight than me) But what the hell is it doing out here?'

And, as we continued on, I could also see that it was a tower. In the middle of nowhere. Still several kilometres ahead, the road ran in

'We waited on the outskirts of town for several hours with nothing happening

'...he insisted on having his photograph taken with us in front of the Ristobar.'

'...a big truck stopped in the town.'

'...the road ahead seemed to be suddenly lifting up into the sky.'

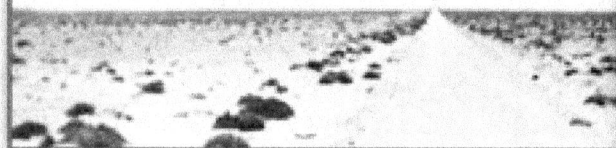

Mussolini's Folly. *In 1973 Gaddafi had it demolished with dynamite.*

a dead straight line towards it...and beyond. Looking around us, the entire landscape was totally flat and empty, with just this tower growing out of the road.

We'd been sitting on a pile of goods in the back of the truck, looking to the front, through a flap that was open to let the air through, when we'd first caught sight of the tower. But we hadn't been able to ask the driver, or his mate what it was. Now our curiosity became too great. I leant over and banged on the roof on the passenger side. An Arab head was poked out.

'What's that?' I yelled, pointing ahead.

I'm not sure whether he understood English or not, but he got the message and laughed.

'Mussolini,' was all he called out, as he pulled his head back in. We sat back to await a closer view and as we neared the structure, we could see that it was not just a tower, but a huge arch over the road.

Nobody had told us to expect this rather large Folly of Mussolini's which he'd had built in his own honour to celebrate the construction of the desert highway during the late 1930s, so we were doubly surprised and amazed as we pulled up in its shadow to take a closer look.

The tower, built of marble, reached a height of around 120 metres, with the top of the actual arch a good sixty metres above the road. It was an extraordinary structure, with terracing and two angled peaks at the top that gave it a vaguely oriental look... like something from old Peking, rather than its present amazing locale, right out in the middle of nowhere. But even more surprising was the fact that it had survived the intense warfare that had raged back and forth in the desert around it in the 1940's.

In fact, as Montgomery's Eighth Army was in the process of pushing Rommel's Afrika Korps westward during December, 1942, the Royal Air Force constructed an airstrip and set up a temporary air base in the flat, sandy desert beside Marble Arch, as it is known. The temptation for some hotshot fighter pilot or tank commander on either side to put a shell or two into it, as the war see-sawed two or three times past it, must have been considerable. There was plenty of evidence of small arms fire; bullet holes everywhere, but nothing substantial enough to have seriously damaged it. The only other sign of abuse had come from standing unattended in the desert for many years. Graffiti artists,

Arab, English, German and Italian had all left their marks over the bottom parts of it, to as high as their arms could reach.

But the arch was a bit too much for the newly-installed revolutionary leader Muammar Gaddafi to tolerate, as he considered the landmark a symbol of Italy's lengthy domination of Libya. So, in 1973 he had the arch demolished by dynamite.

Another hour or so of travelling brought us to the point where our drivers planned to turn south. Here, there was another small village, not unlike El Auegia and with a somewhat similar name...El Agheila. It meant nothing to us at the time, but years later, reading Montgomery's account of the great desert battles against Rommel, during world War II, El Agheila is mentioned as a major strategic point... a 'bottleneck'. Once past this point, the way to Tripolitania in the west was opened up for the allied forces, but twice during the desert war, they had been turned back here, near this inconspicuous little settlement.

After waiting less than an hour at El Agheila, a truck stopped in the town and we were able to clinch a lift on it for the remaining 300 kilometres to Benghazi. We were elated at having been picked up after such a short wait, but, in more ways than one, the trip turned into a nightmare. It was a big truck, carrying about twenty Arab pilgrims... all men, on their way to Mecca, a further 1,200 kilometres across Libya and Egypt, then another 1,000 kilometres by boat from Port Suez to Jeddah on the Red Sea coast of Saudi Arabia and on to Mecca. But big as the truck was, there was standing room only available in the back of it... not just for us, but for most of them too. They were standing the whole way!

And it wasn't a free ride. They were all paying customers, who would have been very much put out at us getting on board without paying. So we had to negotiate a fare with the driver. Fortunately it was relatively small, ten piastres (about two shillings) each. Climbing up into the back, we found ourselves crammed in an upright position, body to body, with the rest of the passengers...as tightly packed as in any Tokyo subway train, but without the advantage of overhead straps.

'Thinking about those poor fish the other day...' Noel said. 'Now we know what it feels like to be bloody sardines...'

'Yeah, but just thank your lucky stars were not on a winding mountain road, with a 400-foot chasm on one side. I wouldn't like to be in this bloody thing on anything but a straight road.'

As the truck travelled along, its movement made the mob in the back sway from side to side...not dangerously, we tried to tell ourselves...but it wasn't difficult to imagine the whole thing tipping over.

The crowd of other passengers seemed to notice nothing untoward. Apart from one policeman, in a khaki uniform and black beret, and a couple of men in long trousers, most were dressed in long djalabeas...white robes that went from neck to toe. Several also wore white cloths loosely wrapped as turbans around their heads. A few others wore the little white embroidered skull caps signifying that they had already made the journey to Mecca, at least once. Conversation proved difficult as only a few of the group seemed to speak any English and they were, unfortunately, towards the front of the truck. To pass the time, we tried to estimate the distances we were covering.

'We must be doing sixty...maybe seventy kilometres an hour, Noel said.

'About that.'

'So if we say forty,' he looked at his watch. '...and we've been going for an hour and a half... that's a hundred kilometres or so.'

'Great,' I muttered disconsolately, beginning to feel the onset of what was to become the real nightmare for me. 'That means we've only got another two hundred to go.'

About ten minutes earlier, I had experienced a tight, clenching sensation in my stomach, accompanied by a wave of slight nausea. Fortunately, within a quarter of an hour it seemed to diminish and, for the time being, I felt reasonably normal... apart from the extreme discomfort we were both experiencing standing, in the 35 degree heat of the direct sun, amidst the packed crowd of Arabs in the back of the truck.

Of course, there was the breeze as a result of our speed across the landscape, which helped somewhat, but we'd been additionally lucky, in that we had been able to secure a position hard up against the boards at the very back of the truck. This meant that, although we were cheek and jowl with other Arab passengers on one side, that is in the direction of the front... in the other direction, to the rear, there was nothing between us and the road behind, but a panel of slatted boards that reached up to about shoulder height. We stood, hanging on to the boards, gazing over the slats, at the receding road.

Then, after another half hour or so, the feeling of illness and queasiness began to return along with a definite feeling of needing to go to the toilet.

'I think I've got bloody diarrhoea,' I said to Noel.

'That's going to be fun.' he replied.

Gradually the symptoms got worse and, as most people have experienced the feeling at some time or another, I'm sure I don't need to spell out the sense of desperation that began to sweep over me as I contemplated the immediate future.

How was I going to ask the truck driver to stop, when we were separated from the cabin by at least twenty other people, who wouldn't understand what the hell I was talking about? In any case the truck driver probably wouldn't stop.

Just as I began sweating with the effort of trying to prevent myself from fouling my own pants, the feeling went away again. But only for another half hour. Then it returned with a vengeance, accompanied by more stomach cramps and nausea.

'Must have been something you ate,' Noel said, not very helpfully. 'But I seem to have missed it.' He tried to go back over what we had eaten in the past 24 hours, but my mind was elsewhere. It was becoming increasingly urgent for me to find a solution.

'I'm going to have to do it on the bloody floor in a minute,' I said between gritted teeth. 'They're not going to like it, but I can't hold it much longer.'

'*They're* not going to like it?' Noel said. 'Jeeze! its not going to be too good for me either. Why don't you do it over the back here?'

'The back? What do you mean, just hang over?'

"Yeah... why not? I'll hold you.'

And that's what I did. I climbed up over the back of the truck, and positioned myself so I was hanging out from the end of it, with my feet stuck between the slats near the bottom of the tray. This first movement... of climbing over the back of the truck, had met with howls of protest from the other passengers , who wondered what was going on and tried to stop me. But with a series of gestures and sign language from both of us, we managed to make them understand. Then, hanging on with my left hand, and Noel also grasping hold of my arm from above, I managed, with my right hand to undo my shorts and lower them and my underpants around my knees so that I could squat, so to speak, in mid air above the tarmac, which was passing beneath me at probably fifty or sixty kilometres an hour. There, in what would have made an extraordinary photograph, I managed to relieve the symptoms of my diarrhoea... and make something of a mess of a short section of the highway across Libya... to the accompaniment of much laughter and cheering from our co-passengers.

But, as things go with diarrhoea, although you get rid of the immediate cause and the feeling goes away... it soon comes back. So this rather embarrassing process was repeated twice more. But, like many things, having done it once, I was much less embarrassed the second time, and by the third, not long before we arrived in Benghazi, I was becoming a seasoned professional.

Benghazi, which is Libya's second largest city, suffered considerable damage during the desert campaigns of World War II, changing hands, between the Axis forces and the Allies, five times before being finally captured by the British in November, 1942. And, to our good fortune, they were still there... at least in the army base... in Benghazi, in June 1955.

As a result of a message sent on from the barracks in Tripoli, we were expected... and welcomed at the Benghazi military base with the same hospitality and friendliness we'd experienced in Tripoli. We were given accommodation, food and, after a few enquiries, an offer of a lift the following day for the 460 kilometres between Benghazi and Tobruk.

'There's a BAPO truck going through from here in the morning,' the Adjutant had told us not long after our arrival.

'BAPO?' we asked. 'What's that?'

'Oh... sorry. British Army Post Office. Its a postal delivery truck and pickup. All mail to and from the base in Tobruk comes through here. It'll be a good ride for you. Some spectacular scenery...up around Derna. Anyway, it'll leave around 7.00 in the morning. You should be in Tobruk by tomorrow evening...probably around six o'clock.'

The following, morning, after a good meal and a comfortable night's sleep, we set off a few minutes after seven in a sand-coloured

Bedford Army truck, that must have been in the Benghazi/Tobruk area since the end of the war, it looked so old. It was one of those snub-nosed, or flat-faced angular vehicles that is completely open at the sides, with a canvas roof over the driver and passenger seats, as well as over the back. For a windscreen it had two flat glass panels that could be folded forward over the bonnet to let the air flow straight through. There wasn't really room for two passengers in the front, but rather than travel one in front and one in the back... Noel and I squashed into the front together. The driver's position remained unaffected. It was only on our side that things were a little cramped.

Nevertheless, it was an enjoyable ride and the scenery was pretty incredible. The topography of the North African coastline near Benghazi forms a huge bulge, some three hundred kilometres across, which pushes out into the Mediterranean and is dominated by a range of rugged and arid mountains...the El Jebel Akhdar, rising to almost 600 metres above the surrounding desert. On the Mediterranean side of the range, the coastal road is forced to negotiate a dramatic 200-kilometre traverse of the northern slopes of Jebel Akhdar. In some parts it is covering the reasonably gentle slopes of foothills, in others climbing rugged escarpments and then zig-zagging up the steep and rocky incline towards the Derna Pass, beyond which are dramatic views of the the distant coastline far below. Our driver, a corporal, stopped the vehicle at one of the high vantage points on the escarpment for us to look down towards the town of Derna, off to the east.

'A lot of your lads fought over this country,' he said, as we stood, in the mid-afternoon heat looking out. 'It was the Aussies who took Derna, in January 1941... after they'd captured Bardia and Tobruk. Then they took Benghazi and pushed the Italians out of Cyrenaica.'

'That was before Rommel came on the scene wasn't it?'

'Yep. When he arrived, with the Panzers, it all changed. We...that is the Allies...were pushed all the way back again into Egypt, except for Tobruk.'

Tobruk is almost as emotive a word for Australians as Gallipoli ... and with good reason. When Rommel took command of the Axis forces in North Africa (March 1941) and quickly carried out a bold thrust against the allied forces...pushing nearly all of them out of Libya and back into Egypt, only the 9th Australian Division held out in Tobruk.

Despite all Rommel's attempts to dislodge them and two unsuccessful British attempts, in May and June 1941, to relieve them, the 'Rats of Tobruk', as Rommel had called them, held the garrison there for almost nine months, against fierce onslaughts from the German army. They were finally relieved by a British offensive, launched from Egypt in November of that year.

Later garrisoned by South African and British troops, Tobruk eventually fell to the Germans on June 21st, 1942, in what was felt by Britain at the time as a national disaster second only to the loss of Singapore. The town was finally regained for the Allies however, in November 1942, when Rommel's Afrika Korps began its retreat across North Africa, following its defeat at the battle of El Alamein.

Noel and I knew some of these things...in a general sense, as did every young Australian who'd grown up during the war. 'The Rats of Tobruk' was a catch phrase all Australians knew and their exploits in defending the town against the Desert Fox were already legend. But, now, to actually be in the area where it all happened was hard to believe...for both of us.

The postal truck dropped us at the army barracks in Tobruk and we were again given something of a red carpet treatment. Another message had apparently been sent ahead of us...about the 'two crazy Australians who were hitch-hiking across the top of Africa.' Of course it wasn't really deluxe treatment; we always had very simple sleeping accommodation and never made it to the NCO's or Officers' Messes, but for us the experience...the feeling of security and of being among friends was good fortune enough and a luxury beyond our dreams.

Here, in Tobruk, we had effectively crossed Libya. All that remained between here and the Egyptian border was 120 kilometres of desert coastline to the last Libyan town, Bardia, with the border only twenty kilometres further on. But the problem we faced was the same as the one on the Tunisian side of the Libyan border...very little traffic between the last town and the actual frontier.

'Why don't you go out to El Adem tomorrow to try the RAF,' the Adjutant said to us, shortly after we had arrived and been allocated a

The British Army base at Tobruk.

'...impeccable, but infinitely sad perfection.'

The memorial at the
Tobruk War Cemetery

Near the Derna Pass

place to sleep. 'You might swing a lift with them to the Canal Zone.'

El Adem was a British air base twenty kilometres south of Tobruk, mainly operating Valetta transport planes, but with occasional combat aircraft being stationed there for brief periods. A lift from El Adem to the British air base at Fayid on the Canal Zone would cut out probably a week of hitching in one sweep.

So, early the following morning, after hopping aboard one of the frequent vehicles running between the two bases, we turned up at the Flight Movements office on the base at El Adem and told them our story.

There was some confusion and initial reluctance on the part of the officers we spoke to there, but after a few phone calls... initially to the army base back at Tobruk and then to their own superiors at the base headquarters, things changed a little. They had been friendly and helpful from the start, but were somewhat taken aback by the whole idea.

'It seems we might be able to help you,' the squadron leader in the Movements Office said. He smiled at us. ' Its just that we don't run up against this sort of situation very often... in fact, we never have.'

'So what do you think the chances are of getting a lift through to Egypt?' Noel asked.

'Well , as I said... in principle we can apparently help you, that is, give you a lift, but....'

'Great,' I said. 'that would be fantastic.'

'No, wait a minute,' he went on, 'the problem is there are no planes. There's nothing scheduled to go through to Fayid for at least another ten days.'

Ten days. Well, we certainly didn't want to wait that long, so after some friendly thankyous and goodbyes, we made our way back to Tobruk to rearrange our plans at ground level.

In Tobruk itself, there was nothing much of a town of any sort to see and without the British army base, it would have been completely dead. The few Arab traders and store keepers who were kept in business by the Army and by the base at El Adem, were the only occupants. All around, was debris and chaos... even ten years after the end of the war. As in so many other parts of Libya, there were the rusting remains of different types of military vehicles and petrol drums everywhere and buildings   still in ruins.   One of the largest in Tobruk, a big and impressive two-storey stone house that stood on a small rise behind the army barracks, was now just a crumbling shell that smelled as if it was being used as an oversized latrine. It had once been the Allied forces headquarters...and then Rommel's, in the period after the German army had broken through the towns defences, to eventually capture Tobruk.

It was still a sorry place in 1955, but in the years since our brief visit to Tobruk, the whole town has apparently been extensively rebuilt and modernized and at one stage became the residence of Libya's former King Idris I.

And, in the chaos of the Libyan civil war, hard to believe, but Tobruk has become the seat of government, well at least the seat of one of the Libyan governments...The Tobruk Government of the Council of Deputies. The government of the General National Congress is based in Tripoli, while the Shura Council of Revolutionaries is based in Benghazi.

Although it didn't have much going for it when we passed through, at least Tobruk was peaceful then. The dry and rugged hills surrounding the town, the scene of dreadful battles that raged there little more than a decade earlier, were silent. The only reminders of those traumatic days, the thousands of rusting bits of metal littering the landscape...many of them still deadly.

I remember, on that first day in Tobruk, just after returning from our visit to El Adem, standing for a moment in the scorching heat around noon, looking up at those surrounding hills, when suddenly a soundless puff of white smoke erupted on one of the plateaus. It was about four or five kilometres away, and rose slowly into the sky. Then a sound like a dull thump came across the still air.

'What the hell is that?' I asked the driver.

'Mine. They go off all the time... in the heat of the day.'

'Mines? Now? Ten years after the war's over?'

'Hell, yes. There are thousands of them still up there...German ... and British. They don't know where they are. They just rust away, until one day they go off...like that. There are unexploded shells in the ground only three or four hundred yards from here. '

'Not the sort of place to go for an afternoon's stroll.'

'Right. You've got to be careful where you go.'

'What about the Arabs...' Noel asked. 'How do they get on...with all their goats and camels and so on,   travelling across country.'

'Oh they do all right. They do have their casualties, but they seem to know where everything is better than we do. And...' he smiled, '...there's the story of how an Arab family crosses a minefield... its a bit prejudiced and anti-Arab, but it goes like this: The Arab and his family and possessions come to a piece of land he has to cross , but he knows its a mine field. So he ties everybody together with a cord and they all go off in single file across the minefield. His wife goes in front, followed by his daughters, then come his sons, followed by his donkey, with him finally bringing up the rear.'

We laughed. ' But they don't really do it that way?'

'Well, that might be stretching it a bit. But they do cross the mine fields...regularly. They go out there and delouse them... to get the explosives and then sell them.'

We told him about our experience with the fish at El Auegia.

'Right. They apparently do it everywhere,' he said.

The knowledge that we would not be able to arrange a lift with the Air Force, returned us to more mundane thoughts about our route eastward. But there was also something we wanted to see before we could leave Tobruk. We'd read of the big Commonwealth War Cemetery that had been built in the middle of the main battlegrounds to the south of Tobruk and we both wanted to visit it before we moved on.

'No sense going there now, its too hot,' Noel said. 'We should go up to there later in the afternoon, when its a bit cooler.' Then he added with a smile... 'Anyway, one of the blokes in the mess told me they're going for a swim in the harbour shortly.'

The harbour at Tobruk is shaped like a 'U' with the entrance to the east and when we were there, was virtually unused. There was no activity, other than the passing of a couple of small Arab fishing dinghies. Once the centre of a vast supply effort to keep the stronghold of Tobruk alive in the face of the continued German siege, the harbour was now peacefully deserted. A few remnants... reminders of those frightful days and all the past frenetic activity remained. The rusting hulks of several half sunken ships lay in different parts of the harbour, with either their prow or stern protruding from the water.

What happened to that ship...and this one? I thought. What happened to the men on board, when it was sunk? How was it sunk? Stuka dive-bombers? Who knows? As in the surrounding desert, other wreckage of every description was spread around the harbour, on the foreshore, in the water, under the water.

We swam, for several hours, with a dozen or so young British soldiers, from some rocks on the northern shore of the harbour, to the east of the town itself. The water was incredibly clear...a beautiful turquoise in the shallows, changing to cobalt as the white sandy bottom dropped away. With a mask and snorkel it was possible to see even more wreckage under the water, almost everywhere we looked.

Later that afternoon, back at the camp, we were able to arrange a short ride in a Jeep, to be dropped off at the Commonwealth War Cemetery. This was a small pilgrimage on our part. Not that either of us had any relatives who had died in Tobruk, but both our fathers, as well as two of my uncles, had fought in those extraordinary desert campaigns that raged across Egypt and Libya in World War II.

Being ten years old at the end of the war, naturally I had no direct experience of it. But the knowledge of Australia's role in Tobruk, as well as in many other Middle East campaigns plus, of course, in the Pacific War and the sacrifices that had been made, had become deeply embedded in the spirit of many Australians, like Noel and myself, who though too young at the time, were now beginning to have some understanding of what those sacrifices meant.

The cemetery at Tobruk had been established in 1951 under the direction of the Imperial War Graves Commission. It is relatively small, when compared to the one we would see later at El Alamein, holding the remains of some 2,479 soldiers, sailors and airmen... of which 559 are Australians.

In 1955 it had, and I'm sure it still has now, a stark and terrible beauty about it. The immaculate whiteness of the scene was almost blinding. Serried rows of white marble gravestones, stretching off in all directions, across white gravelled ground; all perfectly aligned, in every direction, whether you looked to the front, to the side, or diagonally. No parade ground RSM could aspire to such impeccable, but infinitely sad perfection.

And then there was the silence. Only broken by the sound of our boots crunching on the gravel as we walked. Whenever we stopped...in the stillness and drying heat of the late afternoon... absolute silence.

Each identical slab of marble, stood about a metre high. Just below its curved top, each carried the insignia of the Army, Navy or Air Force unit in which the men had served, plus their name and rank. Some carried personal inscriptions that had been arranged by parents, wives, sons and daughters, or other relatives.

'They're nearly all the same age as us,' Noel said as we walked, looking at individual gravestones. 'Plenty of them are younger.'

That was one of the hardest things for me to grasp... (and has been in the intervening years, when I've visited other war cemeteries, in France, New Guinea and Gallipoli) the thought of all those young men, dying out there... just thirteen or fourteen years previously, in those terrible battles, while we...now at that same age...were able to travel through the regions they'd fought over and through Europe, simply enjoying ourselves. And, although we couldn't have known it then, we would never be required to perform the sacrifices that were asked of them.

Worst of all to contemplate was the dreadful waste...the lost potential. Even now, after all these years, I remember one tombstone of an Australian soldier who was the same age when he died, as I was then...nineteen...and which which brought tears to both our eyes. 'In Memory Of Our Beloved Son... So Long Big Boy.'

Having done basically all that one could do in Tobruk at that time; tried our luck at getting an air lift, visited the war cemetery, and had a swim...all on our first day there, we then found ourselves stuck in Tobruk for a further four days waiting for a vehicle...any vehicle, that might be going in the direction of the Egyptian border. Not one came.

After saying tentative goodbyes to our soldier friends on the second day and sitting by our packs on the road out of town for four hours, we returned, disgruntled, hot and sweaty to the barracks for lunch...then went swimming for a couple of hours in the afternoon. We also put the down time to some good use by writing letters to our parents and to the Norwegian girls we'd met in southern France during the summer.

Not wanting to repeat the same waiting procedure the following day, we devised a plan: All vehicles heading towards Egypt had to come almost into the centre of Tobruk before continuing eastward. With the help of the army, we were able to arrange for the local police, to let the guard office at the barracks know if and when an eastward-bound vehicle arrived. If we were at the barracks, we would be able to go to the vehicle immediately. If we happened to be swimming, in the afternoon, a message would be sent to us, while the vehicle waited. Under this system, we were at least able to indulge ourselves, for an hour or so, every day, in the wonderful waters of Tobruk harbour.

Eventually, on the fifth day, a vehicle drove into Tobruk that was heading for Egypt. At first glance it seemed like my earlier horror trip, with the pilgrims to Mecca, revisited. This vehicle was also carrying pilgrims to Mecca, thirty eight of them. Fortunately, however, it was not a truck, but a bus...of sorts. It was definitely of World War II vintage; a converted army bus, that was rusted all over and appeared to be almost falling apart. But certainly better than the truck, even though there were no spare seats. However, as with the previous vehicle, for a fee of five piastres, the driver told us we could sit on our own packs in the aisle as far as El Alamein, a further 500 odd kilometres, which was where we wanted to stop for a day.

After some hasty farewells to a couple of the officers at the camp, plus all of the young soldiers who had befriended us while we there, we boarded the shaky old bus and waved goodbye, to rumble slowly off toward the Egyptian frontier.

oooooo

EGYPT

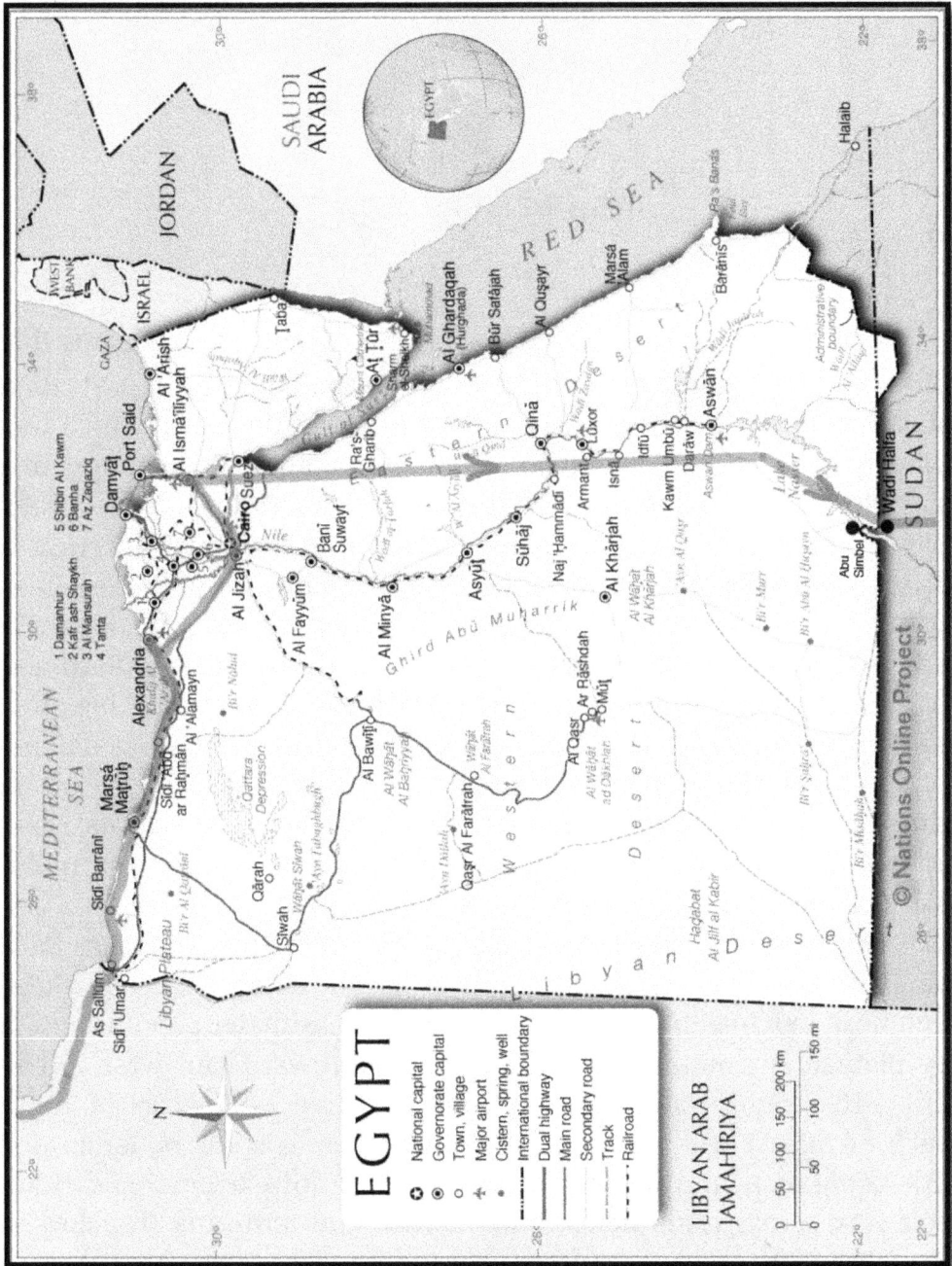

EGYPT

8

ITS A PRETTY RITZY PLACE

Just before we crossed the border into Egypt, the bus came down from a low plateau into the small port of Bardia, built in two parts on the northern shore of a narrow harbour. One part of the town, which in all, probably held less than five hundred inhabitants, was on top of an escarpment overlooking the harbour and the other, down by the water's edge. To the rest of the other passengers, Bardia held little interest, but to Noel and I the small settlement was again a little bit of history. It was here, between the 3rd and the 5th of January, 1941 that Australian soldiers fought their first battle of World War II, the battle of Bardia.

Nine battalions of the Australian Sixth Division, numbering almost 10,000 men, attacked the Italian fortress at Bardia, which was defended by a force more than four times greater...estimated at over 45,000 men with over 400 guns, of 75-mm or larger, at their disposal as well as hundreds of tanks. In three days of fighting the Australians captured the town and took over 40,000 prisoners.

The bus didn't stop...there was really nothing to stop for, as Bardia was in an even sorrier state than Tobruk, but climbed back out of the deep wadi in which the lower part of town was situated, up onto the hot dry plateau surrounding it, to continue southward and west. It was across this same road...and along about three kilometres of it, that much of that World War II action took place as soldiers, laden down with equipment and heavy clothing, because of extreme cold, fought their way across mine fields, barbed wire and anti-tank trenches into the Italian lines.

Crossing the Egyptian border with few formalities, we came, within eighty kilometres, to Sidi Barrani, the site of more early battles in the desert war. We kept travelling however, along an incredibly barren and empty stretch of coastline a further 140 kilometres to Mersa Matruh, another small coastal town which was occupied in June 1942 by Rommel's forces when they pushed the Allies back almost to Alexandria, and threatened Cairo.

The afternoon wore on as we covered another 180 or so kilometres of similarly barren coastline to reach El Alamein. Low clumps of saltbush strewn across the flat and desolate plain provide the only sign of greenery on an otherwise vacant desert landscape. Once again, the settlement here at El Alamein, like many of the others we'd passed through, was a small and forlorn outpost that made one wonder why anyone would wish to live there.

It was not often that we would give up a lift when the opportunity remained to continue further in the same vehicle, particularly when it involved setting down in such an uninviting spot, but we left the the pilgrim bus at El Alamein, late that afternoon, even though we could have stayed with it through to Alexandria...and beyond.

El Alamein, like Tobruk...is one of those places in the Western Desert where, if you're Australian, you cannot just pass by. In fact, no-one should pass by, because here the huge cemeteries commemorating the dreadful loss of life...on both sides...demand and deserve our contemplation and respect, wherever we may be from.

Many thousands of men died in the battle of El Alamein and countless thousands more of their families in Britain, Australia, New Zealand and Canada, as well as in Germany, Austria and Italy...and probably many other countries, still grieve over the loss of sons, lovers, husbands and fathers who lost their lives in a battle for the control of a relatively small piece of desert.

When the Allied forces fell back on El Alamein, in mid-1942, after a series of brilliant strokes by Rommel's Panzer divisions, Alexandria lay little more than ninety kilometres to the east, putting Cairo and the Suez Canal within his reach. Hitler and Mussolini expected that in a matter of days he would be in Cairo and master of Egypt.

But, as it turned out, Rommel had had his last victory. Having come so far and so fast, his forces were exhausted and their tanks were in need of repair and servicing. His first assaults at El Alamein failed to break through the Allies' defences.

My father, who was then 31, was serving as Brigade Major for 26 Brigade, part of the Australian Ninth Division, which occupied the northern end of the Allies' front line, closest to the Mediterranean shore. In what became known as the first Battle of El Alamein in attempting to bring Rommel's advance on Cairo to a halt, it was 26 Brigade that on July 10, 1942, broke through the German and Italian positions at Tel El Eisa, routing an Italian division and taking 1500 prisoners, but most importantly over-running German Intercept Signals Company 621.

This unit had provided Rommel with priceless intelligence gleaned from intercepting British radio communications. That source of intelligence was now lost to Rommel.

Apart from this success, after a week of intense fighting, the overall strategic picture quietened, as the Allied counter strokes were scaled back and suspended because of the corresponding exhaustion of the Allied troops. There followed a brief hiatus while both sides regrouped and were reinforced.

Unfortunately for Rommel, the Afrika Korps received only meagre reinforcements while the Allied armies were strengthened considerably...particularly with new tanks. Consequently, when Field Marshal Montgomery, the new British Commander of the Eighth Army, launched the final battle of El Alamein, on the night of October 23rd, 1942, after a further failed offensive by Rommel during August, he had overwhelming superiority of forces...some 230,000 men and 1,200 tanks to Rommel's 80,000 men and only 210 tanks.

Nevertheless, the Battle of El Alamein is recognised as one of the greatest of World War II. More than 1,000 artillery weapons opened the conflict in the middle of the night with a massive barrage that lit the desert sky for hours.

Within a week, Allied forces had swept around to the north, crossing the coast road and reaching the Sea to encircle the Panzer Grenadiers of the German 164th division. It was the beginning of Rommel's retreat, right across Libya, all the way back to Tunis and the ultimate defeat, by May 1943, of the Axis forces in North Africa.

The British Commonwealth cemetery at El Alamein is much larger than the one we'd seen only five days previously in Tobruk. Officially dedicated by Field Marshal Montgomery just nine years after the Battle of El Alamein, on 24th October, 1951, the cemetery contains the remains of 7,367 British and 1,888 Australian servicemen, as well as the names of 11,874 other Commonwealth soldiers, with no known graves, who died in the campaigns of the Western Desert during 1940-1943.

At the smaller German cemetery, on the opposite side of the road and about a kilometre to the west, we felt the same sense of dreadful waste and loss, even though we had grown up with the knowledge that Germans were the enemy. But reading the headstones, and seeing the ages; all young men, just like their opponents, who had died in the prime of their life, it was impossible to avoid the feelings of sorrow and melancholy. To one side of the German cemetery was a large, but simple, slab-sided marble monument, topped by a German army steel helmet which had been erected in honour of the Deutchen Afrika Korps and its famous commander, Field Marshal Irwin Rommel.

In both cemeteries there was the same incredible and in a sad way, beautiful balance and uniformity that we had seen at Tobruk; the stark white geometrical patterns formed from endless rows of headstones, beneath each of which, in the harsh desert sand, it was almost too confronting to comprehend, lay the decaying vestige of a young man.

The cemetery itself and the graves were well cared for and in immaculate condition when we saw them in July 1955 and even though I have not returned to El Alamein in the years that have passed since then, I'm sure they still are. The Commonwealth War Graves Commission, along with the Imperial War Graves Commission, in Britain, which are charged with and funded for the continued maintenance of British and Commonwealth War Cemeteries around the world, generally does an excellent job of looking after them. I have mentioned some of the other war cemeteries I've visited in different parts of the world, and without exception they have all been clean and well tended. Of course there are huge differences in the circumstances; in northern Europe, green grass and trees surround the war graves, whereas here, at El Alamein, only a treeless, stone-covered plain and the wind-driven sand of the desert provide the backdrop for the final resting place of so many thousands of Allied, as well as German and Italian soldiers.

After spending almost two hours in the British Commonwealth

and German cemeteries, we managed, late on a Saturday evening...at dusk and just as we were thinking of making plans to bed down somewhere for the night, to pick up a truck that was going through to Alexandria, almost 100 kilometres on. This seemed alright to us, except that, as he had a co-driver travelling with him in the cabin, we would have to ride in the back, on top of a load of 44-gallon drums.

We climbed up on top to have a look. The drums looked very greasy.

'What do you reckon?' I said to Noel.

'Its okay, I suppose. They look pretty dirty though. We'll end up in a hell of mess.' He turned to the driver, who had got out of his cabin and was standing watching us, as we checked it out. 'Dirty... very dirty,' Noel said to him.

'Ah... yes,' the driver smiled. 'Dirty. Okay, okay... one moment.' He climbed back up to his cabin and started to pull something out from behind the seats.

'Its a tarpaulin,' I said and Noel and I and the co-driver began helping him to get it out. It wasn't very big, but it was big enough to make a difference.

By folding it over a couple of times we were able to make a small area on top of the drums that was reasonably comfortable for us both to lie on...and where we wouldn't get covered with grease and dirt.

'Okay,' we called to him, holding our thumbs up as we settled into our position... 'very good. Very good.'

Looking back through the cabin window at us, he gave a big smile, then turned to crunch the truck into gear to set us rolling off down the highway towards Alexandria.

We lay on the tarpaulin, in the back of the truck as it rumbled along at probably not much more than about sixty or seventy kilometres and hour, with the warm night air rushing by. We gazed up into the brilliant night sky, filled with countless stars made seemingly brighter by the complete blackness of the surrounding countryside and talked through future plans.

'The first thing we've got to find out about are those river boats in the Southern Sudan,' I said to Noel.

'And how much they cost. We might be pushing to make it. But I reckon we'll be alright. Third class on the train to Khartoum and third class on the boat from, where do they actually go from? I don't think its from Khartoum? Anyway, it should all be pretty cheap.'

The main problem we faced in covering the four thousand kilometres or so to reach Kenya from Egypt, was that most of it would be travel for which we would have to pay a fare and cheap though it may be, we might not have enough.

We knew we could hitch to Aswan, in southern Egypt. From there, however, the only way to get to the Sudan border, 300 kilometres further south, at Wadi Halfa, was by ferry on the Nile River. That meant a fare. Then the only way to cross the nine hundred kilometres from Wadi Halfa to the Sudanese capital, Khartoum was across the Nubian Desert by train. Another fare. Then, to reach the southern Sudan, close to the border of Uganda...the only way through was by train for 350 kilometres, then another Nile River steamer, for a 1,200 kilometre journey lasting two weeks. Yet another fare. We had to find out how much it would all cost.

'Anyway,' I said. 'As long as we can get into the Sudan, even if we haven't got enough money, something'll turn up. It always does.'

The turnoff for the desert road to Cairo from Alexandria is about 18 to 20 kilometres to the west of Alexandria, so, when the driver stopped for petrol, we decided to leave the truck there, instead of going on into the city. There were many things we would have liked to have done and seen there, but we had neither the time nor the money to stay. In any event, although I could hardly have known it, within twelve months time, I would be back in Alexandria, with not a penny in my pockets, trying to find some way to get to Europe. For the moment, however, these events were well in the future and Cairo was our most important goal, where we would have to organize the next part of our journey.

Saying goodbye and thanking our driver, we made our way a little way down the Cairo road and while we thought we might be able to get a lift at night, we decided to bed down by camping next to a low wall, around what appeared to be a deserted house, not far from the road.

In the morning, after some bread and cheese, we picked up a lift by about nine o'clock that was heading for Cairo. It was a van carrying racks of clothing in the back. We sat in the front with the driver this time.

As we jumped in Noel and I looked at each other with the same thought in our minds, we were on our last lift into Cairo, at the end of which we would have crossed North Africa. We had totted up our expenses so far and I note from my diary at the time, that we both had £8-10-0 left. We had spent just over £11 each in the three weeks it had taken us to cover some 5,000 kilometres from Casablanca.

The van trundled along at a steady pace across a desert in which the landscape on either side was universally flat to the horizon. Set well to the west of the Nile delta, the road traverses basically empty country, with no towns or settlements of any size, for virtually the whole 230 kilometres to the outskirts of Cairo.

We weren't travelling fast, by any means, so it was early in the afternoon before we approached the capital and Noel suddenly exclaimed, 'Look! Its the bloody Pyramids!'

Looking ahead, I could see, in the distance what looked like a couple of pimples on the horizon. 'Wow! Even from this distance, you can tell they're huge.'

Neither of us had realized that the road in from Alexandria would take us so close to the Pyramids and, as we approached, and the giant structures grew larger and larger, our astonishment and wonder increased.

Eventually as we entered the now bustling suburb of Nazlet, which encroaches right on the Pyramids, or at least on the Great Pyramid of Cheops, Khufu as it is now known, the van pulled to a halt outside the Mena House Hotel, an imposing colonial-era set of buildings, set back off the main road in well-kept gardens.

'Right next to the Pyramids,' I said in surprise.

'Yes' the driver, who had stepped out of his cabin, waved his arm around. 'This is Giza, where I am leaving you. It is not far into Cairo from here.'

It was very tempting to stay and spend the rest of the day here, walking around and absorbing some of the wonders of the Pyramids, but we decided to continue on into Cairo proper, find a place to stay for a few days, probably the youth hostel while we organized our trip south and to come out to Giza again later to spend some time at the Pyramids.

So we stayed, waiting by the side of the road near the Mena House Hotel, hardly able to take our eyes off the great bulk of stone across the road in front of us, while still trying for a lift from the passing traffic. After no more than twenty minutes, a smart-looking saloon car, a ten-year-old Riley, came out of the hotel drive and pulled up next to us. A well-dressed Egyptian man in his late forties, or early fifties got out.

'Hello,' he said, in cultured English tones, with the hint of a French accent, 'You're heading in to Cairo? Put your bags in the boot and hop in. I can take you right into the centre of town.'

'Thank you, thank you,' Noel and I were both a little non-plussed, as Noel sat in the front and I slid into the back seat.

I saw the "Australia" sign on your packs.' he said. 'We had many Australian soldiers here during the war. Good men. Good soldiers.'

Noel and I nodded and murmured agreement...although we'd also heard some unsavoury tales of pretty rough and boisterous behaviour in Cairo on the part of Australian soldiers during the war but no sense bringing that up now. Certainly such incidents would have been relatively isolated and attributable to only a small minority. If our driver thought favourably of Australians, who were we to argue. We knew we were pretty good blokes and that was all that mattered.

We talked on the way in about our trip, how far we had come across North Africa and where we hoped to go. He was impressed, not to say amazed.

'But this is incredible,' he said. 'You must come to my home, meet my family and have dinner with us. I can organize somewhere for you to stay while you are in Cairo. Unfortunately, my apartment is too small for you to stay there. But I have a cousin who has a bakery. He may be able to help.'

He told us that his name was Jusuf, Jusuf Al Hakim, and we learnt later, at his small apartment in the elegant inner residential suburb of Isma'Ilyah area of Cairo, that he was a magistrate. He had been to a French school in Cairo and studied later in England. His wife was an attractive woman, in her early forties, who worked not far from their apartment in Al-Azbakiyah, the central business district of Cairo, as the personal assistant to the manager of a large insurance company. During an early dinner of lamb and rice, with baba ghanuj and hummus, followed by some super-sweet baklava, their twelve-year-old son and ten-year-old daughter asked us a stream of questions about our trip, which we did our best to answer.

'Now,' Jusuf said, as we completed our meal, 'We must get on our way.' He had telephoned his cousin and had apparently set it up for us to stay with him, somewhere else in Cairo.

I can't remember how we got there. We drove part of the way, past what I later worked out to be Opera Square and eastward toward the old walled Fatimid City. Then we parked and followed Jusuf on foot for about five minutes, through back streets and alleyways. But Cairo itself was such a mind-numbing experience the first time round that, when I think about it now, I'm not surprised I can't recall our route. As it happened we were being led into an area not far from the great Khan al-Khalili bazaar, which first came into being back in the fourteenth century.

The city seemed to us to be all chaos and confusion. It was also dirty and polluted beyond anything we had seen across North Africa. There was extreme poverty, beggars in pitiable condition and as we'd see later people living in deplorable shanty towns on the edge of the city and under makeshift cardboard shelters in streets. All of them somehow finding a way to fit into the endless disorder, tumult and bedlam of everyday life in a Cairo that was home to between five and six million people at that time, with large numbers struggling to make a living in a tough city.

2015 figures put the City of Cairo population at over 12 million, with Metropolitan or Greater Cairo inhabitants numbering over 20 million.

In one of the small back streets, passing robed and turbaned men and veiled women, we suddenly came to a doorway that opened into what was clearly a bakery. Jusuf went in and we followed him. Inside, within a few moments, we were introduced to his cousin Yahya, to whom he explained, in Arabic, something more of our situation.

Yahya's English was not so good, but he gestured to a flour-covered set of wooden steps, not much more than a ladder, in the corner of the room, which led to a hole in the ceiling. 'Up,' he smiled. 'We go up.'

Following him up the stairs, we found ourselves in a upper-level store-room filled with sacks of flour, as well as piles of empty hessian bags, stacked on one side of the room.

'Here. You can sleep here,' he said, pointing to the empty sacks. 'Is it all right?'

'Its great,' I replied, giving him and Jusuf a big grin. 'It couldn't be better. Perfect. Thank you very much.'

It wasn't quite what we'd expected, but really it suited us down to the ground. Our own city pad in downtown Cairo.

We had made up a list of things we had to do while in Cairo, perhaps the most important of which was getting a visa for Sudan and establishing the logistics and costs of getting through Sudan to Kenya, or Uganda. I also felt it might be possible to get a new Australian passport here. So although it was not at the top of our list, we found out where the Australian Legation was and as it was only a couple of short bus rides away went there on the following morning, a Monday.

After we had gone through some preliminary explanations in the offices there about my lost passport, we soon became the focus of increased attention, as they picked up on the fact that we'd had a fairly unconventional journey across the top of Africa.

'You mean you hitch-hiked the whole way?' was the general initial response. 'But... but...?' followed by a range of different questions about everything from the political situation in Algeria, the state of the roads, the amount of traffic to be found, to the attitudes of people we met and so on.

It was during one of these conversations that we met Nick Parkinson, a young third secretary at the Legation, who was able to tell us, after some brief enquiries, that they could not issue me with a new passport.

'At the moment, as a Legation, we're not set up to do that,' he said. 'We could probably organize something, if you were desperate, but as you have a temporary British passport, it would be better for you to get one from the Australian Consulate in Johannesburg, when you get there.'

I was somewhat disappointed by his news, but he quickly made up for it: 'You blokes look as if you could do with decent meal,' he said. 'The Legation closes in the afternoon. Would you like to come out to the house and meet my wife, have some lunch and a couple of beers?'

"...a marble monument had been erected in honour of the 'Deutchen Africa Korps.'

Noel dodging Cairo traffic.

Nick...later Sir Nicholas Parkinson. No reason for him to "...'have put himself out in the way he did to help a couple of young blokes, like Noel and I.'

the view from above the bakery.

The Sphinx and the pyramids: the immense scale of the structures beggars belief.

I don't know what it was about us. We thought of ourselves as a couple of hardy, independent sorts, who'd been around a bit...and we had.   But somehow we must have been giving the impression, or the vibes...or something, that we were just a couple of young lads who needed caring for, because everyone seemed to want to help us.

'Can't say no to that,' Noel said.

Nick drove us to his house in Zimalek, on Gazira Island, where we met his wife Roslyn (who Nick called 'Blue') and sat down to an excellent light lunch of ham and salad and a couple of glasses of icy cold Fosters Lager, brought to us by an Egyptian servant in a white uniform. It was the first Australian beer we'd had since leaving home, the previous year. This was long before Fosters, or any other Australian beer, had gone international. So it was very unusual to find it so far from Melbourne.

'The Legation has a   amount of it sent over specially,' Nick told us. 'It goes down quite well at receptions.'

After lunch he asked if we'd like to see a bit of the city. 'I'm going back to the office later in the afternoon, but I thought you might like to come for a bit of a drive. Have you heard of the City of the Dead?'

'Only the name,' I replied. 'Its a cemetery, isn't it?'

'Well, yes. But one with a difference. In fact its a pretty amazing place.'

Negotiating the heavy traffic along Al-Oal 'ah street, heading to the south eastern corner of Cairo, we passed Saladin's walled citadel and the Muhammad Ali Mosque to arrive shortly at the City of the Dead.

There, on a sloping hillside and only a short distance from where we left the car, we came upon a wall, over which, below us, we could see a vast, ochre-coloured and dusty district, containing hundreds of exquisite shrine Mosques, beautiful memorials and the mausoleums of some of Egypt's early religious leaders. But sprinkled liberally throughout the so-called city, were more modest graves and tombs, as well as, to our amazement, mud-brick and shanty-type housing and even shops.

'There's no water or electricity there, at all,' Nick said, sweeping his hand across the scene. 'But, because of population pressures, people live here without any facilities and without any government approval.'

'And nobody tries to move them out?' Noel asked.

'No point. They'd have to find somewhere to put them. Its easier to leave them here. It is pretty amazing though. There's nothing like it outside of Egypt.'

As Nick dropped us off on Al-Gohar St. not far from the Khan Al-Khalili bazaar, he said. 'You're here for a few more days. Would you like to come to the Gazira Club? Its a pretty ritzy place. You'd probably like it.'

We had vaguely heard of the Gazira Club, in much the same way we'd heard of Cairo's famous Shepheard's Hotel...which was actually burnt down during anti-British riots three years before our visit...but never really expected to have a chance to visit.

'You might as well, while you've got the opportunity. I don't think you'll find much like it in Sudan. What about in a day or so, say Wednesday?'

We agreed to meet him at the Legation offices on Wednesday afternoon, in two days time.

During the following morning, we made our way to the offices of the Sudanese Consulate, there to encounter our first major setback, as far as visas were concerned, that we'd had so far.

'We cannot issue you visas,' the man behind the desk explained, once he knew we intended to travel through Sudan to Uganda, 'unless you can produce train and boat tickets all the way, right to the Uganda border.'

'Do you have information on the trains and the fares?' I asked.

'No. You will have to get those from the Sudan Travel Agency,' he said and gave us an address in the centre of Cairo's business district.

There, not long afterwards, we totalled up the fares, for three weeks travelling third class, by boat and train and boat again, from the top of the Sudan to the bottom, £6 -2-0 each. We had only £8-0-0 each.

'Damn!' I said. 'We could do it. But we won't have much left after we buy the tickets.'

'We could buy the river boat tickets for the Southern Sudan and go back to the Consulate and tell them we're getting a lift as far as Khartoum with someone else.'

'But there's no other way to Khartoum, across the desert, except by train.'

'It could be with some sort of expedition,' said Noel, seeking any formula that might work for us. 'Four-wheel drive vehicles, that sort of thing.'

'They wouldn't believe us. We'd have to prove it.'

'No, you're right. But lets go back and see them anyway. We'll say that we're having more money sent, as a bank draft, to Khartoum and we'll get the tickets there.'

The Consulate was closed for the day when we returned, so we spent a few hours during the afternoon at the rundown and sadly neglected, yet fabulous for its contents, Egyptian National Museum. The wonderful treasures of Tutankhamen and others from the tombs near Luxor. Great statues and monolithic carvings, monuments from Karnak. Sarcophagi from all over Egypt, as well as a vast multitude of smaller artifacts, weapons, paintings, inscriptions and objects from the everyday life of ancient Egyptians, ranging back four and five thousand years, filled the museum to every corner.

'It's terrible that they don't look after all this stuff in a better way,' I said, as we walked down the museum steps. 'Its just as if they put it there and don't do anything to maintain it, or display it properly.'

'And the place itself, the building looks as if its falling apart,' Noel said. 'I read that Rockefeller once offered the Egyptian Government to pay for a whole new building, somewhere by the river.'

We later heard the story that the site Rockefeller was offering is the one now occupied by the Nile Hilton. The Egyptian government apparently knocked the offer back because there were too many strings attached. I don't know if the story is apocryphal, but it sounds good.

The bakery proved to be extremely convenient for us. It was located in an area where there was a multitude of markets and food stalls selling all sorts of things from shish-kebab and tabouli to halva, for amazingly cheap prices and we were able to eat for practically nothing. The baker and his family lived in a small apartment above an equally small shop that was an extension of the bakery. Although it was on the same level, there was no connection from his flat to the flour storage room and our access to it was through the actual working part of the bakery where people were involved in using antiquated machines to knead and shape the loaves and prepare them for a couple of big ovens.

Yahya told us, in a combination of broken English and sign language, that if we came back at night and the shop was closed, we could knock on the entry door of his flat... a little further along the street. But, it was never necessary. As we didn't like the idea of being out too late in this part of Cairo, we were never back later than nine o'clock, and the shop never seemed to be closed anyway.

Sleeping at the bakery was quite an experience, as it became a hive of activity from about three in the morning. We were separated from it all by the fact that we were a floor above most of the action and managed, after getting used to it, to sleep through. But on a couple of occasions during the week we spent there, people came up the stairs to our room to pick up one of the huge sacks of flour which surrounded us and manhandle it back down the stairs again.

On Wednesday morning we went again to the Sudan Consulate to be waiting at its doors when it opened. We spoke this time to another man, who seemed to be more amenable than the first one. We put the suggestion to him that, as we would be able to produce tickets that would be taking us out of the Sudan, that is the river-boat tickets from a place called Kosti, to Juba on the southern border of Sudan with Uganda, how we got into Sudan, should not make any difference to them. We had decided not to say we were having money sent to Khartoum, as that would indicate we were short of money in the first place.

'We can't commit to buying tickets on the train from Wadi Halfa to Khartoum' we lied, 'because we have friends who are planning to drive from Port Sudan to Khartoum and we may be travelling by boat to Port Sudan to join them.'

He appeared to take what we said seriously. 'Yes, yes, I understand. You do not want to spend money on the whole trip first, in order to get the visa, when you might not need the first part.'

'Right, exactly,' we both chorused, thinking, he's got the message. He's on our side.

'It is possible,' he said. 'It is possible, I think. Unfortunately, it is not a decision I can make. You must speak to the Chief of my department, Mr. Haqqi. He will be here later in the morning.'

I thought for a moment that it might have been the same person we'd seen on the previous morning, but then realised that we had already caught a glimpse of him in one of the back offices.

'What time should we come back?'

'The offices close at 1.00 pm. You should come around noon.'

We thanked him and left. But, as this had all taken place shortly after nine, and we had almost three hours to fill, we decided to put into action another little plan we'd been formulating.

'Now's a good chance for us to go to Kodak,' I said to Noel, as we walked out of the consulate office.

'Right. Let's go.'

We had checked on the location of the administrative offices of Kodak in Cairo and as they were in the business area of Al-Azbakiyah and within a short bus ride of the Sudan Consulate, we made our way there as quickly as possible.

Both of us had been taking nothing but black and white pictures during the journey across North Africa, simply because of the cost of colour film. We had taken quite a lot of colour slides in Europe, but generally, the comparatively high cost of colour film had forced us to concentrate on black and white.

Now we had decided to approach Kodak directly, tell them what we had already done and what we planned to do over the next few months and see if they could help us out with a few rolls of colour film each, with the possibility of some later publicity for Kodak. It was pretty naive really, but at the time we thought it worth a try.

'Could we speak to the manager, please?' We spoke to the receptionist in the front office, an attractive young Egyptian woman of about twenty-five.

'Do you have an appointment?' She, like our Cairo benefactor, Jusuf, also had a hint of a French accent, but her English was perfect.

'Er... no. We haven't. But we wouldn't take up much of his time, if we could see him now.'

She looked over her shoulder. 'I'm not sure if he's in right now. Can you tell me what it is about?'

'Well its difficult to tell it all. Um, well, you see...its like this,' I began. 'You see, we're photographers. We've been travelling across North Africa, now we're about to leave on an expedition through Sudan, right down the Nile River, into East Africa, to go...ah, well, um...big game hunting. Yes...big gam hunting and well, you see, we thought... that is, if we could speak to the manager, we...ah, that is, he... could possibly help us out with some free...er, well...that is, cheap colour film.'

'Uh huh,' she nodded. ' So you want to see if you can get some cheap film?'

'Well, yes. That's right,' Noel said. 'Maybe free.'

'Free?'

'....or cheap,' I smiled. 'It doesn't really matter. But free is better.'

Then she also smiled, for the first time. 'Just a moment.' and she disappeared into another office, from which a man in a suit appeared. He was Egyptian, but again spoke perfect English, this time with an American accent.

'The Manager, Mr. Steytler, isn't here this morning. He'll be in this afternoon. You could see him then, if you like and tell him what you're planning to do. He may be able to help. I don't really know. Its a decision he'll have to make.'

'Unfortunately we can't come this afternoon,' I said, thinking of our appointment with Nick Parkinson and the visit to the Gazira Club. 'Will he be in tomorrow morning?'

'Sure, tomorrow morning will be fine.'

Back at the Sudanese Consulate at noon, we met with the department chief, who listened as we went through basically the same story we'd told the other official earlier in the morning.

'Hmm.' He nodded and thought a bit. 'So you could produce tickets for the boat trip from Kosti to Juba?'

This was the two-week... 1,200 kilometre journey through the vast swamplands of the upper Nile that cover much of southern Sudan, from where the only direction we could go would be across the border into Uganda or back up the Nile again, in the reverse direction, on the same boat, which clearly wouldn't make sense.

'I think it may be possible,' he went on. 'This could be acceptable, if you have these tickets. Do you have a visa, or entry permit to Uganda?'

This was an unexpected question. It came as shock, although there was no reason it should have. We'd been planning ahead as far as visas were concerned, all the way across North Africa and now, because we'd run into problems getting into the next country on, in this case Sudan we'd forgotten about checking on requirements for the next country on from there.

'Umm. No, not yet,' Noel said 'We're in the process of organizing all those things at the moment. We'll be fixing that up tomorrow.'

'Well. I cannot guarantee this. It might be possible. I will have to make more enquiries. But, in any case, you must have an entry permit for East Africa. Even with all the train and ferry tickets you still must have the entry permits. Come back when you have done that and I will be able to tell you the results of my enquiries.'

oooooo

EGYPT

9

I CAN'T GO ANYWHERE WITHOUT HIM

The Gazira Club certainly lived up to our expectations. Plush and luxurious, it was a prime example of the way of life that had existed for British expatriates, living in the colonies, in much of the rest of Africa, India and the Far East during the late nineteenth and early twentieth centuries.

Egypt had never been a British colony, of course, but its situation had long been complicated by the fact that Western European powers were continually vying for influence in Egypt: Napoleon's invasion and occupation of Egypt in 1798, though brief (it lasted until 1801), basically inaugurated a different, more subtle type of European invasion that was to be felt increasingly in Egypt over the next 150 years. Protected for centuries by the Mamluk and Ottoman sultanates, the country was no longer immune from European attack and after the opening of the Suez Canal in 1869, Egypt became more and more the object of the rival policies of France and Britain, particularly for Britain, for whom it provided faster, cheaper and vital access to the Indian subcontinent, the rest of Asia, Australia and New Zealand.

Britain gained a controlling interest in the Suez Canal Corporation in 1875, and then in 1882 sent an Expeditionary Force to occupy the Canal and secure sole domination of Egypt, which was to last effectively for seventy years. Rommel's drive to try to snatch the canal for the Axis powers during World War II had only confirmed and heightened Britain's resolve to maintain some sort of control over the Canal. But now, ten years after the war, the whole situation, as far as Britain was concerned, was on a rapid downhill slide. The monarchy of King Farouk had been overthrown just three years previously, in 1952, by a group of young officers led by Colonel Gamel Abdel Nasser and relations between Egypt and Britain were souring daily. Although Britain had no way of knowing it, within little more than a year, she would lose control of the Suez Canal forever.

In July 1956 Nasser nationalised the Canal, prompting an abortive invasion of Egypt by Britain and France, which was brought to a sudden halt by the United States, which was against the invasion, withdrawing support for the Pound sterling.

Some twelve years later, during 1967, Nasser prepared for a war with Israel, declaring: 'The battle will be a general one and our basic objective will be to destroy Israel'. But Israel struck at Egypt first, precipitating the Six-Day War, in which it occupied the Gaza Strip and the entire Sinai Peninsula.

President Nasser died in 1970 to be succeeded by another military officer, Anwar Sadat. Sadat switched Egypt's Cold War allegiance from the Soviet Union to the United States and expelled Soviet advisors in 1972.

However, in 1973, he launched a surprise attack to regain part of the Sinai territory held by Israel, which enabled him to eventually regain all of the peninsula much later, in 1979, in return for signing the Camp David Peace Accords with Israel.

Sadat's assassination by an Islamist extremist in 1981 led to the thirty-year rule of yet another army General, Hosni Mubarak, who held power until the huge riots that erupted during Egypt's version of the Arab Spring uprisings across all of the Arab World during 2011.

Mass poverty and unemployment and the growth of a huge underclass, had led rural families to stream into cities like Cairo, where they ended up in crowded slums, barely managing to survive.

Also, in the lead-up to the uprisings, Human Rights Watch had reported on Egypt's detailed serious human rights violations, including routine torture, as well as arbitrary detentions and trials before military and state security courts.

When Mubarak resigned and fled Cairo in February 2011, the Egyptian military once again took over, calling for a Constitutional Referendum and elections. In the first parliamentary elections in the thirty years since the previous regime had come to power, Mohamed

Morsi, an Islamist, won the presidency.

Massive riots against Morsi's presidency erupted all over Egypt and in July 2013 he was ousted in a military coup, leading to the ascendancy of the current (2016) leader, Abdel Fattah El-Sisi.

Sitting on the verandah of the Gazira Club, sipping a cool beer, gazing out across the lawns and gardens of its huge property on Az-Zamalik Island, opposite the centre of Cairo, naturally, none of this chaotic future for Egypt was apparent to us. In fact, the place had such a timeless air, it was not difficult to imagine the atmosphere there around the turn of the century, of the previous century, that is. It probably wouldn't have been very different from how we found it in 1955, servants in white uniforms wrapped with red cummerbunds and wearing red fez's, rushing to and fro. Foreigners, largely British, in their tropical weight clothes, savouring their pink gins, smoking and chatting about 'how the service has gone off. Not like it was before the war'.

We had been a little worried that the limitations of our wardrobe might prevent us from being admitted, but fortunately some of the clothing given to us by the British Army in Tripoli came in handy. Although we only had shorts to wear, the army safari jackets, with some long socks, gave us a vaguely military air and seemed to be sufficient for admission. At least no one stopped us. We did look a bit strange, but we'd prepared a good line: 'Archeologists. We're archeologists, just returned from a very successful dig in upper Egypt.' But, unfortunately we didn't have to use it. No one even bothered to ask us, probably because we were with Nick Parkinson, who looked eminently respectable.

We didn't stay long at the Gazira Club, only a drink on the verandah and a brief look at some of the facilities, which included a large swimming pool, tennis and squash courts, a golf course, sumptuous dining rooms, billiard and games rooms, a library and reading rooms, as well as accommodation.

'Now its the Pyramids,' Nick said. 'You haven't been there yet, have you?'

'No,' we replied. 'We passed them on the way in to Cairo, but didn't actually get to see them properly. We intended to take a bus out, but this is much better.'

We left the Gazira Club in Nick's car, crossing to the left bank of the Nile and driving south, to take the Giza road out to the pyramids, where Nick turned into the grounds of the Mena House Hotel to park the car.

'We might as well head straight over to take a look now,' he said. 'We can have a drink on the verandah here when we come back.'

That was fine by us. We walked with Nick across the main road and up another paved road along the north side of the Great Pyramid of Khufu, which now loomed, like a giant mountain above us. Khufu, who was called Cheops by the Greeks, lived some 2,000 years before the Greek historian Herodotus wrote about him and the mighty pyramids, which were as much a mystery and a wonder to the ancient Greeks and Romans as they are now to us.

The complex of structures that are readily accessible at the site, are the three main pyramids; Khufu's, Khafre's and Menkaure's, as well as three much smaller Queen's pyramids by each of the Khufu and Menkaure pyramids...and of course the Sphinx.

Important archeological excavations at Giza since the time of our visit have uncovered a host of other wonders, including the incredible boat pits containing the ancient remnants of huge royal barques, the boats that were intended to carry the departed Pharaoh into the netherworld. The first of these was discovered in 1954, a year prior to our visit, but it was not on show to the public. The second was discovered nearby, under thick limestone slabs, in 1985 through the use of extraordinary drilling and micro-camera techniques.

We continued walking around the dusty path that encircles the base of the Khufu pyramid and also leads to the other two, Khafre's and Menkaure's, as well as the Sphinx. The immense scale of the structures beggars belief.

'Its difficult enough trying to imagine how they moved just one of those giant stones into place,' Noel said, 'let alone the whole lot.'

'Yep. Each stone weighs at least two-and-a-half tonnes,' Nick said. ' many of them at the bottom weigh up to fifteen tones and there are around two-and-a-half million of them in the Khufu Pyramid alone.'

Khufu's pyramid, which is the largest in Egypt, measures a fraction over 230 metres on each side, and rises to a height of just under 147 metres... with a total mass of 2,500,000 cubic metres.

'They've estimated that, to finish it during Khufu's reign, the builders would have had to be putting it up it at the rate of over 200 cubic metres of stone a day,' Nick said. 'that's laying an average sized block every two or three minutes, for a ten hour day, over thirty years.'

Unfortunately we weren't able to enter the tunnel that takes you to the burial chamber at the centre of the Pyramid of Khufu, as it was closed for some maintenance work on the steps in the tunnel. (I did manage to get there, twenty one years later, when I returned to Cairo with my family, after travelling overland from Capetown.)

We continued on our walk around the base of Khafre's pyramid, through the ruins of the mortuary temple on the east side, then down the Royal Causeway to what is known as the Valley Temple and the Sphinx. Standing guard before the pyramid of Khafre, for whom it was carved, in around 2,500 BC, this combination of human and lion is considered to be the first colossal royal sculpture in the history of ancient Egypt.

As the sun was now low on the horizon, Nick suggested we head back to the hotel, so, walking only a short distance from the Sphinx to the main road, we turned north along it and strolled back towards the Mena House.

There, as we'd done at the Gazira Club, we sat on the verandah and drank in the atmosphere, as well as a couple of glasses of cold beer.

'I'll try the Stella,' I said. 'That's an Egyptian beer isn't it?'

Nick frowned and smiled at the same time. 'Its up to you. It's the government brewery and it hasn't got much of a reputation. They've been brewing beer for 3,000 years here, but if Stella is the result of all that experience, you wouldn't want to have tried the early stuff. There's the joke about the American chemist who takes a sample of Stella home. He turns it over to a laboratory back in the US and after a week it gives him the analysis: Your camel has diabetes.'

We laughed, but I tried the Stella anyway and more or less agreed with the American laboratory. Apparently Stella has now been privatized and there've been big improvements.

As the great dull-red ball of the sun sank and melded into the desert skyline, with the mountainous bulk of the three huge and ancient pyramids stretching off in diminishing perspective and the darkness to the south west, I felt nothing but awe and could imagine nothing more magnificent.

When Nick dropped us off back in Cairo, we said goodbye. He would be fully occupied, for the next week and in any case we were hoping we'd be sufficiently organized to get underway by the weekend, or shortly after. So we shook hands, thanking him profusely for his kindness and hospitality, leaving him to drive off into the Cairo traffic.

It was fifteen years before I met Nick again, in Singapore. I was based there in the early seventies as a foreign correspondent, covering Vietnam and South East Asia for the Australian Broadcasting Commission. Nicholas Parkinson was Australia's High Commissioner to Singapore. Five years later, in 1976, as Sir Nicholas, he was appointed to Australia's top diplomatic post, Ambassador to Washington, a post he occupied, with a brief break as Secretary for Foreign Affairs from 1977 to 1979 until he retired in 1982.

I've often thought over the years, catching occasional glimpses of Nicholas Parkinson's rise to the top of his profession, about the qualities that make a diplomat successful and about why, as a young, relatively junior diplomatic official, he should have put himself out in the way he did to help a couple of young blokes, like Noel and I. There was really no reason for him to go to such lengths and I'm sure that it is simply because he was that kind of a man all his life, that he achieved the success he did.

The following morning, Thursday, our first call was at the British Consulate, where we filled in application forms for entry permits for East Africa, which included the territories of Kenya, Uganda and Tanganyika (now Tanzania). They weren't visas as such because, as holders of British and Australian passports, we were both 'British Subjects', but the colonial authorities in Nairobi, Entebbe and Dar Es Salaam, had for some reason found it necessary to limit, or at least control, the entry of even their own people into the territories.

'Thank you,' the woman at the consulate reached forward to take our completed forms and passports, but no money, at least they were free. 'You can pick them up tomorrow.'

'Oh,' I said, 'Can't we have them back this morning? We need to show the permit to the people at the Sudanese Consulate, so we can get our Sudan Visas.'

'No. I'm terribly sorry, but its always at least one day, for any visa or entry permits. There's a sign on the wall,' she pointed. 'We'll have them for you first thing tomorrow.'

'That's a bit of a blow,' Noel muttered as we left. 'But we should have time to do it all tomorrow morning, if that Sudanese bloke says its okay. Anyway, lets head back to Kodak now and see what happens there.'

'Mr. Haykal told me something of your story the other day. I'm sorry I wasn't here to meet you.' Mr. Steytler was about 6 feet four inches tall, with sandy hair and moustache, built like a rugby player (which he probably was) and spoke with a strong South African accent. 'You're heading to East Africa?'

'Yes, but we're ultimately heading for South Africa,' I added quickly. 'That's our goal.'

'South Africa?' he said. 'I'm from South Africa. Bloemfontein.'

'Really? Noel said. That's great. we've been wanting to get to South Africa for ages. We're surfers. We hear the surf is pretty good down there.'

'Excellent. Excellent. You'll like South Africa. Its a great country. When do expect to be there? Come into my office and sit down.'

We followed him through and began explaining some of our plans, including the proposed trip down the Nile through the Sudan, to East Africa.

'Hmm,' he muttered, while we were still talking. 'So you need some film. 'Look,' he got up and paced around. 'I could give you colour film at a bit of a discount, but I have something else that might interest you.' He disappeared from his office, for a few minutes, returning with a flat, round tin canister, roughly 30 cms in diameter. 'Would this be any good,' he said, handing it to Noel.

Noel looked at it. 'Its movie film.'

'Yes, 35 mm black and white... Plus X ... exactly the same film as you'd buy in the photo shops, except that its bulk, because its for movies.'

'A thousand feet of it!' Noel exclaimed after reading the label. 'That's probably five thousand shots.'

'At least,' Mr. Steytler nodded. 'You'll have to load your own cassettes, in a dark room or changing bag. But I'm sure you can do that. We can give you some spare cassettes and you can just reuse them as many times as you like. Can you use it? '

'Well, yes,' I said, 'we can definitely use it. But how much will it be?'

'No. No. Its yours. You can have it,' he smiled. 'A gift from Kodak.'

'Wow! Fantastic!' We were both ecstatic in our thanks for what seemed to be a virtually endless amount of film, free. We left his offices with a great feeling of optimism that all of our other arrangements were also going to work out just as satisfactorily.

Friday. If the pieces all fell together during the morning, we could be on our way south, by the following day. But we'd need to have our running shoes on. First pick up the East African permits and take them to the Sudan Consulate to show them. If they approved in principle, we would then dash to the Sudan Travel Agency to buy the river-boat tickets for the journey from Kosti to Juba. Then dash back to the Sudan consulate to show them and hopefully get our visas, all of this before they closed at lunchtime. We'd thought about buying the boat tickets beforehand, so we could present the whole lot to the Consulate, but we'd decided not to because, lurking in the back of our minds, there was still the possibility that they could knock us back.

At the British Consulate, despite the fact that she'd said our passports would be ready for us, there was a wait. A most fortuitous wait as it turned out.

'I believe you're heading down to East Africa?' A young man had been sitting at a desk in an office to one side and came over to talk to us as we stood waiting.

'Well, yes,' I said. 'but then on to Rhodesia and South Africa eventually.'

'And where have you come from? I mean, I know you're from Australia, but how did you get here?'

We gave him a short hand version of our trip across North Africa...looking from time to time out of the corner of our eyes towards the desk where we hoped the woman would appear with our visas. The young man didn't seem to notice, but kept wanting to talk about our travels. And what seemed to interest him particularly was that we had stayed in British Army bases across Libya.

'How were you able to do that?' he asked and we explained our story about being National Servicemen on our way home to Australia and that I had been in the Army and that Noel had been in the Air Force. 'Bit tenuous,' I said. 'But everyone seemed happy enough to let us stay.'

'You know,' he paused a few seconds, 'I am the secretary to the Air Attache here. And it seems to me, from what you've said that there might be a chance that you could organize a lift with the RAF, on a flight from Fayid, on the Canal Zone, down to Eastleigh Air Force base in Nairobi.'

'We've thought about that sort of thing before,' Noel said. 'In fact we went out to El Adem, near Tobruk and the people there said they thought it would be okay for us to fly from there to Fayid. But it never eventuated, because of the time we would have had to wait, so we came overland.'

'Well, its probably possible from here also.' he said. 'So, if you...'

At that point the woman arrived with our passports, which she handed to us.

'Look,' I turned back to our new friend. 'we'd better head off to the Sudan Consulate to see if we can organize our visas there. But, if there's any problems....'

'Please don't hesitate,' he said. 'Come back here and I'll see what I can do. The name's Jeremy. Jeremy Baker.'

Half an hour later, at the Sudan Consulate... the final NO.

'I am sorry.' He was extremely apologetic. 'The rules at the moment do say that travellers across Sudan must produce tickets for the whole journey or evidence of sufficient funds to support themselves. This would be either funds in the Sudan, or sufficient funds here. I didn't ask you that before, but could you produce evidence of sufficient funds?'

'Difficult,' Noel said. 'Difficult. How much is sufficient?

'One hundred pounds'

'Even more difficult,' I muttered.

'I did try, I assure you. I sent a telex to Khartoum, to see if we could accept the way you suggested earlier, with just the tickets   to Juba. But they still insist on some guarantee, some evidence of funds.'

'We're back again,' I said to the woman at the British Consulate, another half-hour later. 'I wonder if we could talk to Jeremy Baker again, please?'

Jeremy emerged from his office a few moments later. 'Ahh. So you did encounter problems?' he grinned. 'Shall we try my suggestion?'

'Yes please,' I said. 'as long as it won't cause any problems or be embarrassing for you.'

'Hell, no. Its no problem for me. Obviously I can't promise anything. Somebody at Fayid would have to make the decisions. But at least I can ring the Air Movements Officer there, to find out if there are any flights going to Eastleigh. I know they fly down there from time to time, but I don't know how often. There may be nothing scheduled.'

'You could mention that we were out at the Movements Office at El Adem...and that they more or less said okay to us, in principle, over there.'

'Yes, yes. I'll tell them that and also that the Army's been putting you up right across Libya. I'll be a few minutes,' he said as he disappeared back into his office to make the call.

'Well, we're on the back foot now,' I murmured, as we sat down in a small couch to await the results of Jeremy's call. 'With the Sudan closed off, we've got problems. The only way south is...'

'To go around it,' Noel put in. 'We'll have to try the ships again.'

'Where? Alexandria?'

'Maybe, but probably Port Said would be better. Anything going through the Canal has to stop there. Anyway, the air base is in the Canal Zone, on the way to Port Said. If Jeremy can set anything up, we could go there tomorrow and then if that falls through, just keep on going, up to Port Said.'

Writing about it now, I recall something of our mind set during this whole journey and one of the things I find most interesting to think about was the extraordinary flexibility we seemed to employ in all our decisions. We seemed quite naturally prepared to make major shifts in direction...as to how and where we were heading (apart from the final destination at the bottom of Africa) with hardly a moment's hesitation. I like to think some of that flexibility stayed with me over the years.

'Right,' Jeremy said as he emerged again from his office. 'You're to report to the Air Movements Office out at Fayid tomorrow afternoon. To be honest, they're not completely sure about you. You'll have to go through it all with them. Presumably you've got some form of Military ID cards, or something like that, you can show them. Anyway, there is an aircraft going down to Kenya on Monday. So, if you can get through the red tape, you might be able to get on it.'

Our hearts lifted. We could hardly believe that we could have had such a turnaround in prospects in the less than one hour that had passed since we had walked dejectedly out into the street from the Sudan Consulate. Even though, as usual, there was no guarantee, we felt entirely optimistic about our prospects and thanked Jeremy, as if he had already performed a miracle.

'Good luck,' he called as we left the British Consulate.

By ten o'clock the following morning, after a bus ride through Heliopolis, on the north eastern outskirts of Cairo, we were on the main road heading north. After a wait of less than ten minutes we found ourselves sitting on our packs, once again in the back of a truck, making up the kilometres towards Bilbays, about half way to Ishmaelia, where the Fayid Air Base was located, a distance of some 100 kilometres from Cairo.

On the previous evening, after Yahya, the baker had notified his cousin, Jusuf that we were planning to leave Cairo, Jusuf arrived at the bakery to say goodbye. We told him of the problems we'd encountered in trying to organize our onward travel, all of which he found hard to understand. 'They have no right to refuse you entry,' he said. 'How can they do that, if you are only travelling through their country?'

We tried to convince him that the Sudanese had every right to refuse whoever they liked, but he was adamant.

'They should realise that you are Australians and that you have come from a long way to visit their country. They should be honoured.'

'I wish immigration authorities, and consular officials really did feel that way,' I said. ' It would make life a lot easier.'

'But, anyway,' he concluded, as we shook his hand to say goodbye, 'you will find good luck at Ishmaelia. I am sure of it. The British will help you.'

We weren't fully aware of it at the time, but the tensions developing between Britain and Egypt were considerable. President Nasser wanted the bases to go, but Britain who owned the Suez Canal company, that operated the Canal, had a big bargaining chip. Egypt was also negotiating with Britain and the United States to finance the building of the Aswan High Dam, in southern Egypt, a mammoth project that it was believed would have a dramatic impact on Egypt's economy. So while Egypt wanted the British bases gone it did not want to cut off its nose to spite its face. Nevertheless in September 1955, just two months after our passing through Egypt, Nasser signed an arms agreement with Czechoslovakia, which was acting for the Soviet Union. This seriously soured relations with the West and set the scene for the dramatic military showdown, between Egypt on the one side and Britain, France and Israel on the other, the following year.

Although no definite plans were in the pipeline for the closure of Fayid, the international situation was such that contingency plans had been drawn up for the eventual movement of all British forces from the Canal Zone, either back to Britain or, as one plan had it, to Kenya. There, the thinking went, they could be relatively close to the Canal, should anyone threaten it, but they could also beef up the strength of the colonial forces in Kenya. British residents, in fact all white residents, were coming under increasing pressure and mounting attacks from Mau Mau terrorists across the country.

'Yes, we got the message from Mr. Baker in Cairo,' The officer, a squadron leader, said to us after we'd arrived at the base and checked in at the Air Movements Office. 'It wasn't me who spoke to him,' he went on, 'but I've been told about you and we're looking in to it. From what I can understand, it rather depends on what sort of identification you have, I mean military identification. As you're not British service personnel, we have to have something to say that you are in the Australian services,'

'Would my Air Force pilot's licence do?' Noel said, handing over a piece of paper with his photograph attached. We waited with baited breath, as he examined the paper, thanking our lucky stars that Jeremy Baker had mentioned the need for some military identification. Noel had delved into the depths of his pack and found it amongst some other personal papers, which he never thought he would have to use. Forewarned is forearmed.

'Pilot Officer Noel Hayes White, Royal Australian Air Force,' he read from Noel's Air Force pilot's licence. 'It doesn't say anything about your actual military service, or present status,' he said. 'But, at least it shows you've been in the Services. It might be enough. I'm not sure. Is that all you've got?'

'Yes. You see we've been studying   in England and we're heading....'

'Uh huh.... and what about you?' He turned to me. 'Do you have a pilot's license too?'

'No. I haven't. Unfortunately we were, that is I, was robbed in Casablanca. I had everything stolen, my passport, my birth certificate, my er, my military papers, everything. All I have is this...' I handed over my British passport. 'They issued me with temporary British papers.'

He studied it. 'But were you in the Air Force too?'

'No. I was in the army. National Service. We are both National Servicemen. And, you see, although we've been in Europe for a year, studying, we still have a two-year obligation to complete back home. Like the Territorials in Britain. So, well, basically we are still in the services.'

He smiled, a good sign I thought. 'Hmm, maybe,' he said. 'What rank?'

'Er...Sergeant.'

'I see.' He took a deep breath. 'With no papers, it'll be difficult... if not impossible. We might be able to do something for Pilot Officer White, but for you. I'm not sure what we can do.'

Noel's piece of paper had suddenly achieved him exalted status. I felt, equally suddenly, as if I was out in the cold.

'He's my batman,' Noel said quickly. 'I can't go anywhere without him. He....'

The officer laughed, '...polishes your boots?'

'Right,' Noel said. That's right. He polishes my boots every morning. Don't you Iain?'

'Yes, absolutely...' Noel lifted his leg to show a dirty old unpolished army boot. 'umm...I missed them this morning though.'

The officer laughed, joined by two other officers who were working in the room who had stopped to listen to the conversation and watch the show. After all it wasn't every day that two bearded backpackers arrived in the Air Movements Office asking for a free, 4,000-kilometre air lift.

'Look, leave it with us for a while. I'll have to check on it with someone a bit more senior. You could hop over to the mess and have something to eat.' He turned to one of the other men. 'Fisher, take them over to the men's mess. There's probably something still on. They could have tea or cakes or something like that.' He turned to Noel. 'You could go to the officers mess, of course, but your friend, er, Finlay, unfortunately can't.'

Another subtle shove for me...towards the outer. Just as well I have a thick skin.

'That's all right,' Noel said with a grin. 'I think I'll be able to get by at the men's mess.'

'Come back at five. We might have some news by then.'

Less than twenty minutes later, before we had even finished our cakes and tea, Flight Sergeant Fisher arrived in something of a hurry.

'You've got to come back to the Movements Office,' he said. 'Apparently the CO wants to see you.'

Back at the Movements Office, the squadron leader seemed even more affable and relaxed. 'You could be in luck,' he lifted his eyebrows, in mild surprise. ' The Commanding Officer, Group Captain Rankin, wants to meet you.'

'The CO? The Commanding Officer, wants to meet us?' Noel and I were both somewhat amazed.

'Yes. He's actually an Australian also. When he heard you were here, he said he wanted to meet you.'

He's Australian? But not in the Australian Air Force?' Noel asked.

'No, No. He's RAF...been in it since before the war. In fact I've always thought of him as English. He doesn't sound Australian.'

Amazing how a stroke of luck, good fortune, just chance really, can change everything. We had to put ourselves in the position of being there of course, of actually going to the air base and asking for a lift to Kenya, but we had no idea that there was an Australian CO on the base, or that it could turn everything in our favour.

'So how long have you chaps been travelling?' Group Captain Rankin asked, after we'd been introduced and were sitting in his office talking.

'Almost a year,' Noel said and we both went into a brief history of our travels in Europe and the journey across North Africa for him.

'But they tell me you're trying to head back to Australia, part of this, completing your National Service, or something. But, going to Kenya is not actually taking you in the direction of Australia.'

I smiled. I felt we could be a little more honest with him. 'Well to tell the truth, technically we don't really have to be back in Australia for another year. We want to be back there for the Olympic Games in Melbourne. But we've got a bit of time, that's why we're heading for South Africa first. We should be able to get a boat from there. So, while its true we do have a commitment back home, what we don't tell anybody, is that there's no hurry.'

He laughed. And we talked about Australia, which he hadn't seen for some years. He came from Victoria and had first gone to Britain in 1937, joining the RAF there shortly after.

'Now look,' he said after a while. I don't think we'll have any trouble getting you on the Valetta to Eastleigh on Monday. I've spoken to the movements chaps about it and while the fact that Iain here doesn't have any military papers does present a bit of a problem, we think we can get around it. We'll have to fit you both out with air force clothing, just some flying suits will do, but apart from that, I think it'll be okay.'

'Wonderful.Incredible,' we both laughed a little uncertainly, 'Thank you very much.'

'No. Its nothing really,' he said. 'There's plenty of room and its not as if its costing the British taxpayer anything. Its just the regulations, getting around a bit of red tape. Now, ' he got up from his chair, 'unfortunately a little bit more bull, as far as dinner tonight is concerned. You'll eat with me at the Officers Mess. Now, Noel is technically an officer, so he can come in. But Iain is not. So,' he turned to me, 'for the purpose of the exercise, we'll say you're not service personnel at all. You're a civilian. And I'll just sign you in as a visitor. Crazy stuff isn't it. But there you are.'

The following day, a Sunday, we had little to do except keep out of peoples way. We read and as there was a swimming pool on the base, we swam in the afternoon and wrote letters to our parents, friends and again to the two Norwegian girls we'd met in Europe. Lise was the girl I wrote to while Noel's girl was called Bibby. The morning had also been taken up partly in recovering from a slight hangover, as both of us had had a little too much to drink the night before. We did have an excuse however as in addition to celebrating our forthcoming flight, we had realised that that actual day, July 17th, was the first anniversary of our departure from Melbourne, bound for Naples on the MV Otranto.

As things turned out, it was decided that it was not necessary for us to be issued with the grey flight suits that Group Captain Rankin thought might be necessary. Our army safari jackets apparently gave us a sufficiently military air. We were told that the plane we were to leave on would be taking off at 6.30 the following morning. The CO invited us for drinks with him that evening and we were able to thank him for his generous help. We then had dinner at the mess and after an hour or so talking, over a couple of beers, with some of the young airmen, went off to our quarters for an early night.

ooooooo

SUDAN

10

A HUGE ROAR RENT THE AIR

As the big old Valetta rolled down the runway, with its two engines roaring, slowly gathering enough speed to lumber into the thin morning air, Noel and I smiled and gave each other the thumbs up. We were on our way. Even in those days I think I must have felt, as I do now, that whenever there is something you really want to happen, never take it for granted that it will happen, until it actually does. Until the contract is signed, until the money is in your pocket, or in this case, until the plane is in the air. We had taken off about an hour later than scheduled.

The Valetta was a sort of Royal Air Force equivalent of the DC3, basically a transport plane with seats running down the opposite walls of the fuselage. There were no creature comforts, like reclining seats or tray tables, sound proofing, pressurization or even toilets. Only eight other passengers, a couple of flight crew, as well as some engineering and ground crew personnel, who sat opposite and beside us, were on the flight. It was difficult to have any conversation from one side of the aircraft to the other, because of the noise, so we confined ourselves to twisting around and gazing out of the small windows at the landscape below.

Because the aircraft was unpressurized, we stuck to relatively low altitudes of only 1500 to 2000 metres. Looking down and checking on our map, it seemed as if we were heading due south, across Egypt's Eastern Desert and not following the course of the Nile, which was somewhat to the west of our flight path. After a couple of hours, however, the co-pilot came back and gestured for us to look below. We had just crossed the Nile and were now travelling to the west of it.

'That's the Valley of the Kings,' he shouted above the noise of the aircraft.

Immediately below we could see a great arid plain stretching westward from the edge of the river, to a low line of dry and barren hills. With the colour of the landscape almost white and the rising sun, still low in the eastern sky, reflecting into our eyes, the view was almost blinding.

'That's where they buried all the kings and queens' the co-pilot said. 'after they gave up on pyramids.'

'Not much there.' I noted.

'Oh, there is,' he looked out himself. 'Its just all underground. They were trying to hide the graves, secret tombs, trying to make them safe from robbers.'

Not with a huge degree of success apparently as most of the graves were robbed in antiquity. Nevertheless, it was here, in 1922 that Howard Carter discovered the fabulous tomb of Tutankhamen.

Off to our left, also back-lit by the morning sun, we could see the modern city of Luxor as well as some of the ruins of the ancient temples of Luxor and Karnak passing below us.

The barren, uncultivated area occupied by the Valley of the Kings, on the western side of the Nile, was something of an exception, in that, for most of the rest of the way to Aswan, a further 300 kilometres, the river is edged on both sides by intensive cultivation and irrigation. From the air it presents the image of a muddy brown river, running down the middle of a wider, undulating ribbon of green, that varies in width from a few hundred metres, to a kilometre or so. Beyond the green ribbon, on either side, is the harsh and apparently endless desert.

But once we had passed over the city of Aswan, the green ribbon shrank considerably, so that now the desert and dry cliffs and wadis often encroached close on the river. And there was far less sign of habitation. This whole area, for over 400 hundred kilometres to the south, would in the future be flooded, by the building of the High Dam at Aswan. The huge body of water created by that dam would be known as Lake Nasser. In the meantime however and for many years to come it remained that narrow, but deep, ribbon of muddy water.

Some 250 kilometres south of Aswan and only about thirty kilometres before we landed at Wadi Halfa on the Sudan border, the co-pilot came back again to point out of the window.

'That's Abu Simbel,' he shouted. 'The great temple built by Rameses II.'

We had come down low enough to get a good view and as we were to the east of it and looking to the west, with the sun shining directly onto it, we had a clear view of the four giant statues carved in the cliff face to guard the entrance to Rameses' temple.

'How incredible,' I said. 'that it should be way out here, so far from everything else in Egypt. Are there other temples or towns nearby?'

'Temples, yes, and tombs, dozens of them, all the way back along the river to Aswan. But no towns.'

I could hardly have known, that within a year, I would be on a small boat on the Nile river, approaching and stepping ashore at Abu Simbel.

We landed ten minutes later at Wadi Halfa, an uninspiring river town of a few thousand inhabitants, not long after mid-day to spend about an hour there, during which time the plane was refuelled. The flight crew also cleared the aircraft and passengers' paperwork with the Sudanese customs and immigration officers at the airstrip. You could hardly call it an airport. It was all relatively straightforward and uncomplicated and after a cup of tea and a sandwich in a small shelter we were on our way, lifting off and heading south once more, towards Khartoum.

Now from the windows of the plane we could only see the deep blue of the sky fading and gradually blending, closer to the ground, into a sandy colour,   so that the horizon was hazy and not clearly distinguishable. On the ground below, only a totally flat featureless desert, the great Nubian desert that stretched the whole 750 kilometres (as the crow flies) from Wadi Halfa to Khartoum.

'You'll love this place,' The pilot, whose name was Harrison, said to us as an Air Force van dropped us off at the Country Club in Khartoum. The building, near the centre of what otherwise seemed a dusty and unimposing city, was white and impressive. Inside it was even more so. Another fine example of how the Brits looked after themselves in the colonies. In the midst of the squalor of Khartoum, this was like a luxury hotel. But having had our own fair share of discomfort over the past few weeks, we had no qualms about taking

Our Valetta. Noel with others prior to takeoff.

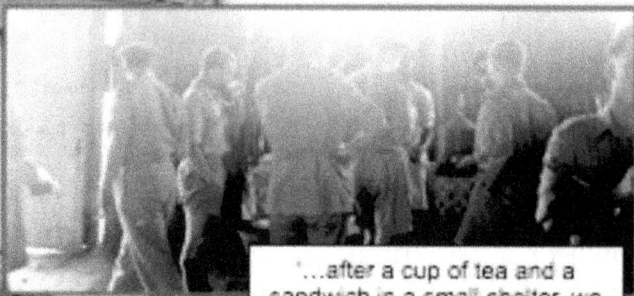

'...after a cup of tea and a sandwich in a small shelter, we were on our way.'

The Country Club in Khartoum. 'It looked for all the world like a Roman bath

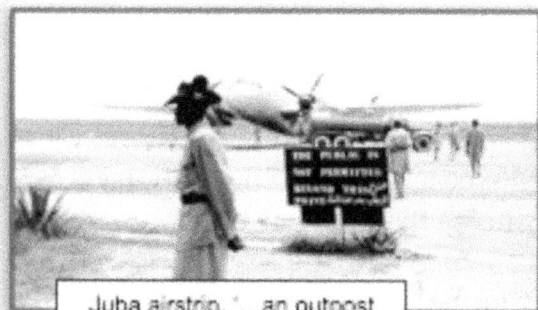

Juba airstrip. '...an outpost with very primitive facilities

'...we managed to hitch a ride with an Automobile Association officer in a Land Rover.'

advantage of any comforts that now presented themselves.

There was an elegant lounge, a comfortable bar, a reading room, a huge dining room and an inner courtyard which opened onto a swimming pool surrounded by columns. It looked for all the world like a Roman bath. All we needed were the couches around the sides, the togas and grapes and the scene would have been complete.

Neither Noel nor I had expected anything like this, but took to it all quite readily. We swam, had drinks and dinner and slept in a comfortable bedroom with an overhead fan humming softly all night.

'If only all our travelling could be like this,' Noel said the next morning as we ate a full English breakfast of bacon and eggs, toast and marmalade and coffee, before being driven back out to the airport.

'Oh, I'm sure you'd get sick of it after a while.'

'Try me,' he laughed.

This situation we found in Khartoum, the hangover from colonial days, had seemed extraordinary to us but like the British position in Egypt, it was all about to change. Within less than six months, on January 1st 1956, the colonial era would be out the window and Sudan would be declared an independent republic, with an elected representative Parliament. A little more of that in Chapter Eighteen however.

There was only one more stop we would make on the 4,000 kilometre journey from the Canal Zone to Nairobi and that was at Juba in the far south of Sudan. In fact our flight was touching down at three of the major points we would have passed through had we been travelling on the surface. On this third leg we had a birds eye view of the sort of territory I would encounter at close quarters a year later on the river boat trip north from Juba.

Gone now was the desert, replaced by a vast green carpet stretching from one horizon to the other. Not jungle but the world's largest swamp, tens of thousands of square kilometres of almost trackless swamp; with only the meandering, zig-zagging course of the Nile to give it any perspective. But it was not a swamp that could be viewed at eye-level. Papyrus reeds grew to a height of almost three metres over much of the swamp, which meant that from ground or river level you were   effectively in a jungle and could see only as far as the next patch of papyrus or to a turn in the river.

From the air however we could see the enormous extent of the Bar El Jebel, as the huge swamp is called and on one or two occasions we caught a brief glimpse of a dugout canoe creating a spearhead pattern in the waters of the river far below.

As we neared Juba the country opened up. In parts there was what appeared to be dense areas of jungle-like foliage and trees then more open rolling hills covered with flat-topped Acacia trees that was teeming with animals.

'We're going down a bit lower for a look at some of the game,' the co-pilot told us. 'There are huge herds of elephant in these parts.'

And as the plane came down to almost tree-top height we glued ourselves to the windows with our cameras and although somewhat anxious at first soon ignored the fact that we were less than a hundred feet from the ground. We found ourselves shouting with excitement.

'Look. Buffaloes!'

'And a hippo! Look there's a whole lot of them.'

Crocodiles. Crocodiles. Did you see the crocodiles?'

Then the elephants. A magnificent herd of more than a hundred elephants came in to view, spread over a broad green plain off to our right.   Turning and climbing slightly, so as not to be so low as to frighten them, the pilot swung the aircraft in a wide arc around the herd, so that we were able to see them more clearly. The animals were obviously a little disturbed by the sound of the aircraft...and some of them moved suddenly and nervously in alarm, but it was not sufficient to panic them and after our one turn around them, we straightened up and continued on to land at Juba hardly more than ten or fifteen minutes later.

Juba at that time had little more claim to fame than the fact that it is the most southerly border town in the Sudan. It was an outpost, with very primitive facilities. The simple airstrip at which we landed had a tin shed at one end. Refuelling was done from a truck which carried drums of avgas from which the fuel was pumped into the aircraft's wing tanks by hand.

We'll return to Juba later, in Chapter 18, to tell of our journey by

Riverboat down the Nile, as well as touching on some of the tragic events that have befallen the southern Sudan during the sixty years since we first called in at Juba.

We stayed there an hour, bought a soft drink from a man who pedalled up on a bicycle, pulling a metal container with ice in it, and then took off for the last leg of our flight, of about 900 kilometres, to Nairobi.

Flying southeast towards the Kenyan capital, we were told by the co-pilot, after about two-and-a-half hours in the air, that we were crossing the imaginary line of the equator...a little tidbit of comforting information that made the two antipodeans on board feel a little closer to home.

At the same time we passed over the north-eastern corner of Lake Victoria. Looking to the south, across the lake for as far as we could see... there was no land in sight. It was like a huge sea set in the middle of East Africa, with a surrounding countryside at the top end that looked green and fertile...very different from the deserts of North Africa or the Sudan. As if to underline that impression, as we approached Nairobi the sky seemed suddenly filled with dark and lowering clouds and just as we landed at Eastliegh Air force Base on the outskirts of the city, the heavens opened and a torrential thunderstorm broke over us.

The actual city of Nairobi, when we finally got there, after clearing immigration authorities, saying thankful goodbyes to our Royal Air Force friends and then catching a bus, had been washed clean by the rain. It had that wonderfully fresh ozone smell that always seems to accompany heavy tropical downpours. But even without the rain, we could see that Nairobi was a clean and well-cared for town. It looked modern...in an African sense...buildings were well constructed. People were laughing and moving around, as they do after heavy rain...emerging from shelters, or from restaurants, or offices, to pick up where they had left off when the deluge started. They were jumping puddles or making diversions on the footpath and roads to avoid water that had not yet run off. The place looked in a strange way, as if it could be somewhere in Northern Australia. And because everybody spoke English, I suppose we felt it was a little like home. But there were big differences.

'Look,' Noel said. 'That woman is wearing a gun.' He pointed to a blonde woman in a floral dress, walking along the opposite side of the road. She had a leather holster containing a pistol, on a belt around her waist.

'And this bloke over here...' I pointed to another armed civilian getting into his car. Within the space of fifteen minutes, we saw at least half a dozen white civilians carrying weapons that were obviously meant to be obvious.

In the Poste Restante section of the central Post Office we were pleased to be able to pick up mail from our parents and from our Norwegian girlfriends that had been waiting there for us for some time. While there, we saw three more Europeans, including another woman, who were wearing weapons. Yet, we were assured by people we spoke to later, that the Mau Mau situation was not dangerous enough to warrant this sort of display or precaution on the part of civilians in the capital.

The Mau Mau rebellion had begun in late 1951 and early 1952 when members of the dominant tribe in Kenya, the Kikuyu, formed a secret society whose activities were directed against the presence of Europeans in the country and their ownership of land. Outbreaks of violence, sabotage and assassination, as well as attacks on European-owned farms, led to the declaration of a State of Emergency in October 1952.

Oddly, the ones who suffered most at the hands of the Mau Mau were those members of the Kikuyu tribe who failed to support the secret society. Some 2,000 of them were executed or assassinated by the Mau Mau, compared to little more than a hundred Europeans. On the other hand, around 11,000 rebels were killed by the government's forces during the first four years of the rebellion, while a further 20,000 other Kikuyu were held in detention camps, where efforts were made to convert them to the political views of Kenya's British Government.

Jomo Kenyatta, one of the suspected leaders of the Mau Mau movement, was jailed in 1953, along with five others, for seven years.

Released in 1959, Kenyatta was held under house arrest until Kenya was granted independence in 1963, with him as Prime Minister. A year later he became President of the newly formed Republic of

Kenya.

Kenyatta remained President until his death in 1978, which saw his Vice President, Daniel Arap Moi take over the job and remain in power for 24 years. Moi actually won five elections during that period, for three of which he was unopposed in a one-party system. However, after the introduction of the first multi-party elections in 1992 he was re-elected...and then again in 1997, although both campaigns were marred by political violence on both sides.

Moi was constitutionally barred from running again in 2002 after widespread reports of corruption and of accepting bribes from international developers. His Vice President, Mwai Kibaki won the Presidency and soon gained respect for transforming the country's poorly-performing economy to produce a bustling 7% average annual growth rate as well as introducing a plan to make Kenya a middle-income nation by 2030.

Despite suggestions of corruption on his part, Kibeki managed to successfully introduce a new constitution which started a process of wide ranging institutional and legislative reforms in Kenya.

However, his Party of National Unity lost the 2013 elections to Jomo Kenyatta's son Uhuru Kenyatta, whose Jubilee Alliance Party now holds power.

Of course, in mid-1955, when we passed through Nairobi, the country was still under British rule and had been through about two-and-a-half years of the Emergency and, according to the information we received, the Mau Mau were largely under control and confined mainly to the area around Mount Kenya, roughly 300 kilometres to the north of the capital. But it would be a further five years before the State of Emergency was officially brought to an end in 1960.

Despite the Mau Mau situation then, we nevertheless felt that Kenya...or East Africa in general, presented us with a whole new range of possibilities and opportunities. Although our permit was only for a brief transit through either one, or all of the three East African territories, Kenya, Uganda and Tanganyika, we felt there was a reasonable possibility of finding work here.

'It doesn't say anywhere that we can't work,' I said, looking over the stamp that had been put in our passports.

'In any case, if we got a job. I'm sure we'd be able to extend it pretty easily.'

We managed to find an extremely cheap, though decidedly down-market, hotel in which to stay for our first night. This was one of the difficulties we would encounter, which up until now we'd been able to avoid... that is, paying for accommodation and unlike Europe, East Africa was not the sort of place you could readily find youth hostels..in those days anyway. And white people just didn't sleep by the side of the road.

On the following morning, we made a few desultory attempts at enquiring about jobs...at the central government offices, the Shell Oil company and a large department store...but our hearts weren't really in it and, around noon, we sat down in a small Indian café to talk about it.

'Look, our main aim has always been to get down to South Africa,' I said. 'We could stay here and get a job, but we'd just be delaying things.'

Noel nodded. 'Well, I've got roughly seven quid left,' He flipped through the few notes in his wallet. 'You're about the same, aren't you?'

'Yep.'

'Then I reckon we should keep going... heading south.'

'Me too.' Neither of us required much convincing. 'We should at least be able to get to Northern Rhodesia, before we run out. And we could try for some of those jobs on the copper mines there.'

'Spot on.' We both laughed, as we always did, whenever we reached a joint decision that both of us favoured. 'Well, we're on the road again.'

On the southern outskirts of Nairobi we joined a road heading south, which ironically is called, 'The Great North Road'. In those days, given the right resources; namely a decent car and enough cash, you could stay on that same road and without any trouble, or likelihood of getting lost, or hurt, drive some six thousand kilometres, through five British colonies, territories, or dominions, to Capetown... at the bottom tip of Africa.

Well, we didn't have the right resources, but nonetheless, we felt the surge of excitement that came from setting out on that road and knowing that it was all laid out there in front of us...waiting.

After only two short lifts, we managed to hitch a ride, with an Automobile Association officer in a Land Rover that was heading some two hundred kilometres further south to a place called Namanga River, on the border of Tanganyika and Kenya. Straddling the border, a little further to the east, in the midst of the great Amboseli National Park, stands Mount Kilimanjaro.

'Will we be able to see Kilimanjaro from the road?' I asked our driver, a white Kenyan in an AA uniform, who'd introduced himself as Michael.

'You certainly will. It'll be about a hundred kilometres off to the left as we get down near the border, but its 19,000 feet high, so you won't have any trouble seeing it. That's if there's no cloud about. It could be clouded in with all this weather though.'

As luck would have it, although there were no storm clouds and the day was sunny and hot, the small, fluffy white clouds that were sprinkled across the sky, kept us from seeing Mount Kilimanjaro. We did, however, see what for us was a surprising amount of wild game from the car...off on the plains to the side of the road. True, we were quite a distance from Nairobi before we started to see them, and most were a good way off the road, but we saw eland, gembok, gazelles and springbok...at least that's what our driver told us we were seeing, as well as wild buffalo and giraffe...even three elephants in the distance.

We both knew that this was what to expect in East Africa, but somehow it still seemed incredible that these animals, which in the rest of the world are confined to pens in zoos, should be free to roam around, in a habitat that was as much theirs as ours.

Of course this was well before the advent of Open Zoos... or Plains Zoos in Australia and other countries, which approximate the idea of an open, free environment, but which still, in the end, have boundaries and fences.

'I'm stopping here overnight,' the AA man told us, as we reached Namanga River and pulled into the yard of a small hotel with the same name. 'I have to meet up with some people in the Serengeti tomorrow, but this is as good a place as any to stay. They've got a good bar... and, if you want to try to get out into Amboseli, you should try here. The owner of the hotel is also a game warden. So he generally knows what's going on at Amboseli.'

There was not much of a town at Namanga River...more a collection of stalls selling all manner of food and vegetables as well as souvenirs, beads and artifacts along the roadside as you approached the border and the small bridge across the river to Tanganyika (now Tanzania). The Namanga River Hotel was a collection of low brick buildings with thatched roofs, set amongst shady trees, shrubs and lawns a short distance back from the actual border crossing.

'Its pretty difficult...in fact its impossible to get out into Amboseli on your own,' the hotel owner, Alex Portman, told us as we sat in the bar with Michael shortly after we had arrived. 'Unless you've got a car, of course. There are also safari wagons that bring people down from Nairobi to go out into the park all the time, but...' he raised his eyebrows and smiled. 'I don't think they're likely to pick up any non-paying passengers.'

The bar was an attractive room, done in dark timber, with exposed beams and comfortable lounge chairs and tables spread around. The walls were covered with African artifacts and memorabilia; dozens of photographs of big game hunting...many, of course with the snow-capped Kilimanjaro in the background. There were spears, shields, masks and carvings, antelope heads, leopard skins and so on. Two ceiling fans were spinning quietly, providing some respite from the heat of the late afternoon.

Then, in another of those little turns of fate that seemed to be constantly working in our favour, the owner came out from behind the bar, where he'd been serving some drinks for a couple of other customers, and said to us, 'You know, I'm just thinking, there's a chance you could get out into the park tomorrow, with a friend of mine who's coming down here tonight. He's a hunter...a big game hunter. Normally takes hunting parties out into the bush, in northern Kenya and some of the other parts of the country, but he knows Amboseli well. He's coming down with a couple of friend I think, to show him around. But, I'm pretty sure its a private trip, not a commercial one, so he may just feel that he could fit you in.'

'But what sort of vehicle is it? Would there be enough room?' I asked.

'Oh yes. He's got a long wheel-base Land Rover, so there shouldn't be any worries, unless he's got extra people along.'

'The only problem we have,' Noel said. 'Is that we haven't got enough money to stay in the hotel tonight. We're heading for Rhodesia and South Africa and we've got to try to stretch the pennies out.'

'Is there somewhere else around here that we could stay.. a bit cheaper.' I asked.

He laughed. 'There's nowhere else here at Namanga. This is it. We're the only Europeans here...and there's nothing the natives have in the way of accommodation.'

'We've got sleeping bags,' I said. 'Do you think it'd be alright if we slept in the grounds of the hotel...like on the lawn, perhaps. Just for security.'

'Absolutely. You're welcome to do that. In fact, I've got a couple of camp stretchers you can have later.'

We talked more about the park and his various experiences in the area over the years...particularly in the other major parks just across the border in Tanganyika...Serengeti, Lake Manyara and Ngoro Ngoro Crater.

'Of course, Tanganyika used to belong to the Germans before the First World War,' he told us. '...and then we, that is Britain, took it over. And up until recent years...well, it was almost as if there was no border...particularly for people like us, hunters. I used to be a white hunter...as they called us, also. We could just come and go, whenever and wherever we liked.' He paused to light a cigarette. 'Oh, perhaps it wasn't quite like that. People...that is the authorities, knew we were out there. But they also knew that we knew what we were doing, so it was all left pretty much to us. Its all changing now though.'

We also talked of our own travels, across North Africa and down through the Sudan with the RAF, all of which tended to amaze him and another man at the bar. In turn, they both had plenty of good advice for us about what to expect as we travelled down the Great North Road through Tanganyika.

During the time we had been sitting there, we had bought a round of beers...a practice we tried to...and generally succeeded...in keeping to a minimum. Fortunately the drinks were not too expensive, but as darkness approached and it came on to dinner time, we insisted on making our own meal. We had bread and cheese and sardines, as well as some fruit, in our packs and, so as not to confuse or disturb any of the other guests, of which there were only about a dozen, we prepared and ate our meal at a small garden table out of sight of the rest of residents.

'The chap I mentioned earlier won't be arriving from Nairobi until late,' the owner, Alex told us later, as he gave us the camp beds to use on the lawn. 'There's no sense you waiting up to see him. I'll talk to him about you when they arrive and let you know in the morning.'

The stretchers he had given us were of canvas, with folding legs... but of the low type that are only about 15 centimetres above the ground. It was around nine thirty when we set them up on the lawn in front of a small verandah that came out from the bar. The light from the bar and the sounds of voices there provided a sense of company...and some security for us as we settled down.

The Namanga River, which, at this point, formed the actual border between Kenya and Tanganyika, was not much more than about 200 metres from the hotel. At the river's edge, the owner had told us, was a drinking place, where very often zebra, buffalo, different kinds of buck, monkeys and other somewhat more fierce game came to drink during the night.

'What sort of game do you mean?' I had asked.

'Oh all sorts... We've seen lions, leopards...elephants come there too.'

'And...er, do they...do they ever come near the hotel?'

'No... not really. Not very often at all.'

'Not very often...? So, they do actually come... occasionally?'

'Very rare... very rare. I shouldn't worry too much if I were you.'

This was the message we were left with as we settled down, side by side on our stretchers on the grass, gazing up into a moonless, but star-filled sky, listening not just to the low undertone of voices from the bar, but the other sounds of the night; the humming of insects, the sharp cackle of some strange night bird, the sudden crashing of monkeys in the trees. And then, as the customers of the bar moved off to their beds, we were left with only these sounds...these vague murmurings...which tended, as we listened more carefully, to become intense, distinct and frightening.

Nevertheless, despite our tenseness, we eventually fell asleep.

Then, at about 2.00 am, we both sat bolt upright on our stretchers simultaneously at the unmistakable... (after all those MGM movies)...sound of a lion's roar, followed a second or two later, by another.

'Jesus,' I said. 'How about that?!'

Both of us were instantly wide awake. From somewhere in our bodies a jolt of adrenalin had brought us from being deep asleep to totally awake and alert, with nothing in between.

'Its... they're... I reckon they're a fair way off, don't you.'

'Do you think there's more than one?' I whispered.

As if to answer... a roar came across the night air, accompanied by a second, obviously from a different lion. This time the roaring continued for several minutes.

'How far... how far do you reckon they are?'

'How the hell could you know? Couple kilometres? More maybe.'

The roaring tailed off and soon there was quiet. We were able, once more, to distinguish the gentler sounds in the trees and the night air. But we were awake. We whispered back and forth for several minutes and then fell into an uneasy silence.

About fifteen minutes later, like a clap of thunder, a huge roar rent the air...followed, almost immediately by that of another lion. This time much closer.

Neither of us spoke. We were both already out of our sleeping bags and running in sheer terror...with the bags and our packs slung over our shoulders, across the intervening twenty metres or so to the hotel, and up three steps, onto the verandah. There we stopped for a moment and looked back out into the garden and the night. Another tremendous roar.

'Christ. That's only a hundred yards away,' Noel said. 'But where?'

'We can't stay here on the verandah. The bloody thing'll come here for sure.'

I tried the glass door to the bar. It was open.

'Oh, Jesus,' I breathed, as we dashed inside.

In the bar, we stood, looking out into the darkness, trying to see the animals that had caused our flight. We settled into a couple of lounge chairs and remained awake for a further half hour or so, listening to the spine-tingling roars as they came close by... somewhere in the grounds of the hotel...and then were gradually lost in the distance.

'I thought I'd find you here,' Alex said, waking us when he came into the bar at around seven in the morning. Came quite close didn't they?'

'Close?' Noel laughed. 'I thought you said they didn't come close to the hotel.'

'Well,' he chuckled. 'I didn't say *didn't*. I said it was rare.'

'Oh yeah. Rare. How close did they actually come last night?'

'Well, there are spoor marks on the drive and across parts of the garden out there.' He pointed across the lawn where we'd been sleeping. 'So they passed about thirty yards from where you were.' Another smile. 'Anyway, you did the right thing to come in here. And ... the good news is that Harry Alderson...he's the hunter I told you about, says you can go along with him this morning when he heads out into Amboseli. Now, how about a coffee?'

ooooo

KENYA

SOUTH SUDAN

ETHIOPIA

UGANDA

SOMALIA

UNITED REPUBLIC OF TANZANIA

INDIAN OCEAN

Administrative Boundary

Lake Chew Bahir

Lake Turkana (Lake Rudolf)

Sibiloi National Park

Marsabit National Park

Towns and places:
Konso, Yabelo, Houdat, Negele, Guenale, Kelem, Lolimi, Todenyang, Banya, Sabarei, Mega, Banissa, Ramu, Mandera, Dolo Odo, Lokichokio, Kakuma, Lokwa Kangole, Moyale, Takaba, Kaabong, Lodwar, North Horr, El Wak, El Beru Hagia, Moroto, Lolyangalani, South I., South Island N.P., Buna, Lokichar, Marsabit, Tarbaj, Girito, Wajir, Lokori, Baragoi, Laisamis, Habaswein, Dif, Losai National Reserve, Tot, Marsial Game Sanctuary, Mbale, Kitale, Maralal, Kisima, Archer's Post, Mado Gashi, Libol, Lorule, Isiolo, Kinna, Bilis Qooqaani, Tororot, Busia, Webuye, Butere, Eldoret, Marigat, Nyahururu (Thomson's Falls), Nanyuki, Meru, Hagadera, Kakamega, Solai, Mt. Kenya 5199 m, Kisumu, Londiani, Nakuru, Nyeri, Embu, Nguni, Garissa, Homa Bay, Molo, Kericho, Gilgil, Naivasha, Murang'a, Thika, Mwingi, Migori, Narok, Nairobi, Machakos, Kitui, Bura, Kolbio, Buur Gaabo, Musoma, Kajiado, Sultan-Hamud, Hola, Kaambooni, Magadi, Namanga, Kibwezi, Mtito Andei, Tsavo, Garsen, Lamu, Pate I., Manda I., Arusha, Moshi, Taveta, Voi, Malindi, Kilifi, Mariakani, Mombasa, Same, Moa, Wete, Tanga, Korogwe, Pemba I.

Kilimanjaro 5895 m

Tsavo East National Park
Tsavo West Nat. Park
Amboseli Nat. Park
Masai Mara Nat. Res.
Meru Nat. Park
Mt. Kenya Nat. Park
Aberdares N.P.
Kora National Reserve
North Kitui Nat. Res.
Rahole Nat. Reserve
Bisanadi Nat. Res.
South Kitui Nat. Res.
Tana River Primate Nat. Reserve
Arawale Nat. Res.
Dodori Nat. Res.
Boni Nat. Res.
Shimba Hills Nat. Park

L. Victoria, L. Baringo, L. Naivasha, L. Magadi, Lake Natron, Masinga Reservoir, Nyumba Ya Mungu Reservoir

Ewaso Ngiro, Tana, Galana, Ungama Bay

KENYA

- ⊛ National capital
- ◉ Provincial capital
- ○ Town, village
- ✈ ✈ Airports
- –·–·– International boundary
- —— Main road
- —— Secondary road
- ········ Other road or track
- – – – Railroad

0 50 100 150 200 km
0 25 50 75 100 mi

© Nations Online Project

N

161

KENYA

11

THOSE LIONS AREN'T THE ONLY PREDATORS

About forty kilometres out from Namanga, over rough unmade roads, we came to a great dry lake. The glare of the brilliant morning light on its sun-baked surface forced us to squint through half-closed eyes, almost as if we were travelling across a wasteland of snow. A huge column of fine, powdered dust rose probably a hundreds metres in the air behind us as we travelled fast, for several kilometres in an easterly direction across the totally flat, hard bed of the lake. At its eastern end we continued on over grassy, savannah plains, dotted, here and there with flat-topped acacia trees and clumps of thorn bush. In the distance...and to the south now, we could see the snowy peaks of Kilimanjaro above a layer of clouds.

'This is the sort of country where we should start to see a bit of game,' Harry turned to tell us. 'We're still a bit far from water... but we'll be spotting some soon, I'm sure.' He was probably about fifty years old. His leathery face was deeply creased around the eyes... almost certainly from years of squinting, as we'd just been doing, across the dry lake. His hair was close cropped and grey. He wore the defacto uniform of a white hunter...drill trousers and desert boots, a short-sleeved safari jacket with lots of pockets and a broad-brimmed white hat.

There were four of us in the vehicle. Noel and I had been pleasantly surprised when we were introduced to Harry's travelling companion, who was female, rather than male, after they had eaten breakfast at the hotel. It was his twenty-four-year-old niece, Uta, the daughter of his sister who had married a German architect and now lived in Germany. Harry drove, with with Uta at his side in the front, while Noel and I were on the bench seats along the sides, in the back of the vehicle.

'When do we enter the park,' Noel asked.

'We're in it. The Hotel is in it. You've been in it since yesterday. The main road south, from Nairobi, cuts across one corner of the park. There're no fences or boundaries. The animals just come and go as they please. They don't know it, but they just happen to be much safer in here...from people like me.'

We drove now on a succession of different and often indistinct trails, just wheel tracks through the short grass, that seemed to follow no particular direction. Sometimes we would leave them altogether, as we made for a particular landmark, or low hill.

We began to see quantities of buck, of different varieties.

'Zebras over there,' Harry pointed to his left where, in the distance, a large herd of Zebra was grazing. We turned toward them. 'Could be some lions around too, near them.'

'There's a giraffe...' I said, excitedly, spotting first one, then two others some way off to our right.

We slowed down as we approached the zebra herd and, while still two to three hundred metres away, we stopped as Harry looked around. He pulled a big set of binoculars from a holster by his seat and began scanning the landscape to his front and either side.

Casually...but absolutely as if it was to be expected, he said, 'There's a lion over there, under that bush.' He pointed. 'A big one. Male. Another over there.' He moved his finger slightly to the right. 'Probably more somewhere nearby.'

The bushes he'd pointed to were between us and the zebras. We all took turns at looking through the binoculars. The second one he'd mentioned we could see relatively easily, but the first one wasn't entirely clear...even with the aid of the binoculars. We drove slowly towards the bushes. As we came nearer, we could see the the shape of the big male lion, lying on his side, propped up on one elbow, looking out at us from under the bushes. It was an incredibly exciting feeling to be so close to something, so big and powerful....and so potentially dangerous, that we had only previously seen in zoos.

'Look at his mane. Its black.' Uta whispered.

'Yes. Some are black...others are more or less the same colour as their coat,' Harry explained as the vehicle came slowly to a halt side on and not much more than seven or eight metres away from the huge animal. I found myself gripping the back of the seat as I turned around to look out at it. And I knew my heart was going quite a bit faster than normal. I lifted my camera.

'Open the hatch. You'll get a better view.' Harry said.

The Land Rover had two specially-built hatches in the roof for hunting and photographic purposes...one over the front seats and one over the back. With the hatches open, you could stand up and get a clearer view of the surroundings. So far we hadn't used them.

I slid back the cover of the one above us. 'Is it okay...do you think... I mean, he won't jump up on the car?'

'No...no. He's not going to do anything like that,' Harry said softly. 'Although, I should try not to make any noise...and don't make any sudden moves. They're quite used to seeing cars and vehicles really. And anyway, he's just had a meal. He's not hungry. Look at him licking himself. He'll be asleep before too long.'

'So, You think there's been a kill?' Noel asked.

'Yep. Probably a zebra. If we looked around, we'd probably find it. More than likely where those vultures are.' He pointed to the north where, about half a kilometre away, we could see vultures circling above a low line of acacia trees.

We poked our heads through the hatch to look at the splendid animal, who appeared supremely disinterested in the whole proceedings. I, on the other hand, found myself experiencing an extraordinary mix of sensations; amazement, excitement and awe...at the idea of not only being able to enter the same free and open environment of such a wonderful beast, but to be able to approach within a few metres of it. We took several photos from the hatch and then, giving him a little goodbye wave through the windows, we moved slowly off.

As Harry turned the vehicle around we were suddenly presented with a fantastic view of Kilimanjaro. The line of clouds had moved to one side leaving the whole of the great, almost perfectly cone-shaped mountain, with its gleaming snowy-white summit, exposed. It stood out now, majestically alone, above the flat surrounding plains.

'I'd like to climb that one day,' I said as we drove off. 'Imagine what all this looks like from up there. It must be sensational.' (*Thirty one years later, I found out. And it is.*)

We drove on, slowly, towards the zebra herd and past it, making more or less towards the northern slopes of Mount Kilimanjaro.

'Look,' Uta exclaimed in amazement. 'People.' She pointed to two lone figures moving in the distance.

'Masai,' Harry said. 'This is all Masai territory. Even the Reserve. They can come and go as they please...also across the border into Tanganyika.'

'But...what are they doing out here?' I asked. 'Where are they going?'

'They just move where they want to. They're nomads. They haven't accepted the white man's civilization. They don't want to.They just herd their cattle. See...they have three or four with them now. They'll have a camp somewhere...a temporary camp, probably fifteen or twenty kilometres from here...that'll be where they're heading.'

'But how can...what about the lions out here? Aren't they scared of them?'

'Yes...' he smiled, '...they are. That is, the lions are scared of the Masai. It might seem hard to believe, but the Masai are not concerned about the lions at all. In fact, the story goes...and I believe it, that, for a young Masai to become a man, he has to kill a lion, single-handed. I'm not sure if they still stick to the practice. But it certainly used to be the case before the white man came along.'

'How? How can they do it?'

'With their spears. You see those spears?'

We were coming near to the two figures now...tall, thin, brown men, both almost totally naked, with only a simple piece of ochre-stained material hanging loosely over one shoulder, but covering nothing. They wore elaborately beaded arm bands and necklaces and each carried two long spears. They were heading south, with four thin and bony, brown cows, one of which was on a lead, following at a brisk pace. We slowed almost to a stop, as they passed us at an angle, and waved to them. They waved back and kept going.

'Aren't they beautiful?' Uta said to Noel and I as we continued driving. '...so tall.'

'You like tall men?' Noel asked her, smiling.

She laughed, turning around to us and lifting her eyes, as if thinking... 'Oh yes, but...' She paused, glancing a little embarrassedly at

Noel and Uta in Amboseli.

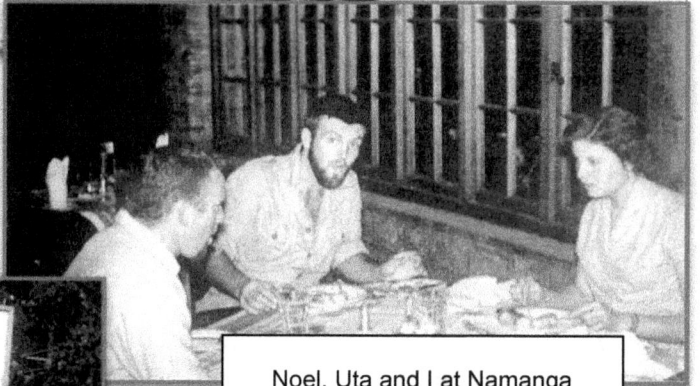

Noel, Uta and I at Namanga River Hotel. 'I was now definitely

At Namanga

Noel with Masai

Harry. '...they don't have to be tall.'

'Aha... I see,' Noel also laughed.

This brief interchange had occurred as we were bouncing over a rocky stretch of terrain, and it seemed to go unnoticed by Harry in the front, who was preoccupied with the track. However, sitting opposite Noel, I noted a familiar glint in his eye and thought, those lions aren't the only predators out here today.

We had a small ice chest on board, which held water and soft drinks, as well as luncheon packs of sandwiches and fruit, that had been prepared by the hotel for Harry and Uta, but also...very kindly... for us. We stopped in the shade of a big acacia tree to eat and slake our thirst. As we sat in the wagon, we watched a large herd of wildebeeste off to our left and several giraffes nibbling at foliage high up in a couple of trees about two hundred metres away to our front.

After about twenty minutes we moved on again and for the rest of a hot and dusty, but wonderful day, we were treated to a superb assortment of wild game: many different types of buck, three separate herds of elephant, many more giraffes, quite a few extremely ugly hyenas and a single, very large, black rhinoceros. He...or was it a she? you couldn't tell...stood and stared at us as Harry manoeuvred the vehicle slowly (but as quickly as was possible without causing alarm) in order to be facing away from the animal. We had come upon it while driving through some patches of low thorn bush and could go no further forward without being unnecessarily intimidating to him/her.

'We don't take too many chances with these buggers,' Harry muttered as he backed away slightly, then turned, so we could look at the creature through the rear window and from the hatches. We were about thirty or forty metres away from it at most. Harry stayed sitting in the driver's seat, turning to look back between us and through the rear window. He left the engine idling.

'Tell me if he starts to move this way,' he said. 'They're very short-sighted, so he probably can't make out much of us at the moment...except by smell. Which way is the wind now?' He looked around. 'Hard to tell... its pretty still, I guess. But if he doesn't like the smell, or the sound, or the look of us, he can do one of two things... move off...or move towards us. And they can move pretty fast if they want to... whichever way they go.'

Fortunately, he didn't move at all. Just stood there looking at us...or in our direction, until we eventually moved off ourselves.

We also saw scores of monkeys, baboons, wild dogs, warthogs, two herds of buffalo, a tremendous variety of game birds such as hawks, eagles and vultures, as well as water birds like herons and flamingos. And we saw two cheetahs. They were standing on a rocky outcrop, about a fifty metres from us as we drove by. They stood, looking at us for a minute or so as we came to a stop, then loped slowly off away from us, and eventually were lost from sight behind a slight rise in the ground.

'You're lucky to see them,' Harry said. 'Cheetahs are pretty reclusive, by comparison to other cats. They don't seem to be quite as at ease with people and vehicles as the lions and other animals are.'

And finally, as if to end the day as we'd begun it, we saw more lions; a pride of four lions stalking a lone...and very nervous zebra that had become isolated from its herd. We watched for some time, but the zebra, which did not seem to be disabled in any way, was able to avoid capture, until we had to move off, heading for Namanga River again.

That evening, back at the hotel, we sat in the bar and enthused over what we had seen during the day and thanked Harry for having allowed us to come along. We also had to thank Alex, the hotel owner not only for having arranged it for us, but for inviting us to spend another night at the hotel. This time, he said, we could sleep on the verandah...and move into the bar when it closed.

'Its nothing,' he smiled. 'And as you are heading off south tomorrow, you might as well eat properly as well. Its on us tonight.'

'No, no..' we both insisted. 'We have food. Its not necessary. You've been kind enough already. How will you ever make a profit here if you give food and accommodation away?'

'Ah well,' he smiled. 'Its not often someone comes through here with plans like yours...to travel all the way to the Cape.'

Over dinner Noel continued to pay attention to Uta... and, for her part, she seemed to appreciate his interest. She came from Limburg, she told us. 'It's very small though. You would not know it.'

But Noel was quick to let her know that we had been there. 'We passed through Limburg last year on our way up to Denmark and

Norway from Italy and Austria. 'We stayed at the Jugendherberger there,' he said.

'Yes. I know it well.' Uta said. 'I had many friends from other towns who would stay there during the summer vacations.'

The conversation at table changed several times during the course of our meal...as conversations do. Sometimes Harry was talking to Noel, while I was talking to Uta. At other times we were all listening to Harry recount some of his experiences of hunting wild game in various parts of East Africa...but I noticed that whenever the opportunity arose, Noel would turn back to Uta and they'd talk animatedly together.

After a while, Harry said good night to us and, leaving Uta with Noel and I, went to his room. For a time the three of us sat talking in one corner, while a few other people sat by the bar, but Noel and Uta were by this stage touching and whispering to each other in a way that left no doubt that I was now definitely superfluous to the scene.

'I'm going to hit the sack also,' I said to them.

'Okay,' Noel said. 'I'm coming too, in a moment.'

Our packs and the camp beds were on the verandah, so, leaving Noel and Uta together, I stepped out onto the verandah, closing the door behind me and slipped into my sleeping bag. Again there was the slightly apprehensive sensation of the previous evening, hearing the muted sounds from the surrounding bush...but somehow, being on the verandah seemed much safer. As soon as the bar closed, however I would have no hesitation in moving back. Alex had said that it was unlikely the lions would return again tonight, but we weren't really convinced.

Less than ten minutes after I'd settled down, Noel came out from the bar to get into his own sleeping bag.

'She's got her own room,' he whispered. 'As soon as the bar closes and we move in there...I'll give it about ten minutes for everything to quieten down ... then I'll go to her room.'

'But... she's expecting you? She said its okay for you to come?'

'Yes... yes,' Noel chuckled... She's hot.'

'Lucky bugger,' I muttered.

oooooo

TANGANYIKA

TANGANYIKA

12

'I AM THE CHIEF OF THE GOROWA TRIBE"

The town of Arusha, about a hundred kilometres south of Namanga River, inside present-day Tanzania, is now the main centre for the large number of tourists who travel out into the great game parks of Serengeti, Lake Manyara, Ngoro Ngoro crater as well as Olduvai Gorge...and also to Mount Kilimanjaro. Here, if you're making something of a tour of Northern Tanzania, you can take any of a dozen major brands of rental cars...or hire a four-wheel drive vehicle, either chauffeured or drive-yourself, to go on safari. Or you can stay in fairly luxurious hotels much closer to the action.

Even at the time we hitched through, Arusha was something of a base from which safaris were organized, albeit on a much smaller scale...and far less sophisticated. Most of the territory in Northern Tanganyika, as it was then, that was not taken up by game reserves, consisted of vast areas of open veldt, or savannah grasslands, populated only thinly by the Masai and other tribespeople, as well as large numbers of wild animals. The country, unlike that of Kenya and Uganda, which are both quite varied topographically, is relatively open and flat. This is where the vast Central African high plateau stretches out, at an altitude of over 1500 metres, for thousands upon thousands of square kilometres.

We'd been dropped in the centre of Arusha, after a single lift from the border post at Namanga River, by a British businessman, who ran a hardware store in Moshi, to the east of Arusha at the base of Mount

Kilimanjaro. He'd been up to Nairobi to pick up some stores and was returning via Arusha to his home. As he drove off and we began to walk through the bright and well-cared for little town, (*population now over 2 million*) we came immediately upon a large sign, outside one of the town's two hotels, the Hotel Arusha, which proclaimed: 'This spot is exactly half-way between the Cape and Cairo and the exact centre of Kenya, Uganda and Tanganyika.'

'Wow... look at that,' I exclaimed. 'Half way between Cape Town and Cairo.'

'Yeah...only another 4,500 kilometres to go,' Noel added dryly.

I'm not sure whether its still there at the base of the big stone clock tower at the roundabout in the middle of town. It was when my wife and I climbed Kilimanjaro in 1987.

Somehow all those old connections; highways through British territories, linking one end of the continent to the other had a different meaning then. Now, with all of those countries independent, and many of them...like Sudan, Uganda, Zimbabwe and South Africa, having gone through major upheavals over the years and others, like neighbouring Rwanda and Burundi, still experiencing them, the whole idea of a road running to the tip of the continent and what the distance is from Cape Town to Cairo, has little meaning or relevance to the present day inhabitants of those countries. At the time, however, I recall that we felt buoyed and encouraged by the sign. It was as if it were saying... "you're on track. Keep it up and you'll get there."

Although the Great North road was the main artery running through central Tanganyika, it was stretching a point to call it a highway, particularly in those days. It was a wide dirt road, with a flat and very dusty surface in the dry season and a shockingly muddy and often impassable surface in the wet. Fortunately, at the time we were on the road in Tanganyika, it was dry, but we had to accustom ourselves to a continuous pall of fine, red-brown dust that hung inside just about every vehicle we travelled in and which settled thickly on everything and everyone.

From just outside Arusha we scored a lift of about seventy kilometres, in a large Dodge pickup truck driven by a white tobacco farmer, who was returning from Arusha to his farm near Oldeani, not far from the big game reserve at Lake Manyara. He had been to Arusha to pick up some machinery he needed for his farm. The equipment, whatever it consisted of, occupied most of the back of the truck in a couple of large crates. Fortunately, there was sufficient room on the bench seat in the front cabin for Noel and I to sit with the driver, otherwise, by the end of the journey we would have been caked, like our packs were, with dust.

About forty kilometres west of Arusha, we pulled up behind a large safari wagon, and a truck that had both stopped by the side of the road. Two or three Europeans, that is white people… were hunched around a couple of black men working by a rear wheel and three or four other Africans were gathered by the truck.

'Better stop and see if they need any help,' our driver had said while we were still some distance away. The landscape on either side of the road, although studded with low bushes and acacia trees, was otherwise empty. 'Its probably just a flat tyre and they look like they've got plenty of people to deal with it, but out here, its best not to take chances.'

As it happened, it was only a flat tyre and no help was needed from us. But, in the few minutes that we stood talking there, we were introduced…or rather 'exposed' for the first time to one of the most successful technical innovations of the second half of the 20th century…the Polaroid camera.

The party in the safari wagon, who had been out into Serengeti and Lake Manyara, and were now on their way back to Arusha, were all Americans…relatively wealthy ones at that. We exchanged a few brief stories about where they'd been and where we'd been and where we were going…at which one of the Americans, a large cigar-smoking man wearing a cowboy hat, produced one of these new Polaroid cameras.

'Just come onto the market,' he said as he took our photo. 'They're really fantastic.'

We didn't know what he was talking about, until a minute later, he handed the picture to us. 'There you are. How do you like that?'

We were amazed. 'How does it work?" I asked.

'Its a new system. The developer is in the film itself.'

Then, as we looked at the first picture, he took another…and, as we stared in astonishment at the second one gradually taking shape, he took a third. I still have those small, black and white, early Polaroid prints from sixty years ago... in reasonable condition.

Continuing on some thirty kilometres or so, our driver dropped us off at a fork in the road, where he took the fork heading north west towards Lake Manyara and eventually to the Serengeti game reserve. We would have loved to have made the detour to Serengeti, but with dwindling funds and having had a great experience at Amboseli the previous day, we resigned ourselves to the fact that we needed to press on southward, so we settled down to wait by the roadside.

There was not a great deal of traffic and what there was seemed to be heading mainly for Serengeti. About mid-afternoon, however, a late model black Ford Consul pulled to a stop to pick us up. Surprisingly, it was driven by a large, well-dressed African man in his late thirties. He wound down the window of the car.

'How far are you going?' he said in perfect English, with a rather pronounced British accent.

'We're heading for Dodoma' I replied.

'Hop in. I can take you some of the way.'

We didn't need asking twice. It was always much better travelling inside a comfortable saloon car than a truck, so it was an opportunity not to be missed. Noel sat in the back seat with the packs, while I sat in the front beside Amri Dodo, as he had introduced himself.

'I'm from the Mbulu district, a little further south. But what about you...?' he turned with a smile. 'I see from your packs that you've come from Australia. 'How did you get here and what are you doing in Tanganyika...and where are you going?'

'That's a bit of tall order,' I laughed, but we began to tell him something of our story so far...and that we were heading now for the Northern Rhodesian Copperbelt and then hopefully on to South Africa.

He seemed fascinated and asked many questions...firstly about Australia, but also on the political situation in French North Africa, about which he appeared to be quite well informed. For a time, while we were answering these questions, we had little opportunity to find out anything about him, which was frustrating in a way, because he was clearly something of a paradox. He was certainly somebody quite out of the ordinary for East Africa: a relatively affluent, well-dressed African, driving his own car, in a country where the vast majority of black Africans lived relatively simple, materially poor lives, with no chance of any real status in the commercial or political world of a white-dominated colony.

'And you...' Noel asked. '... your English...er, you have a bit of an accent. Have you lived in England?'

He laughed. 'Yes. Yes I have. I went to university there and... well, I spent a bit of time working in London afterwards.'

'But how...how did that come about?' I asked him. 'I mean, surely its a bit unusual...' I felt awkward, not wanting to sound prejudiced in my question. '...there can't be too many people from...ah, the Mbulu district who have been to university in England. How...?

Another laugh. 'Yes, you're right. I am the only one and it is unusual. But you see, I am the Chief of the Gorowa Tribe, who live all over the Mbulu district. My father was the Chief before me. He is dead now, but he was a real tribal Chief...in the old sense, with feathers and spears and shields and drums. He wanted me to have a British education, so he sent me to school in England and then to university.' He tossed his head to one side slightly. 'So you see, I am a bit of a mixture.'

He was a tall, well-built, good-looking man whose self-assurance and confidence had made us consider him in a different light, to anybody else we'd met in East Africa so far...even before he told us of being a chief.

'You must stay with me tonight, at my home,' he said, as we drove into the small town of Mbugwe, a little less than fifty kilometres from where he had picked us up. 'Have dinner with my family.'

His house, at one end of the town, had also been the house of his father. It was a large brick bungalow of European design, with a tiled roof. The walls were cement rendered and painted a tasteful cream. A big open verandah with polished earthenware tiles on the floor, and reached by half a dozen steps, extended across the front of the building.

A group of men, both young and old...most in western clothes, that is, slacks and shirts, but also two or three others, probably tribal elders, wearing toga-like robes, greeted him on his arrival. They had apparently been waiting for his return. We were viewed by them with some surprise and puzzlement, but, after explanations from our host, with nods and smiles.

He introduced us to his wife and his mother, who lived with them, then left us with them, while he attended to business with the other tribal members.

I don't recall a great deal about the details of the evening meal, but I remember that the conversation revolved around the future of Africa and the idea that one day Africans would rule themselves and not be colonies or under the administration of white European powers thousands of kilometres away. Somehow, I think he felt...and we certainly encouraged him in the idea that, as Australians, although we were white, we thought a little differently than their British administrators.

'After all,' he said at one stage to us, '...you've also been colonies at one stage yourselves.'

India had won its independence from Britain just eight years earlier, on August 15, 1947, the but there was at this stage no real independence movement for East Africa as a whole. The Mau Mau terrorists in Kenya...or Freedom Fighters, depending on which side you viewed the situation from, were a crack in the veneer but, according to what we'd been told in Nairobi, their influence was fading. There was also no sign that the Belgians were going to give up their hold on the vast riches of the Congo...or Ruanda-Ruindi which they administered and which both bordered on Tanganyika.

'Tanganyika is in a slightly different situation,' Amri said. 'We were a German colony, of course, for a while. But after World War I, we became a League of Nations mandated territory. Then we were administered by Britain, but we were never a colony. Quite different from Kenya in that respect.'

'But the League of Nations...?' I began...

'...no longer exists,' he said. 'Yes. that's right. We became a United Nations Trusteeship, with Britain still the administrator. But things are changing for us now... quite quickly. Dr. Nyerere has formed a political party...the TANU, that's the Tanganyika African National Union and he is at the United Nations right now, asking that a target date be set for our independence.'

'Dr. Nyerere?'

First Polaroid pictures. 'Its a new

'Wow, look at that,' I exclaimed. 'Half way between the Cape and

'To our Australian friends, from Honorary Chief Amri Dodo of the

A 400-kilometre lift to the Northern Rhodesian border. '...they had been trying to track

'Yes. Julius Nyerere....Its not as if we want to reject Britain entirely,' Amri said. 'Not at all. We have much still to learn from

Britain. We have to educate our people. But the day *must* come when we will be in charge of our own destinies. When black people can have the same opportunities as whites.'

It was the first time either Noel or I had heard the name of the man who was to become, within five years, Chief Minister of a self-governing Tanganyika.

When we parted, to continue on our way south, after spending the night in his house, Amri Dodo gave us a photograph of himself, writing a note on the back:

'To our Australian friends, from Chief Amri Dodo of the Gorowa Tribe ...in the Mbulu district.'

Although, unfortunately, neither Noel nor I ever had contact with him again, I've read that, after independence, in December 1961, Amri Dodo became prominent as a member of parliament in a number of roles, particularly in efforts to promote and protect women's rights. He was appointed Chairman of an investigative commission, which resulted in A White Paper On The Law Of Marriage in Tanzania, published in 1969 and later enacted into Law.

He eventually became Arusha Regional Chairman of the TANU/ CCM coalition around 1990... a post he held until his death in 1993

On the wider stage, Independence for Tanganyika in 1960 saw Julius Nyerere elected Prime Minister and a year later, when the country became a republic, he became its first president... a post he held until 1985, when he handed it over to his successor, from the same political party, President Mwiniji.

But it was during the years of Nyerere's rule that his grand experiment in social, economic and agricultural reform... 'Ujamaa'...was undertaken in Tanzania. Under the scheme, which promoted the grouping of dispersed villages and homesteads into ujamaa or 'familyhood' villages...communal production systems would be introduced as well as the expansion and improvement of community services in rural areas. It was a concept, not unlike the forced collectivisation of farmlands in China in the 'sixties and in the Soviet Union prior to World War II...But, by the late 1970's and early '80s, for much of the same reasons the idea did not work in those countries, it had also been recognised as a failure in Tanzania.

In 1992 opposition to the ruling CCM Party was allowed for the first time... and in elections held in 1995, Benjamin Mkapa won the presidency. Then Jakaya Kikwete, won office in contested elections in 2005. The current President, John Magufuli was elected in October 2015.

The son of a peasant farmer, Magufuli worked his way through university to eventually be elected to parliament in 1995 at the age of 36.

The fact that he could rise from such underprivileged circumstances, through several important government posts along the way, to eventually lead his country, speaks volumes for Tanzania's overall political stability.

I can remember something of my own general attitudes at the time and, though I recall them being different from those I hold now...in that I thought it quite acceptable for Britain to be holding political and economic sway over half of Africa, I also recall feeling very strongly that the black people of Africa, the native inhabitants ...the real owners of the land, if you like, deserved a better deal; better education, a more even chance in life, greater opportunities. At the time I saw no clear way in which this could come about, but listening to Chief Amri Dodo convinced me that one day the opportunities would come.

And they have come... for virtually every country in Africa. Unfortunately, what has been done with those opportunities over the years, is a different and, in many cases, sad story.

From the outskirts of Mbugwe we were lucky enough to find a long lift for the whole distance to Dodoma, some 300 kilometres down the road in central Tanganyika. It was with another farmer although this time, one who was raising peanuts. He, like the tobacco farmer of the day before, was white, but of German descent, and he was accompanied by two black workers. Despite our protestations, he shifted them from the front cabin to the back of his truck, to make room for us. We both felt extremely embarrassed and a certain immediate antipathy towards him, but found ourselves not sufficiently strong-minded to argue the point with him, or to turn down the lift.

At first, conversation in the cabin was somewhat strained and sporadic, although I believe he felt no discomfort...or even realised our own sense of irritation. After a while, however, as the kilometres rolled by, we talked more easily, with him telling us a little of how his father had come to Tanganyika during the German colonial era and had remained, despite the takeover by the League of Nations and Britain...and in the face of considerable hardship and prejudices, to persevere with his farming, which was originally raising sisal.

We stopped at a small settlement for petrol and a soft drink. Beside the road, where the truck pulled up, there was a group of Masai tribespeople... both men and women. And, like the two we'd seen in Amboseli, they were all extremely tall and thin and all wearing similarly elaborate bead work. Their ears had been pieced and large holes had been 'grown' in the lobes, so that plugs of wood, or in the case of one man, black 35 mm film canisters, in which he carried his small change, could be pushed through and carried in the lobes.

Three women were sitting in a group on the ground in the shade of an acacia tree, working at making beaded arm bands. One was naked from the waist up, but wore a piece of red material tied like a sarong around her waist. The two others were naked, apart from a piece of ochre-coloured cloth tied over one shoulder, that hung loosely over their bodies. They also wore much bigger and more intricate beaded necklaces than the men. These were made into large, flat round discs with circular patterns of beading, that fitted around the neck and looked more like a big coloured plate than a necklace.

A herd of probably twenty brown cattle stood nearby, also trying to find some shade under the few trees available. All of them, though not emaciated, appeared very thin.

'The Cattle look as if they could do with a good feed,' Noel said to the farmer. As a teenager he'd worked for his uncle on a cattle station out from Julia Creek, in Northern Queensland. 'Two of these wouldn't weigh as much as one beast back home.'

'Ah, yes...' the farmer said. 'But the Masai never slaughter their cattle, or sell them for meat.'

'You mean they just milk them? They don't look as if they'd be able to give any.'

'Well, they do...but they also 'milk' them for blood.'

'Blood? How...what do you mean?'

'Their entire food supply comes from the cattle. They puncture a vein in the neck of the animal... make a small hole so they can drain off a bowl of blood, then mix it into a sort of porridge with milk, often from the same beast and that's their meal.'

'Good grief,' I grimaced, looking at them now slightly awed. 'Don't they eat anything else?'

'Oh, they do now, I suppose,' the farmer said, as we stood by his truck. 'But not much. That's the way they've lived and made their livelihood for centuries. The cattle are their wealth. They don't want the white man's civilization and so far they've been remarkably unaffected by it.'

'What about their children. Don't they go to school?'

'No. They have absolutely refused to allow their children to go to Western, or even African schools. Because, you see, they are quite different...a different tribe altogether, from the ordinary native you might see in the town or countryside. They consider themselves to be far superior.'

'What about the government. What are they doing?'

'Its a bit of a dilemma for them. They can't really force the issue without wiping out the Masai. They're nomads, you see. They move across the borders of East Africa as they please. How do you put a halt to that and make the kids sit in classrooms, without destroying a people and a culture?'

We warmed a little more to our driver, after he bought sandwiches and soft drinks for his two workmen and joked and chatted with them in Swahili, before we all continued on our way to Dodoma.

'Are peanuts a good crop to grow?' Noel asked him as we drove.

He laughed. 'Its a living, I suppose. There are a lot of people doing it. I took it up after the war (World War II)...one of those who got caught up in the British government's plan make Tanganyika the world's biggest peanut producer. It was pretty much a disaster... and I'm one of the survivors I guess.'

He told us of the vast British experiment for Tanganyika soon after the end of World War II...a venture in which some 1,200,000 hectares of land were to be turned over to peanut production, with an input of around £25,000,000 from the British government.

The project failed because of the lack of preliminary investigations and the need for a substantial rail network to be constructed in southern Tanganyika. It was subsequently carried out on a greatly reduced scale...sufficiently large enough though to ensure the continuation of the peanut industry, which still forms a significant part of present-day Tanzania's agricultural production and export earnings.

I recall the Dodoma that Noel and I passed through, after being dropped off by the peanut farmer, as being a relatively quiet, reasonably attractive town of about ten or twelve thousand people. It may have been more...but that's the impression it gave then. Situated at an altitude of about 1,100 metres, on the great central plateau of East Africa, it has a dry, pleasant climate. Its location within Tanganyika also works in its favour. Being more or less in the centre of the country, where the main north-south road crosses the east-west railway line, linking Dar es-Salaam on the coast and Lake Tanganyika to the west and Lake Victoria to the north, Dodoma has long been an important cross-roads.

So important, in fact, that in 1974, the Tanzanian Government, under the leadership of President Nyerere, designated Dodoma as the future national capital of Tanzania. The transfer of official functions from Dar es-Salaam began in the 1980's and was competed in the 1990's, by which time the population of the hugely expanded city was already around 160,000, and has grown to over 2 million people at present.

ooooo

TANGANYIKA

13

'THOSE SOUNDS...THE DRUMS. WHAT ARE THEY?'

South of Dodoma, the flat landscape of the high plateau continues, broken only occasionally by low lines of rugged and arid hills. For long stretches, as we travelled south, sending great clouds of dust spiralling high into the air behind us...from whatever vehicle we were in, the countryside was open savannah, untouched by western civilization or farming. Small native villages of no more than half a dozen huts, could be seen from time to time, either near to the side of the road, or off in the distance. Generally they were clusters of small, circular mud huts with pointed thatched roofs, or often just simple grass huts. Nearly always, however, they were surrounded, for protection from wild animals, by a wall of thorn bushes.

From the back of a truck, one of our various lifts on the sector between Dodoma and Iringa, I took a photograph of a bronze Hillman Minx passing us, little realizing that it would be a future lift for us further down the track.

Although the distance from Dodoma to Iringa was only about 250 kilometres, there was virtually nothing in between, apart from two or three very small settlements. Because of the large distances between towns of any size in this part of the country, the Tanganyika Public Works Department had established, in a number of places along the Great North Road and other routes to the west, stopping places called 'Road Camps'. These consisted of a group of huts, solidly constructed with bricks and mortar, with timber and metal roofing, that were set up in various parts of the country on long stretches of remote roads, as an aid to travellers. Anyone could stay there, for no cost.

We were dropped off at one of these camps at dusk, after a long, hot afternoon in which we had travelled south from Dodoma with an architect who was heading to a game park, the Ruaha National Park, about a hundred kilometres to the west of the Great North Road. He had told us about the Road Camp, which was not far from where he would be turning off the road.

'I've never stayed in one,' he said. 'But I've heard they're okay. They're pretty basic.'

Checking out the facilities, after we'd said goodbye to him, we found them to be in the charge of a couple of African attendants sitting outside one of the huts. They were both bare footed and wearing khaki shorts and collarless khaki tops.

'Jambo,' Noel and I said together, as we walked up to them.

'Jambo Bwana,' they both replied.

'Can we stay here tonight?' I asked.

'Yes, Bwana,' one of them laughed. 'Of course, you can stay here. come.' He led us to another of the huts.

The little complex comprised several sleeping huts with simple metal beds and mattresses, a separate hut for toilets and another which contained a spartan kitchen. The kitchen was really little more than a few benches and a couple of sinks with tap water provided from a large rain tank.

We prepared ourselves a meal from our more or less standard menu while travelling: tinned sardines, or tuna, cheese, tomatoes and bread. Usually with sultanas or dried apricots for desert.

As there was only a simple kerosene lantern for light, it was quite early, probably no later than eight o'clock, when we spread our sleeping bags out on the beds and prepared to settle down for the night. It was too hot to get into the bags, so we just lay there on top of them, listening once again to the soft sounds of the evening; crickets and a dog barking a long way off.

But, within fifteen minutes or so, while we were both still awake, we heard the faint sound of drums in the distance...as well as the chanting of many voices.

'What d'you make of that?' Noel whispered.

'Wouldn't have a clue. Where do you reckon its coming from?'

we both got up and stood in the door of the hut, then walked around it, trying to ascertain the source of the sounds. They appeared to be coming from the east, where, against the dark silhouette of some low hills we could see the glow of what could only be large fire.

'Those sounds... the drums...' I said to one of the two attendants, who were still sitting outside another of the huts, smoking, '....what are they?'

'Singing, Bwana. Singing...dancing.'

'Why? I mean... is there a reason... some special occasion?'

He looked puzzled. 'Occasion...?'

'You know, a ceremony... birthday, wedding, something like that?'

'No. No. just singing...dancing.'

'I guess he's not really sure,' Noel said as an aside to me, and then to him, 'Can you take us there?'

'You want to go there?' He was astonished.

'Yes. That's okay isn't it? Is it forbidden, or something?'

'No Bwana,' He smiled with what seemed to be genuine pleasure and surprise that we should want to go to see the source of the drumming and chanting. 'Come... I will take you.'

Its difficult to describe the feelings we experienced as we followed the man across those darkened grasslands for probably a couple of kilometres towards the glow of a fire, with the sound of the drums and tom toms and rhythmic chanting growing louder as we approached. There was something totally primeval about it. This, in a sense, was the real Africa. Not Nairobi, not the game parks, the towns and farms and vehicles on the roads that we'd seen. This, I felt, was a taste...a very small taste of Africa as it must have been for thousands of years. And as the drums grew louder and we approached what was clearly a native encampment, it was also frightening in a way. Even though we had our guide with us, there was still a little uneasiness and apprehension in our minds as we came out of the darkness and up to the circle of figures around the fire.

There we saw a group of about thirty men, women and children sitting and standing outside a small collection of wattle and daub huts, in a circle around the flames of a large fire. The men, some young, others older, were beating drums of various sizes made from an assortment of materials. The women sat and clapped their hands to the beat of the drums, accompanying their clapping with a rhythmic, wailing chant. Several children danced and pranced to the sounds of the music.

For a few moments as we stood there on the edge of the light, the sounds struck a primitive chord and I felt goose bumps on my arms and my hair stand on end.

Then the music faltered and some of the drummers stopped playing as they saw us. A couple of young men came over to us. Our guide, the attendant who had led us from the Road Camp, spoke swiftly to one of them in Swahili, explaining our interest in the music. He laughed and welcomed us in faltering English, then he shouted to a young child, who dashed to the fire and pulled three corn cobs...or 'mealies' as they are called in Africa, from the ashes at the side and brought them to us.

'Please... eat. Sit down,' the young man said.

A buzz of conversation ran around the circle and for a minute or so we felt acutely embarrassed as all eyes were focussed on us.

'Please... continue,' I said. 'Don't stop for us.'

Our guide shouted to them in Swahili. Several of them shouted 'Jambo...jambo Bwana' to us and waved, laughing and then the drums, the clapping and the chanting all started up again.

For two hours we sat there entranced and amazed. Their energy, vitality and exuberance was simply stunning. But what we found most interesting was their clothes. Many of the children were naked. Some of the women wore rather shabby western style dresses, while others wore more traditional native clothing...a small fabric skirt and bare breasts. But the men were all wearing khaki shorts and short-sleeved shirts, some of which appeared new, while others had obviously seen a lot of good service.

As we walked back across the grassy plain, having said goodnight and thanked them all, I asked the attendant why the men were all wearing khaki clothing. He didn't answer, but looked at me puzzled... as if my question was very strange.

I tried again: 'Why do the men all wear the same... their clothes...their shorts and shirts? why are they all the same?'

'It is the uniform Bwana. They work for PWD.'

'They all work for the Public Works Department?'

'Yes Bwana...the men. The men are working on the roads around here. And the women...the wives and children, come to live close by them while they work.'

I went to sleep that night amid a welter of mixed emotions about the future of Africa...about the 'advance' of civilization, as we were seeing it then, under the administration of colonial governments. The dramatic effect that even something as relatively straightforward as a road was having now...and would have even more in the future, on the simple lives of native African people was hard to grapple with.

And yet, as we travelled further south on the road through Tanganyika, we were to have one more experience that would illustrate for us even more vividly...and leave a more indelible impression than any book, or movie...of that so-called 'real Africa'.

It was well after we had passed through Iringa and were on our way to Mbeya. We seemed to be on the edge of the vast plateau, with the Great North Road snaking precariously down some some three or four hundred metres to another wide, flat savanah landscape.

I can't recall exactly where we were dropped off, but it was somewhere on a long and lonely stretch of the road probably about two-thirds of the 400 kilometres between Iringa and the border town of Mbeya. Once again we'd been travelling in the back of a truck and we'd been dropped during the afternoon at a fork in the road. At first glance there appeared to be nothing in sight for seemingly endless kilometres over the veldt, whichever way we turned, except the three dusty trails winding their way to different parts of the horizon; two roads that split in different directions at the fork and the one back in the direction from which we'd come.

There was a small, straggly tree, off to one side of the road, which gave some shade and we sat there waiting for a vehicle to come along, travelling in the direction of Mbeya. As we sat and looked around more carefully, we now saw that the landscape around us was not entirely empty. A tiny mud and grass hut, was just visible, low in the grass, a couple of hundred yards away and from time to time we could see the shape of a person...it seemed to be a woman, moving nearby.

As far as we could see, however, there was no wild game apparent, which was unusual, as we'd seen plenty of buck and wildebeest, as well as some buffalo, earlier in the afternoon.

'Hope there's no bloody lions around,' Noel muttered.

'Yeah...with no game about, we'll just keep our fingers crossed there's no lions.'

We waited and the afternoon wore on...but nothing came. In four hours, not a single vehicle came by. The sun was now low, like a big red ball suspended in a haze of dust in the west. To the east, night was coming fast. Near the equator, as the millions of people who live there know...there is virtually no twilight. One moment the sun is setting, the next its dark.

'Doesn't look too promising,' I said. 'Looks like we'll be sleeping out.'

'Yeah...I suppose we'll be okay here, although you can't help feeling a bit bloody jittery.'

'What do you reckon about going over to the little hut over there and asking them if we can stay there.'

'I don't know...it looks pretty small. They wouldn't have any room.'

'We can give it a try. Even just sleeping outside would be better than sleeping here. Be safer, I reckon.'

We picked up our packs and made our way across to the little hut where the African woman, who looked as if she might be about thirty years old, was squatting by the low entrance to the hut grinding corn in an earthenware bowl. Beside her, a naked two-year old girl played in the dust.

She was surprised and disconcerted...possibly even a little frightened...at our approach. She had obviously seen us sitting under the tree during the afternoon, as we had seen her. But she had evidently not expected us to come across to the hut.

We smiled and looked as friendly as we could and, with gestures...as she spoke no English, we tried to make her understand that we wanted to spend the night by the hut. Although sleeping outside would have provided us no more real protection from anything like a lion or a leopard than sleeping by the tree at the crossroads, there was a low thorn-bush fence, which somehow made it feel more safe.

She seemed totally non-plussed at the idea that two white men would want to come and spend the night on the ground by her hut. Gradually though, she appeared to grasp the fact that because we did not have a car, as most other white people did, our only alternative would be to sleep by the roadside.

While we were going through a sort of pantomime to get this message across, the woman's husband, a tall thin man, of indeterminate age, but probably forty or so, and wearing nothing but a loincloth, arrived. Behind the hut there was a small vegetable patch surrounded by thorn bushes, which because of a slight dip in field, had not been visible from the road where we'd been waiting during the afternoon. He had apparently been working there and heard our voices. She spoke to him in Swahili and, once he understood what we'd been trying to say, he smiled and made welcoming gestures for us to enter their hut.

We tried to make it clear that we only wished to sleep *near* the hut, and even unrolled our sleeping bags to demonstrate the fact that we could sleep on them outside, but he was insistent.

We crawled into the hut on hands and knees, as the entrance was only about three feet high. Inside, the earthen floor was as smooth and dust-free as if it were cement. At some stage the soil would have been wetted down and then allowed to dry to a hard, flat finish which would have been reasonably easy to maintain. In the centre of the floor some hot coals glowed among the ashes of a small fire, which also provided the only light in the hut. The woman immediately placed some mealies on the coals and set to work to fan the fire to life. A large hole in the centre of the roof allowed most of the smoke to spiral out into the night sky as the fire grew, leaving the room smoky, but not smoke-filled. The little girl sat quietly to one side, playing with a large spoon.

In addition to the smell of smoke, the hut was permeated with a strong musky body odour. But crude and humble though it may have been, it was certainly not squalid. In fact, in its own context, the hut was extremely clean and tidy. A few simple possessions were placed around the circular wall of the structure; some rough wooden shelves on which more earthenware cooking utensils were stacked and some low stools. A wooden fruit box held some mealies and there were a few woven mats and some rolled up bedding lying to one side... and that was it.

When the corn on the fire had been turned several times and was well 'toasted', she handed us and her husband a cob each and took one herself. We opened our packs and took out some bread and cheese to share with them. The toddler took a small piece of cheese too and began to suck on it. We also carried a couple of mugs and a small tin of Nescafé, which they were fascinated by... and, after she had boiled water, we made some coffee. They had had coffee before, as Tanganyika produced coffee beans in abundance, particularly to the north, but they had never seen instant coffee. They laughed and made appreciative nods of approval as we drank it.

'Why do you think they're out here on their own like this?' I said to Noel at one point. 'There are no other huts... there doesn't seem to be a village nearby.'

'Its also a bit funny that they've only got one child. Normally there'd be half a dozen running around,' he said.

We never discovered the answers. After some understandably awkward attempts at sign conversation in the flickering light of the low fire, in which we tried to ask a few questions about their life, as well as struggling to explain, without success, where we came from (they had never heard of Australia), we eventually made signs that we would like to sleep. She spread two mats end-to-end for us on one side of the hut, and one slightly larger mat for her and her husband and the child on the other side. Then we laid our sleeping bags on top of the mats and, leaving our clothes on, settled down for the night. I found it quite an amazing thought ...the five of us in this little round mud hut, out on the African plains.

Despite a few mites and bed-bugs which revelled in finding some new and tasty fare, we slept soundly...thankful for a roof over our heads and, in a very real way, thrilled at having had the opportunity of such an extraordinary experience.

Although that may sound condescending or patronizing, its not intended to be. Noel and I both knew that our own lives were infinitely richer in a material sense and in terms of opportunity than that of the native farmer and his wife and that, realistically, there was little we could do individually to change their lives. And yet we both felt later, as we talked about it, that we had been enriched by the experience... through gaining a deeper understanding of life and human relations at a very basic level, as it has been for thousands of years and still is, in many parts of the world.

In the morning we had some more roasted mealies and coffee and packed our bags in order to return to our position on the road, where we would continue our wait for a passing vehicle.

'We should leave something with them,' Noel said as we rolled up our sleeping bags.

'Well, we can give them some money,' I replied.

'Yes, but something else. Something of ours, like...' He laughed. 'I mean, I'm not thinking of giving my camera or anything, but...'

'I've got that old pair of shorts that have a couple of holes in them,' I said.

'Yeah... right. And I've got those thick socks that I don't wear. And we could leave the rest of our coffee.'

We pulled the shorts and socks and the tin of coffee out of our packs and offered them to our host, along with about ten East African shillings...equivalent to about a dollar at the time.

At first he tried to refuse, indicating that he and his wife didn't want us to give anything, but we insisted. Eventually he accepted, smiling and shaking our hands in genuine delight and we left them to walk back over to our position under the tree by the road. Within an hour were on our way in a truck that was travelling another hundred kilometres or so to Mbeya.

As the truck had pulled to a stop to pick us up, the farmer and his wife stood by their hut looking across at us. We climbed into the back of the vehicle and, when it moved away to drive off down the dusty road, we waved to the man and his wife. They waved back and in a few minutes, when the little hut had grown smaller in the distance and was about to pass from our view, they waved again... and we waved to them.

The Rhodesian border lay only seventy kilometres beyond Mbeya. If no other tribal, cultural, or societal event or encounter presented itself before we crossed the frontier, we would have had more than our fair share in Tanganyika.

'I've got to admit,' Noel said during that day as we talked about our recent experiences, 'Its not what we came here for, but I'm sure as hell glad its all happening the way it is.'

ooooo

NORTHERN RHODESIA

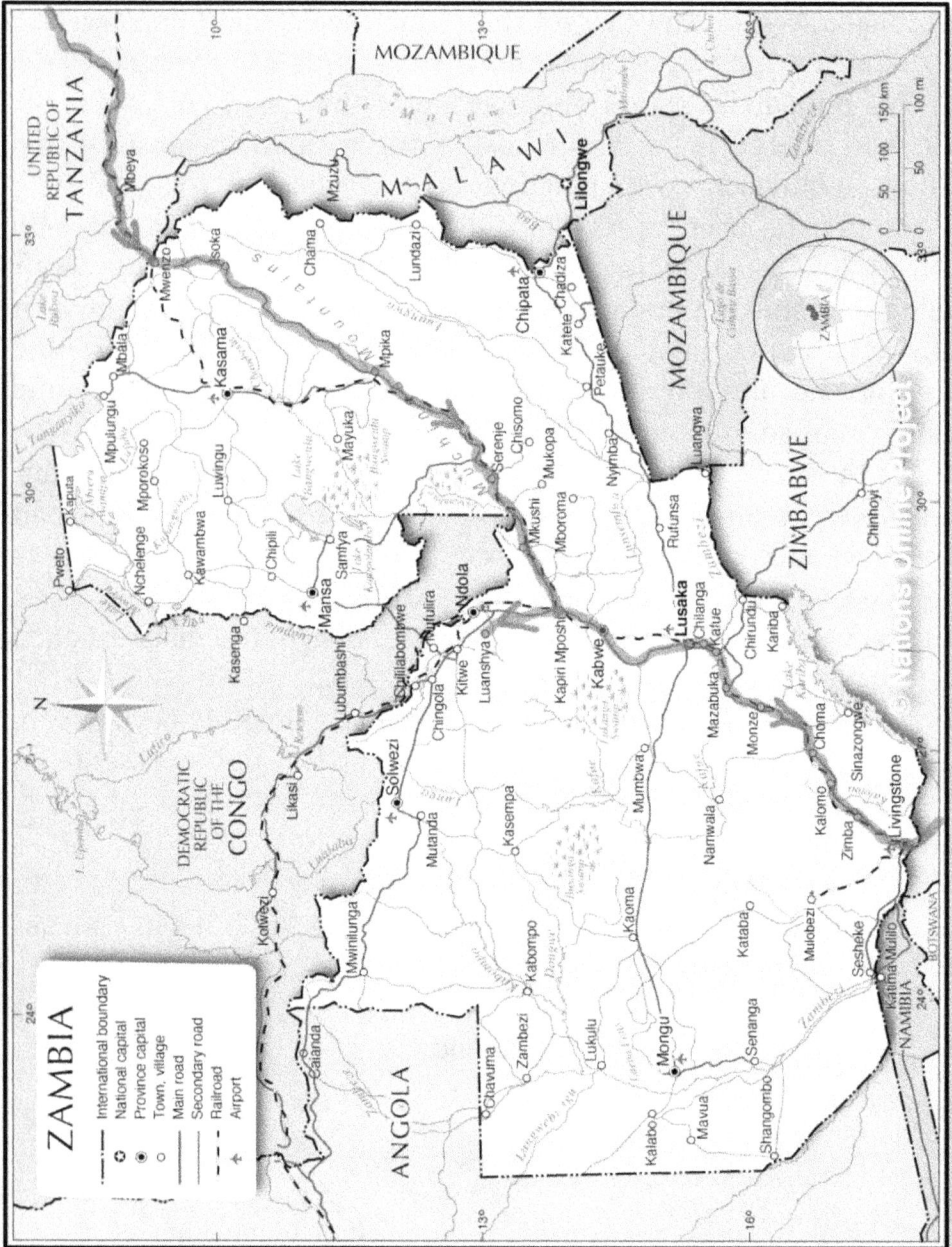

NORTHERN RHODESIA

14

'THIS PLACE LOOKS FANTASTIC,' NOEL WHISTLED.

The area just before border between Tanzania and Zambia... or as it was then, between Tanganyika and Northern Rhodesia... presented us with a sharp physical and topographical change. For here, as we left Mbeya and approached the frontier at Tunduma, we were leaving the great central tablelands and wide rolling plains of East Africa to pass through the Kipingere range of mountains. The range runs in a more or less north-westerly direction for several hundred kilometres parallel to the border, with at least one peak of almost 3,000 metres.

Although there is no great difference in altitude... most of Northern Rhodesia also forms a plateau some 1,000 to 1,500 metres high, the Kipingere mountains however, do present a natural dividing line between two quite different types of country on either side. In Northern Rhodesia, as we moved south from the border, the vegetation changed rapidly from the open landscapes of grass, low shrubs and widely scattered acacia trees we'd been used to for the past couple of weeks, to thick bush country.

Further south, the country was particularly rich and fertile and swarming with game. It was this enormous territory...comprising the entire countries that are now known as Zambia and Zimbabwe, that the young Cecil Rhodes claimed for his British South Africa Company...and for Britain, in 1890 and 1891.

Founder of the giant de Beers diamond mining empire and Prime Minister of the Cape Colony by the time he was thirty eight years old, Rhodes had an enormous impact on the social, political, and economic history of southern Africa. Although he visited the territories that soon bore his name only briefly, and died in 1902 at the age of forty nine, the Commissions granted to him and the British South Africa Company by Queen Victoria, for the opening up of central and southern Africa, effectively gave his company the right to govern the whole of Southern and Northern Rhodesia right up until 1924, when the British Government finally took over administration of the territories.

Southern Rhodesia (now Zimbabwe) became a British colony, while Northern Rhodesia (now Zambia) and the neighbouring territory of Nyasaland (now Malawi) became British protectorates, effectively run by the British Colonial Office. However, the British South Africa Company retained its mineral rights in Northern Rhodesia, from which it reaped large profits up until 1960...most importantly from the enormously rich 'Copperbelt' in the central-western corner of the country.

In 1953, the three territories were amalgamated into The Federation of Rhodesia and Nyasaland, also known as the Central African Federation. Its first Prime Minister, Godfrey Huggins, was just as much an advocate of white minority rule as the leaders of South Africa continued to be for years to come. He retired in 1956 and was elevated to the British Peerage as Viscount Malvern.

It was during these few years between the mid-'fifties...the time of our journeys and the beginning of the nineteen-sixties that these East and Central African nations were going through the turmoil of throwing off the shackles of their colonial past. Tanganyika, as I've mentioned, attained independence in 1960.

In Zambia, widespread disturbances in 1959 and 1960 led to a declaration of a state of emergency and many black nationalist leaders were detained without trial. Among them, Kenneth Kaunda, a brilliant young former teacher and founder of the Zambian African National Congress, a militant organization opposed to the white dominated Federation of Rhodesia and Nyasaland. Kaunda's arrest elevated him almost overnight to the status of a national hero and, upon his release from jail in January 1960, he was elected President of the UNIP, the United National Independence Party.

At the end of the same year, when the British government decided the time had come to discuss the future decolonization of Northern Rhodesia, Kenneth Kaunda was invited to the discussions in London. A further four years of complicated constitutional procedures passed before Northern Rhodesia became independent in October, 1964. But, thanks largely to Kaunda's leadership and political skills, the process occurred without bloodshed. Naturally enough, he became the first president of the new republic, which was named Zambia.

Throughout the 1970s and into the 1980s, he led the so-called 'front line states' in their opposition to apartheid...South Africa's practice of political, economic, and social oppression along racial lines. But, in 1991, Kaunda lost power when, in the country's first multi-party elections...which he introduced, he lost a closely-supervised race to a colourful and controversial rival politician Frederick Chiluba.

Chiluba, who was President of Zambia for ten years, was followed by five other short- term (2-3 years) leaders, including 70-year-old Guy Scott. Scott, a Rhodesian-born politician of European descent, was serving as the country's Vice-President when the incumbent President, Michael Sata died. Scott then served in an interim capacity as Acting President for three months, during which time he temporarily became the only white leader of an African nation since the fall of the apartheid regime in South Africa.

New elections in January 2015 brought the current President, Edgar Lungu to power.

As we crossed the border into Northern Rhodesia, we knew only a little about what was then the relatively new Central African Federation. All we really knew or cared about was that the Copperbelt, in the north-west corner of the country, was our planned destination...the place where we thought we might be able to make lots of money.

It was a cluster of towns that, in the years since 1924, when large deposits of copper had been found in the area by British prospectors, had mushroomed into life, attracting hundreds of thousands of people...both black and white, to settle and work there. It was a corridor of bush country, roughly 120 kilometres long by about fifty kilometres wide, alongside the south western border of what was then the Belgian Congo. The towns, which were separated from each other by less than thirty or forty kilometres, bore names like Ndola, Kitwe, Nkana, Mufilira, and Luanshya, and were each the sites of huge copper mines... amongst the richest mines in the world at the time.

Amongst the series of lifts we picked up over the next three days which eventually brought us to the Copperbelt, was the little Hillman that had passed us between Dodoma and Iringa. It pulled to a stop to pick us up about 400 kilometres south of Mbeya, at a small town called Mpika. We found it was driven by two Englishmen who had been working in the Kenya Police Force for the past two years and were now heading down to South Africa for two months leave. The driver introduced himself as Jeremy, the other as Charles.

They told us that just prior to taking their leave they had been posted to the Mount Kenya area where they had been trying, not very successfully to track down Mau Mau terrorists.

'It wasn't very pleasant or popular duty,' Charles said. 'We were not very pleased to be assigned there... and happy when it came time to leave.'

'What was wrong with it?' Noel asked.

'Bit dangerous basically. The Mau Mau are pretty well on the back foot right now and the chances are that nothing would happen to you...but if anything was going to happen, that was where it would be.'

We stopped on a couple of occasions over the next four hundred kilometres or so at small inns to have sandwiches and beer, before they dropped us off at Kpiri Mposhi, where we were turning north to the Copperbelt and they were continuing south.

Little more than a hundred kilometres separated us now from our goal and with one lift, from outskirts of Kpiri Mposhi, with a mining engineer called Frank Partridge, we arrived the at the Copperbelt on August 1st, 1955. We were fortunate in this last lift, mainly because our driver worked on the Roan Antelope copper mine, around which the town of Luanshya had developed. And Luanshya, although we didn't know it before we arrived, was one of, if not the most physically attractive of the copper towns. But Frank had also prepared us for the task ahead by telling us something of the facts of life on the Copperbelt, as well as giving us some advice on how to go about getting jobs.

'There are roughly 5,000 whites here,' he said. '...and that's just in Luanshya alone...and about 80,000 blacks. The whites and blacks live in separate towns, but there're no problems. People basically get on well together... mainly because everybody's got a job and is making good money. You can live a pretty good life here, if you want to stay. The money is fantastic, depending on where you're working. And you can save a hell of a lot.'

He went on to explain the differences in earning potential between working for the actual mining company...in whatever capacity, or working for a separate company, commercial or ancillary organization. It took a while over the next few days for us to understand the complexities of it, but it appeared to be clearly much better to be working for the mining company itself, than for anybody else, or any other company in the surrounding towns.

'You see...' he went on. 'Anyone working for the mining company...and there are several different companies operating on the Copperbelt...anyone working for one of those actual companies, whether they're working underground, or on the surface, and whether they're black or white, qualifies for the Copper Bonus. That means they get an automatic 100 percent increase on their basic monthly salary, every month. It has been as high as 108% and the basic salaries are very high to begin with.'

'For blacks as well?' I asked.

'Yes, but of course their base salary is much lower...nowhere nearly as high as the white's,' he said. 'But, in their own terms, the money they're getting on the mines is fantastic...an absolute fortune. They come from hundreds of kilometres to work here. Whites come from all over the world. You'll be amazed. '

'But, what about us?' Noel said. 'How do we get a job on the mine... if we've got no mining experience.'

'Yeah...well, that is a problem. I mean it will be if its underground work you're going for and that's where the really big money is, because the base salary is much higher. But surface jobs are easier to find. I'm not sure how you'd go about it, because I'm not in that side of it, but I'm sure you'll be able to get a job somewhere on the mine.'

We were driving into the town of Luanshya as he was speaking. He was silent for a moment and then began nodding his head, as if having a conversation with himself. 'I tell you what... I won't drop you here in town...I think I'll drop you at the Mine Club. There may be some people there who could help you.'

The actual town of Luanshya appeared, as we drove through it, to be very much like a small Australian country town; cars, covered in ochre-coloured dust and angle-parked on wide streets, along which low, verandahed shops lined either side. In that limited sense we felt immediately at home. But we were far from it in reality. We had no job, nowhere to live and virtually no money...on our last examination, just four pounds between us.

Driving to the Mine Club, just a kilometre or so from the town centre was in many ways like driving through a leafy semi-tropical suburb in some Queensland town. The streets were unsealed and a deep red colour, but beautifully lined with jacaranda and flame trees. Many of the houses, which were of low, ranch, or bungalow design, had well-cared-for gardens that bloomed with hibiscus and bougainvillea. T h e Mine Club itself was a sprawling, but attractive single-storey building that was also encircled with lawns, large tropical shrubs and shade trees as well as colourful flowering shrubs. Directly opposite its main entrance which was reached by a paved pathway through the garden, was a full-sized Olympic swimming pool, which was also surrounded by lawns and gardens.

'This place looks fantastic,' Noel gave a low whistle as Frank led us into the club.

'Wait till you see the rest of it,' he said, taking us immediately on a brief tour of the place. At the rear of the main entrance lobby was a 200-seat cinema. To the left was the largest of three bars, connected to an even larger restaurant. To the rear of this, linked by corridors and open verandahs, the complex included a beautifully set up billiard room with half a dozen tables, a huge ballroom, a play theatre, a camera club with darkrooms, tea rooms and lounges, and a soda fountain and milk bar for children and teenagers. There was also a reading room and lending library as well as ten squash courts within the building itself. Other sporting facilities that were spread out around the Club consisted of a cricket oval, separate rugby, soccer and hockey fields, a bowling green, a baseball diamond, six tennis courts and an 18-hole golf course. All this, for just one town, in the middle of 'deepest, darkest Africa'.

After about half an hour, Frank led us back into the main bar

Luanshya Township, 1955

The Mine Club

A photo and story about Noel and I appeared in the Mine magazine

These two Australians pitched up at the Club last month in the course of a world-tide. They got jobs immediately. Ian Finlay (left) in the Club Office and Noel Whistler (right) as a Pool Attendant.

Bryce Courtenay. '...he smiled. 'I'm...well, I'm just a miner, really.'

Our rondavel in the single quarters

Fooling around at the pool

near the front of the club, where he bought us a couple of South African Castle beers. 'Wait here for a moment.' he said. 'I'd like you to meet somebody.'

Shortly afterwards, he returned with a tall, solidly built man beside him.

'This is Syd Hall, the Club Manager. I've been telling him a little bit about your trip and what you're hoping to do.'

We shook hands and he and Frank sat down to join us. He was interested in hearing more of the details of our North African and East African journeys. Although nothing was said about job possibilities, and we had no clue as to what Frank had said to our new companion, Noel and I both sensed the potential and immediately, although not obviously, we hoped, began putting our best and most charming feet forward...that is, we told our story once more, but in such a modest and unassuming way as to make some of the events appear even more incredible.

'Fascinating,' he said after we'd run through some of our adventures. 'Absolutely fascinating. Look. I'm sure our Mine Magazine would like to do a little story on you...and your trip. You know, how you've been wanting to get here to find work on the mine and some of the experiences you've had. Would you mind if I contacted our magazine editor, to see if he'd like to come and talk to you?'

'Not at all,' I said. 'That'd be fine.'

'Good. Good. You're not in a tearing hurry are you?'

'No.' Noel laughed. 'We've got all the time in the world.'

'Right. I shan't be long,' he said as he left us to return to his office. 'See you shortly.'

'Hmm, what do you make of that?' I said to Frank.

'Well, hard to say. He's a good bloke, Syd. If there's anything around he'll know about it. Looks like he's on your side anyway. I didn't press your case when I first spoke to him. Just mentioned that you were on the lookout for jobs.'

'But we didn't talk about it...just then,' Noel said.

'No, but he knows.'

'Hello Frank, how are things?' A slim young man in his early twenties had walked up to our table. 'Playing this evening?'

'Bryce. Hi...' Frank replied. 'Yes. Definitely. We'll have a few rubbers.' He turned to Noel and I. 'This is Bryce Courtenay. Bryce is one of our local squash champs.'

Bryce, who was carrying a duffel bag with a couple of squash rackets sticking out one end, was wearing the defacto uniform for white men in Eastern and Southern Africa; shorts, long socks with suede desert boots and a blue-checked, short-sleeved shirt (the blue-check was not compulsory).

'Oh now, come on Frank...that's stretching the truth a bit.' He said ... and then to us, as we stood up to shake hands, 'Its really Frank who's the hot shot.'

'Oh Bull, Bryce. Sit down and have a beer. These two blokes are Aussies. They've come all the way down from Cairo...and before that they hitch-hiked across North Africa.'

'Good Lord. That's fantastic,' Bryce said. 'How long has it taken you?'

We were about to go into yet another of our routines to tell Bryce something of the story...(we had developed several versions: the extra long, long, medium, short and extra-short, the choice of which depended on the circumstances and who was being told)...when the Club Manager, Syd, suddenly returned.

'The magazine editor is coming. He's very interested. He was around at the library. He'll be here in a minute or two.'

'I'll wait until you tell it to him.' Bryce said to us. '...that is, if you don't mind me sitting in?'

'Not at all,' I said. 'Do you work at the club...or for the mine?' I thought perhaps he might have a job in the mine offices.

'On the mine... underground.'

'Underground,' Noel was as surprised as I. 'What do you do?' he said.

Bryce smiled. 'I'm... well, I'm just a miner, really.'

'Bryce is a supervisor,' Frank put in. 'There are about fifty white supervisors of different ranking underground at any one time. And all of them work with teams of native miners. How many in your team Bryce?'

'Twenty four... twenty five, including the 'baas boy', most nights.'

'Nights,' I asked. 'You work at night?'

'Sure. The mine works twenty four hours a day. Down there it makes no difference whether its day or night. I've been on night shift for the past month. Start at midnight.'

At this point the magazine editor, Martin O'Brien arrived and was introduced to us. After some preliminaries we set about telling him our story, starting with our departure from Australia (the medium length version) while Frank , Syd and Bryce sat by listening in.

There were a few questions about details as we talked and Martin took notes, but before long we had brought it all up to date with our arrival in Luanshya. The editor took a photograph of us sitting in a small couch.

'So now, what are your plans?' he asked.

'Well,' I said, '...it all depends on what we can find here. We have been hoping to get jobs on the mine.'

'Underground?'

'We don't know,' Noel replied. 'That's not really possible if you have no training, is it?'

'Oh yes. The mine has training programs,' the editor said. 'And there are 'learner miner' positions, where you are trained as a supervisor... that is to work with the teams of black miners. Those courses come up from time to time. But there's always people waiting to do the them. I'm not sure when the next one is.'

'Look,' Syd said suddenly. ' I think I can fit one of you chaps in here at the Club. There's quite a few general jobs around here... and in the office, that need doing. If you think...'

'Yes, certainly...that'd be great,' I interrupted.

'So which of you...' he smiled, looking from me to Noel.

Noel laughed. 'On the road, we always decide these things by tossing a coin.' He pulled out a Rhodesian two shilling piece and flipped it, caught it and covered it with his other hand.

'Heads or tails?' he looked at me.

'Tails,' I said.

He lifted his hand to look. 'Tails it is. You take the job.'

'Good,' said Syd. 'I'm just sorry I can't make it two jobs. But it really is only...'

'No. No. don't worry about it,' Noel said. 'Its terrific for us to get even one job so quickly. Something else will come up. We hadn't even started to look around.'

Then Bryce suddenly leant forward to Noel. 'Hey, didn't I hear you say that you were both life-savers back in Australia?'

'Yes,' Noel said. '...that's right.'

'Does that mean you've got some certificates or something to prove it?'

'Yep....bronze, silver and gold medallions, in Surf Life-Saving. They include all the stuff you do for the Red Cross Life Saving certificates and more.'

Bryce turned to the others. 'You know, "Watty" Watson might be able to help out. I was talking to him the other day.' He's the manager of the swimming pool across the road,' he explained to us. 'He told me he was run off his feet, trying to give swimming classes and couldn't keep up with things. Maybe he'd be interested in talking to you.'

'Good idea,' Syd stood up. 'Come on Noel. We'll go and talk to him now.'

The two of them disappeared through the doorway to the lobby, heading for the swimming pool, while I remained, talking to the others.

Within less than half an hour Noel and Syd returned, both beaming. 'Got the job,' Noel laughed. 'Its fantastic over there. Start tomorrow.'

Neither of the two jobs we had landed carried the so-called Copper Bonus, because we were not employed directly by the mine company. Nor did we receive a cost of living allowance of approximately 10 percent of the basic salary which was apparently also paid to mine employees. And our base salaries, at £54 a month, were lower than those on the mine. But they represented, to put it mildly, a big step up on our previous situation. We were both absolutely elated over our good fortune in being able to find jobs literally within hours of arriving.

For weeks there had been the vague idea of 'getting a job on the Copperbelt '...a place thousands of kilometres away and amongst people who were completely unknown. Now, in a matter of moments, it seemed, we'd accomplished it.

We were also pleased to learn that, although the Mine Club was not actually run by the Roan Antelope Copper mining company, it was considered to be an ancillary organization. As such, the club's employees, in which we were now numbered, did enjoy at least some of the perks that mine employees did. Firstly, we were entitled to accommodation in the single quarters provided for mine personnel. These consisted of rondavels… round huts solidly built in bricks and mortar with a conical corrugated iron roof, with a small, mosquito-netted verandah, or sleep-out, attached to one side. Although liberally coated with the ochre-dust from the unsealed roads that seemed to cling to everything, they were comfortably furnished with two single beds and cupboards, as well as a small table and chairs. Communal showers, washing and toilet facilities were close by. For this we were required to pay the princely sum of 10 shillings (a half-pound…or about one percent of our salary) a month in rent. For a further £12.10.0 a month, in other words a quarter of our salary, all meals were provided at the mine mess.

'People generally have a servant to clean their place, as well as doing all the washing and ironing,' Bryce explained to us as we were settling in to a rondavel not far from his in a large complex of these uniquely African buildings grouped together and labelled simply: The Single Quarters. Married miners lived nearby in an even larger complex… more like a suburb really, that consisted of small, fully-detached bungalows, which, depending on their owners' energy, had their own well-kept gardens and garages.

The idea of having a servant was amazing to me. 'I'm sure we won't need a servant,' I said. 'We're pretty used to doing our own washing and cleaning up.'

'It'll only cost about two quid a month… each,' Bryce said.

'Two pounds each? Four pounds for all our washing and ironing… and keeping this place clean, for a month? We couldn't do that. Its highway robbery.'

'You mean its too expensive?'

'Hell no. I mean its highway robbery on our part. I wouldn't feel right.'

Bryce leant against the wall as we pulled all our crumpled and dirty clothes out of our packs and spread them on the floor. 'I can see what you're getting at,' he said. 'But there are a couple of other things to think about. Firstly, you provide employment and income for someone who might not have it unless you did get them to do your cleaning and washing…although, I'm suggesting you could use the same m'fuzi I do. She has a number of chaps in the single quarters she washes and cleans for. Secondly, by comparison to her friends and relatives, she can make pretty good money this way.   She takes the washing back to the township and distributes it amongst her friends. So she ends up making a good living and the money gets spread around a bit.'

We considered Bryce's comments and, after looking once more at the crumpled, dirty pile of clothes in front of us, decided in favour of employing Bryce's 'm'fuzi'... the Bantu name for a washing woman .

My job turned out to be a bit more than I expected. In fact, it was quite a trusted position. I became, for want of a better description, an Assistant to the Chief Accountant. Each morning I had to go around to all of the various departments in the club and collect the takings from the day and the night before. These came from the cinema, the three bars, the restaurant, the milk bar and soda fountain, the tea room and the swimming pool and amounted, generally, to more than £1,000 in cash each day. I then had to count it, in the main office, and balance the books, something I had never done before.

Once this was completed, usually be the end of the morning, and checked by the accountant, it was then also my job to drive the Club van in to the bank in Ndola, about thirty five kilometres away, to deposit the money.

I enjoyed it from the start...because it was new and a challenge, but I was nevertheless supremely envious of Noel's job.

'You can't believe what its like,' he said, as we sat down to eat in the nearby mine mess during the lunch break on our first day. 'You should see the birds. There's some great sorts over there...lying out sun-baking. There's one shiela who...'

'You lucky bastard,' I said. 'How come you always get the good jobs?'

'We tossed for it, remember?'

'Yeah, I remember.'

I also remembered, but only with feelings of friendly rivalry, that Noel always seemed to have the better job. Back home, before we left Melbourne, he was the young super salesman who had a brand-new FJ Holden, and made fifteen to twenty pounds a week. I'd been an office boy, sharpening the pencils of the General Manager at the Shell Company and earning seven pounds a week, followed by a quick succession of part time jobs, like selling door-to-door the idea of people having their children's photographs taken and working as a waiter, in an effort to save enough money to join Noel on the sea trip to Europe.

In London, where I'd also been earning seven pounds a week, as a salesman at Hamleys toy store in Regent Street, Noel found a job making ten pounds a week at the British Vinegar factory. Then I'd taken a job for fourteen pounds a week cleaning lavatories at the Pyrene Fire Extinguisher Factory, on the Great West Road, thinking that I'd well and truly eclipsed Noel, for a change. Only to find that I had to work twelve hours a day, six days a week, to earn that amount... and then to have almost four taken in tax! I quickly swapped the lavatory cleaning for an 8-hour-a-day job as a sales person for Thomas Cooks Travel Agency in Berkeley Street. It only paid eight pounds a week, but at least I only had to work forty hours to get it.

'But what do you have to do at the pool?' I asked him. 'Surely you have to do some bloody work?'

'Oh yeah. I've got to help on the gate...you know, take the money as people come in, when Watty's busy. I've got to keep an eye on the filtration system, see that it doesn't clog up and so on, supervise a couple of natives in keeping the place clean and doing the gardening... And that's about it.'

'What about the swimming lessons?'

'Aha, I think that might be a little while. You see, I've found out why Watty was so willing to have the Club hire someone...so that *he* can give the swimming lessons. They're not free. He charges separately for them, so if there's someone like me looking after all the odd jobs, he can spend more time giving lessons.'

'And will you get to give any lessons?'

'Not straight away...but there's apparently a lot of people who want them, particularly young women,' he chuckled, '...so who knows.'

ooooo

15

A SENSE OF ALONENESS

One of the first things we did, after having been given the two jobs, was to each buy some new clothes on credit in one of the clothing stores in the town; a pair of long slacks and a couple of shirts, as well as a reasonable pair of shoes. This came to about £15 each which, with our payments for food and accommodation, took a good chunk out of first month's pay.

We began, however, to settle in to our roles at the Club and the pool quite quickly, as well as entering into a range of other activities. Noel and I would sometimes work as ushers at the movies, in the evenings which would brings us an extra 7/6 an hour on top of our normal earnings...and also a free movie. We joined the Mine Camera Club, which included, for a fee of only £2, special evening classes in which we started to learn the whole process of developing, printing and enlarging, in a set of excellent darkrooms,with up-to-date equipment. Before long we were haunting the place, printing off large quantities of the black and white shots we'd been taking on the journey.

Also, at the urging of Bryce, we joined the mine's baseball team, the Luanshya Dodgers. I had played baseball in my early teens, when I lived in Canada with my parents for three years, but had not played it since. Now Noel and I found ourselves suddenly kitted out in full baseball gear and mitts... travelling around with Bryce and a bunch of other young guys on the weekends to play against mine teams in Ndola, Kitwe, Nkana and the other Copperbelt towns. I really enjoyed it. And, as I remember it, we didn't do too badly.

Noel and I also started playing quite a bit of squash with Bryce and other members of the club. Noel, as usual, was a far better player than me. He used to play regularly at the gym he belonged to in Melbourne, whereas I hardly ever played back home. But Bryce left us both for dead. He was slight in build and not as tall as me and carried no fat. He really was one of the top players in the Club and, competing in the Copperbelt championships he generally did very well, although I don't know if he ever won.

As time went by Bryce became our closest friend in Luanshya. It was strange, to begin with because, while Bryce was working night shifts, our lives were completely in reverse. He was working while we were sleeping and vice versa. And yet our non-working hours were basically the same. Although, as a miner, he was in a totally different financial league to us, we ate together, played sport together, spent much of our general leisure time together and he would do everything possible to help us, particularly in the early stages, to settle in and meet people. He seemed in away to latch on to us...not, I thought, because we were the newest arrivals in Luanshya, but in a genuine need for real friendship. He had been on the Copperbelt for about a year, working underground for most of that time. He had come up from South Africa, where he'd grown up mainly in the Johannesburg area. And, although I'm not positive of this, I don't think he had made a great many friends in Luanshya.

He presented a complex and rather contradictory persona. To only see him coming up out of the mine, with his hard hat on and his face covered in grease and dust...having spent the night some six thousand feet below ground in darkened stopes and grizzlies, working with a team of African miners to the constant sound of drilling, punctuated by frequent blasting and the ever-present danger of rock falls... it would have been difficult to imagine the other individual. This was the quiet and seemingly unflappable Bryce, who spoke with an accent that sounded, if anything, English. His enunciation was soft, with no harsh South African gutturals. In fact it was hard, judging from his accent, that he came from South Africa at all. He was well educated, well read and longed to travel, as he had never been out of South Africa, except to come to the mines in Rhodesia. Perhaps it was the stories of our own travels and of Australia...in both of which he was always greatly interested, that made us friends. In any event Bryce talked frequently of his plans to travel and of his future:

'I'm going to spend the first third of my life making money,' he said to us on more than one occasion. '...the second third will be travelling and having a family and the last third writing...writing books.'

By now the reader might have guessed that the twenty-three-year old miner of whom I write is the same person who, some 30 years later penned one of the world's most successful first novels, The Power of One and went on after that, to write a string of more than twenty other successful books earning him more than a million dollars each in advances. I'll return to Bryce and how he came to Australia later, but for the time being, suffice to say that without his help and friendship in Northern Rhodesia at that time, our stay there would have been much the poorer.

It was during this time in Northern Rhodesia, as Noel and I settled down to a routine of working and saving, that we were able again to talk more seriously about future plans. Although visiting South Africa remained important, the idea of returning to Australia for the Olympic Games in Melbourne, which were now little more than a year away, became central to any discussion about where we might be heading next.

We started to dream up fantastic schemes as to how we would get back there.

'If we write to a whole string of companies,' Noel said at one stage, '...like Holden or the Shell Company, for starters, we might be able to organize a car for an overland trip across the Middle East and India.'

'Holden provides the car...and Shell gives us the petrol,' I added enthusiastically. 'We could also write to Leica, or one of the other German camera companies and get them to give us cameras and sponsor us. And Kodak could give us more film.' (Interesting to think that the host of Japanese camera companies we now know so well, simply did not exist in those days. Canon and Nikon were there, but were definitely down-market when compared to Leica.)

We even went to the Rhodesian Automobile Association in Ndola to get maps and information to help us plan a route we could travel up through Africa and across Western Asia to India and Australia.

Naive though these schemes may seem now, we felt at the time that, if we could save enough seed money, we could at least make an effort in that direction. The fact that we had already done some pretty out-of-the-ordinary travelling in Africa should also add some weight to any proposals we might put to different companies.

As a result of these plans, the need to get employment on the mine proper, where our earnings would be dramatically increased, became more important for us. To illustrate the difference: even a Learner Miner, that is, someone selected to go through a three-month training course as an underground supervisor, was paid £63.14.0 a month as a basic wage. The 100% copper bonus, brought earnings up to £127.8.0. Then, with the cost of living allowance of £6.10.0 a month added, total earnings would be almost £134 per month...about two-and-a-half times our present salary. After the three-month training period, an underground supervisor could be earning well over a £100-a-month base salary, with the extra's pushing it up around £250...five times our earning capacity at the moment. With that sort of money we could really save quickly... enough perhaps to do the sort of trip we'd started to dream up.

These thoughts started developing probably about six weeks after we'd arrived. We'd been told at the time of our arrival in Luanshya, that no vacancies on training course would become available for at least three months, but we'd considered it was worth waiting for something to come up. Then, after a couple of months, an opportunity suddenly arose for one of us to join the mine company...not as a miner, but working above ground. A vacancy had come up in what was known as the Pool Gang.

The Pool Gang was a party of hourly-paid native labourers who presented for employment each day to work on a huge variety of general tasks throughout the whole of the mine area. These consisted of anything from watering and mowing the grass on the golf course, shifting earth for landscaping projects and keeping the mine buildings clean and free from litter, to washing the fleet of mine vehicles, or road repair jobs.

The job that had come up was as a supervisor of the day labourers... and although it didn't carry a base salary much higher than our present jobs (around £60 a month), it did include the copper bonus and the cost of living allowance... which pushed it up to around £126 a month. A dramatic increase... for one of us.

'Heads or tails?' It was my turn to flip.

Noel paused a moment...'Tails again,' he said.

I peeked under my right hand which covered the coin in my left and smiled, as if I'd won... and then revealed it. 'Its yours...you bastard.'

'Yahoo!' Noel leapt into the air. 'You little beauty!'

So Noel migrated from the swimming pool to the pool gang.

The jobs couldn't have been more different, of course, but he was pleased to make the move. The swimming pool job had been easy and pleasant, but he had tired of it...partly because of the lack of talent, I think. There were a few attractive girls that came to the pool... but, as we found to be almost universally the case in Northern Rhodesia, they were invariably spoken for. You had to be quick off the mark on the Copperbelt, to have any sort of decent looking girlfriend...either that, or have a pretty ritzy sports car.

We also found it to be true... although its a sad comment, that the girls who weren't presently attached to someone, seemed only too well aware of the dynamics that operated on the Copperbelt...where white men outnumbered white women by about twenty to one and played the game to its limit. In other words they were on the pedestal and had to be treated accordingly. Neither of us seem to have much luck in the girlfriend department while working on the Copperbelt...not so much from an unwillingness to play the game, they simply weren't available.

On the job front however, I have to admit to a feeling of envy when Noel got the job on the Pool Gang, and thinking back over the years that he and I have known each other, I'd also have to acknowledge that there was always something of an element of competition between us. On occasions where one of us won out over the other in some way...whether it was for jobs, or pulling birds, as the saying went, or whatever, there might have been some degree of envy, although never jealousy or dislike. If anything, there would be a little sneaking admiration for the other's ability, or luck. Travelling in each others pockets as we did for so long, living in such close proximity to one and other for months at a time, we inevitably disagreed on some issues, or became irritated with certain of the other's habits or idiosyncrasies.

On two or three occasions we actually came to blows...over nothing.

In fact on the night before we left London, heading for France, at what was to be the start of our trip through Africa, we had a party in our South Kensington flat at which Noel and I got horribly drunk and fought with each other. We rolled down the stairs of the apartment, punching at one and other as we fell. Noel ended up at the bottom with a dislocated shoulder. We took off for France the next morning, however, him with his arm in a sling and the two of us the best of mates.

We had another big brawl in Rhodesia... actually in the Mine Mess over dinner. It had been preceded by several minutes of increasingly robust argument which developed into vitriolic abuse across the table...all over some issue which was forgotten within minutes of the fight. But we sent the table, plates and food flying over the floor as we again threw punches and wrestled with each other.

Bryce pulled us apart and calmed us down. Half an hour later, as we drank a beer together, we were both able to give the other a hug and say something like, 'I'm sorry mate, I don't know what got into me.'

I'm not sure whether that fight was before or after Noel got the job on the Pool Gang. I tend to think it was before... not long after we had arrived on the Copper Belt and that it was over something as stupid as the way he ate his food, or the way I did. In any event, Noel's job on the Pool Gang did gradually begin to separate us in a way that could probably have been predicted. At the time, I don't think either of us would have even acknowledged that there was any sort of dynamic at work to force us in different directions, but looking back on it now... it seems quite clear.

As Noel's earnings and savings increased, he became, in a way, more secure in his planning than I, in that the resources at his disposal, (in other words money) were greater. Its true that for months we had shared and shared alike with the extremely limited funds at our disposal, but now, when we we both earning, there was no similar imperative. There was just a big differential in those earnings. We still talked of our plans for travelling by car back to Australia, but they seemed to gradually fade. And this effect was compounded by the fact that, in his new job Noel found himself... de facto...in line for a little more good fortune that would lock him in to working on the mine for some time to come.

I still held the hope that a similar job there would come up for me, but as the weeks rolled by, I began to doubt that a position on the training course would become available in time for us to be able to do some of the other things we'd always talked about, such as travelling and surfing in South Africa... before we'd have to start heading home, in order to be back in Melbourne in time for the '56 Olympics.

Then we learnt that a vacancy would be coming up for a 'Learner Miner' position in November, that is, within about a month's time. But, we were told, it would be filled first by any applicant who was at the time an employee of the Mine Company...which meant Noel, as he was now employed on the Pool Gang.

I don't recall any particular conversations at the time of the news, only a sense of disappointment and the slow realisation, over a period of a couple of weeks, that I would have to do something different...probably make my own way to South Africa. There was no animosity, or ill feeling between Noel and I, but a sense of aloneness began to creep into my thoughts.

At times I felt a little homesick, a longing for things Australian. It was all very vague and ephemeral...like gum trees or Vegemite, or Saturday arvos in the beer garden at the Torquay pub, none of which I'd felt for the entire time we'd been away from Australia. Now, as I lay in bed at night, thinking of what lay ahead, these thoughts came drifting in. And yet, I found that I also missed Europe and the sort of free and easy lifestyle we'd experienced on the road there. I missed Lise, her blonde hair and beautiful high cheek bones, her sea-blue eyes and sexy laugh. I had received several letters in Luanshya from Lise in which she'd said how much she wanted me to return to Europe to see her. I found myself thinking of the way we made love wherever and whenever we could...of our first meeting at the Youth Hostel in Cannes and making love in the darkness on the beach, by the wall below the Esplanade.

Is that what I should do? Head back to Europe to see Lise? Did I love her? Did I want to marry her? I don't think I even asked myself those questions in such definite terms. I just knew I missed her then more than before...and did want to see her again. But... but....

But first I had to get to South Africa. I don't remember exactly when it was, I think it was about a week after my twentieth birthday that I made up my mind that, if Noel did not want to come now, I would head south without him.

'I think I'm going to head south pretty soon,' I said to him one Saturday evening. '...and make for Durban. See if I can get a job on the beach there.'

'Don't you think it'd be better to wait a bit longer...save some more money?' Noel asked.

The subject was a difficult one for him also, because he understood the nuances of the situation just as well as I. He recognized that while there was an economic rationale for him to stay working there, it made no sense for me.

'No. I've more or less made up my mind. I'm going to give Syd my notice on Monday and then take off two weeks from today.'

oooooo

SOUTHERN RHODESIA

THE RHODESIAS
AND
SOUTH AFRICA
16
THE SMOKE THAT THUNDERS

When I left Luanshya, I travelled south towards Broken Hill (now known as Kabwe) and Lusaka on a form of road that I've since realised must have been unique to Southern Africa... strip roads they were called. I'm sure someone will tell me they exist now, or did exist somewhere else in the world, but I know that I had never seen them before and have never seen them since... and I'm sure they have long disappeared from the two countries that are now Zambia and Zimbabwe.

They consisted of two strips of tarmac, no more than about forty five centimetres wide, that had been laid down on a narrow dirt road to correspond roughly with the width of a car's wheels, or a bit more. As they were separated by a dirt strip in the middle, the driver had to concentrate in order to keep the vehicle's wheels on the strips of tar. Whenever a car or truck approached from the opposite direction, it was necessary for each driver to move their vehicles further to their left (as they drive on the left of the road in eastern and southern Africa), so that one set of wheels were on the dirt shoulder of the road, while the other set stayed on one of the strips of tarmac. It was sometimes a fairly unnerving experience, as it was easy to slide on the thick, red dust (or mud, in the wet season) at the sides...and oncoming trucks often took up more than their fair share of the road. It was also very never easy to pass a slower vehicle.

Broken Hill was about 200 kilometres south from Luanshya, but, as the lift I had picked up in Ndola was going all the way to Lusaka, a further 140 kilometres, we passed straight through the big mining town, which is a major lead and zinc producing centre. I had no real desire to spend time in Broken Hill, nor in Lusaka, the capital, but was intent on continuing as quickly as possible to the former capital, Livingstone and what has become one of the greatest attractions for travellers in southern Africa...Victoria Falls. Ever since David Livingstone became the first European to lay eyes on what the local inhabitants called *Mosi-oa-tunya*...The Smoke That Thunders...the falls have remained one of the half-dozen or so must see sites of the African continent. And rightly so.

Situated on the Zambesi River, which forms much of the border between Northern and Southern Rhodesia (Zambia and Zimbabwe), the falls dwarf Niagara in height, width and volume of water. The Zambesi is the fourth largest river in Africa...after the Nile, the Niger and the Congo, but, at the point where it flows over the falls...even though it still has almost 1,500 kilometres to flow to the sea, it is nevertheless one-and-a-half kilometres wide. In the rainy season the water flowing over the 110-meter cliff that extends across the whole width of the river, is three meters deep...a flow that has been calculated to be almost a thousand cubic meters of water a second.

On occasion, as you travel towards the Falls...even from as far as fifty kilometres away, you can see, above the thick bush country, a broad column of 'smoke'...that is, a dense mist, rising like a cloud from the Falls into the sky.

The structure of the giant chasm into which all this water falls is such that, while the river has a width of 1.7 kilometres at the top of the Falls... at the bottom it is suddenly constricted into a narrow gorge with only one outlet...a fissure between the steep, black cliffs that is only 20 meters wide; a wild, seething mass of water which is called, appropriately enough, 'The Boiling Pot'.

I'm not sure if it can still be done, but in 1955 it was possible to hire a small canoe some distance above the Falls and be paddled a few hundred meters out into the Zambesi to one of several small islands that run right to the edge of the Falls. Its a hair-raising experience, because it is so easy to imagine being caught by the current and swept over the edge. But the two or three canoeists competing for my business were adamant that it was safe.

I had left my pack with the owner of a small roadside café nearby, while I investigated the canoe journey at the river's edge.

'No problem sir. We are safe here. We go across and down to that Island...' One of the men, dressed...encouragingly, in a faded white sailor's suit, pointed to a jungled island about three hundred meters out in the river and perhaps two hundred meters further down towards the Falls. The island extended right to the lip of the Falls. 'We go out into river,' he continued, pointing straight out at ninety degrees from the shore. '.... we drift down to top end of island. Not to worry sir...I do plenty of times. Very safe.'

Yes... well, maybe. I looked at him, hesitating momentarily.

'Livingston land there,' he said.

'Livingstone? David Livingstone?'

'Yes, sir. 1855... that is Livingston Island.'

What the hell, I thought... if David Livingstone could do it, I should be able to. And this guy does it for a living. He's got to be on top of it.

'Okay, lets go,' I said, getting in to his canoe.

As we left the shore we were immediately picked up in the current. He had pointed the nose of the canoe out into the river and upstream and was paddling hard. Even so we were moving down-stream towards the Falls at a good pace. I could clearly see where the river stopped amidst continuous clouds of rising mist no more than four hundred meters away. A muffled roar from the Falls filled the air.

But, just as he had predicted, we were able to get far enough out into the river to drift down onto the island, where he pulled us in beside a fallen tree that had also been carried down to lodge itself securely between some rocks. I scrambled ashore onto the thickly-wooded island while he tied the canoe to another, smaller tree.

He started off down a narrow, overgrown path in the direction of the Falls and beckoned to me to follow. After we'd covered about a hundred meters he stopped by a large tree and pointed up.

'This... Livinston tree. See his name.'

I stared up to where he was pointing, about three or four meters above us and there I could quite easily make out the old and by then somewhat spread out and distorted letters, DL.

'David Livingstone carved those initials?'

'Yes sir. Livinston carve.'

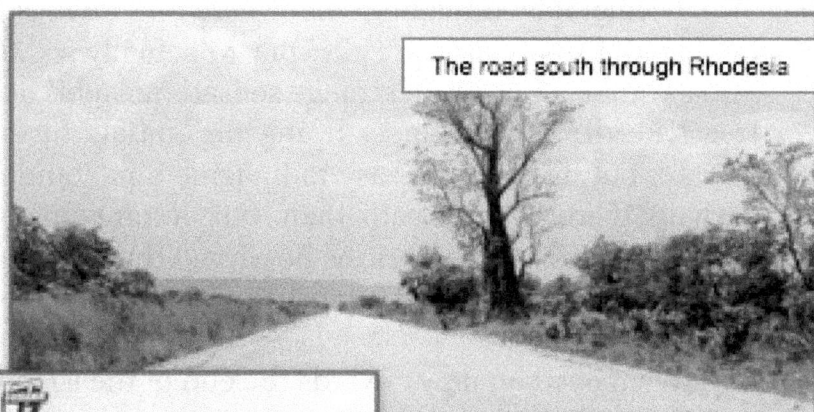

The road south through Rhodesia

Lusaka, 1955

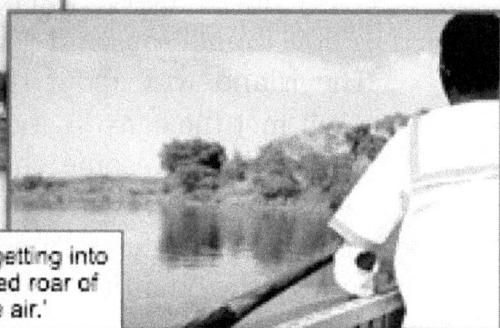

'Okay, lets go,' I said, getting into his canoe...The muffled roar of the Falls filled the air.'

Victoria Falls: '...we could manoeuvre and clamber to the very rim of the vertical drop.'

I remembered reading somewhere that Livingstone had carved his initials in a tree near the Falls. But to actually see the tree, with those initials still legible, was a strange sensation... a bit like a time warp. The tree had grown, of course, lifting his initials further away from the ground, but it was quite easy to imagine him standing here... although perhaps there was no path then, but accompanied perhaps by a few puzzled guides and bearers, as he carved those meaningless symbols in the tree a hundred years, almost to the day, previously...on November 17, 1855.

We moved on now towards the end of the island that went right to the edge of the abyss, where the roar of the falls now filled the air.

As we came towards the cliff, the path opened up to reveal dark, black and wet rocks amongst which we could manoeuvre and clamber to the very rim of the vertical drop. The sound of the Falls all around us was by now thunderous and deafening.

The island was about thirty or forty meters wide at the point where it it met the canyon and it was possible for me to stand, close to the edge of that awesome chasm and look down into the turmoil of water at the bottom, then to my left and right to see huge volumes of water pouring over the rim on either side. It was incredibly impressive, even though the quantity of water in the current dry season, was only a fraction of what it would be in the wet. To the left, the width of the river was only about three hundred meters or so, but to the right, it extended off out of sight, for more than a kilometre, with several other small islands punctuating the enormous flow of water over the rim.

Eventually, after taking plenty of photographs, I returned, with my guide to the canoe for the trip back...and the sudden realisation that we could not just paddle back to where we started from. We'd already been carried probably two hundred meters downstream. Even pointing and paddling upstream again, we would be carried much further down towards the falls, as we attempted to make it back to the river bank.

But, once again, he knew his business and we made it safely to the river shore, but almost half a kilometre below our starting point and not much more than two or three hundred meters above the falls.

I stayed for a couple of days near the Falls in the equivalent of a small pension...a relatively cheap hotel, while I made several journeys around the Falls. There is a road and a spectacular bridge across the chasm that linked Northern and Southern Rhodesia and still serves as a border crossing now between Zimbabwe and Zambia. The bridge was built in 1905 as part of the projected Cape to Cairo railway...a grand plan to traverse the entire African continent, through British territory from south to north which never came to fruition. From the bridge, there is a stunning view of the 'Boiling Pot', where the river is reduced to only twenty or thirty meters width.

There was also, at one end of the Falls, an impressive statue of Livingstone gazing and pointing down along the length of the great gorge into which the Zambesi is falling. Close by a path runs through dense jungle along the cliff top on the opposite side of the Falls, called 'The Rain Forest' because it rains there for 365 days of the year, as a result of the continual mist caused by the Falls.

And then there is the Victoria Falls Hotel. An incredible and quite beautiful colonial edifice, built at the same time as the bridge and set amid sculptured lawns and gardens at one end of the Falls. Providing its guests with an unsurpassed view of the whole sweep of the great canyon into which the Zambesi plunges, it was far too upmarket for me to stay at, at that time, but I felt a cup of tea on the terrace was in order.

I sat there, amongst a few other Europeans at nearby tables sipping my tea and eating my scones with clotted cream and strawberry jam, gazing down over the lawns, towards the Falls. White-uniformed black waiters moved amongst the tables, serving drinks, as well as Devonshire Teas. The Union Jack fluttered on a tall white flagpole in the centre of a grassy terrace below the hotel.

Because of the nature of the geography of Northern and Southern Rhodesia, if you're heading towards South Africa from Lusaka, you can either take the south-western route through Livingstone and Victoria Falls to Bulawayo, or the south-eastern route through Salisbury (now Harare) to Bulawayo. But its difficult to go to both places without back-tracking and covering a lot of extra kilometres. Consequently, at the end of my stay at the Falls, I decided to press straight on south, through Bulawayo to Beit Bridge, on the South African border...a distance of just over a thousand kilometres.

It was strange to be travelling on my own. It took a while for me to feel it...to realise that I was by myself, going from place to place, seeing incredible things like Victoria Falls, without someone to share it with. I far preferred being on the road with Noel. I suppose it was easier to get lifts as one person rather than two, but I missed the company more than anything...being able to discuss where we were going, what we were seeing and so on.

We had split up to go off in different directions once before... when we'd been working in Norway, during the previous year. After a six-week stint at lumber-jacking in the forests in the south of the country, we'd moved off together, as winter approached, to find work in a paper factory in Lillehammer...the beautiful little town in the centre of the Norway, which, forty years later became the site of the 1994 Winter Olympics. But, after several weeks there, I made up my mind to hitch-hike across Sweden and up through Finland to the Arctic Circle, in mid-winter, after which, I worked my way on a Finnish timber ship to Rotterdam, to eventually turn up in London on New Years Eve, 1954.

There's more to it than that, of course, but the point is, although Noel and I were the best of mates and had been through a lot together, we both knew we could could get on without the other. As it happened, on that first occasion Noel eventually turned up in London a couple of months later anyway, in February '55, to share a flat with me and several other Australians. And now, eight months later, as I departed Luanshya for South Africa, he'd indicated that it might not be too long before we joined up again.

'If this job on the mine doesn't turn out well...or if I don't like it, I'll be off like a shot to meet up with you in Durban,' he'd said.

Southern Rhodesia, as I continued south, was noticeably different from its northern partner in the Federation. At the time it had a population of white settlers that would have been around 130,000...much more than in the north. And they were settlers in the real sense of the word, in that they considered themselves permanent residents...farmers, graziers, business people and so on, whereas in Northern Rhodesia, on the Copperbelt, there were huge numbers of whites, who, like Noel and I, were just there to make money, with no intention of settling permanently.

The move to set up the Federation of Rhodesia and Nyasaland, in

1953, mentioned in the last chapter, had been urged on the British Government by white political leaders and industrialists, who felt the advantages of an amalgamated territory would be the creation of a larger market and the ability to draw more freely on black labour in the territories. Strong opposition...largely from the black population in the north, was on the grounds that the policies of the Federation would work mainly in favour of the white population in the south, that is Southern Rhodesia.

So, the white settlers in Southern Rhodesia, did not like the break-up of the Federation, when it came in 1963... leaving them reverting to the status of a colony.

Nor did they like Zambia and Malawi gaining independence in 1964. So, in 1965, the conservative white Rhodesian Front government, under the leadership of Prime Minister Ian Smith, unilaterally and illegally declared Rhodesia independent of Great Britain under a constitution that guaranteed the continuation of a white dominated parliament.

Economic sanctions, installed first by the United Kingdom and later by the United Nations, caused financial hardships, but the regime endured through the 1960's and 70's thanks largely to help from South Africa. Numerous and continuous guerrilla attacks by black freedom-fighters for over a decade, in which thousands of people died, finally led to consent by the white minority to hold multi-racial elections supervised by Britain in 1980. The Zimbabwe African National Union party, ZANU, won a landslide victory and its leader, Robert Mugabe became the first Prime Minister of Zimbabwe.

In 1987 he became President and has ruled the country under an authoritarian and corrupt regime since then, using the state security apparatus to commit widespread human rights violations, suppress freedom of the press and crush any realistic opposition, as well as rigging successive elections.

In a gesture towards the seriously oppressed opposition party...the Movement for Democratic Change (MDC), led by Morgan Tsvangirai...which was forced on Mugabe by allegations that the MDC had actually won the 2008 elections, the President negotiated a power-sharing agreement with Tsvangirai, in which the MDC leader became

Prime Minister in 2009. But Mugabe was left in control of the Army and security forces.

As of mid-2016, 92-year-old Mugabe's Zanu PF party faces the first-time possibility of a coalition of all other opposition parties, as well as the growing influence of an anti-government cleric, Evan Mawarire, who has fled the country in fear of lengthy imprisonment.

He nevertheless intends to contest the 2018 elections.

At Beit Bridge I suddenly came not only to the northern border of South Africa, but up against a virtual brick wall. The South African immigration authorities at the frontier wanted me to produce steamship tickets away from the country, or one hundred pounds in cash, to prove I could support myself during a maximum of three months stay as a tourist. And I didn't have a hundred pounds to my name. In the three months I'd spent on the Copperbelt, I'd managed to save little more than thirty five pounds. I put a story to the official similar to the one Noel and I had tried to spin at the Sudanese Consulate in Cairo.

'Look, I've got more money back on the Copperbelt,' I told him. 'I'm only going down to South Africa for a bit of a holiday. Then I'm going back up to Northern Rhodesia to work again.'

'I'm sorry pal,' he shook his head. 'The regulations say you must have £100, or your ticket out of the country. There's nothing I can do about it.'

'So, if I get some money sent from Rhodesia, you'll let me in?'

'Sure. We've got no objection to you entering South Africa, so long as you have sufficient funds.'

I left the border post and walked back into the actual township of Beit Bridge still on the Southern Rhodesian side of the frontier, to sit in a little cafe and curse all manner of officialdom.

'Damn, damn, damn!... stupid bloody drongos!' I muttered to myself, as I tried to think my way through it all. I felt like telephoning the Prime Minister of South Africa...at that stage Johannes Strijdom, the extreme right-winger and one of the main architects of apartheid, to tell him that I had hitch-hiked across and down the whole continent of Africa to get to his country, only to be denied entry because of the lack of a few pounds. Don't you realise what South Africa is missing by not letting me in? I would say... but I didn't.

I could telephone Noel, of course, and ask him to send me some money. But I couldn't bring myself to do that. It would be like admitting defeat, or that I'd made a mess of things within days of leaving Luanshya. I also started thinking about trying to enter South Africa at a different border crossing...perhaps through Bechuanaland (present day Botswana) which was a British High Commission territory. It would have been a reasonably short trip...about 250 kilometres back through Bulawayo and then about 100 kilometres to the Bechuanaland border at a place called Plumtree. Once in Bechuanaland, it might be easier to enter South Africa...although I wasn't sure. I realised that I was clutching at straws and that I could easily run up against the same barriers. Nevertheless, I started to think seriously about it.

After sitting, brooding for some time over a cup of coffee in the small café, I learnt that the Indian owner of the place had a couple of rooms which he rented cheaply. As I had arrived at the border late in the afternoon, I decided to stay there overnight and do something... whatever it might be, the following day.

During the evening, I hit upon another plan. Ever since we'd made up our minds that South Africa was one of our goals, Noel and I had been collecting names and addresses of people we'd met on the road, while hitch-hiking in Europe during the previous year, who either lived in South Africa, or who knew people there. Amongst the names in my address book was that of a South African farmer we'd met for a very brief period on a ferry crossing the English Channel from Dover to Calais the previous April. His name was Jan Pieterson and he lived in Klerksdorp.

'If ever you get to South Africa,' he'd said. 'Look us up. You're welcome to come and stay on the farm.'

I telephoned him that evening to explain my predicament. He was sympathetic and wanted to help.

'Listen,' he said. 'I can send you the money, but it will probably take some time. Try asking the officials there, if I could guarantee you while you are in this country. Ask them if I could go to one of their offices, or to some government office here and sign some papers. They could telephone from there and confirm that it had been done... and then let you in.'

It sounded a bit complicated, but I was willing to try it. However, as I was approaching the South African frontier post the following morning, fate intervened on my behalf.

'Iain!' a voice called out from the car park behind me. I turned to see a young Canadian fellow, Karl Petersen, who'd been working on the mine at Luanshya and who had played on the same baseball team with Noel and I and Bryce. He was just stepping out of his car and also heading for the border post. 'Hi, I wouldn't have expected to find you here,' he laughed as we shook hands. 'I thought you'd be in Durban, in the sea already.'

'Well, I've been taking my time,' I replied. '...I didn't want to rush by Victoria Falls and, well, I'm on my way now... er, that is, I should be on my way, but I've run into a problem.'

'What do you mean?' He looked concerned. 'What sort of problem?'

I explained the whole thing to him.

'That's no problem,' he said with a big smile. 'I'll just lend you the £100, you show it to the guy...and when we're on our way, you can give it back to me.'

Which is exactly what I did. We went first to the little café/guest house to pick up my pack and then returned to the frontier office. Fortunately I didn't even have to make any explanations about where the money had come from, because the man who had dealt with me the day before, was not on duty. So, within less than ten minutes, I was on my way, heading down the road with Karl towards Louis Trichardt, Pietersburg, Pretoria and Johannesburg, almost six hundred kilometres distant.

'If you want,' he said, 'you can come with me all the way to Durban. I'm staying in Jo'burg for a day or so, but I'm driving straight on to Durban after that ...and then down the Garden Route to Port Elizabeth and Capetown.'

Karl and I shared an inexpensive hotel room in Johannesburg, which we reached after driving all day. We stayed in the city for two days while he did some business there, bought a few clothes and did some other shopping. I telephoned the farmer friend who had offered to guarantee my stay in South Africa to explain what had happened and to thank him for the offer. As he lived near Klerksdorp, about 150 kilometres south west of Johannesburg and we would be heading south east to Durban, I said that I would try to get to visit his farm later, after I had found a job there.

Johannesburg was quite a shock to me...in more ways than one. By comparison to every other city we'd seen on the African continent, it seemed modern, clean and efficient. The population at the time was under a million (*around 4.5 million now*). There were new highways running into and out of the city, office buildings twenty-five storeys high, smart shops and restaurants, Cadillacs and other large American cars in the streets. In other words, lots of money about. But there was a disquieting side that took a while to sink in. Of course at that time, I hadn't even heard of Soweto, let alone seen it...or any of the other shanty settlements that existed on the fringes and beyond the city.

They were there, however, and it was patently obvious, even at first sight, that blacks in South Africa were forced to live quite separate lives, with far less opportunities. Although this was just at the beginning of the era of serious apartheid, all of the trappings were evident. There were separate seats in buses and in the parks, separate areas in restaurants and cafés, separate counters in the post office, separate cinemas, separate public toilets, and many other places which carried signs saying: 'Whites Only'.

The black people, it had to be admitted, looked relatively prosperous, busy and well-dressed when compared to the inhabitants of any of the other major African cities I'd seen so far... the operative word though is 'relatively', because they were obviously far poorer than the poorest whites in South Africa and oppressed in a multitude of subtle and not-so-subtle ways. The reason they...or anybody else in Johannesburg were comparatively well-off, in material terms, was pretty basic... full employment.

Johannesburg then was a boom town and had been ever since gold had been discovered there in 1886, just sixty-nine years previously. It was difficult for me to imagine then... and in a way even more difficult now, when 80+ years is the present length of my life, that this huge, bustling city of skyscrapers was just virgin grassland and open veldt one lifetime prior to my first visit.

By the time Karl and I arrived in Durban, we'd been in South Africa three or four days and we were getting used to the fact that it was very different from the rest of Africa. True, most of the other countries Noel and I had travelled through had had some form of colonial administration or influence, in which whites were in a position of relative power. But somehow, under the British colonial administrations of East Africa and the Rhodesias, where blacks lived separate lives, those systems seemed to have a softer edge. They weren't compelled by such harsh legislation, or confronted so blatantly with public signs that reinforced the big differences between their own social and economic positions and potential... and that of whites.

Perhaps...thinking about it now, this was something of an underhand approach; appearing to do one thing, while the reality was quite different. In any event, there was another distinction: South Africa was not a colony. It was a member of the British Commonwealth...an independent nation of Dominion status, similar to Canada and Australia. However, the structure of its constitution and makeup of its parliament was very different. Blacks, who formed the majority of the population, could not vote, nor be elected to parliament and coloured people, that is people of mixed race, who had enjoyed these rights since 1910, had them removed shortly after my visit in 1956, after various legislative expedients and considerable political tumult. The bottom line in South Africa, in 1955, was that whites were clearly in command. You felt it and saw it everywhere.

Durban was almost as amazing as Johannesburg, but in a different way. A thriving port city in the heart of Natal Province's sugar cane country, it was then, and still is, one of South Africa's premier resort towns. As such, its long esplanade, fronting on to kilometres of excellent white-sand beaches, was lined with high-rise commercial and apartment buildings, parks, restaurants and cafés, as well as fair-ground and entertainment facilities for families and children. But the other immediately noticeable thing about Durban was its large Indian population.

Britain annexed the Natal Republic from the Boers in 1843 and, from 1860 onwards, began bringing large numbers of indentured labourers into the colony from India to work on the sugar plantations. The Indians settled in, worked and prospered, as they did in East Africa, Fiji and other parts of the British colonial world. They soon dominated the small business economy of Durban and became an extra element in the already tense racial mix of Natal.

The Zulus were the original inhabitants of the area and fought ferocious battles against the Afrikaners at Blood River in 1838... and then against the British in the Zulu War of 1879 in futile efforts to prevent the takeover of their territory.   And although whites have effectively ruled there since the mid 19th century, the Zulus have remained a strong and important factor in Natal's and South Africa's racial politics ever since. In the mid-fifties, however, they were, like the rest of the country's black population, second-class citizens and employed only in menial jobs...with one extremely colourful exception.

Along Durban's beachfront, the Zulus had established a thriving business amongst the white tourists and holiday-makers as rickshaw pullers. Although there is almost nothing that can be said in general defence of a practice that seems to treat human beings as beasts of burden, it's worth noting that Durban's Zulu rickshaw men made quite a good living at it...much better, for example, than other black workers in hotels or factories or other more prosaic jobs. Unlike the rickshaw boys of pre-revolutionary China, Hong Kong and Singapore, the Zulu's made the whole thing into entertainment and art, for which they charged entertainment prices. They were big men and they dressed in the most elaborate costumes, painted their bodies and wore huge feathered head-dresses. And the tourists were willing to pay a premium for the privilege of being pulled along the esplanade by such magnificent men. The Zulu rickshaw men were one of the most dramatic and colourful sights along Durban's beachfront during the four months I spent there from November 1955.

And they're still there. Despite a downturn and disruption during the transition from apartheid-era white rule, to complete independence and black rule in South Africa and, although there's only about twenty of them, the rickshaw pullers have not only survived, but prospered...with recognition and support from the City Administration.

ooooo

SOUTH AFRICA

17

'WHITES WERE CLEARLY IN COMMAND'

Karl didn't stay in Durban more than a day. He had friends to visit in Port Elizabeth some 600 kilometres down to the coast towards Cape Town and wanted to get there as soon as possible. He dropped me at a tourist information office near South Beach, where I planned to start looking for some reasonably priced accommodation. We had a coffee at a nearby restaurant and, after thanking him profusely for what had turned into a great lift, we shook hands and he was on his way.

As it was early November and just before the main summer holiday period, I was fortunate in being able to find a small, very cheap room in a guest house, the Beach Mount Hotel, in Seaview Street, about a hundred meters from the beach. The bathroom was separate and had to be shared with two other guests, but the room itself was clean and bright and had a basin with hot and cold water, a radio and its own private entrance from a verandah...all for £8 a month.

The following morning brought a clear sky and the feeling that it would be a hot day... a good day for the beach... and for checking out the job situation. Noel and I had talked for months about getting jobs as lifeguards on the beach in South Africa, just because we'd heard in London that the lifeguards there were paid professionals. In Australia, by contrast, the surf beaches were then all patrolled by volunteer lifesavers trained and qualified through the surf clubs. We'd been told that life-guards in Durban were paid around £12-10-0 a week, but we had no idea if it was true, or how the system worked, how one was employed, or by whom. To find out, I set off down to the beach.

The beaches, of course, were all segregated. There were two beaches for Whites, plus others for Indians and Blacks, spread over a distance of several kilometres along the coast. The two white ones, North Beach and South Beach were closest (naturally) to the commercial centre of the esplanade, while the Indian and Black beaches were further north.

South Beach at ten in the morning had a reasonable number... perhaps fifty or so, people in the surf and on the sand, sun-baking, reading, children playing and so on. I had been directed to a large building facing right onto the beach, which contained changing rooms and toilets. It also included an observation tower and other facilities for the lifeguards there.   But as I approached it, I saw two guys on the beach standing by a large umbrella, who could only have been lifeguards. They wore bright-red, old-fashioned one-piece costumes, with straps over the shoulders and 'Lifeguard' embroidered across the front in white letters. I walked across to talk to them.

The conversation was a bit strained at first as they took me for one more tourist coming to ask endless questions like, 'Where are the toilets?', 'Are there any jellyfish in the water today?', 'What time does the restaurant close?' or 'Do you sell suntan lotion?' But when I mentioned that I was from Australia and that I was a member of a lifesaving club there, their manner changed.

'We've just had an Australian lifesaving team out here... last year, touring around,' one of them said. He was a big guy with a blond crewcut, who introduced himself as Dave Jamieson. 'They went all over South Africa, demonstrating the Australian methods of surf lifesaving. It was good stuff. They came here too.'

'Yeah... and we've already picked up on some of your techniques,' the other guy, Bobby Burdon...also with blond hair, added with a friendly grin. 'You see the belt and line?' he pointed to a red box down nearer the water containing a surf rescue belt and line. 'We've been training with that for a good while. Used it in a couple of rescues too.'

We chatted for a while about the surfing scene in Australia...a subject in which they were greatly interested, and about my trip with Noel through Africa, without any mention of jobs. Then, fortuitously I thought, the suggestion came from them rather than me. I didn't want to appear desperate.

'So, what are you plans now? Having a look around South Africa?'

'Yep...that's right. I might look around for a job in Durban though.

The surf looks pretty good. Be good to stay a while.'

'Why don't you try for a job on the beach... here?' Bobby Burdon said.

'What do you mean... as a lifeguard?'

'Sure. Its not too bad. £16 a week... and...'

'*Sixteen* pounds a week?'

'Right. You've got your certificates and so on haven't you?'

'Oh... yeah...sure. Got em all; bronze, silver and gold medallions. But...but what sort of... I mean, how do you...?

'You have to do it through the Beach Office. Its up in town... part of the Durban City Council. I don't know if there are vacancies... but you might as well try.'

He gave me the name of someone to contact at the Beach Office, but...not wishing to appear too keen, I sat under the umbrella with them for a while talking, then went off for a swim to catch a few waves on the body. As I swam out beyond the shore break, I felt as though their eyes were on me the whole time... of course, it was just paranoia I'm sure but, if they were watching, I wanted them to know that I was at least capable of catching a few decent waves. Little did I know, I was about to enter a world where this sort of macho competitiveness was the order of the day.

But to cut a long story short, I got the job. I had to fill in forms, produce proof that I was qualified, go through a number of physical and proficiency tests, as well as medical examinations, but, within less than a week I was on duty, alternating, as the others did, between being on patrol on either South Beach or North Beach.

To say it was the best job I ever had in my life, might be stretching things, but its up there amongst them, that's for sure. Of course, once I started work, it was true that the lives of the people on the beach *were* our responsibility... literally, so we had to be alert to any dangerous situations that might arise and to keep a constant eye on what was happening in the water and on the beach itself. And, on many occasions we had to warn people of rips and currents, pull others out of the water, rescue some and in a couple of cases actually save their lives.

But to do that...to be aware of what was going on, meant we had

The boys at South Beach. (Chookie in sunglasses in the deckchair behind me)

Shorty and I on the line

A rescue

to be sitting on the beach, where inevitably there also happened to be a very reasonable collection of attractive young women. And, after a while one got to be quite good at chatting up the talent, while still keeping an eye on the people in the water. And it was surprising how many young women there are on holidays who seem to enjoy talking to lifeguards on the beach.

There were about a dozen full-time white life savers employed by the Beach Office on a complicated roster system for the two white beaches under which there were never less than two lifeguards on duty on each beach. And during the middle of the day, that is, from 10 am to 2 pm there were four on each beach. On weekends and holidays, the numbers went up to six on duty on each of the two white beaches. The Black and Indian beaches ran a similar system, but with not as many lifeguards because there were not as many Black and Indian swimmers.

Settling in to the system and being accepted by the other lifeguards took a while. And, as in every workplace there always seems to be a boss-cockey, or someone who fancies himself to be king of the heap, lifeguarding on Durban's beaches in the fifties was no different. The king of the heap during my time, was a guy called Chookie Salzman. I never knew what his real name was, but he was a tough little bugger... about five foot seven (1.67 meters) tall and probably 28 or 30 years old. He obviously worked out at a gym as there wasn't an ounce of fat on him. Dark hair, brushed straight back made him look a bit Italian, but his name and his accent were Afrikaans.

Not that he ever spoke much. He was the strong silent type, even in his dealings with us, his workmates. And yet, somehow everyone deferred to Chookie. When I came into the group, it was something you just learned by osmosis. There were legendary stories about Chookie's prowess as a swimmer and a lifeguard, most of which I've forgotten now, though the memory of his aura as a superior being remains. Whatever Chookie said within our somewhat limited world...went. I suppose he was the senior lifeguard... the one with the longest service. He probably got paid a bit more money...I don't know. I just know that if Chookie wasn't happy, nobody was. And it took a lot to make Chookie crack a smile. When I think about him now, I feel he would have been perfect in the Mafia. A bit taller and he would have given Robert De Niro a run.

But there was one day when Chookie's ascendancy over the rest of us led to a frightening situation which I've remembered in stark clarity all my life.

The surf in South Africa can be big...very big. And I can picture in my mind plenty of really good days there when there were some of the best waves...for board or body, that I've ever seen. Hot days with beautiful, big, clean swells rolling in under a clear sky. A slight off-shore wind just pushing the crest back a bit...keeping it from breaking until the last minute. And big waves...so that with just a few strokes you were on then and sliding down a long slope with your whole head and chest out of the water, ahead of the foam.

This particular day though was not like that. There had been a full-blown gale out in the southern Indian Ocean and Durban was being lashed by a storm. We still had to turn up for work on those days, however, and I remember running across the esplanade, through driving rain, to the Lifeguards' rooms below the observation tower on South Beach. There was not a soul on the beach itself, or anywhere else along the beachfront.

On rainy days, which didn't happen very often in the summer months, we would normally sit in the observation tower and play cards. And that's what we were doing on this day. As the rain continued bucketing down and was whipped by the wind against the big windows of the tower, four of us sat there playing Pontoon. There was Chookie, Bobby Burdon, Shorty Bronkhorst and myself. Shorty and I should have been working on North Beach during that morning but, as there were no facilities for lifeguards there, other than a small wooden hut, literally no more than a meter-and-a-half square, it was accepted that on rainy days the two lifeguards from North Beach would go to the tower in the South Beach bathing pavilion.

This would have been about a month or six weeks after I had taken up the job there and my relationship with Chookie had not really gelled yet. By that I mean we were polite and superficially friendly to each other, but he never seemed to be really amiable. He never initiated a conversation, or talked directly to me. He seemed to regard me with either suspicion, or perhaps as a threat...although I was anything but that. I never could tell. In any event, there was a tension which I, and I think some of the others felt when Chookie was around. It was as if I was the new boy, the initiate, who had not yet been accepted into the club...or the gang.

We played for about two hours, in a reasonably relaxed and joking atmosphere. And then at the end of one hand, Chookie looked out the window across the wind and rain-swept beach and suddenly got up to say, 'Who's coming to catch a few waves?'

The rest of us glanced quickly at each other in stunned silence for a few quick seconds before Shorty (whose real name was Leonard, but was never called anything but Shorty) stood up and stared through the window. 'Yeah... good one,' he said with a casual air, although I knew he was just putting a good face on it. '...there's some big ones out there. You coming Aussie?' (No one ever called me by my name either).

Bobby and I stood up and muttered something like, 'Yeah...beauty!... yeah! good one... right, let's go!'

We opened the door to a small balcony where we could see more clearly. Even though the rain was still pelting down, I saw much more clearly than I wanted to, that the sea was huge. Ginormous! Out beyond the lines of breaking waves, the sea was covered with white caps with the wind blowing furiously. I gulped quietly to myself and followed the others downstairs and out onto the sodden beach... Chookie in the lead, saying nothing.

We walked up and down the beach with the rain pelting on us for probably seven or eight minutes looking for a way to get out. The waves were breaking a hundred to a hundred and fifty meters out and the turmoil of foam and broken water in the lines of waves charging towards the shore was formidable. The wind had been whipping the foam into an aerated spume that blew all along the beach and had built up at the water line to a depth of half a meter. At first I thought... and hoped... its going to be impossible to get out. Chookie won't do it. But I knew really, with a sinking feeling, that I was wrong.

There were a couple of big rips running...one at the far right hand end of the beach, the other nearer the middle. Chookie was checking them out.

'Right?' he said, turning to the rest of us. And that was all. He was off and into the seething torrent of the middle rip and within seconds was being carried fast into and under the foam of the broken waves. Shorty and I ran straight in after him, with Bobby close by. I guess we all figured that, if we were going to do it at all, we might as well stay close together.

The power of that channel of water in the rip, that was streaming outwards from the beach, tended to slightly moderate and flatten the giant waves coming in against the rip. But they were still breaking well beyond where the rip started to dissipate and we found ourselves swimming hard without make any apparent progress. Chookie was out ahead of us...probably one or two breaks further out. We'd swim for a few strokes, then gasp for a breath, hold it and dive under a roiling mass of broken water, surfacing only to see another mass powering down on us. Even between the waves the water was white and wind-whipped all around. The sky was black and it was still pouring rain. This is madness, I remember thinking. But there was no way I could turn back. I'd be finished in Chookie's...and therefore everyone else's eyes.

We had to get out past where the waves were first breaking. Once there, we could tread water and catch our breath...but getting there was proving to be a dangerously exhausting process. For a period, it seemed as if we wouldn't make it and then we found ourselves in deeper water where the swell was deeper and we could see the waves before they broke. Under a couple more of these and we were finally out beyond the break.

It had taken us nearly fifteen minutes of full-on effort just to get out there. All four of us were now treading water in a loose group spread out in a line, with probably only a couple of metres separating one from the other. We dropped and rose dramatically as the huge swells swept under us to break fifteen or twenty meters further in. Looking down from the crest to the bottom of each wave as they passed through, I guessed them to be at least six to seven meters high 'Jesus! what a sea,' Bobby shouted.

'Yeah. That rip wasn't as good as I thought it would be,' Chookie responded. 'Probably have done better on the other one.'

'Shit,' Shorty cried. '...there're the bloody shark nets.' He pointed to a couple of small buoys about thirty or forty meters further out which came into view on the top of a huge swell as it moved towards us .

'Well they're about four hundred meters out,' Bobby yelled, 'So we must be three hundred....three hundred and fifty, at least.'

Although we were in the midst of a storm, the mountainous swells coming in along the beaches were not the direct result of the local tempest we were experiencing. They had been formed out in the Indian Ocean and would have been big, even without the present violent winds. As such, they were not choppy and irregular waves... but reasonably even, well formed swells that almost certainly would have been incredible... but equally scary, as body or board waves, on a sunny day.

We spent a few minutes just floating around catching our breath before anyone went for a wave... and of course it was Chookie first. He swam for one huge swell that came in and looked as if it would break where we were, but it was too full and didn't crest soon enough. Shorty swam for another and missed it too. Then Chookie was on a big one and disappeared from our view.

A minute or two passed. We each went for a couple of waves and missed them. I backed off one huge one in horror at the drop that yawned beneath me... and yet I was determined not to be left out there on my own.

'Chookie's coming back out.' Shorty said, and for a second, as a wave lifted us high, we glimpsed a tiny figure battling out in the white foam about a two hundred meters further in.

Shorty went for another wave and caught it. I went for one and again dropped off. Bobby and I waited. One suddenly broke beyond us and we had to dive deep to get under the broken water and then swim a little further out to stay beyond the break. We glimpsed Chookie again, still struggling through the broken water, but closer now. He would soon be out with us again.

Bobby and I went for one together. This is it, I thought...now or never. I was swimming hard and kicking, the wave was breaking already to my right. Then I felt myself picked up and surged bodily forward. It was the biggest wave I've ever caught. As the lip curled and the wave broke beside me, I tried to corner to my left where the water was for a moment still unbroken. There was suddenly clear air beneath me... and in the water, just to my left, Chookie was looking up at me as I flew for a second through the air. His head disappeared. I threw my hands out in front and slapped them hard down against the water when I landed, trying to propel myself forward. I was instantly engulfed in a tumult of white water hurling me towards the beach. All I could do was hold my breath. The power of the wave was enormous. Ten seconds, fifteen...it could have been more, or less, I don't know, but suddenly my head and shoulders were clear. I could lift my head and grab a breath as I powered inwards at the front of all that white water, for probably a further hundred meters or more. Then, equally suddenly the wave weakened and dropped me off...still a hundred meters from the beach.

'Yahoo!!' I yelled into the storm and punched towards the sky. A wave of euphoria swept over me. I heard an answering shout off to my right and saw Bobby waving.

But then he turned and started heading out again.

'Oh no... Jesus,' I moaned. '...not back out there.' But I knew I had to follow.

Eventually I was back out there treading water again...dreading, though also, inexplicably, looking forward to the amazing thrill of another ride like that. Chookie and Shorty had already gone again... So just Bobby and I were there again together.

'I think I'm going in after this one,' Bobby called to me from about ten meters to my left.

'Yeah, me too,' I shouted back with a sense of inner relief. 'It makes you hungry. I could do with a hamburger.'

Bobby swam for another wave and caught it. Now I was on my own. It was strange enough to be out there with the other guys, but on my own it was quite surreal. Deep water, black clouds covering the sky, a storm raging, the rain pelting down and me treading water three hundred meters from the shore. Hmmm.

Shorty was swimming out about fifty meters to the right. He dived beneath a couple of breaking waves and started to swim across towards me.

'Bobby's just gone in,' I called to him. 'We're going to get some hamburgers.'

'Good idea... great. I'll come too. I'll tell Chookie.'

I swam for a wave and caught it. Again I was hurled out and suspended in the air before being swallowed up in the churning maelstrom of broken water. But this time was different. I held my breath, waiting to be spat out from the front of the wave... and held it and held it... but it just kept churning around me. Suddenly I needed air. I stopped lying prone, like a torpedo and flailed my arms, struggling to get to the surface of the foaming water and gasped a breath of water-laden air. I coughed and spluttered and let myself be tumbled forward until the wave dropped me. Then I swam in to the shore.

It was over. I had done it.

It took me some time to realise it, but on that morning I'd passed some sort of unofficial test without really knowing it, because from then on Chookie spoke to me directly. He was never effusive...with anybody for that matter, but I could tell that, in his eyes, I was okay now.

Life on the beach was extraordinarily good and always interesting. Lifeguards meet all sorts of people: millionaires and hoboes, farmers, journalists and hoteliers, race course touts, Johannesburg gangsters and film stars... they all came down to our beach and spent time talking to us.

But what was best of all...girls seem to just run after us. It was amazing. Most of them were on holidays from inland cities like Johannesburg or Pretoria or Bloemfontein and were down at the coast for a couple of weeks of sunshine and swimming. They would sit around, sometimes in groups of three or four talking to us...even when there were only two lifeguards on duty. They were beautiful... of course. And we could just take our pick.

Having my little room only a hundred meters, or so back from the beach proved to be a godsend...like hitting the jackpot every few days. It worked particularly well when I was on the morning shift. Starting at six and finishing at two in the afternoon, I could chat up a new girl while I was working during the morning and we could spend the rest of the afternoon back in my room. 'You mustn't get too much sun all at once,' I would say.

And the really good thing was that it was an ever changing population. At the end of their holiday, they were off back home and a new lot were already there waiting for their chance.

Most of the other guys had rooms or a flat where we used to have parties and barbecues, but Shorty was still living at home with his parents and did not have quite the freedom of action, as far as the girls on the beach were concerned, that I enjoyed with my little room. Nevertheless, we were able to work a system.

Hard at work on the beach at Durban

With Milton Mfulu, one of the lifeguards from the Black Beach.

'They were big men and they dressed in the most elaborate costumes.'

'Have you got the key to your room?' he'd say to me on various occasions when I was working the afternoon shift and he'd been on in the morning. I'd hand him the key and off he'd walk, hand-in-hand with some smart little number in a bikini. 'Be careful of that bed ,' I'd shout nearly every time...to roast him. 'Its not very strong.'

I also recall one girl from Johannesburg... she was blonde, petite and attractive and about eighteen or twenty years old... who's appetite for lifeguards seemed to be somewhat more developed than most. During her first week on holidays in Durban, she had taken up with Marty Viljoen, another of the lifeguards, for a couple of days, then, in the following week she was with a second one, Tom Bergman, although I was too busy with my own affairs to know anything about this until the next weekend, when she was apparently due to return home.

That Saturday was a dull and rainy day, like the day described earlier, except that it wasn't stormy. But, with the beach deserted, we were once again in the tower playing cards...although on this occasion there were six of us. At one point, about eleven o'clock in the morning, Cliff Honeysett, who hadn't been playing, came into the room without saying much to anyone and picked up one of two collapsible stretchers, normally used for first aid, that were standing against one wall... and disappeared, carrying it down the stairs.

We all looked at each other without saying anything and back at Cliffy's departing figure. If it had been a cartoon, you would have seen those little electric globes lighting up over each of our heads... with the realisation that something interesting was going to be happening soon in the lifeguard changing rooms downstairs.

'Sshhh,' Shorty said, and we all got up quietly from our chairs and began to tip-toe silently down the stairs.

'Just in here,' we heard Cliffy say softly to someone we couldn't see. Six of us were lined up along a wall, with Marty closest to the door to our locker rooms. He took a quick look around the edge of the door...and then turned back to us in amazement, 'Jeeez!' he whispered. '... its that bird I was with last week, Cliffy's on to her now.'

'You mean Karen?' Tom said. 'Hell!' Tom who'd also spent the last few days with her, was also one of us lined up along the wall.

We were like a bunch of little boys, as we whispered and stifled giggles and at the same juggled for position, taking turns at peering around the corner of the door at the two naked bodies humping away on the First Aid stretcher.

As we listened to the increasing tempo of the action, Tom moved up towards the door and then, just as Cliffy finished, he walked casually into the locker room.

'Oh, hi Karen...Hi Cliffy,' he said. 'How are things going?'

'Pretty good,' Cliffy smiled, rolling off Karen onto one elbow. 'You know Karen, don't you Tom.'

'Sure,' Tom laughed, taking off his swimming costume, 'Like a little more of the same, Karen?'

We heard her laugh and say something in reply...and the next thing we knew was from Shorty, who was now at the door position, and reported with a whisper, 'Tom's on the job now!'

Shortly after this, Cliffy walked out the door, saw us all lined up and was only just able to suppress his laughter. We decided on a strategy; when Tom finished, Marty was in position by the door and walked in with the same banter.

'Oh, hi Karen, hi Tom. How's everything going?'

Both she and Tom burst out laughing...and within moments the changeover had taken place.

Next it was Shorty.

'Hi Karen, hi Marty how's everything?' He said.

Again the laughter, although Shorty was the first one whom she didn't know...other than having seen him on the beach.

'Oh my God,' she giggled, 'How many of you are there?'

'Only three more.... after me,' Shorty said.

'Where are they?' she asked.

'Just outside.'

At which point, I, Bobby Burdon and Dave Jamieson stepped in from the doorway. 'Hi Karen...Hi Karen...' we all said together. 'How's everything going?'

'Fine... just fine,' she laughed.

Shorty was already hard at work, while she lay on the stretcher giggling.

Eventually Karen had her turn with all of us...me last, number seven, because I was the 'new chum', the most recently employed. Shorty, Dave and Bobby had insisted on the last four being in strict order of seniority.

Karen took the train to Johannesburg that evening, happy, I'm sure, in the knowledge that she had cut something of a swathe through the Durban Lifesavers...but perhaps a little disappointed that there were still another five she'd missed out on.

Within my first six weeks or so of starting work on the beach, I'd written a couple of letters to Noel spelling out some of the more pleasant details of my job and he'd written back, in a somewhat envious tone, saying that he'd started work as a trainee miner, but felt dissatisfied with it and might soon be heading down to Durban to join me.

I had also written to Lise, in Norway, telling her about plans that were formulating in my mind to head back to Europe for the summer of 1956. I found that, despite all the young women in my life here on the beach, Lise was often in my thoughts. Even though we'd known each other only a few weeks, while hitching in France, Italy and Austria, I missed her and wanted to see her again. If all went well, I told her, I would be able to save enough money to come to Europe. I felt I could spend say three months there, during which time I could meet up with her and try to figure out if there was something serious between us and still be able to make it back to Australia in time for the Olympic Games in Melbourne, which were due to start in November.

There were always other plans in the background, of course, including those which Noel and I had formulated, but they would change constantly, depending on what new information or opportunities arose. However, even though Noel and I were corresponding and talking of joint projects, I was now also making plans that were independent of him... in case he decided to stay on the mine.

The idea of returning to Europe for a while, before heading home, grew out of the realisation that there would be quite a bit of time to fill before November. Also, I'd had news that my parents would soon be arriving in London for a two-year period. My father, an officer in the Australian Army, was being sent there to attend the Imperial Defence College. It would be a good opportunity to see them again.

I was joined in these plans to return to Europe by Shorty

Bronkhorst, who became after a while, my best friend amongst the lifesavers on the beach. Shorty had never been out of South Africa, except once, to nearby Lourenço Marques in Portuguese East Africa, and he had a burning desire to get to Europe. He was fascinated by some of the stories I told about the trip through Africa and was always trying to extract more information from me about it...and to contribute ideas about future trips.

It would have been around Christmas 1955 when we first started talking about it. But I knew I needed a few months to save some money...and anyway, I wanted to spend the summer on the beach. The simplest plan I could see at the time was to take a Union Castle liner from Cape Town to England some time in April or May, so as to be in Europe for the summer. But life is never simple.

'Whichever way you go, I'm coming with you,' Shorty said on one of those early occasions. From then on, although the objective slipped into the background for a couple of months, and there was always the possibility that Noel would arrive and we would make new game plans, it was more or less assumed that Shorty was coming to Europe and then on to Australia with us.

ooooo

18

'HERE WE GO-O-OO!'

In the years that have passed since I spent those halcyon days on the beach in South Africa, I've often been asked how I shut my mind to the racist bigotry and discrimination that existed there. Its not an easy question for me to answer, because I guess I must have shut my eyes. But its interesting to look back and realise that, apart from the 'Whites Only' signs already mentioned and the segregation in buses, toilets and the like... I never actually saw any racial abuse or harsh treatment of black people while I was there.

This is not to say it didn't happen...I'm sure it did and in quite unacceptable ways. What I'm saying...and I've heard it said by other Europeans who visited South Africa at the time...is that it was possible in those days to live in South Africa and feel almost as if you were living in a country populated mainly by white people...so rarely was it necessary to interact with black people on a personal level. This, despite the fact that the reverse was actually true, as blacks outnumbered whites in the overall population then by some 3 to 1. Now its closer to 7 or 8 to 1. The sensation was there because virtually all whites lived...as its so often described... in a cocoon.

For example, as I've mentioned, there were no blacks or Indians on the white beaches, expect perhaps a black person cleaning the beach of litter, or an Indian selling soft drinks and ice creams. White people owned and ran the major stores, white people lived in all the houses and apartments along the beach. Black people and Indians, if they worked in white areas during the day, went home to their own townships every night... except for domestic servants, who might have their own accommodation provided in some apartments.

In the apartheid years that were still left, when so many of the evils and iniquities of the system were exposed and publicized, I often asked myself how I could have lived there. And I found myself relying on the rather weak excuse of being young and ignorant, which was a bit hard to sustain, as I generally took a keen interest in what was going on around me.

Its interesting to consider that, during the period I was in Durban, the dynamic young black lawyer, Nelson Mandela, was enjoying a rare period of six months (September, 1955 to March, 1956) when there were no banning orders applied to him. Government banning orders, which were applied to large numbers of black leaders, effectively confined them to one town...forbad them from attending meetings and from talking to more than one person at a time. Mandela complained that the bans effectively prevented him even from attending his son's own birthday party.

It was during this unbanned time that he drove from Johannesburg on an extended tour to Durban, and down the southern coast of South Africa to Cape Town, holding open, as well as secret meetings with branches of the African National Congress (ANC). At the centre of their discussions was the Government's plan to implement the so-called Bantustan Program. This was in fact Dr. H.F. Verwoerd's blueprint for separate development, or Grand Apartheid. Verwoerd, then minister of native affairs, wanted to set up separate ethnic enclaves, or homelands for all African citizens, as a way of muting international criticism of South African racial policies, but at the same time institutionalizing apartheid...a status quo, in which three million whites owned 87 percent of the land and ten million Africans owned 13 percent, would thus be preserved.

In March 1956, Mandela was given a five year banning order. In December of the same year he was arrested and put on trial for treason. After an on-again, off-again trial that dragged on for five years, he was acquitted... but jailed the following year for five years. While still in prison, Mandela was linked to an organization seeking to overthrow the Government by violence and was sentenced to life imprisonment.

Twenty six years later, in February, 1990, he was released. Four years after that, he was elected as the first President of a free and multi-racial South Africa.

Declaring his intention of only serving one five-year term as

President, he successfully dismantled the hated apartheid system before his retirement in 1999. He died in December, 2013.

Presidents Thabo Mbeki and Kgalema Motlanth followed and the current president, Jacob Zuma, was elected in 2014

I knew nothing of the banning order on Nelson Mandela in March, 1956. It would only have received relatively small coverage, if any, in the Natal Mercury. And during those great days on the beach in Durban, I have to tell myself now that my mind was elsewhere. However, I do know...in my heart, that I personally never acted in a racist or abusive way to any non-white person in South Africa. Nor do I recall any of the guys I was working with on the beach being aggressive or abusive.

In fact we had a reasonably good, though very limited relationship with a few of the black and Indian lifeguards who worked on the other beaches. From time to time they would come and ask for our help or advice in certain situations. Because there were fewer of them on duty, if ever there was an unexpectedly large number of bathers on their beaches, or the sea was particularly rough or dangerous there, as a result of rips or sand banks, it was sometimes necessary for one or two of the white lifesavers go to the black or Indian beaches to help out.

This generally involved walking up and down by the water's edge blowing a whistle and signalling to people to either come out of the water, or to move to a safer part of the beach. Sometimes it meant going in and helping a person in deeper water to make it to where they could stand or make their own way back to the beach...or perhaps shouting to someone to swim across a rip instead of against it. But on a couple of occasions the situation turned quite serious.

One day I recall more clearly than others because it got a bit of a write up in the local press. It was a hot weekend...I think in the week between Christmas and New Year, with a big crowd of people in the water and I was one of six guys on duty at North Beach. The morning had been relatively trouble free, but shortly after noon, Milton Mfulu, one of the black lifeguards, came running across the sand to us, shouting. He'd cycled down from the black beach with the news that a large sandbank had collapsed just off the shore and that a big rip had quickly developed and carried a lot of bathers well out from the beach. Many of them were in trouble, being unable to get back in and it was beyond the ability of the three lifeguards on duty there to handle it themselves.

'We need an extra belt and line,' too Milton said.

Grabbing a box with a belt and line in it, four of us; Bobby Burdon, Dave Jamieson, Chookie and myself ran with Milton to Dave's car, which was parked just twenty meters away, and roared off to the black beach, arriving there within minutes.

We found to our relief that the situation had improved dramatically in the time taken for Milton to bring the news and for us to return. The majority of people had managed to get themselves back to shallower waters and to the beach. The two lifesavers who had remained had pulled several others out and were in the process of hauling one woman in with the belt and line when we arrived. But there were two others apparently in serious trouble a long way out, and quite widely separated. A crowd of Indian and black bathers gathered around us, shouting and pointing out their bobbing heads as they came sporadically into view beyond the waves in what was a reasonably large surf. One of them waved a couple of times. They were both about four hundred meters from the shore.

'You and Aussie go for the one on the left,' Chookie barked at Bobby. 'Dave...you swim the belt out. I'll go for the one on the right.'

We all dashed for the water...Dave hesitating for only a moment or two to jump into the belt and shout at some of the Indians standing around to pay out the line to him as he swam.

'...and don't start pulling me in until I've got the guy in my arms,' he said. 'Wait for my signal before you start pulling.'

It was not a situation that any lifesaver swimming a belt out would have liked. Dave would have far preferred it if one of the other lifesavers was there to supervise the line, but Milton had run off to help his colleagues, who were still struggling in the water with the woman and another young boy who was now in trouble.

Without having to pull a line out, Bobby and I could swim much faster. We were under the first few lines of breakers and swimming out towards where we'd last seen the man waving his hands. But it was a long swim...and tiring. We would stop every twenty or thirty meters to look around.

'There he is,' Bobby shouted. 'Over to the left.'

We swam another fifty meters or so to where a young black man, probably about twenty-three or twenty-four years old, was floundering weakly and coughing and vomiting up quantities of swallowed and inhaled water. For a second or two we held off from him...what drowning people do can be as dangerous to a rescuer as it is to themselves.

'Listen to me,' I yelled. 'Just do as we say. Don't struggle. We can help you...but you mustn't struggle. Just keep still.'

But he was beyond it. He wasn't going to struggle. He was about to go under... for the last time, I guessed. We moved in and Bobby slipped around behind him, taking the boy's head in his hands and holding it face upwards, clear of the water. Then he started to frog kick back towards the beach. I swam beside them, trying to buoy him up, by lifting underneath his body. But we were a long way out and after about a hundred meters or so, Bobby was tiring, so we changed roles. From behind, I put my right arm over his right shoulder and grasped him underneath his left armpit... and started swimming side-stroke. Resting on the right side of my chest, his head was still clear of the water, but I wondered for a moment, as I started to swim with him, if he was still alive.

'He's like a bloody dead weight,' I said to Bobby, who was swimming beside me and trying to keep the rest of the man's body up.

'He's full of water,' Bobby said. '...that's why.'

At which he suddenly gasped and coughed up some more water. At least he's still alive I thought. Then, after I'd also swum with him for several minutes, we met with Dave swimming out with the belt.

'How is he?' Dave asked.

'Pretty crook,' I replied. '...but he's still alive.'

We passed him over to Dave, who positioned himself behind the young man, holding him with his hands, this time under the armpits. Looking to the shore I couldn't see Milton and the other two black lifeguards. They were apparently still occupied with other rescues.

'There's only those Indian guys there with the line,' I said to Dave. I can't see Milton. What do we do?'

We were now faced with a situation that could not only lose the patient...but also endanger Dave's life.

'Give 'em the signal,' he muttered. 'We haven't any choice.'

Bobby waved to the shore and twenty Indians and blacks immediately grabbed at the line and started pulling. Dave and his passenger moved away from us towards the shore at a cracking pace... and we swam after them as fast as we could.

The danger in pulling a rescuer and a drowning person in together on a line through the surf is that, unless you use the right technique, you can have a disaster. Firstly, there shouldn't really be more than three people...maybe four, maximum, pulling on the line; Secondly, there's a way of crossing one arm in front of the other, in a seamless pulling motion, that ensures a steady, non jerky ride for the rescuer, who is travelling backwards through the surf with the person he's trying to save; Thirdly, the people pulling on the line have to constantly watch the waves and see where the belt-man is in relation to a wave that is about to break. Then everybody has to *stop* pulling at the same time, allowing the wave to pass under or over the two people at the end of the line, before resuming pulling. If that doesn't happen, then they are simply pulled backwards into the cauldron of white water at the front of a breaking wave and then along in it... unable to get out, or to come up for air, because the pulling on the line tends to keep them down.

And this is exactly what happened to Dave, as the twenty or so amateur linesmen, with the best of intentions, pulled as hard as they could on the line. Fortunately, he had been pulled more than a hundred and fifty meters through big but unbroken swells, where he was able to keep both his own and the young man's head clear of the water, before they reached the shore break where the real danger lay. Then, as the fierce pulling on the line continued unabated, they were suddenly engulfed in a breaking wave and pulled down and under. There is nothing you can do in such circumstances, but let go of the person you're rescuing and try to save yourself. Dave did exactly that... and struggled desperately to release himself from the belt. Pulling on the safety release, he burst to the surface, looking frantically around for his lost charge... to find him floundering a few yards away.

Luckily, they were by now only fifty meters or so from the shore and Milton and one other lifeguard were swimming out to help. Bobby and I had also caught a couple of broken waves that brought us in to Dave's aid a few moments later. In no time the young man was on the beach and although he was better than when we first found him, he lay down and gladly accepted the ministrations of some ambulance paramedics who arrived shortly after.

Chookie meanwhile was still out there. He'd also swum some four hundred meters out and searched in an area just to the south of where Bobby and I had picked up the young African...but without any luck. He was now on his way back in, still looking everywhere, when people on the beach started yelling and pointing to an object in the water between him and the beach only about fifty meters from the shore. Chookie swam furiously towards it and found the second young man, an Indian, floating face down and unconscious. He had managed to swim, or been washed in by the waves. We all ran to help Chookie pull him out onto the sand where, after being given artificial respiration and oxygen by the paramedics for about fifteen minutes, he was partially revived and then rushed to hospital to eventually make a full recovery.

Early in the New Year I decided to do a course in shorthand and typing that had been offered in one of the Durban newspapers. I think I was first motivated to do something like that by one of the bunch of Australians with whom I'd been sharing a flat in London, Keith Byron. He was a press photographer, working at the time for the London bureau of United Press (Later UPI), the American wire service...having previously been employed on a newspaper in Sydney. Keith was often sent off on interesting assignments in Europe and what he was doing had appealed to Noel and I enormously, as we were both interested in photography. But I remember him cautioning us on several occasions.

'Its no good being just a photographer,' he said. 'Okay, I do alright out of it. But you really have to be able to put some words with the pictures too. If you can do that and know how to type properly and do some shorthand, you can become a photo-journalist. Now that's where the real money is.'

Photo-journalist. I turned the expression over a few times in my head. I'm a photo-journalist...its got quite a good ring to it, I thought. Maybe that's what I should be.   There was also a more distant and somewhat nebulous motivation. My grandfather, A.P. Adams, had been the Principal Parliamentary Reporter and Chief of the Hansard Staff at Parliament House in Canberra. I can clearly remember him squiggling away in Pitmans shorthand on many occasions when I was a young lad living in Canberra with my grandparents and my mother, while Dad was away at the war. So it had been sitting in the back of my mind, for some time when I saw the ad in the Natal Mercury.

There were night classes as well as day classes available over a period of six weeks in either one...or both of the subjects. The shorthand courses could be continued for longer periods, in order to develop greater proficiency, but I started on a six week course for both. I was able to arrange things so I could attend afternoon classes when I was working morning shifts on the beach...and evening classes, if I happened to be working afternoon shifts.

'What the heck are you doing that for?' Chookie had snorted, when I'd told the guys on the beach I was starting the course. 'Typing and shorthand are for women. You want to be a secretary or something?' he laughed, along with the others.

They all laughed on the the other side of their faces though when I came back from my first lesson and told them that I was the only guy in a whole class of young women...none of whom had ever met a lifeguard before. It opened up a whole new world for me.

Life in the New Year progressed well. The job on the beach continued to be wonderful. I completed the typing course and the introductory shorthand course, but decided not to continue with more shorthand studies at this stage. Perhaps later. Noel had written a few times indicating that he'd overcome his initial dissatisfaction with the mine job and, as the money was so good, he was staying on there and continuing to stack the money away. We discussed in our letters returning to Europe in the summer, but our plans were now vague and it even seemed as if Noel might stay on the mine for most of the year and return directly from South Africa to Australia at the end of the year. Everything seemed up in the air.

Shorty, however, was now more certain than ever that he would come to Europe with me, whether Noel was coming or not. And he had an advantage over me in that he knew he would have sufficient funds to make the trip without any trouble...even without saving for it. Shorty had a Morris Minor that he was paying off on a hire purchase plan, but he'd had it for eighteen months and, even though there was still a substantial amount owing, he knew, from the current second-hand prices, that he'd be able pay off the balance after selling the car and still have more than enough left over. At least that was the plan before something rather dramatic and unexpected happened.

Occasionally on a weekend when we had a rostered day off together, which was quite rare, Shorty and I would take off in his car for one of the string of other good surfing beaches at Isipingo, Amanzimtoto, or Umkomaas, along the coast road to the south of Durban. So one Sunday in late February we drove off in Shorty's car, heading for Umkomaas. He'd arranged to meet up with some friends who lived there for a breivleis (a South African barbecue) after we'd spent a few hours in the surf.

We'd been travelling on a relatively open stretch of road, with practically no traffic in either direction, when, not far from the town of Umkomaas, we reached a long shallow curve in the road leading onto a high bridge over a river. The road had been built up above the flat surrounding countryside on a sloping embankment to a height of about ten or fifteen meters, so as to meet the bridge.

As we entered the curve at about eighty kilometres an hour, something suddenly went wrong. There was a loud noise and for no apparent reason, the car lurched violently out of control.

'Shit!' Shorty yelled struggling to keep it on the road.

There was a terrifying tearing, scraping sound for a few seconds as we swung around 180 degrees, with both of us hurled sideways ...and no seat belts! This was long before they'd even been thought of. Then we were thrown violently to the other side of the car as it switched fiercely back towards our original direction...but not quite far enough to stay on the road. One of my most vivid memories...the image presented to me over the next few seconds, has remained with me all my life. It was seeing the landscape through the front windscreen disappear and blue sky come into view, as the front of the car tipped upwards and we flipped over backwards down a fifteen meter embankment, at probably sixty kilometres an hour.

'Here we go-o-o!' I remember shouting... rather superfluously.

The car did several somersaults down the steep bank and ended upright at the bottom. I was about three or four meters away from it with the passenger door, which had been completely detached from the car, bent around me, with my head through the glass window. But I

'...we flipped over backwards down a fifteen metre embankment, at probably sixty kilometres an hour.'

'...during the next couple of hours we watched a fantastic exhibition of drumming and dancing and music.'

On the road to Lourenço Marques

was conscious...and felt, initially, as I pushed the car door off, that there was nothing broken. I was bleeding from several cuts, but nothing seemed serious.

'Are you okay?' I yelled to Shorty as I looked across at the car.

Most of the passenger side of the car was gone, so I could clearly see Shorty, sitting upright in the drivers seat, still holding on to the front wheel and looking straight to the front. He didn't reply. I ran across to the car... and stopped for a moment shocked. The whole top of his head and face was covered in blood that was pouring down his front.

'Jesus Christ! Shorty! What the... are you...?

He moved his head from side to side... 'Yeah... yeah. I... er, I think I'm okay.' He looked at the blood. 'What's happened to my head?'

Shorty had blond hair which he always wore as a crew cut. Some part of the car...the steering wheel, or the dash, or something had connected with the top of his head and cut a neat unfinished rectangle, about five or six centimetres long on two sides and about two centimetres wide at one end, raising a flap of skin that, for want of something better to compare it with, looked like a doormat that had been lifted up at one end and curled back on itself.

'Are you all right?... how is he?' Shouts of half a dozen people, as they clambered down from the road and ran towards us, made me turn around. Up on the road above us several cars had stopped.

'Jesus man...are you okay?' one of them said as he ran up. 'That was terrible. I thought you were finished. I was behind you. I saw it all.'

'What the hell happened?' I asked.

'Your bloody wheel fell off...the back wheel. Christ, man...is your pal all right?' Two other people were trying to open the driver's door to help Shorty out, but it wouldn't open.

'Its okay,' Shorty mumbled. 'I think I'm okay. I can come out this side.' He started to clamber out over the passenger seat.

'Sit down...lie down,' several people gathered around to help him. 'Both of you should lie down...or sit. Someone's gone to call for an ambulance.'

We sat down in the long grass, now flattened not only by the rolling car, but by the increasing number of people who'd come down the embankment to help. Several people were checking Shorty's head wound...which although it had produced a lot of blood, had apparently not cracked his skull...and were making positive sounds, but there was no way of knowing until we got him to hospital. I felt surprisingly unhurt. I pulled several chunks of safety glass about as big as a fingernail out of my leg as well as one from the side of my nose and a couple of other smaller bits from my cheeks, but apart from that, after a cursory all-over check, I felt reasonably sure that nothing was broken, at least.

'You say the back wheel came off?' I said to the man who'd first arrived on the scene. 'But...how? I mean...it wasn't a blow out? You mean it just...came off?'

'Right. That's it. We were driving behind you...I suppose about 100 yards or so, doing about the same speed as you, and I saw it happen. It just came away...the wheel just came away and kept rolling on the side. And your car just dropped to the ground at the back. There was a huge spray of sparks...and then you spun around...and went over the edge. It was shocking man. Terrible. You're lucky to be alive.'

Shorty sat quietly beside me, apparently listening, but not saying anything.

'Jesus, I'm cold,' he suddenly muttered.

'He needs a blanket, or a jacket,' A woman said. 'He's probably in shock.'

People started calling out to the others up on the road, for a blanket or anything to wrap around Shorty and someone ran down with a picnic blanket which Shorty held around himself.

'I think we should go up to road to wait for the ambulance,' he said, getting up.

'No, no, you should stay here and wait,' several people said. 'You shouldn't move. They won't be long.'

Within a few minutes the ambulance arrived and two men came clambering down the bank with a folded stretcher. They examined both of us where we were for several minutes, cleaning up Shorty's head wound a little so they could properly see the extent of the injury.

'I'm okay,' I said. 'I can get back up there myself. I don't know about Shorty.'

'I'm alright,' he insisted. 'I can walk.'

There was some urgent discussions between the two ambulance officers. They looked at the embankment and saw that if would be impossible to carry Shorty up on a stretcher, but they were nevertheless worried about his condition. They decided to let him walk...that is climb, but with one of them supporting him on either side...in effect half-carrying him up the bank in an upright position.

At the top, someone had found the wheel that had fallen off and brought it back.

'The nuts are all in place,' he said. 'But the bolts have just sheered off. There's only three bolts, instead of four.'

We later learnt that Shorty's car wasn't the only one this had happened to. In later models, Morris changed the wheel design to the more standard four bolts instead of three that they had used in all earlier models.

Shorty was laid on the bed in the back of the ambulance and, after thanking the people who'd helped us, I got in to sit opposite him and we took off for the hospital in Umkomaas.

They kept us there for four hours, during which time they stitched up the tear in Shorty's scalp and put a few patches on my cuts and abrasions. They said that Shorty had mild concussion and should rest for a few days...and that was that. We were on our way. Thinking back on it, I'm not sure if they should have released us, because I remember that Shorty wasn't really talking any sense at all...and didn't for another couple of days. Anyway, one of his friends in Umkomaas who'd been telephoned and told of the accident had come to the hospital and now drove us back to Durban to Shorty's mother's apartment.

Shorty's mother, his older sister and a girlfriend of hers were at home when we arrived. They were all shocked and upset when they learnt what had happened. Shorty had decided not to telephone his mother in advance from the hospital, so as not to worry her. Now, however, she was extremely distressed.

'You hop into bed,' she said. 'Right now. I'll make you a hot drink and some aspirin.'

'No, Mum. I'm going to stay up for a while. I'm all right.'

'Leonard... they said you've got mild concussion. You should be in bed.'

But Shorty was equally insistent on staying up and for a time we sat around over cups of tea just talking about it all, going over the accident... how it had happened, what it felt like and so on, until Shorty, of his own accord, decided to lie down.

'I'm feeling a bit tired now,' he said. 'I think I'll have a rest.'

He went off to his bedroom where his mother helped put him into bed.

'I think you should go to bed too, Iain,' she said to me when she came back out. 'You can stay the night here. I can make up a spare bed on the balcony. Some times there are delayed reactions to these things and it would be better if you were with people you knew... where there's a telephone, in case anything goes wrong... you know.'

Although it was only about five in the evening, I didn't feel at all like arguing. I was beginning to feel a few uncomfortable aches and pains and to be overwhelmed with tiredness.

'Thank you very much,' I said. 'If its not too much trouble...'

The flat had a balcony, enclosed by windows, where Mrs. Bronkhorst and her daughter quickly made up a bed on a small divan there. As soon as it was ready, I stripped down to my underpants, slipped into the bed and was asleep within minutes.

I slept deeply for about fifteen hours. Then, when I awoke, shortly after eight in the morning, to the sound of someone moving in the kitchen, I found I couldn't move. I was wracked by excruciating pains in almost every part of my body. I felt as if a truck had run over me... or like an old man of 99, with arthritis and rheumatism all over. Gradually, I forced myself up on an elbow... then to sit up on the edge of the bed. Examining myself, I found bruises all over that I hadn't felt the afternoon before. I had a corked right thigh, a sprained left ankle, a sprained right wrist, a strained back with two dark bruises over my kidneys, pulled muscles everywhere, a black eye and my nose was badly swollen.

I managed to stagger into the kitchen, where Mrs. Bronkhorst and her daughter Kirsty were making some breakfast.

'Hello,' I said. 'How's Shorty? I hope he's better than me.'

'Good morning,' they both replied...and Mrs. Bronkhorst went on, 'Yes...you don't look too bright and I don't think Leonard's much better than you look. He's awake and he's going to have some breakfast soon, but he can't go to work... I'm going to ring the Beach Office shortly. I don't think you should go either.'

'No,' I nodded. 'I think I'd be pretty useless there today.'

'I'll ring for you as well then, when I call about Leonard. I'll tell them what's happened. I'm sure you'll be able to have a few days off. There's milk and sugar if you need it...' she said, handing me a cup of coffee. 'I've got to go to work... and so does Kirsty, but you should stay here today. I'm sure it'll be best for you and for Leonard.'

Shorty and I sat around during the morning and read and talked and drank a Castle beer each and slept a bit more and then... around noon, the doorbell rang. It was Kirsty's girlfriend, Sophie, who had been there when we arrived the previous evening.

'I came around to make you guys some lunch,' she laughed. 'Kirsty said you were both pretty incapacitated, so I thought I'd help out.'

'Great!' Shorty replied. 'There's salami and cheese and tomatoes in the fridge and bread in the cupboard. We can have some sandwiches... and a beer. Do you want a beer Sophie?'

'Sure... I'll get them. You guys sit down.'

Sophie had reddish brown hair... and a few freckles on her face which, fortunately she made no attempt to cover with makeup. She was tall...about 1.7 meters and slim, with small breasts that were tantalizingly evident beneath a thin tank-top type blouse that was tucked into a pair of dark slacks.

I wondered why I hadn't seen her before at the beach. Shorty's sister would come down to the beach from time to time and would always come to say hello to Shorty when she was there, but I couldn't recall ever having seen Sophie with her. Kirsty was a few years older than Shorty, so I guessed Sophie would be about the same age... probably around 25.

She made the sandwiches and we lounged around in the sitting room for almost an hour talking about the accident and various other things, including our plans to head for Europe within a couple of months. We talked too about the trip that Noel I had made through Africa... and Sophie began asking me questions about Australia.

'I think I'm going to have a kip,' Shorty said and got up to leave. 'I'll see you guys a little later.'

He told me the next day that he'd seen the way things were going and decided to make some room and, as I was to discover, his perception of the situation had been faultless.'

Sophie chatted about Australia for a few minutes after Shorty had gone and then she said, 'How are all the aches and pains now? Are they getting any better?'

'A little,' I said. 'But I just feel bruised all over.'

'I've done some training as a masseuse,' she said. 'Lie down out on the balcony. Take your clothes off and I'll massage you.'

Well, if anything was designed to take away those aches and pains, it was a suggestion like that.

'Really,' I smiled, getting up to walk out to my bed on the balcony. 'You think it will help?'

'I'm sure of it,' Sophie said. 'I'll get a towel and some baby oil from the bathroom.

Amazing what a bit of that sort of exercise will do for bruised and aching muscles. I returned to my room that evening and Sophie visited me there for more of her special massage treatment the following day...and several subsequent days thereafter. I had been able to return to work on the Wednesday, that is within two days... and Shorty was fit enough to return by the end of the week.

The accident, as well as a new letter from Noel, crystallized a lot of things about our proposed trip to Europe. The car was a total write-off. Fortunately, it was insured, but not for as much as Shorty might have got for it, had he been able to sell it in good condition on the second hand car market. In fact, he lost quite a lot of money on it... so that, after paying off the company he was buying it from, he didn't have as much money left as he'd anticipated. Neither of us had enough to pay for the sea voyage to London, the idea of hitch-hiking back up through Africa again became a more serious issue.

Shorty and I had discussed travelling overland before, because he was keen to experience some of the things...or at least similar things to those which Noel and I had met up with on our way down through Africa. On several occasions he'd suggested hitching. 'I'll come with you,' he'd say. 'We could take a different route... so you won't be seeing the same things twice.'

'No, no,' I'd always reply... 'I did it the hard way coming down. I'm going back the easy way...by boat.'

But now, as we moved into March, it seemed clear to me that I wouldn't be able to save sufficient money for the boat trip to England, and have anything left over. I was forced to start thinking of hitching again. One of the problems with doing it this way however, was that it would take much longer than the boat trip, so we would have to leave earlier. I estimated we could probably do it in three months...which would leave a couple of months in Europe during the summer... but then there still wouldn't be enough money to buy a passage on a ship home. The only way I could see myself getting back to Australia in time for the Games at the end of the year was by somehow getting another job on a ship... from Europe.

But that was still a long way off. And yet, down in Durban, we had to make decisions pretty soon about what was happening next. Another letter arrived from Noel confirming that he was staying on at the mine until later in the year and would probably go back to Australia directly from Cape Town. That more or less decided me to head off with Shorty as soon as possible. We set a deadline for ourselves for the end of March... just four weeks away.

Our plan was to head across through Portuguese East Africa to the Capital, Lourenço Marques, where we would try to find deck passage on one of the small coasters running from there up to Mombasa or Zanzibar, then on an Arab dhow up into the Red Sea. Many of these old trading vessels are said to be up to two hundred years old...or more, and still follow the routes that were plied by similar vessels trading ivory, slaves and spices between Mombasa and Aden for more than 2,000 years. From Aden we'd try to get up through the Suez Canal to Egypt and from there across to Greece or Italy...and so on. Its a good idea to have plans, I suppose, but its incredible how differently things turn out in the end. And this one was no exception.

During the period I had been working on the beach, I had sent my temporary British passport, which had by now expired, plus my birth certificate, with an application to the Australian High Commission in Pretoria, for a replacement passport. The new passport arrived early in March...one less thing to worry about.

In the five months I'd been living in Durban, I'd collected various extraneous items; clothing, books etc. that I obviously couldn't take along on the trip, so I packed some of them up, plus a few souvenirs and sent them off as a parcel by sea mail to my grandparents address in

Melbourne, to be collected at some time in the future. From now on I'd be travelling light... with just the same backpack that I'd had for the past two years. In addition to the map of Australia on the top, it now had a colourful map of Europe and Africa painted down one side with the route that Noel and I had followed marked on it as a red line.

I have to admit, that despite my initial reluctance to do it all again...and the dreams of travelling the easy way on a liner to London, once I got my pack out and started into the preparations and planning, I became excited and enthusiastic. It would be good to be on the road again after such a long time in one place.

Shorty bought a similar-sized pack and painted the words South Africa across the top. We also painstakingly stitched pieces of leopard skin, which we'd bought in the Durban markets, over the length of the shoulder straps of both our packs. We talked a lot about what Shorty should and shouldn't take...he bought a few bits of clothing and some hiking boots, so that by the middle of March we were ready to go.

Shorty had more money than me...a little more than seventy pounds, whereas I had only saved about fifty.

'I think I'll send twenty quid on to London,' he said at one stage. '... and keep fifty here, so that we both start off with the same amount.'

I would have liked to have done something similar, but I reckoned I'd need every bit of the fifty to get to Europe. I'd just have to react to the situation, as far as money was concerned, when we got there. We both gave our notice to the Beach Office two weeks before we planned to leave and I set about doing several of the things that I hadn't found time to do...mainly tourist-type things, like taking a ride in one of the Zulu rickshaws...which was great...and going to a big Zulu tribal dance, an event which was staged at a sprawling African housing estate not far from Durban.

Dances were put on there from time to time during the year on occasions of tribal importance among the Zulus and Shorty and several of the other boys on the beach insisted that it was something I should not miss.

'We could take Aussie along to see it,' Dave had said. 'I'll bet they don't have anything like it in Australia.'

So we and a few of the other lifesavers and some of their friends drove out to the Zulu estate in a couple of cars on the Saturday before

Shorty and I left. It was naturally a big event for black people and there were more than a thousand there. There was also quite a large number of whites...mainly tourists I suppose. We were charged admission to a dusty soccer field where during the next couple of hours we watched a fantastic exhibition of drumming and dancing and music. The costumes, with bells and feathers around the mens' legs and arms and huge feathered head-dresses were quite incredible, as they and a number of women danced around in a circle to the heavy, pulsating beat of scores of drums, accompanied by a chorus of reed flutes and the melodic tones of men playing musical bows with calabashes attached for resonance.

Going to this dance suddenly brought home to me how little I had actually seen of South Africa during the period I'd been working there. I had been down to East London, but hadn't even been as far as Port Elizabeth, on the Garden Route, let alone Cape Town. Nor had I seen any of the other wonders of South Africa, like the Drakensburg Mountains, Kruger Park, the gold mines of the Witwatersrand, the Kimberley, the Karoo desert and so on. There was a long list of things I could have seen and done, but had not.

I felt this even more strongly in the last few days before we left. It seemed ridiculous to be going, when all I'd seen of the country was the beach.

Some twenty years were to pass before I managed to see and do many of the things that I'd missed. I returned to South Africa in 1976 with my wife and children to spend three months travelling throughout the country. It was in the depths of the apartheid era...only a few months before the dramatic Soweto riots, which shook South Africa to the core...and there was quite a different atmosphere than the one I had known on the beach in 1955.

On the 1976 trip we were researching two books about Africa... one a jointly-written non-fiction book, the other a novel...by myself. When published in 1977 and 1978, I felt that both of them, in their own ways, gave something of the true picture of what was then, and still is an amazing and complex country.

oooooo

MOZAMBIQUE

19

'I HELPED TO BUILD THAT DAM'

In the mid-1950's, Mozambique, or Portuguese East Africa, as it was known then, was still twenty years away from independence. For most of the twentieth century it had been a colony of Portugal. But in 1951, just five years prior to our visit, the territory had been declared an overseas *province* of Portugal, prompting widespread dissatisfaction in the black population. Antagonism, particularly among the educated urban elite, led to the birth of a nationalist movement and a war of liberation.

Samora Machel, emerged as the man who would ultimately lead the country to Independence in 1974 after that long and bitter civil war. He died in a plane crash in 1986.

(An happy footnote to the Independence struggles of both South Africa and Mozambique is that Graça Machel, his widow, married President Nelson Mandela in 1998, a year before Mandela's retirement.)

Samora Machel's successor, Joaquim Chissano, introduced sweeping reforms, moving the country, in stages, from Marxism towards capitalism. After three terms, Armando Guebuza assumed the presidency for two five-year periods and in January 2015 Philipe Nyusi took over as the country's fourth President.

Nyusi, is leader of FRELIMO, the Front for the Liberation of Mozambique... the original revolutionary organization formed in 1964 and the only party to hold power in Mozambique since Independence.

Back in the 1950s, although nowhere nearly as wealthy as its neighbour, South Africa, Mozambique was able to sustain a reasonable (comparatively speaking) standard of living for most of its black inhabitants. South Africa and the Portuguese colony were on good terms, so large numbers of black Mozambiquians were permitted to travel and work on the mines around Johannesburg and in other parts of the country, taking back, or remitting their earnings to their families at home in Mozambique.

Lourenço Marques, the capital (now called Maputo), was a thriving port city of about 300,000 inhabitants (now above 1.5 million), about 650 kilometres by road from Johannesburg. Because of its continental atmosphere of outdoor cafés, small bars and wide-open, 'anything goes' night-life, 'LM', as the South Africans called it, was a popular watering hole and holiday resort, particularly for people from Johannesburg, but also from the rest of South Africa. Shorty had described LM in glowing terms, so as we approached the Mozambique border, I found I was looking forward to something different.

Shorty and I had finally said goodbye to everyone, in what became something of an event...or series of events, with a lot more ballyhoo than we'd expected. A couple of reporters and a photographer turned up at his mother's flat to do a little story about our proposed trip and a group of lifesavers were also on hand to see us off and to continually thrust beers into our hands. When at last we managed to leave, around noon, we were a little sloshed, but fortunately someone... I think it was Bobby Burdon, gave us a lift to the northern outskirts of Durban to set us on our way. And within a few minutes of him setting us down, we had a lift and were waving Bobby goodbye.

Our route took us initially in the direction of Johannesburg, but, as we had started rather late, by the time we reached Volksrust, about 350 kilometres from Durban, the sun was setting and we decided to spend the night there in a small and cheap guest house on the outskirts of the town. Continuing in the morning towards Johannesburg, but not wanting to spend time there, we turned north at Standerton, cutting up through Bethal to Middleburg, which was on the main road east from Johannesburg to Lourenço Marques. The traffic wasn't so heavy, so we may have waited slightly longer for the two lifts that got us there, but avoiding Johannesburg had saved us a hundred kilometres or so.

From Middleburg to the frontier of Mozambique is about 250 kilometres, the last eighty or ninety of which runs parallel to the southern border of the great Kruger National Park. Had it been something a little further along the way...in another country, Shorty would probably have agreed to a brief visit, but that wasn't how it was.

'I've been to Kruger a couple of times already,' he said. '...and you've seen game parks in East Africa. I think we should give it a miss and keep going. We've got a long way to go.'

He was right, of course, but there is only one Kruger National Park...and I felt that it was something of a loss, not being able to spend the time to stop and see a little of it. Not that I protested...I didn't, because, as with many things, I generally tend to think, oh well, I'll come back and see it some other time. Of course it generally doesn't turn out that way.   But in this case, and with many other parts of South Africa...as I've mentioned, I did come back, twenty years later, to see it all properly.

Reaching the frontier post at Komatipoort, on the South African side, we crossed into Mozambique a few kilometres further on, at Ressano Garcia, to continue on our way towards Lourenço Marques, 120 kilometres further, reaching the city about four in the afternoon.

It was like suddenly finding a little bit of continental Europe in Africa. I guess I hadn't really thought about it much during the trip south with Noel, because all of the countries we travelled through after we left Cairo were run by the British, and everyone spoke English...and even in North Africa, like all English-speakers world wide, we tended to take it for granted that at least *somebody* would be able to speak English. Now we found that people were speaking Portuguese and didn't have much of a command of English at all.

In the centre of Lourenço Marques, particularly in the areas mainly frequented by tourists; the waterfront cafés, the old Portuguese fortress, built in 1787, and on the fine beaches, many people spoke and understood English...which was just as well, because trying to understand or speak Portuguese for an English speaker is particularly difficult...much more difficult, for example, than Spanish. At least that's the way I've found it.

Anyway, LM was an interesting town for me because it was so different from South Africa and the other British colonial territories I had been through before. I was vaguely aware of some of the undercurrents of tension that existed in Mozambique... that were also present, of course, in dozens of colonial territories across Africa at the time, although during our brief transit through the Portuguese colony they had no direct impact on us. Nevertheless, the history of Portugal's repression of the inhabitants of Mozambique was such that they could not remain submissive for much longer.

The economic policy pursued during the colonial era by Portuguese administrators had shamefully neglected domestic development... particularly for rural Africans, in many ways denying them access to technical skills and managerial experience. Industrial development was basically discouraged and little was done to exploit the country's mineral resources, or to develop systems that might make the territory economically independent.

A significant portion of Mozambique's foreign earnings came from migrant workers travelling each year to work on the gold mines in Johannesburg. Under agreements signed with the Witwatersrand Native Labour Association, a body of South African mine owners, Mozambique supplied up to 150,000 contract workers each year. Under what would seem to be a totally unethical payment system, the workers were deprived of the full benefit of their labours.

Apart from taxation on their income, which was withheld and paid directly to the Portuguese government in Mozambique, South Africa also paid a separate fee for every worker who came to the mines for contract work. This added up to around sixty percent of the miners wages and it was paid to the Mozambique Government in gold at the official gold rate. The Portuguese administrators in Lourenço Marques then resold the gold at much higher free-market prices making a substantial profit, which was used to help balance the countries foreign exchange debt. Over $150 million a year was earned in this way from the pool of Mozambiquian labourers.

Despite this iniquitous, and basically unprincipled treatment of Mozambique's African workers, another eight years would pass before the FRELIMO guerilla campaign started. A shooting in 1960 of 500 peasants during a peaceful demonstration against a program of forced labour on the Portuguese cotton fields in the north led to serious unrest.

But, while it took until 1964 for people who actually lived in Mozambique to begin organizing some form of resistance to the

government, in 1956 it was fairly easy for a couple of young hitch-
hikers from outside the country to sail through without being too
aware of the underlying Machiavellian dealings of the Portuguese
government.

As far as Shorty and I were concerned, we were pretty much preoccupied for much of our time in LM in working out our next moves. In some of the planning we'd done, we had also discussed, in addition to the idea of going up the East African coast on a series of different boats, another itinerary that would take us up through Mozambique and into Nyasaland, (the present day Malawi) and after travelling around one side of Lake Nyasa, we could then head for Dar Es Salaam, where we could also try to get on one of the Arab dhows heading north.

Plans, plans, plans. They were always changing. On the morning after our arrival in LM, where we stayed at a small campground near the beach, we checked with the Tourist Office in the centre about roads that we could follow north towards Malawi...only to discover that Mozambique was a very different country from South Africa... not only in language. There was no road, we were told, between the capital, Lourenço Marques and the country's other major port and second largest city, Beira. Well, there was a road, or roads of sorts, but heavy rains and flooding rivers to the north had apparently made many of them impassable at the moment. At any rate, from our point of view, at the moment there was no way of heading north by land.

So we set about finding a boat that was going to Beira, roughly a thousand kilometres further up the coast, by sea. Finding one was not a major problem. The problem lay in getting one that we didn't have to pay for. In starting off on a journey of this scope, the tendency is always, in the early stages, to spend money on things that you would never spend on later in the venture...particularly as you always have more money in the kitty at the beginning than at the end. Anyway I knew we should try to look around for some way of getting to Beira for nothing...by working our passage as deckhands, or something like that. But after a fruitless search among the ships in port, we had to settle for paying the three pound fare for the two of us as deck passengers for the three to four day trip to Beira.

As the ship was not due to leave until the following day, Shorty and

I went swimming during the afternoon from the beautiful little beach near the camping grounds where we were staying. There the water was crystal clear with an amazing variety of colourful fish that teemed on a small coral reef just offshore. Unfortunately, while swimming over the coral, I managed to badly scratch the top of one foot on a piece of it. It bled profusely for a while and I came out of the water to wash it, cleaning the tiny bits of coral out, and to put a dressing on it. It seemed to clear up quite well over the next few days, but, as I was to find out, coral cuts can't be taken too lightly.

Beira was, like Lourenço Marques, another fishing and trading port...although on a much smaller scale. And while it also had something of the continental atmosphere of LM, it also presented that oddly pleasing combination of tropical decay and run-down colonial architecture.

We tried the same approach in Beira, that is, to find a boat on which we could work our passage further up the coast. And it seemed at first as if this is what we would be able to do. The captain on board a small Portuguese coaster, which was sailing shortly to Dar Es Salaam and Mombasa, told us we could work our way there on board his ship... once we had clearance from the Portuguese Police.

Here, where we expected it to be just a formality...although I should have known better, we came once more to a dead stop.

'I am sorry,' an officer of the Port Police told us, '...but if you are landing anywhere in the East African Federation (That is, Kenya, Uganda and Tanganyika) you will be required to produce a through ticket, an onward sea or air ticket, or a bond of one hundred pounds.'

'But that's crazy,' I said. 'I have just come down through Kenya and Tanganyika a few months ago...last year.' I pulled out my old (and now cancelled) British passport to show him the stamps. 'I wasn't required to put up a bond then.'

'That may be so,' he said. 'But, you did not come in by ship. If you come in by sea...if you get off a ship, that is what the East African authorities require.'

'So what do we do now?' Shorty muttered, as we sat disconsolately on the steps of a nearby building.

'The Information Office should be able to give us a few details on the roads up into Nyasaland and Rhodesia,' I said. 'I just hope they're in better shape than the road from the South. But that's about all we can do for the moment.'

But at the Oficie Informaçao we were greeted with equally gloomy news. There weren't many roads of any consequence in Mozambique anyway, but those that did exist, heading to the west and to the north were completely blocked, or flooded out in a number of places. Mozambique was not like South Africa, or the Rhodesias. It was no where nearly as wealthy, of course, but it also had to be admitted that, over the years, the Portuguese had put relatively little into the infrastructure of the country and when the rainy season came, the whole interior deteriorated into a impassable mess. Fortunately, there was one alternative...the train. A rail link between Beira and Umtali, the small town on the border of Mozambique and Southern Rhodesia, was still intact, despite the heavy rains in the interior.

And so, early the following morning, after reluctantly paying a fare equivalent to about one pound each, we found ourselves on board a crowded little train chugging slowly out through the dense and sparsely populated bush country of Mozambique, heading for the Southern Rhodesian border...only 260 kilometres in distance, but almost nine hours travel away.

Umtali (since renamed Mutare) was an attractive little town, set in in the foothills of the densely vegetated Eastern Highlands, where it sprawls up the sides of what is known as Christmas Pass, through which the road descends from the tablelands. The town, which was originally built by prospectors around 1890 and has wide streets lined with flowering trees, sits on the halfway point of the rail line that we had travelled from Beira, and which continued on to Salisbury (now Harare), the capital then of the Federation of Rhodesia and Nyasaland.

In the mid-1970's, some twenty years after our passage through Umtali, the town became something of a regular battleground for the struggle between Rhodesian forces and Zimbabwean nationalist guerrillas operating out of Mozambique. Since the early 1980's, however, Umtali (Mutare) has resumed its more peaceful role as a rail and commercial centre for the highly productive eastern region of Mozambique.

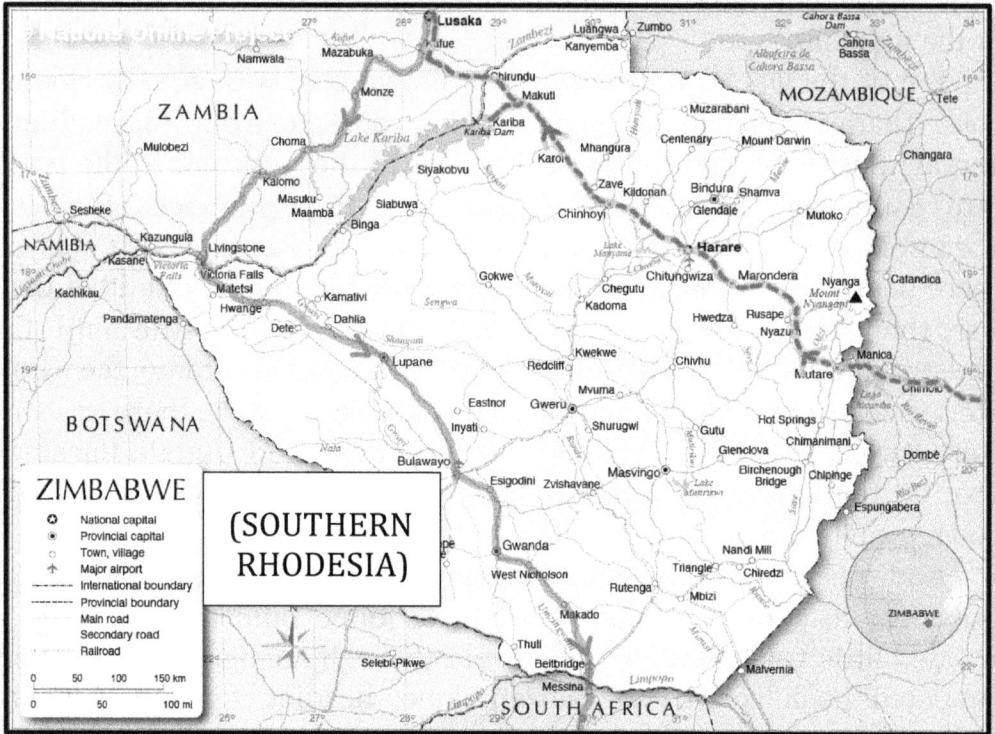

Shorty and I could have continued on by rail from Umtali to Salisbury, as that was our next destination, but we knew it would be cheaper to hitch... and probably quicker. Although we had both found Mozambique interesting and different, there was something quite reassuring to be back in an English-speaking environment and one where the roads were in reasonable shape and everything else seemed to work.

Once in Salisbury, which I had not passed through on the way down to South Africa, we would be able work out the best way to proceed... either up through Nyasaland, or back up through Northern Rhodesia again, where we hoped we might also be able to convince Noel to join us. But it was on the road to Salisbury that our plans got a bit of a shakeup once again.

We were picked up by a white South African truck driver, who was employed by a construction firm involved in the building of the Kariba Dam. I had vaguely heard of it while living in Durban, from reading small snippets of information in the newspapers about an enormous dam to be built across the Zambesi River. But neither I nor Shorty knew much about it at all.

'Its going to be huge,' the driver, whose name was Geoff, said to us. 'They're going to build a dam across the Kariba Gorge... its a deep gorge out in the bush about 450 kilometres from Salisbury. Its going to be the biggest in the world...four times larger than Boulder Dam, in the States.'

'For hydroelectric power?' Shorty asked.

'Right. Its going to create an artificial lake 350 kilometres long by over a hundred kilometres wide. Say... you guys could get a job there. Its really good money.'

'How much?' I asked.

'Well... an average weekly wage is between £42 and £48.'

'Forty eight pounds!?' I said. 'Wow. What sort of jobs are available?'

'All sorts. The labouring jobs are all done by blacks...but there are plenty of other jobs, driving trucks, and other vehicles, handling machinery, mechanical jobs, plumbing, welding, that sort of thing. How are you at that sort of stuff.'

'Not bad...it depends, I suppose. Not very big on welding, or plumbing. But... we're quick to learn,' I laughed.

'Yeah... well, they've got an office in Salisbury, where you could get some info. But I think all the employing is done on the site. But check it out.'

In Salisbury we found an equally attractive, though much bigger city than Umtali. Salisbury was a modern, well-planned metropolis, with multi-storied buildings and tree-lined avenues. It too was founded in 1890 by explorers...the emissaries of Cecil Rhodes, who halted their pioneer column, on its march into Mashonaland, at the point where the city eventually grew. They named the place after Lord Salisbury, who was then the British Prime Minister.

When the British South Africa Company's pioneer column halted there in 1890 and decided it looked a pretty good place for a town, they had simply seized land occupied by the local tribal chief Neharawe. The city's commercial district eventually grew in this are and the name Salisbury was changed to Harare...a derivation of Neharawe... after Zimbabwe's independence in 1980.

At the Government Offices in Salisbury we were given some

promotional material about the Kariba dam and its various statistics...who it would be built by and so on, as well as the local addresses of a couple of the large contracting companies, but were told again that workers were not employed from Salisbury. We would have to make our own way to the construction site, some 500 kilometres out in the bush and check with the main contractors there.

Two days later we arrived at the site...although there was nothing there that was recognisable as a dam, or anything even approaching it. It was difficult to grasp even where the site was, the project was so vast. 10,000 black workers were involved, as well as some 2,000 whites and there seemed to be dozens of sites spread over twenty or thirty kilometres, with dusty roads snaking two and fro through the thick bush country linking them together. The actual dam was to be built in a part of the Zambesi valley where the river flows through mountainous gorges and ravines, but at the time much of the work was being done in areas remote from the point where the dam would rise. First, proper roads had to be built to bring all the concrete, construction material and equipment to the right places and at the moment that was the main activity under way.

There were big workshops under construction. Accommodation for workers, both black and white, was temporarily in tents with wooden floors, while more substantial living and messing quarters... in prefabricated huts, was being built in various places. People moved like so many ants across the hot and dusty landscape.

We had hitched a ride into one of these locations in a truck carrying steel reinforcement rods and now sought out someone who might be able to tell us where to go and who to see about getting a job. We stopped a young man in a hard hat, who was carrying a surveyor's tripod and who looked as though he might be about the same age as us.

'I'm not sure, where you go to see about jobs, generally,' he said in response to our question, '...but, I did hear the other day they were looking for experienced bulldozer operators.'

'Bulldozers....?' Shorty nodded slowly.

'Yeah... you driven bulldozers?'

'Ah... well....'

He laughed. 'I think they're pretty hard pressed at the moment. Just tell them you've driven D-6's and D-8's'

'D-6's and D-8's...?' I said.

'Yeah... Cats.... Caterpillars.'

'Okay... but where do we go? Who do we see?'

'The Plant Foreman. He's not here, but you could grab a lift from somebody down to the main workshop area... its about seven or eight kilometres from here. Just ask around for the Plant Foreman.'

Thanking him, Shorty and I sat down for a moment to make a plan of action. 'I could tell him I've been working with D-6's and D-8's on the Snowy Mountains project in Australia,' I said. 'He'd know about that. 'And with Wimpeys...they're the big construction company in England....on London Airport.'

'Yeah, and I could say I've been working on the mine dumps in Johannesburg,' Shorty said.

Which is what we did. I can't remember the actual conversation with the Plant Foreman, mainly I suppose, because it seems so incredible to me now that anyone could believe such a far-fetched tale.

Not that he necessarily did. I think perhaps he was desperate enough for qualified people that he just *wanted* to believe our stories. He wanted to think they could be just partly true. If so, he probably reasoned, we might be able to pass muster on some simple jobs and then gradually improve our performance. Having decided to take us on, he then sent us off to see another foreman.

'Jim Bolton is the man on the job out on the new north bank approach road. Its about 30 kilometres out towards the main Lusaka road,' he said, showing us the location amongst what seemed to be a maze of roads on the blueprint plan in his office. 'Go out and tell him I sent you. There's a truck leaving here in about half an hour...you can get out there on that. But first, take this over to the pay office,' he handed us a slip of paper. '...tell 'em your names and sign on.'

In the intervening period, after we'd registered at the pay office and were waiting for the truck, Shorty and I found ourselves a quiet place out of the now searing heat, in the shade of tree, where we tried desperately to formulate the next stage of our plan . We were thankful that we'd been able to get this far...but equally sure in the knowledge that we were fast approaching the moment when we would have to 'put up or shut up'.

'There's no way we can bullshit this guy when we get there,' Shorty said. 'He's going to see straight away we don't know one end of a D-8 from the other. I mean, how the hell do you even start one up? Just turn the key?'

'No...you're right,' I said. 'I think we can only be honest with him. Everything depends on what sort of bloke he is. All we can do is throw ourselves on his mercy... tell him we got the job under false pretences, but that we're willing to work hard and learn fast. I mean, really we've got nothing to lose.'

And luckily Jim Bolton was that sort of bloke. There were several other white bulldozer, front end loader and grader operators out there who were experienced and qualified. They were working away, with large numbers of black workers on various aspects of the road construction over a distance of a couple of kilometres or so from where we met with Jim Bolton. He took us under his wing...but on very straightforward and conditional terms.

'I'd say you've got a couple...maybe three days to get it together,' he told us. 'Patrick (the plant foreman we'd spoken to) probably won't be out here for two or three days. If you can learn how to operate the D-8's and grade the road... roughly, by the time he comes around, he'll more than likely let you stay on.'

'Trouble is...' I smiled embarrassedly, 'We don't even know the first thing.'

'You mean you've actually *never* driven one?'

'Right.'

'Mmm... I see. Okay, lets get going.'

Jim taught us as much as he could, as fast as he could, about a D-8; how to start it up, how to operate the lever controls...forward, reverse, turning right and left...lifting and lowering the blade and so on. I got to be quite good, even on the first day, at pushing trees down, but this was not going to get us past Patrick when he turned up in a few days time.

'To make Patrick happy, you're going to have to do a rough grade on the road,' Jim told us. 'To see a wheeled grader moving along over a road, it looks easy. But that's hard to do with a bulldozer and yet that's what we're going to need you to do...pushing the road through and then levelling it up a bit so the grader can come through after you and do a proper job on it. I'll get you onto it tomorrow afternoon and you can start to practice a bit.'

We spent most of that first hot afternoon, just getting used to the machines. Shorty was also on a D-8, under the guidance of another driver...an Italian called Marco, but we were both working within sight of each other and could each hear the occasional yelling from the other's coach when something went wrong. For my part, it wasn't as if Jim had the time to devote solely to educating me in the finer points of bulldozer driving. On occasion, after we had gone through the basics, he had to go off to do something else nearby for brief periods, leaving me to my own resources.

'Just clear all the trees and bushes out of the way from here to here,' He'd say, marking out a stretch with me on foot. 'Try and push all the stuff you've knocked down off to the sides of the road as you're doing it. I'll be back in about ten or fifteen minutes to see how you're going.'

Fortunately the actual terrain, underneath the trees and bush and shrubbery, was totally flat in the area we were working. If it had been hilly, I'm sure we'd have had a great deal more trouble. As it was, it was an amazing experience to find ourselves, within hours of arriving on the project site, to be operating these huge machines virtually on our own. I'm sure that, without an operator's license, there wouldn't be the slightest chance of ever being allowed to drive machinery like that on present-day projects of that size.

'Okay, switch 'er off,' Jim called out to me at five o'clock. 'Knock off time. Just leave her where she is. Nobody's going to pinch her. We'll pick up her first thing in the morning.'

'You swimming?' Marco said to both of us as people started to gather around the trucks that would take us back to our tents and the black workers to their own camp. 'Everybody's going for a swim.'

'Sure,' we both replied. 'Where do you go?'

'In the River...' Marco said. 'There's a good swimming hole in a bend, about five or six kilometres from the main camp. Quite a few people go in the evenings before tea.'

In a lifetime, most people do some pretty unusual things, but late afternoon swimming in the Zambesi River has always remained as one of the more bizarre experiences I can remember. The sun was still an hour and a half from setting when Shorty and I and several others arrived in a small pickup truck to join a crowd of probably thirty other men in their swimming costumes and shorts, on a big sloping sandbank on the outer edge of a bend in the river. The Zambesi was about two hundred meters wide at this point...and deep. At one end of the sandbank there were some rocks and a large, deep pool where the opaque water curled in from the main river current in small eddies and this is where a number of other men were swimming.

'Look,' I cried, pointing across the river. 'There's bloody crocodiles over there...and there.' On two sandbanks...one about three hundred meters upriver from us and another, some two hundred meters below us, were at least a dozen large crocodiles, basking in the late afternoon sun.

'Jesus... you won't get me in there,' Shorty muttered.

'Its all right,' someone beside us said. 'Take a look up here,' he pointed to the back corner of the sandbank, where a man was sitting on one of two red boxes, holding a high-powered rifle as he watched the swimmers. 'But that's not all...' he smiled. 'You watch.'

As he spoke, a second man opened the other red box and took out what looked like a couple of sticks of dynamite tied together and walked towards the Pool. Someone else blew a whistle and everybody in the pool left the water. Then, lighting what must have been a sodium fuse, the man threw the sticks together far out into the water, where within seconds a huge eruption sent a column of water flying into the air. With a cheer, everybody then dashed back into the water.

'Holy smokes...' Shorty whistled. 'That's amazing. But that won't keep them away for long, will it?'

'Oh... a good while. Anyway, they do it every ten or twelve minutes to be on the safe side. And the crocs seem to have picked up on the idea that its better to stay away from here, than to come nosing around.'

We did go swimming. Nervous at first, but as they continued to throw dynamite in every ten minutes or so, for another hour, we became accustomed to the routine and began to feel reasonably secure. In any event, none of the crocodiles moved from the other sandbanks while we were there.

Our second day on the dozers progressed along much the same lines as the previous afternoon. We were learning as fast as we could and doing small, simple jobs at the same time. In the afternoon, as he promised, Jim started us in to grading.

In principle, the procedure seems the essence of simplicity. You set the bottom of the blade right at ground level and you start moving forward. Where there's a bump, or slight rise in the level of the road ahead of you, the blade will dig in to it and just push the earth aside, creating a continuance of the same level your tracks are travelling on. But, when there's a slight dip in front, while your blade goes over the top of the depression, the tracks of the dozer, following just behind the blade, will go down into it. It doesn't have to be a deep dip... it can be very shallow, only a matter of centimetres... but as the tracks go into the dip and the dozer tips slightly forward, the blade also tips forward...just a fraction and digs in, creating another dip a little further on, which the tracks then run into. And so on, and so on... until you have a road which looks like permanent wave.

There is a technique that bulldozer operators learn, to avoid these results, but its subtle and doesn't come easy. And that is what we were trying to get on top of during our first days at Kariba.

We went swimming again at the end of the second day, which, like the first had been hot and dusty. Then in the evening, after dinner in the big mess hall, we were treated to another rather offbeat spectacle.

In the whole camp of more than two thousand white men, there were apparently only seven white women (of which I only ever saw two) so the general atmosphere and ambiance was, to say the least, somewhat rough and ready. Because everyone was earning such high salaries and their social life was nil, drinking and gambling were basically the only forms of entertainment in those early stages of the construction program. There was no drinking allowed during the day, of course, but at night, after dinner, the mess hall doubled as a sort of bar and general meeting place. And two nights a week it became a cinema where recent release movies were shown.

Our second evening in the camp was a movie night and we saw Stalag 17, starring William Holden. But, while I can't recall a great deal of the plot...apart from the fact that they were escaping from a German prisoner of war camp, I'll never forget the image of many of those construction workers sitting on the wooden benches in their shorts and big boots, watching the film as they drank Moet & Chandon and Veuve

Clicquot from the bottle.

Back on the job the following day, both Shorty and I were gaining in confidence...and competence. Well, that's the way we felt about it anyway. But it was not good enough for Patrick. When he came out to our site that afternoon, he asked to see where we'd been working.

'Hmmm. Is that all?' he said to Jim.

'Oh, I've had them doing a few other things I needed doing. They haven't been working on these bits very long.'

'Hasn't been graded yet....' he said, glancing at a stretch of track that I thought didn't look too bad.

'Ah... no,' Jim replied. 'he was about to do it... pretty soon.'

'Okay,' Patrick waved to me. 'Lets see you straighten that out.'

Well... there's no sense going into the sad details. Suffice to say it wasn't up to Patrick's standards... apparently by a long way. 'Christ, I could find chimpanzees that'd do a better job than that!' were his exact words. 'Why didn't you send 'em back?' he said to Jim.

'I need men out here. You send 'em out, I work with what you send.' Jim turned towards us, with an apologetic lift of his eyebrows.

Patrick shrugged and then also turned to us: 'Sorry, but we do need qualified men. I knew you weren't fully experienced, but its not good enough.' He slapped me on the back. 'But no hard feelings matey. Go up to the pay office and collect your money and we'll call it quits.'

And that was that. £22 each for three days work on the Kariba Dam. As we sat in the back of a truck driving up out of the gorge we paused for a few moments at the top of one of the many hills that surround the camp below. We'd met a truck coming from the other direction and the two drivers stopped for a brief conversation. Looking around from our vantage point, I could see nothing, in any direction but rugged, thick bush country, which, like most of Southern Rhodesia at the time, was full of wild game...everything from springboks and eland to rhinos and elephants. But there was not a house, not a road, not a sign of life, right out to a distant line of hills on the horizon, even though we knew that just a few kilometres back, vast works were under way. The dam was finished in 1959.

Twenty years after Shorty and I had worked there, I returned to Kariba, while on the trip through Africa with my family. We drove on a perfectly tarred road to a vantage point near the dam where we could gaze out over the great, 5,000 square kilometre expanse of water that is now Lake Kariba and on which we then travelled some 300 kilometres, from one end to the other, by ferry. None of the countryside was even remotely recognisable to me, expect for the fact that the surrounding and more distant hills were still cloaked in dense, bush.

Earlier we had been to see the huge dam itself... 128 meters high, 625 meters long, embodying a hydroelectric power generation plant that turns out almost seven billion kilowatt hours of electricity annually for Zimbabwe and Zambia. Our children, Sean and Zara were at that stage eight and nine years old. 'I helped to build that dam...well, a bit of it,' I told them with my tongue firmly in my cheek. And their eyes opened wide in awe.

'Wow!' Sean said.

For Shorty and I, Luanshya was now our new destination. In the wake of our failed attempt at bulldozing, we changed our plans once again. We now actually had a bit more money than we'd started out with and felt that we should travel up through Northern Rhodesia to visit Noel and Bryce briefly to see if they might come north. As they would have considerably more money than us, Shorty and I felt it might even be possible to talk them into buying a vehicle between them, that we could all travel in.

We crossed the border into Northern Rhodesia at the Victoria Falls, which Shorty was determined to see and I certainly didn't mind visiting once more. We spent a day touring the length of the rim and walking in the rainforest opposite the huge cataract before moving on to Lusaka, from where we pressed on the next day towards the Copperbelt.

I was having some trouble by this time with my right foot. The cuts from the coral reef in Lourenço Marques had not healed properly and it was clear they were infected in some way. Even though I had kept a dressing on it, my foot was red and swollen and quite uncomfortable to wear inside a walking boot.

'Maybe we should get a doctor to look at it,' Shorty had said on a couple of occasions on our way north after we had left Kariba.

'No. I'll wait until we get to Luanshya,' I kept saying. I'm sure it'll be all right.'

In Luanshya, once we'd met up with Noel and Bryce again, I forgot about the discomfort of my foot, or at least pushed it into the background as we celebrated over a few beers in the Mine Club. Noel was really pleased at us meeting up again...and also glad to get to know Shorty, as I'd written and told him something of our plans for travelling north through Africa with Shorty.

'But I thought you were going to head up the coast, on the dhows,' he said. 'I didn't expect you to be coming through here.'

'We weren't. But it all became so difficult with the boats and the regulations for getting into East Africa, that we decided to come inland through Umtali...and that's when we heard about Kariba.'

We told Noel and Bryce some of our stories about Kariba, at which we all laughed and gradually, as the evening wore on, and the beers kept coming, we became increasingly merry.

'Why don't you guys come with us?' I kept saying.

'Yeah... in a way, I'd really like to, but... well, I guess I've made up my mind now to stay here and keep stacking the money away, so that I can get back to Australia and still have dough left over. And anyway, its no good hitching with four... or even three.'

'I know that,' I said. '... but we could do it like we did in Europe with the Norwegian girls...split up, two and two, and then keep meeting up somewhere further on.'

'Why don't you guys *buy* a car and we could all travel overland to Europe in it?' Shorty said to Noel and Bryce.

'Yeah...' I said. '...you must have the money to do it now... between you. And you could always sell the vehicle when we got to London.'

'Now you're talking,' Bryce said. 'That's the sort of trip that I'd really like to do. A good, strong car... maybe even a second-hand Land Rover.'

Everybody became enthusiastic and talked about which routes we could follow. Up through East Africa, Ethiopia and the Sudan to Egypt, was an early one. 'Or we could go through the Congo, and up through French Equatorial Africa, to Nigeria and then across the Sahara,' Noel suggested later. We sat discussing the pros and cons of the various different approaches, what they would involve in terms of equipment and so on...and all the time more beers kept coming, until finally we staggered, pretty plastered, back to Noel's rondavel, still talking loudly about our grandiose plans. There we collapsed asleep on a few cushions laid on the floor.

In the early morning I awoke with a splitting headache, sweating with a high fever and a badly swollen and painful groin. Sitting up, I looked at my leg in dismay. The whole leg was red and swollen. And my foot...well, when I saw it, I knew I was in trouble. My right foot had swollen up like a pink balloon, but more frightening than that was the thick yellow line that ran under the skin, following a vein, from my foot, past my ankle and up the inside of my calf.

'Jesus!' Noel said, when I woke both him and Shorty to show them. 'You've got to get to the hospital.'

Three days later, after some fairly serious work on my leg, which included draining copious amounts of pus, and dosing me with all manner of antibiotics, I was able to contemplate leaving the hospital.

Noel and Shorty and Bryce had visited me, of course, at various times, but for long periods I slept...better, perhaps than I had slept in ages. Interesting how, in hospital, once you accept the fact that you have to stay there and you know that really everything is going to be all right in the end, you relax in a way that you never do in the outside world. You know there's nothing you can do about it all...that there are people who are going to look after you and feed you, so you think, Ah, well, might as well make the most of it. That's if you know its only going to be two or three days. Of course, if its longer and you don't know the eventual outcome of your stay, that's a totally different matter.

By the time I was ready to be discharged, I'd already accepted the fact that all of our big talk about buying vehicles and travelling overland had evaporated. It had been the booze talking that night and once more sane and sensible thoughts came into play, there was no way that Noel and Bryce were going to jump into anything like that at such short notice.

'Maybe later on,' Bryce had said. 'Its the sort of thing that needs proper planning.'

Which was true. I knew it as well as they did and realized the difficulties of setting up a trip like that. Realistically it could take months of preparation.

So, from Shorty and my points of view, we were now more or less back to Plan E... in other words, moving on, hitching north again. But all of our talk over the previous days, particularly something that Noel and Bryce had mentioned, had sparked a couple of new ideas and different possibilities for Shorty and I.

'There's a good route from the Copperbelt up through the Congo now,' Noel had said during our first night's discussion. 'Some of the blokes from here have driven right up the eastern side of the Congo and then across into Ruanda-Urindi and Uganda and they say the roads are rough, but drivable, in an ordinary car.'

Now we started to go over this idea with a little more serious intent. It seemed, from looking at our map that, if we crossed the border into the Congo, which was about 80 kilometres from Luanshya, there was a good road on to Elizabethville (now Lubumbashi), the capital of Katanga (now Shaba) province, about a hundred kilometres further on. From there, there seemed to be a loose network of secondary, or tertiary roads linking a series of small towns, all the way up to the beautiful lake district of Central Africa around Kivu and Costermansville, or Bukavu, as it is now called.

Anyway, the end result of all our discussions was that we thought there was a route that could be followed and, from my point of view, the fact that it was different from one that Noel and I had travelled south was good enough for me. Shorty was happy to follow any route, so long as it led northward.

So, within two days of leaving the hospital, and after more protracted farewells, Shorty and I shouldered our packs and took to the road, heading for the Congo border.

'I'll see you back in Melbourne, for the Games,' Noel yelled, as we drove off...once again in the back of a truck.

oooooo

BELGIAN CONGO

BELGIAN CONGO

20

'A THREE-THOUSAND KILOMETRE LIFT

The actual frontier between Northern Rhodesia and the Belgian Congo was at a place called Tshinsenda. We had travelled up through another mining town called Chingola and been picked up by a truck carrying supplies to a little store on the Rhodesian side of the border, but which was going no further. After showing our passports to a white Rhodesian policeman in a small office there, we walked for about a kilometre along a narrow and winding unsealed road, through thick bush, to the Congo side of the frontier. It consisted of three small brick and cracking plaster houses beside the road where there was a customs and immigration office. A small village was visible some distance away through the trees.

We were anticipating some problems in entering the Congo, as the word we'd been given, back in Luanshya was that it was difficult for anyone to get in unless they were either Belgian, or Rhodesian. Rhodesia apparently enjoyed reasonably good relations with the Congo with whom it shared (in a geological sense) the great wealth provided by the Copperbelt. The enormously rich deposits of copper ore mined on the Rhodesian side, also extended well into the Belgian Congo and there were several large Belgian copper mines not far from the border. Rhodesians crossing at Tshinsenda were evidently presented with a minimum of formalities by the Congo authorities... and vice versa. But other nationalities were apparently meeting with greater restrictions.

Ever paranoid about these potential problems, we'd decided to say that we were working in Rhodesia...at Luanshya and that we were just going up to Elizabethville (now Lubumbashi) for a short holiday. But, as usual something totally different happened.

A single Congolese officer, dressed in khaki shorts and shirt, was on duty at the immigration post, a tiny one room structure, which had an open window facing, like a ticket booth, onto the road. He was just leaving the building as we walked up.

'Manger... manger,' he said pointing to his mouth... indicating he was heading off to eat.

'But...we are going to Elizabethville,' I said. '...Elizabethville. Can we...? I held my passport up.

He waved his hand and shook his head. 'Pas de vehicule... No cars,' he said. 'Je vais manger.' And he walked off towards the small village, disappearing among the trees.

We looked around. Another dirt road came in at a tangent from the west, presumably connecting the border to another part of the Congo's own Copperbelt and the mines there. But there was not another person...and no vehicles in sight in any direction. Not that we could see very far. The immigration post and the roads coming in to it were in an area of dense vegetation... not exactly jungle, but beginning to feel more tropical than the sort of bush country we'd become used to. We sat down in the shade of a big tree to wait.

Two hours passed without any movement on the road and without a sign of the immigration official, who was obviously enjoying a long lunch. We got up and walked around. We ate some bread and cheese and fruit. I strolled up to the little immigration office and looked in the window. There was a small table, with some papers and pens spread over it... an ink pad and a couple of rubber stamps. I walked back to the shade of the tree...thinking. Then suddenly, from the side road, we heard the sound of a car. A big Humber Hawk, carrying a Rhodesian number plate and followed by a cloud of dust, was approaching us. We leapt to our feet, held out our thumbs and the car pulled to a stop beside us. We were amazed to see two white women in the front seat.

'Hi, where are you guys from?' The driver, a dark-haired woman of about thirty-five, sounded American.

'South Africa... Australia,' we both replied at once.

'And where ya heading?'

'Elizabethville,' Shorty said. 'Can you fit us in?'

She turned to her companion, a woman, I guessed to be in her early to mid-sixties. 'What d'ya say Mom? Can we take 'em along?'

'Sure,' her mother replied. 'I don't see why not. We've got room.

You'll just have to shift a few things from the back seat,' she said to me.

'What are we going to do about our passports?' Shorty whispered to me as we went to the tree to pick up our packs.

'Well... yeah,' I paused. 'I wonder if they have to see this guy here also, or if they've already been through immigration somewhere else.' I turned back to her, 'Do you have to go through immigration here?' I asked.

'No, we've already been through yesterday. We've been down the road in Kasumbalesa, on the mine there... so we're set.'

'Ah... well, um...we've just got to pick up our passports,' I said, indicating the little brick office to one side. 'We'll only be a minute or two. Come on Shorty.'

We walked across to the open window, which was partially obscured from the women's view. I reached in, leaning over as far as I could, and picked up the two rubber stamps and the ink pad.

'Open your passport, quick,' I said to Shorty, stamping it first with the Kasindi frontier stamp, then with a date stamp. I immediately did the same with my own and, returning the pad and the stamps to their place on the table, turned to walk back to the car, stuffing our passports in our pockets.

'All okay?' the younger woman said, as we settled into the back seat.

'Sure,' I replied. '...just fine.'

She moved the car into gear and off we drove towards Elizabethville. I turned to look out of the rear window, to see if the Congolese official might reappear, but he didn't and as we passed a turn in the road, I lost sight of the building, breathed a sigh of relief and settled down for the ride...not realising for a moment how long it would turn out to be.

'Where do you come from in the States?' I asked, by way of starting the conversation, as we drove.

'Minneapolis. Do you know where that is?' the younger woman replied. 'By the way, my name is Jodie, Jodie Hurst...and this is my mother, Elaine. Elaine Fisher.'

Shorty and I introduced ourselves also.

'Minneapolis is in the middle somewhere, isn't it...and sort of north, I think,' I went on.

'Very good,' Elaine seemed surprised. '...and you've never been to the States?'

'Well, yes, I have. When I was ten or eleven years old...and again when I was about thirteen. My family lived in Canada for three years. So we got to go to San Francisco... and New York.'

'And what the heck are you doing here?' Jodie asked. 'how did you two get here?'

We told them a rather disjointed version of our two separate situations...a bit about Noel and my trip south, Shorty and I meeting in Durban and our trip north, so far. All of which seemed to fascinate them.

'But what about you and your mother,' Shorty said. 'Its pretty unusual...amazing really, to find a couple of American women on their own, driving through the Congo. How come you're here?'

'Ahh...' Jodie chuckled. 'Its pretty simple really. My husband is South African. He's a mining engineer and we're living in Ndola. My mother's been out here visiting us from the States and we've got a couple of weeks to ourselves now, while my husband is on a special mining course in South Africa. So...we just thought we'd take off and see a bit of the Belgian Congo.'

They explained that, after Elizabethville, they were thinking of heading to Jadotville (now Likasi) and then branching off on a minor road to Mitwabe and Manono from where they could reach Albertville (now Kalemie) on Lake Tanganyika. From there they would head north to Lake Kivu and Uganda. Their planned route was quite a different one, for the first half, from the one we had been planning, but one which ended up in the right place. We let them know in as subtle and as diplomatic a way as possible that we were also hoping to find our way to Lake Kivu and Uganda.

But...'Great. Well, I'm sure we'll meet up somewhere along the way,' was the best response we could get.

Arriving in Elizabethville after taking four hours to cover eighty kilometres over a second class road made worse by long stretches of road work underway, but no workers in sight, we said goodbye to Jodie and Elaine, thanking them for the lift, as they left for a four-star hotel and we went off to find a cheap pension for the night, not far from the centre.

Elizabethville (now Lubumbashi) was a big town... the second largest in the Congo at the time, after the capital, Leopoldville (now Kinshasa) and it had a population then of around 200,000. Lubumbashi now is pushing up towards two million. It was at the time, and still is, the main industrial centre of the Congo's south eastern mining district and, like neighbouring Northern Rhodesia, immensely rich in minerals, including cobalt, zinc, cadmium, tin, manganese and coal... but more particularly, copper, of which there are vast deposits.

As the capital of the former Katanga (now Shaba) province... Elizabethville became a centre of disaffection immediately after the Belgian Congo gained its independence in 1960 and Katanga Province, under the leadership of local politician, Moise Tshombe, seceded from the new Republic of the Congo, to form the independent Republic of Katanga. The ensuing political crisis and bloodshed, involving Congolese, Belgian and United Nations forces was not resolved for many years.

In the midst of that turmoil, in 1965, Colonel Mobuto Sesi Seko, having assumed the role of Army chief of Staff, engineered a coup d'état that brought him to absolute power as President of the Republic of Congo, whose name he later changed to Zaire. Over the succeeding three decades of his rule, notorious for corruption, nepotism, brutal suppression of human rights, and the embezzlement of a reported US $15 billion into his personal bank accounts, he drove the country to economic collapse and its people into the ground.

He was finally forced from power in 1997 by opposition forces and died of prostate cancer three months later. His successor, Laurent Kabila was assassinated in 2001 to be replaced by his son, Joseph.

The second Kabila has held on to power since then over a period in which an array of opposing forces continue to struggle for overall power in the once again renamed Republic of Congo and thousands of people continue to die annually from disease and starvation in one of the most resource-rich nations on the African continent.

As a town, Elizabethville didn't strike me as being particularly memorable...certainly not as a tourist destination. One thing I do recall and which I bet is not there now, was an amazing street market for ivory. Almost half a city block in length, along the footpath, under the colonnades of office buildings and large stores, handicraft traders were lined up with their wares laid out in front of them. Rows and rows of elegantly carved elephant tusks, ivory heads, human and animal figures, chess pieces, all manner of things for which God knows how many elephants died.

The following morning, after croissants and big cups of coffee in a sidewalk café, Shorty and I set about getting some up-to-date information and more detailed maps of the roads to the centre and north of the country, which, we were told, carried more traffic than the ones Jodie and Elaine were planning to take. After doing so at the Government Tourist Office, we were referred to another smaller travel agency nearby, which, we were told, should have details of occasional buses that ran between some of the towns to the north. Arriving shortly afterwards at the travel agency, we found Jodie and Elaine inside.

'Hi,' we said as we walked in. 'what are you doing here? Not checking on buses too?'

'No...but its almost as bad, ' Jodie muttered. 'All of the roads to Mitwaba...where we were going, are down, washed out.   Also to Manono. So we're looking into some major changes in our plans.' She swung the map around to show us...our first hint that something might be in the air. 'We're thinking of going through Jadotville, Kolwezi and Kamina. None of the roads are sealed, from here on and they say its pretty tough going...because of the rains, but we should get through. Its more like the way you said you were thinking of going, I think.'

'Yeah. That's right. We've been around to the Information Office getting some maps.'

At this stage Elaine, who was on the other side of Jodie, must have nudged her. 'Excuse me,' Jodie said and turned to talk to her mother in soft tones...not much above a whisper, that we couldn't quite hear.

'I'm sorry,' she said, turning back to us. 'Its just that we've been thinking about asking you if you felt like coming along with us. It would be good from our point of view to have a couple of guys like you who could help out with the car, if we got into any trouble along the way... which seems likely. And it should be good for you guys too, getting a lift to Uganda.'

A three thousand kilometre lift... good? You could say that again!

But somehow we managed to maintain our cool, as they'd say now, instead of leaping in the air and yelling our heads off.

'Great. Yes we'd love to come. Thanks very much. Terrific.' we said.

Jadotville, which is now called Likasi, 125 kilometres north west and Kolwezi, a further 260 kilometres, were both part of the Congo's own Copperbelt. Seven or eight large copper mines, operated by the Belgian-owned company Union Minère du Haut Katanga, were sprinkled along the route. The road between was through country much the same as that of Northern Rhodesia, monotonous, thick bush and, as I've said, somewhat more tropical in nature, but from any point of view, thick! Once off the track, on foot, you'd have had trouble covering three or four kilometres in a day. The track itself...once we started out, left everything to be desired. It was an unsealed dirt road, like every other one in the southern...and most of the eastern and central parts of the Congo as well. In the rainy season, which was now, all roads turned to mud...sometimes deep mud, that made them impassable.

The one fortunate, or sensible, aspect of the route we were taking was that, most of the time it followed a watershed, where the road was generally higher than the surrounding countryside, running along the top of ridges where possible, so that most of the rain water drained to either side. Nevertheless, we were often in difficult and muddy conditions and during the first and second days, we had to fit the equivalent of snow chains to the tyres, several times because of the mud.

These were the first occasions that Shorty and I were able to show that we had been a worthwhile investment for the two American women. Each time it was a messy and physically awkward job which they probably would have had a lot of trouble doing. In some small appreciation of this, on the evening of the third day, Jodie and Elaine had shouted us to dinner and now, in the bar of the small hotel where they were staying, Jodie was buying the drinks.

The hotels were one of the more surprising things we were to discover about this southern part of the Congo. So long as we could reach a small town, there always seemed to be a little inn, or hotel run by a Belgian, where European meals and accommodation could be found. Shorty and I hadn't been staying in the hotels, as we would have soon exhausted our funds by doing so. Instead, we'd arranged with Jodie and Elaine that we would sleep in the car...which would be good for us and also meant that we'd be able to keep an eye on the car during the nights.

'I don't know what we would have done without you guys, really,' Jodie said, as the second round of beers for Shorty and I and gin and tonics for her and her mother arrived. 'We expected the going to be a bit rough, but not quite as bad as this.'

'And who knows what it gets like further on,' Shorty noted. 'The hotel manager says he thinks its not too bad as far as Kamina, but after that, he says he's got no idea what its like.'

'Yep...' Jodie nodded. '..although the people back in Elizabethville told us that beyond Kamina, the roads become more rocky and sandy... and there's not so much mud.'

Elaine sipped on her G&T and also nodded. 'I guess we'll just have to wait and see,' she said profoundly. '...and where will you guys go when we eventually get up into Uganda? I mean which way?'

'We've been thinking about trying to get the ferry boat that runs from Juba, in southern Sudan, down the Nile towards Khartoum,' I replied. 'But we're also working on the idea of trying to head West, through French Equatorial Africa, and Nigeria and then the Sahara.'

'But surely it's impossible to hitch-hike across the Sahara?'

'You'd think so, but we've just read about an English girl who's done it...on her own.'

We talked for a while about the article we'd read and some of the exploits she'd had during the journey.

'Hitching... across the Sahara?' Jodie murmured, looking at me in a rather strange way. 'That's incredible.... Another beer?'

'Ahh... well, yes. thank you very much.'

'Shorty?'

'Yeah... great. Thanks a lot.'

'Mom?'

'Thanks darling... just one more.'

The drinks arrived and the conversation continued for about half an hour on diverse subjects, from the politics of the Congo, to copper mining in Rhodesia and the weather back home in Minneapolis. Then Elaine got up.

'Well, I'm off to bed...got to get my beauty sleep,' she smiled. 'See you in the morning boys. Goodnight Jodie.' She leant over and kissed her daughter and then turned to leave the bar.

'Night Mom. See you in the morning.'

Jodie settled back in her chair, and drained the rest of her drink.

'Same again?' she asked with a little laugh, beckoning a waiter.

The drinks came and we continued to talk on about various things...safaris she'd been on in Rhodesia and Kenya on other occasions and then it turned again to our projected route north. She opened a map and came to sit next to me. Elaine had been sitting next to me on the sofa and when she left, the space was vacant.

'Now you see, there is an alternate route around this way, from Kolwezi,' she said, pressing quite hard up against my side. I flashed a quick glance at Shorty, raising my eyebrows in surprise, while Jodie was examining the map, and Shorty raised his own in response. But he also grinned and nodded energetically. '.... but the roads to the north don't look too good,' she continued. '...unless we cut back through Kamina. Not much choice.'

'Yeah. What do you think, Shorty?' I turned the map around to him and pointed out the route she'd been discussing.

'Uh huh. It looks like pretty low-lying country...runs parallel to the river. That probably means it could flood. Hard to say. The one to the west looks better, I think.' He turned the map back. 'Anyway, I'm going to leave you guys to work it out. I'm just about flaked out. I think I'll head back to the car and catch some sleep. Do you have the keys, Jodie?'

'Sure...' She fished in the pocket of her slacks for the car keys and handed them to him. 'See you in the morning Shorty.'

Once Shorty had left, the situation developed rapidly. Jodie relaxed back into the sofa, half leaning against me and laying her head on my right shoulder. I lifted my right arm and put it around her. Since she'd looked at me like that and then sat beside me, my mind had already been in a overdrive working through the possibilities. I mean, I was only twenty years old and she was at least thirty-five...almost old enough to be my mother!

Also, for Chrissakes, I thought, she's married. Maybe she isn't getting enough at home. How was I to know? Anyway, the other problem was to do with our trip north. By hopping in the cot with Jodie, I could jeopardize the whole thing. What if her mother found out... Jesus, maybe she wants it too! I thought. But also, and most importantly, I had to consider what Jodie's reaction would be if I didn't do the right thing. That'd be the end of it for sure. I might have been only twenty, but I knew about 'Hell hath no fury....'

'Have you got a separate room?' I asked.

'Yes. Its opposite my mother's.'

'Okay, lets go,' I said.

From then on, Shorty and I had a hotel room between us each night, instead of sleeping in the car. I don't know what Jodie said to her mother to justify them paying for the extra room, but presumably it was along the lines that it was only fair that we should be treated as equals, and not as second-class citizens...or something like that. Neither Shorty nor I were particularly worried about what sort of story Jodie told...we were just pleased to have a decent bed at the end of the day.

'Now, all you've got to do,' Shorty said to me, '...is keep up the good work each night .'

And it was each night... and often through the night. And what beat me was that, while I could at least drop off to sleep in the back seat of the car from time to time during the day, Jodie had to keep awake to drive. And she did... no problems.

The road from Kolwezi to Kamina, then turning north to Kabongo, was hardly different from the one we'd been travelling from Elizabethville...bush and more bush, with what might be a passable road on one stretch, changing in moments to medium-poor, poor, then terrible, then back to passable again. At various points along the road, we would see simple native villages, mud huts with thatched roofs, but there was little else in the way of civilization between the towns that were marked on the map. Nor was there much in the way of traffic at any point, in either direction. Yet we were by no means the only white people travelling. Over a period of five days, which brought us to Kabongo, we'd seen a number of four-wheel drive vehicles, as well as a few cars and trucks driven by Europeans, many of whom would have been involved in mining, or commercial projects of one kind or another in the south eastern parts of the Congo.

On our seventh day out from Elizabethville, after travelling some 1,300 kilometres, we came at last to Kongolo and to the mighty River Congo...or at least its major tributary, the Lualaba. Where it passes

Kongolo, a small town nestled on the west bank of the river, the Lualaba has already flowed over 1,000 kilometres from its source in the southern Congo, about a hundred kilometres west of Elizabethville. And though it still had some 5,000 kilometres to run before it reached the Southern Atlantic Ocean, it was almost a kilometre wide, at the point where we would cross, and it looked very impressive. This great expanse of muddy water, deep and swollen with rains from a vast jungle catchment area, was moving relentlessly along at a speed of three or four knots.

Now there is a bridge across the Lualaba at Kongolo, but when we were there, there was only a ferry...well, a sort of ferry. The barge that carried us and about ten other vehicles across the river was flat and wide and rusty. So rusty, in fact that we all wondered if it would fall apart in mid-stream. Then, as we slowly chugged across, a sudden downpour of thick, warm rain temporarily obscured the low line of thick green vegetation on the far side of the river and it was easy to imagine the whole barge just disappearing...like something in 'The Twilight Zone', never to be seen again. However, the squall passed and we drove off safely on the northern shore, to shortly find our way to a small, rough road leading north towards a town called Kasongo, about 200 kilometres away.

As we drove, the vegetation on either side of the road grew thicker and the road itself changed imperceptibly from dirt to a sandy texture. Soon we were travelling on just two sandy tracks with grass growing in the middle. Then the grass in the middle seemed to be higher and there was grass growing on the actual tracks we were driving on. I felt this was not a particularly good sign, because it meant that very little traffic had been over it. At the same time the vegetation on either side had joined in a great canopy over the top of us, so that we seemed to be driving through a tunnel of overhanging trees and vines. And the fact that it seemed to make everything dark in the middle of the day didn't help.

'I'm not so sure about this road,' I said to Jodie. 'Is this the one that's supposed to be going to Kasongo?'

'As far as I know. We followed the sign back at Kongolo...and there haven't been any since then.'

But, while we soon left the tunnel effect of the overhanging canopy, the road continued as just a grassy track, with the grass growing to a height of thirty or forty centimetres all over.

Belgian Congo: One of several river crossings

'...I can't believe this can be right,' I said. 'There hasn't been any traffic over here for ages.'

Shorty and I with Jodie and the geologist at Kamituga.

'I can't believe this can be right,' I said. 'There hasn't been any traffic over here for ages...not with grass this high. It can't be the road to Kasongo.'

But just then we passed another track coming in at an angle, which appeared to have had more traffic over it... and we saw a small village ahead. Stopping there, we attempted to ask directions. Fortunately there was a young man there who spoke some French.

'Kasongo?.. non, non,' he shook his head at our question and pointed back the way we had come.

'He says its back the other way,' I said to Jodie.

'But it can't be,' she frowned. ' We've just come from Kongolo. I wish their names weren't all so much alike.' She turned to the young man again. 'Kasongo...this way?' she pointed ahead, the way we had been going... ' dans cette direction, n'est pas?'

'Non, non,' he replied more vehemently than before. 'La...c'est Kakole. Kakole.'

'Kakole. He says that's the way to Kakole,' Jodie muttered as we pulled our map out to consult it, '...where the hell's Kakole?'

'There.' Shorty pointed to a tiny village about 120 kilometres north east, as the crow flies, from Kasongo. 'We must be on this little track that branches off. ' He ran his finger along a thin dotted line on the map.

Jodie looked at the map. 'But it looks like Kakole is still on our route north to Lake Kivu. This track cuts about 200 kilometres or more off it. Maybe we don't have to go back through Kasongo. How far do you think Kakole is...from here on this track?' She turned again to the young man. 'Kakole... combien de distance?'

He shrugged his shoulders. 'Sais pas. Cinquante.'

'Fifty... fifty kilometres that'd be.' She looked at the map again... and the track. 'But the map says its only for cross-country vehicles. What do you think?'

We all looked at the grassy track. At least it was dry. 'Might as well,' I said.

'Yep. Lets do it,' said Elaine.

So on we went, pushing our doubts aside. And after almost three hours of the same sort of track; grassy, then sandy, then grassy again....we came at last to Kakole, a small town which brought us once more back to the main road from Kasongo to Lake Kivu. After filling up with petrol, we continued in a north-easterly direction, following a road that wasn't really much different from the track we'd been travelling on. The tyre tracks were better defined, through more usage, but grass still grew high in the centre, and always it was closely bordered with dense foliage and rainforest. At least its not muddy, I thought, and we aren't pulling chains on and off.

With our minds slightly more at ease, I began to drop off to sleep in the back seat. I had developed a facility of being able to doze briefly, even though the car might be bouncing over extremely rough and uneven roads...and then to be instantly awake and participating in the conversation, as if nothing had happened...at least that's the way it seemed to me. I don't know how long I'd been napping on this occasion, when suddenly, I was brought to an abrupt awakening by a tremendous jolt accompanied by a loud and ominous crash, with the car coming to a shuddering halt.

'Jesus... what was that?' Shorty sat up, grabbing the front seat.

'We've hit something,' Jodie cried. 'Sounded awful.'

We all jumped out of the car to try to see what had happened. Shorty and I and Jodie went down on our stomachs to look underneath the car and immediately saw that a whole section of the chassis, supporting part of the motor, had been knocked right off... or rather, was hanging by one or two broken bolts. We had hit a rock hidden by the grass in the middle of the road.

'I don't think this is the sort of thing we're going to be able to help with... unfortunately,' I said.

'Shit! Shit! Shit!' Jodie burst out. 'Oh God, what a place for it to happen. What the hell are we going to do?'

It didn't bear too much thinking about. We were more than 200 kilometres from Kasongo and it was probably the same distance ahead to Costermansville, the main town on the southern shores of Lake Kivu, with virtually nothing in between...in either direction, except perhaps an occasional village of mud huts in the middle of dense forest.

'Its not as though we're going to be able to walk anywhere, either,' Elaine noted glumly after we'd all sat down to try and think it through. 'Everything's too far.'

'We'll just have to wait,' Jodie said. 'Something will come along .'

'Yeah... I'm sure it will,' I nodded hopefully. 'There is other traffic on the road. Its been pretty thin, but I guess we would have met...what would you say, probably one car an hour, as we were driving.'

'I suppose so. But they were all going the other way. Not much heading this way.'

'Didn't seem to be,' Shorty said. 'But, it doesn't really matter. If we could get back to Kasongo, or even Kakole, we might at least get some help from there.'

Yeah... well, I guess so,' Jodie punched her fist into the palm of her other hand in frustration. '...although we don't really know. We didn't go through Kasongo. There may be nothing there. Its amazing to feel so totally powerless...not being able to do anything.'

I got back down on my stomach to look under the car. 'I'm pretty sure there's nothing we can do. If we could somehow get the car lifted and tighten the bolts up... but it looks as if the whole section has been bent... and the bolts actually torn out on one side.'

'Don't worry, Iain,' Jodie said. 'Lets' just wait and see what happens.

Within five or ten minutes of the accident, several naked children had appeared from nowhere, to stand slightly off to one side and stare in amazement at us. We tried to talk to them in both English and French, which were naturally of no use at all, but Jodie overcame the language barrier by giving them some sweets, which she had in the car. From then on they came in close, laughing and chatting away in some tribal language as they inspected the car... and us.

We sat for almost two hours surrounded by a growing number of children and one or two adults, who were also almost naked...wearing just loin cloths, who usually stayed for fifteen or twenty minutes and then moved on.

'Well, if we get people coming by at this rate, eventually they'll know about us in Kasongo, just by bush telegraph,' Jodie laughed.

As she spoke, we all jumped to our feet at the distant sound of a vehicle coming from the direction of Kasongo and within minutes a Land Rover rolled into view, eventually coming to a halt behind our car.

'Well... you look as though you're in a spot of trouble,' the driver, a sandy-haired man in his early forties, said in English.

We all looked at each other in amazement and laughed... with immense relief. Not that there was any guarantee he could help us, but just the fact that we now had someone with whom we could communicate was a huge leap forward.

We explained what had happened and he looked under the car.

'Hmm,..' he scratched his head. 'You're right. I don't think it can be fixed here. But..not to worry,' he said with a smile, almost as if he appreciated his saviour-like status with us. 'I think we can get it done another way. You see, I work at the Kamituga Mine, up the road... I'm a geologist there...from Rhodesia originally. We could probably get a breakdown truck back to help you.'

'That'd be fantastic,' Jodie said. 'But where is Kamituga? I haven't seen it on the map.'

'That's no surprise... its not very big. There's the gold mine, where I work and a small settlement nearby. Its about a 120 kilometres.'

'A hundred and twenty kilometres!' Elaine exclaimed. 'I thought you said it was just up the road?'

The Geologist laughed. 'Well, it is up the road... and there's only a couple of villages between us and the mine, so the actual distance doesn't really matter. But, anyway...' he glanced at Shorty and I, '...I could take the two ladies on with me, if you like...' and then turning back to Jodie and Elaine, '...there's a small bar and guest house where you could put up for the night. It'd probably be a good idea though, for the men to stay here to look after the car.'

Jodie and Elaine looked at us.

'Sure,' No problem,' I said. 'We'll stay and keep an eye on things here.' And... I thought, have bit of a rest.

The two women then set about getting a few clothes and other things together in a small bag to take with them, as it was clearly going to take at least a couple of days, maybe more, to sort the car out properly... if it could be done at all.

All of this took place in front of a growing audience of locals that had grown now to about twenty...most them not much more than ten or twelve years old. I wondered what they thought as they stood and watched as Jodie and Elaine climbed into the Land Rover, which then negotiated its way around the Humber to take off up the track, heading north, with us standing beside the crippled vehicle waving goodbye.

OOOOOOO

21

'ALMOST AS IF IT WERE A DREAM'

As sign language was our only means of communication, we set about trying to make friends with the people gathered around us. I showed them a little match-trick ...where you stick two matches in the sides of a matchbox and spread a third one at right angles and under a bit of tension, between them and then, with a fourth match, light the middle of the third one. It burns for a while and then suddenly flies forward a couple of metres like a miniature firework. There were 'oohs' and 'aahhs' of surprise and fascination from the group as they thronged around to get a closer look, while I did it again. Then Shorty suddenly stood on his head and the whole crowd just burst into uproarious laughter. They ran around and slapped their thighs and yelled in delight. Then I did it also and they went into an even greater frenzy of shouting and laughter.

'We should try to make a fire and some sort of shelter,' Shorty said. 'So we don't have to sit in the car all the time...particularly when it rains.'

We began to gather some twigs and branches from the ground around us, but they were totally sodden. All of the thick foliage was in a thoroughly damp condition, being subjected to a regular downpour almost every afternoon in the rainy season. But once the mob of children saw what we had in mind, they flew into action as a group, running here and there collecting branches, big palm leaves and vines...and within minutes had begun constructing, with incredible ease, a rough shelter by the side of the road near the car. Completing that, they then set and lit a fire in a few more minutes...an impossible task, with such drenched materials, for anyone not skilled in bushcraft. Now it was our turn to stand around in awe and admiration.

Next we managed to make them understand we wanted food... and water. Several of them ran off...there must have been a village nearby, although we couldn't see it, to return within less than ten minutes, with corn and eggs. Another showed us where there was a stream of clear water only fifty metres away. We offered money for the food, but they weren't interested. They wanted the empty Coca Cola bottles that they'd seen in the boot of the car. So, for four empty Coke bottles, we received four ears of corn and six eggs. We also gave them two full bottles...as a bonus, which delighted them.

As dusk and darkness closed in around us, we sat under our little shelter, by the fire...still surrounded by a score of onlookers. We boiled our eggs in a small camp saucepan and cooked the mealies on the hot coals. It was a strange feeling...being so remote from anything connected to our own culture, the two of us alone, in a vast stretch of territory where we were probably the only white people. And yet, apart from slight initial feelings of unease at the prospect of spending a night and possibly more in such circumstances, we had no really serious fears for our safety...nor need we have had.

The people of the territory we were in, were so removed from day-to-day contact with European civilization and so unused to meeting white people, that they really had no reason to be hostile or unfriendly to us. At least that was what we told ourselves at the time. Of course, closer to cities, where shanty town conditions and unemployment create resentment, we might not have been justified in feeling so secure.

As it was, however, we ate an enjoyable meal and not long afterwards, said goodnight to our friends to settle ourselves down in the front and back seats of the car for a good night's sleep.

'Your night off tonight,' Shorty said...with a laugh...but, also I thought, with a hint of envy.

Next morning we awoke to find almost as big a crowd as the previous evening, just sitting and standing around looking at the stranded car and its two occupants. I remember thinking that perhaps they hadn't gone home to sleep and had remained there all night, just in case something happened. Anyway, they stayed with us all through the morning, bringing us bananas and mangoes and listening in fascination and delight to the car radio.

Around midday some of them offered to take us into the jungle to catch monkeys...at least that's what I think they were offering. While we weren't particularly interested in *catching* monkeys, Shorty thought it might be interesting to see some, so he was preparing to go with them, while I stayed with the car, when we suddenly heard the sound of a vehicle approaching from the north. It was the breakdown truck from the mine.

To our amazement, after lifting the front of the Humber with a hoist, so the damage could be examined more clearly, they were able to effect sufficiently robust temporary repairs on the damaged piece of chassis, to allow us to drive the car. The process took a couple of hours, but by shortly after two in the afternoon, we were waving goodbye to the crowd of native onlookers, which by then numbered almost fifty, and driving off slowly down the track behind the truck. The crowd of villagers waved and the children ran after us, yelling and laughing, until we left them far behind and, as the track took a number of turns, we soon lost sight of them.

The region surrounding Kamituga is quite mountainous and, after the relatively dull and vista-less scenery of the south, it was a wonderful change. But this, according to the proprietor of the small guest house there, was only a prelude to the beauty of the Kivu district...the country surrounding Lake Kivu, now only a hundred kilometres to the north of us.

'The Kivu district,' he said, 'is the most beautiful territory in the whole of Africa.

Although his words made us keen to push on, we had to wait for a further day while more expert repairs were done on the underside of the car in the mine workshops. Of course, we could hardly believe that we'd been so lucky as to come out of an accident like that and be driving on again, within forty eight hours. And yet, by early afternoon of the second day after we'd been brought to such a frightening halt, we were on our way...making for Costermansville (now known as Bukavu), at the southern tip of Lake Kivu and less than three hours drive away. .

Its a tricky business to talk these days about what were former European colonies, in nostalgic terms...and I'm not one who would ever encourage a return to those days of European rule. I'm a Republican. I think my own country, Australia has waited far too long to drop its maternal ties to Britain, so I'm never going to say that those central

African nations would have been better off staying as they were. In fact, much of the blame for how they are now rests at the feet of those same European powers...Belgium and Portugal in particular, who handed independence to populations which had purposely been denied access to education and any real experience in how to run an independent nation.

In Congo's case, of course the blame is sheeted home to Belgium...and more particularly to its heartless 19th century monarch, King Leopold II, who has been described as one of history's greatest mass murderers. For decades he exercised personal control over the Congo Free State, as it was then known, milking an immense fortune from rubber, using slave labour and organized slaughter of the native population. The near-genocidal numbers and the scale of the terror, in which estimates for the number of people killed range from two to fifteen million, easily invite comparisons with the Holocaust in Nazi Germany, Stalin's Kulak campaigns or Cambodia's Killing Fields

Although independence and chaos were only four years away, at the time we were passing through the country, in 1956, Belgium still had a firm hold on Congo. Joseph Mobutu was just a 26-year-old clerk who'd been working for seven years in the finance department of the Force Publique, the Belgian Congolese Army. He left in that same year...1956, to become a reporter for the daily newspaper *L'Avenir* , in the capital, Leopoldville. He joined the Mouvement National Congolais (MNC) and planned his rise to power from there.

So this was the partial background to a country which, with the exception only of South Africa, was the richest nation, as far a resources are concerned, on the whole continent of Africa. The Congo has immense mineral wealth...in copper and gold and uranium, as well as a host of other rare and strategic ores, like zinc, cadmium and magnesium, as well as large reserves of silver, diamonds, coal and offshore deposits of petroleum. It also has a hydroelectric potential equal to about one sixth of the world's total.

And yet, in 1997, the year of Mobutu Sesi Seko's departure from the scene, the Republic of Congo, this vast territory of some 2.3 million square kilometres, with a population of almost forty million people, had a gross national product equal to not much more than half of the

Microsoft Corporation's annual turnover.

When we arrived in Costermansville, however, one had the impression that the country had a great future. It was apparent in the obvious prosperity of its inhabitants...mostly the white ones of course, because they earned much more money, but also, in relative terms, as in South Africa, in the black people, for whom prosperity also meant jobs. Costermansville, which was a city of probably sixty or seventy thousand people, was physically very attractive. Built on a peninsula extending out into Lake Kivu, its buildings and streets were clean and well-cared for and its position on the southern shores of Lake Kivu was one of considerable beauty.

Along parts of the lake shore, sidewalk cafés, reminiscent of France or Italy, lined the waterfront and expensive American and European cars were in evidence throughout the city...though where they could drive in the jungled hinterland beyond the Lakes District was a difficult question.

From Costermansville, we took the well-sealed road running around the western shores of Lake Kivu, still moving north, to the volcanic region of Goma and Kisenyi. These are two of the names appearing in the news over the years, in reports about the troubles in neighbouring Rwanda and Burundi, or Ruanda-Urindi as the combined territory was known then, just across the lake, because of course, the Congo, or Zaire, (as it was... and now Congo again) had been drawn into the brutal conflict and hundreds of thousands of refugees from Rwanda and Burundi have fled there. But nowhere have I read of the incredible beauty of the country. I guess the horrors of what is happening in the region now make any mention of beauty impossible...and sadly irrelevant. And yet, I remember the whole area as so astonishingly attractive. And re-reading what I wrote in my diary at the time, brings it back to me even more clearly:

"This is the heart of the famous Kivu District. A beauty so fantastic that it is hard to be imagined, surrounds us on all sides. We are on the shores of the highest lake in Africa, where the two towns of Goma and Kisenyi nestle by the lake, at the foot of three active volcanoes. Thick vegetation grows up

from the water's edge to cover the other non-volcanic mountains which encircle the calm, glistening lake and, on the opposite shore, wisps of cloud hang to the sides of the mountains just above the surface of the water."

In this magnificent setting we found what was dubbed at the time, the 'Riviera of Central Africa'. Both towns enjoyed a continental atmosphere, with the ubiquitous outdoor cafés and restaurants, similar to those we'd seen in Kivu. But there was also a bustling holiday feeling, with beaches and swimming clubs, and people in paddle boats and canoes, women in bikinis diving off swimming platforms out in the lake...scenes one would expect in the south of France, but not in central Africa. And yet, further out in the lake and all around its shores, the real Africa persisted. Unfazed by all the trappings of civilization around them, local fishermen, in long dugout canoes, continued their calling...earning a livelihood for their families in the same way it had been done there for hundreds, probably thousands of years.

From Goma, the road north ran for a short distance just inside the border with Ruindi (Rwanda), and through the Belgian Parc National de Virunga, one of only two or three places where the wild mountain gorillas survive. Just 20 kilometres to the east, was the Mount Visoke region in which the great American naturalist Dian Fossey carried out her amazing long-term studies on the lives of the mountain gorillas...and where she was tragically murdered by game poachers on December 26, 1985. Our journey was long before these studies even began and there was no mechanism in place by which tourists could get to see these magnificent animals.

Some thirty years later, however, and only two years after Dian Fossey's murder, I returned to Rwanda with my wife and a small group of other Australians to trek up into the jungled mountains of the Parc National des Volcans, on the Rwandan side of the border. There we saw, at extremely close quarters, a group of about ten or a dozen big and, in their own way, beautiful gorillas. But, even that visit...in the mid 1980s, is itself already three decades in the past. With the gorilla numbers less than 300 at that time, they were clearly threatened with eventual extinction.

Fortunately, serious and sensible conservation and preservation efforts were put in place, including a well organized and controlled process for tourists to see the gorillas. A charge of US$750 per person, per visit is now required to join a small group on a trek into the jungled mountains to see gorillas. The income from tourists, has been well managed, with a percentage of funds directed to building schools and health centres and improving roads, while providing work for locals as trackers and porters and in tourist lodges.

So... a little good news from this part of Africa for a change. Its hard to find much of it in the 21st Century, but I keep trying.

In all of the news reports about the dreadful massacres and mass killings perpetrated on each other by the Hutu and the Tutsi tribes of Rwanda and Burundi, I don't recall reading anything describing the extraordinary physiques of the Tutsi. Again, I'm sure its because of the fact that, in the context of holocaust-scale killings, the unusual height and stature of one tribe...like the beauty of the surrounding area, is almost certainly irrelevant. And yet, in a historical sense, the amazing tallness of the Watutsi as they used to be called, played quite a significant part in the relationship with their neighbours, the Hutu.

Large numbers of the Watutsi are 2.05 to 2.12 metres tall. (In imperial terms that's 6 feet 9 inches to seven feet) In other words, they're extremely tall... and also slim.

The Watutsi came to this part of central Africa from the north-east in the 14th or 15th century, seeking new rangelands. Though they were skilled warriors, they gained dominance over the resident Hutu tribespeople through a slow and basically peaceful infiltration. The Watutsi became an aristocratic minority, comprising about 10-15 percent of the population, who were, in effect, feudal overlords of the Hutu. this was achieved mainly as a result of their possession of cattle and their more advanced knowledge of warfare at the time.

Of course, at the time we were travelling along the shores of Lake Kivu and the eastern border of the Congo, all of the troubles in Rwanda and Burundi were still in the future. It was definitely a happier time. So when the opportunity came for us to see more than a hundred of the Watutusi warriors dress up for a tribal dance, we took it. It was a vivid and unforgettable experience that we were privileged to witness about forty kilometres outside of Goma, while heading north, into those crumpled ranges of the Virunga mountains running down the Great Rift Valley between Lake Kivu and Lake Edward, that are also the habitat of the mountain gorillas.

Although technically the Trust Territory of Ruanda-Urindi (now known as Rwanda and Burundi) was a separate country from the Belgian Congo, it was administered by Belgium at that time and there were, to all intents and purposes, few border formalities between the two, so tribal populations spread with relative freedom across what to them were artificial borders. And while we may have seen the Watutsi living and performing their tribal dance in what was part of the Belgian Congo...in 1956, the border was of no importance or relevance to them.

The dance of the giant Watutsi warriors was first given a mass audience in the West in the hollywood movie King Solomon's Mines, starring Stewart Granger. The dance we saw, accompanied by twenty or thirty drums and tom toms, although not hyped up with Hollywood backdrops and costumes, was still mightily impressive. A hundred of these imposing men, each holding a long spear and a small bow and arrows, and led by the eldest and tallest of the village, danced themselves into a frenzy.

But it was a dance that was totally different from the Zulu dance we had seen in South Africa. Here, in addition to chanting and moving around in a circle, bobbing and turning and waving their arms, the Watutsi would periodically stop and just start...well, bouncing... bouncing up and down. Standing straight and erect and looking directly to the front, with elbows bent and arms held loosely in front of them, though still holding their spears and bows, they would bounce themselves to extraordinary heights, as if on pogo sticks. It wasn't a leap, where the legs are bent...and the body is hurled upwards, but a bounce. With only a slight bending of the knees, it appeared as if most of the movement was achieved simply with the calf and ankle muscles...for the rest of the body remained stiffly upright, as it lifted what appeared to be about thirty centimetres off the ground. That doesn't sound much, but try it...with the rest of your body rigid and without bending down before springing up. Anyway, to see a hundred of these men...each one as tall, or taller than American basketball players, all leaping up and down like this, apparently tirelessly, was an intense and memorable experience.

Even though there were other uncommon and intriguing events to come for us, I remember thinking at the time, of the dance of the Watutsis as one of the highlights of our travels in Africa. And yet now, in the light of the horrific acts of genocide that have been perpetrated there in recent years, acts of which both the Tutsi and the Hutu have been guilty, and which have destroyed the lives of so many innocent people in that part of the world, I look back on that naive and happy journey through central Africa... almost as if it were a dream.

Once out of the mountains we headed for Ruindi Camp in the great Parc National Albert...the Prince Albert National Park, a huge game reserve covering a vast tract of flat, open territory that included the whole of Lake Edward (and through which the frontier of Uganda passed). On the other side of the border it was still a national park and game reserve, but in Uganda it was called the Queen Elizabeth National Park. The Prince Albert Reserve teemed with game, particularly elephant and buffalo. We stopped overnight in Ruindi Camp, which consisted of a large collection of comfortable rondavels, linked by garden paths to a central common area of dining and sitting rooms and surrounded by a high brush and thorn-bush fence.

In the morning when the gate was opened for us to leave the enclosure, we found a large herd of buffalo grazing right up to the entrance. They moved slowly away as Jodie edged the car out through the gate, with two other vehicles following behind and we set out onto a network of tracks within the park to see some of the other game. For much of the morning we just cruised and stopped to admire giraffe, buck, wildebeest and large numbers of hippopotami...some sleeping on the mudbanks others cavorting in the water of a small river which ran through the park...and everywhere, hundreds of elephants roaming the plains off into the distance.

Later in the afternoon, as we followed the dusty trail leading out of the park, we were brought forcibly to a halt by a herd of elephants crossing the road about fifty metres in front of us. Switching the engine off we sat immobile in the car for about half an hour counting almost eighty of the giant animals, including several young ones, as they slowly ambled across the trail, before we were able to proceed.

Leaving the park in the south western corner, we followed the only road heading north, paralleling the western side of Lake Edward for about 150 kilometres, through Butembo, to the town of Beni. Stretching off to the west of us, there was only the vast equatorial rain forest of the northern Congo, where, in some areas, one could scan the map for 200 to 300 kilometres with no sign of a road or settlement.

Not far from Beni, at a place called Oichi, we paid a visit to The African Inland Mission, which I recall being told was the world's largest leper colony. I'm not sure how accurate that was, but at one stage the widely spread and well-equipped hospital complex at Oicha housed some four thousand leprosy patients.

It was possible in those days to visit the mission...not so much as to see the patients, but the facilities, which the missionaries were happy and reasonably proud to show off to foreign callers like us, who came by relatively infrequently. The missionaries were apparently mainly drawn from the United States, although there was a New Zealander there named Bennett Williams, who introduced himself to us while we were being shown an area where hand crafts and other skills were taught to the patients.

'I understand one of you is from Australia?' he said, shaking our hands. 'Its not quite New Zealand...but its about as close as you can get to it and...I suppose the next best thing.'

We laughed and began questioning him about what he was doing at the Mission and how he'd come here. He was tall and rangy with dark hair and appeared to be about forty years old.

'I've been here for two years now,' he said. 'I was in New Guinea for five years before this and I thought for a while, when I first came here that I was destined to live the rest of my life in the tropics... but at the end of next year I'm going to spend some time in Britain.

'What will you be doing there?' Elaine asked.

'Its one of the main offices that deal with the activities of the Mission...because we do have other Missions in several different parts of Africa. I'll be doing administrative work there for a year. It'll be a good change... although I really love it here.'

'How long would you normally spend in any one place?' I asked him.

'Oh two to three years would be the general rule, but it can be longer... or shorter.'

An older man...an American missionary, joined us briefly as we sat and talked, and for a while we discussed other missionary work in different parts of the world, as well as advances in the methods of dealing with leprosy. These involved the long-term use of sulfone drugs, which apparently brought about an immediate arrest of the infection and improvement in most cases. (In the early 1980's however, health officials began to notice a worldwide increase of resistance to these forms of chemotherapy and predicted that the incidence of leprosy might once again begin to rise.)

'Oddly enough, we've noticed that the pygmy people from these parts hardly seem to be affected by the disease...' Bennett said. 'probably because they rarely come into contact with other native tribes.'

'Pygmies?' I said. 'We were talking about them the other day... about them being somewhere in this area. Are they near here?'

'Oh yes...' he replied, '...in the Ituri Forest...that's the huge area of jungle which begins about 35 kilometres north of here. But they are a nomadic people...always on the move, so they are hard to keep track of. We do know of one small group that has apparently been camped in the same place for the past week. I've been thinking of going to see if I can find them. Would you like to come along tomorrow?'

Shortly after breakfast on the following morning, five of us...that is, Shorty and I, plus Jodie and Elaine, with Bennett driving, set off in one of the mission's Land Rovers, on a rough dirt road that wound its way into increasingly dense rain forest. The Ituri, one of the world's great equatorial forests, is believed to cover almost 50,000 square kilometres...about two fifths of the whole country, but in 1956 its southern and western boundaries had not yet been defined.

After almost fifty kilometres, we stopped at a small village of wattle and daub huts on one side of the road, under giant trees, that was inhabited by normal-sized tribal people. Descending from the vehicle, Bennett began to talk haltingly to one of the men in the local dialect. After a few minutes, during which the man had nodded several times, Bennett turned to us.

'He's going to lead us to the pygmy settlement. Its a couple of kilometres from here. He's not sure if they're still there, but he thinks they might be. He also understands a bit of the pygmy language.'

Following in single file, along a barely visible track, we splashed through mud and slush to keep up with our guide as he led us deeper and deeper into the jungle.

'What do the pygmies live on in here?' I asked Bennett as we walked. 'I mean what do they do?'

'Well, as I mentioned, they're nomads, but they are also superb hunters, so it is very easy for them to live off the land. They collect jungle fruits and edible plants and they can kill almost any animal they come upon...monkeys, jungle cats, even elephants. They trade ivory, for example, with local villagers for arrowheads and other types of food.'

We had covered almost a kilometre and, as Bennett was about to go on, three pygmy women carrying bunches of bananas on their heads suddenly appeared on the trail ahead of us, emerging from what appeared to be impenetrable undergrowth on either side of the track. After a brief conversation accompanied by many hand gestures, between our guide and the three women, they took over the forward position and began leading us.

All three of them were no taller than 1.3 metres and were dressed in nothing but a small piece of soft bark, about 12 cms by 5 cms, which hung loosely from a leather thong tied around their waists.

For another kilometre we followed them, through an archway of tall trees, hanging vines and creepers, walking all the while on a silencing carpet of grass and lichens. To our sides and above us were a host of multi-coloured flowers including scores of different varieties of wild and beautiful orchids which clung in big clusters on almost every large tree, while high above, an incessant chatter from hundreds of monkeys accompanied us, as they followed through the branches.

Then suddenly we came to a little clearing, not much more than about ten metres square, in which five tiny palm leaf huts were erected. This was the pygmy village...a temporary settlement which would probably have been erected in half a day and abandoned whenever they decided to move on. About fifteen men women and children were the inhabitants. The children ran and hid in the huts, while the men and women stood staring at us in quiet fascination. They spoke first to the three women with the bananas who had led us in and then to our native guide. Several of the men held small, but lethal bows and arrows in their hands, as our guide addressed them. The guide turned and spoke at intervals to Bennett.

'Don't worry about the bows and arrows,' Bennett said to us shortly. 'They're not intended to intimidate us. Apparently they were about to leave on a hunting foray when we arrived.'

After a few minutes, curiosity got the better of the children and they began to emerge from the huts. They were both amazed and puzzled by us all, but particularly Shorty, whose blond hair and blue eyes fascinated them. As they came closer, they gathered around him, prattling away, pointing and laughing. They seemed to be similar in size and shape to normal sized children...although we didn't know how old they were. Their parents, though not much bigger than their children in height, were perfectly proportioned people... in miniature.

For a few sweets (money was of no use to them) we bought some of their weapons as souvenirs and after looking inside their huts, delighted them by taking some photographs, although I'm pretty sure they didn't know what it was all about.

As we examined their bows and arrows, one of the older men showed us a little container of poison in which the tips of the arrows were rubbed when they went hunting. Through Bennett...our guide explained that with these tiny arrows and spears, they could hunt and kill a huge elephant. Once hit with dozens of poisoned arrows, the pygmies would run in and out underneath the dying beast, as it raged and thrashed about, jabbing at its heart with more poison-tipped spears until at last, overcome, it would fall to the ground dead. The pygmies then performed what was called 'the elephant dance'. Only witnessed by a few white people, it is apparently an incredible spectacle.

Our walk back to the first village, where we had left the Land Rover, was interrupted by a sudden torrential downpour of rain. The thunderous roar as it crashed on the canopy of thick foliage overhead was deafening. The cover was so dense that little direct sunlight could penetrate in mid afternoon even under clear conditions. But now, with storm clouds overhead, the jungle path was darkened. For a while the great arch of trees and vines above protected us from the deluge, but soon it was coming through...thick, drenching, warm rain that soaked us to the skin and made hundreds of little rivulets on the path. But the rain stopped almost as quickly as it had begun and in the sudden quiet and stillness, we made our way along the sodden path back to the car.

Shorty and I were walking at the end of the file when, about ten minutes before we reached the road, a tall native emerged from the bushes and motioned for us to come aside while he talked to us.

At first we were taken by surprise and slightly frightened by his appearance, but seeing his smile and sensing something a little out of the ordinary, we let the rest of the group walk on and waited to see what he wanted. From his pocket he produced two ink bottles full of small gold-like nuggets weighing together, we guessed, about a half a kilo. He spoke no French or English, so our only communication was by gestures and sign language. He indicated that he would give us both bottles for the equivalent in Belgian Congo Francs of about £20.

'What do you reckon?' I said to Shorty. 'Do you think its real ?'

'I wouldn't have a clue. But if it is, its worth a hell of lot more than that.'

'I know. But how can we tell? I mean it *looks* real.'

'Yes... but I don't know if there's any gold around here, and sometimes they can make things look like real gold that aren't. Anyway, if we spent £20 on this, we wouldn't have much money left to get through to Europe.'

'True... but it sure is tempting.'

In the end we told the man that we didn't want the bottles, even though he dropped the price to the equivalent of fifteen pounds. H e disappeared down a side track while we hurried to catch up to the others. The whole encounter had lasted only a few minutes, but it left us talking about the possibilities for days. The gold, if it had been real and we'd been able to sell it in Europe, would have been worth at least ten to fifteen times the price asked and at today's gold values would be worth over $20,000.

Of course engaging in gold transactions of that nature would probably have involved heavy penalties...although we weren't sure. In any event we decided to keep what money we had intact for the road ahead and leave the gold for our dreams.

From the Inland Mission, where we said goodbye to Bennett, we turned south for the first time since we'd joined Jodie and her mother, and made for the Uganda border at Kasindi. Emerging from the close confines of the Ituri Rainforest, we drew near the great range of mountains known as the Ruwenzori. We had caught distant glimpses to the east of the rugged, snow-capped line of mountains as we were driving north to Beni, but now they came into much sharper focus.

These dramatic mountains were first described by Ptolemy, (Claudius Ptolemaeus) the ancient Greek astronomer, geographer and mathematician, in the second century AD. He called them The Mountains of the Moon and identified them as the source of the Nile. There is no suggestion in his description that he actually saw them, but just the fact that a range of mountains thousands of kilometres south of the Mediterranean, in central Africa should be known and described with surprising accuracy in such ancient times, is amazing in itself. More than seventeen centuries passed...until the late nineteenth century, before the European world heard again of the Mountains of the Moon, when the American explorer, Stanley 'rediscovered' them during his African journeys from 1887-89.   Now known as the Ruwenzori Mountains, they form a spectacular central African scene which, from almost any angle, is quite stunning.

Standing out over the jungle, huge, dark and craggy peaks rise to permanently snow-capped summits, of which the highest, Mount Stanley, is over 5,000 metres high. And here, right on the equator, they form a giant ridge known as the Congo/Nile Divide, down which, on opposite sides, run the tributaries of two of the mightiest rivers in the world. Those tributaries joining the Congo River fall to the west and travel some four thousand kilometres to the Atlantic Ocean. Here too, on the western side of these ranges, were the tributaries of the longest river in the world, the Nile...which we were destined to see at closer quarters in the weeks to come and to follow it for much of its 6,000 kilometre length, all the way to its mouth, at Alexandria, on the Mediterranean Sea.

Visible for hundreds of kilometres on either side of the border with Uganda, the majestic Mountains of the Moon formed our last view of the Belgian Congo as we crossed into Uganda at Mpondwe and continued on towards Fort Portal and, on the following day, to the Ugandan capital, Kampala, on Lake Victoria.

oooooo

UGANDA

UGANDA / SOUTH SUDAN & SUDAN

22

'I SHOULD ARREST YOU'

Kampala was the end of the line for Shorty and I as far as our seemingly endless lift with Jodie and Elaine was concerned. They planned to head across to Nairobi and then turn southward through Tanganyika to eventually return to Jodie's home in Northern Rhodesia, while we would be continuing north to the Sudan.

'If you guys ever make it to Minneapolis, come and say hello,' Elaine said as we made our farewells and they prepared to drive on. We had spent three weeks with them and covered over three thousand kilometres, in what I suppose you could call a successful symbiotic relationship. They had insisted we spend one final night at their expense at a hotel in Kampala and, as usual, after Elaine had gone to bed, I had spent much of the night in Jodie's room. Now she would be returning, within a couple of weeks, to her husband.

It was a strange feeling and I'm sure I was rationalising it all, but I didn't feel as if I had been an adulterer trying to win her affections... or that she was really being unfaithful to her husband. Of course she was...and it was adultery, but somehow I didn't feel the least bit guilty. We had naturally become close to each other, but she was not in love with me, nor I with her. It had just been sex rearing its enjoyable head and we had taken advantage of it for three weeks...and that was the end of it.

Jodie gave me a circumspect hug and kiss on the cheek and then settled into the driver's seat of the car, beside her mother. 'I just don't know what we would have done without you two. It made a hell of a difference having you along. Maybe we can meet again.' She started the car.

'Yes,' I said. ' You never know,'...although we both knew we would never meet again. 'And...we feel the same way too,' I said. 'We don't know what we would have done without you two. It was a great ride!' I smiled and winked at Jodie.

She winked back, and also smiled. Then she slipped the car into gear and, with a wave, turned into the bustling traffic outside the hotel and was gone.

In Kampala we tried in vain to obtain permits to enter the Sudan. It seemed that, firstly, a separate permit was needed to enter the southern provinces of the Sudan, as a bloody revolt had just been quelled there and the whole area was still under martial law. Then, naturally, a visa for the Sudan was required, plus a visa for the next country on...in this case, Egypt, plus tickets for the whole of the journey by boat and train through the Sudan. It was our Cairo dilemma revisited.

But the big problem was that there was nowhere in Uganda where any of these things could be obtained...nowhere in East Africa in fact, except for the Egyptian visas, which could be obtained in Nairobi, almost seven hundred kilometres to the east.

'But what's the use of going and getting our Egyptian visas in Nairobi,' Shorty said, '... if we can't get the rest of the stuff. We'd be no better off.'

'We could just hitch to the border and see what the story is there.' I said.

'I'm game,' said Shorty. So off we headed towards the tiny town of Nimule on Uganda's northern border with the Sudan, some 500 kilometres north of Kampala.

Passing through Uganda so quickly, as we did, we had little time to appreciate what a fantastic place it was then...a mini-paradise in central Africa. Like the area around Lake Kivu, Uganda used to be described by people who lived there, both black and white, as The Pearl of Africa.

But in the decades that have followed its independence, in 1962, Ugandans, like their neighbours in Rwanda, Burundi and the Congo have been subjected to almost equal amounts of sorrow and prolonged brutal genocide.

Nearly all of its woes have been due to tribal conflict. Milton Obote, of the northern Langi tribe, was elected the first prime minister after independence. He soon ousted Sir Edward Mutesa, who was the hereditary King of the Baganda tribe, to install himself as President. Next, Obote abrogated the constitution and destroyed the political structure Uganda had inherited from Britain at independence, and established a one-party police state with an elaborate network of spies. Using the army, under the command of a young colonel (later self-styled General) Idi Amin, he systematically oppressed various ethnic and tribal groupings in order to stay in power.

In January, 1971 Idi Amin led the army in a coup d'etat from which Obote escaped into exile in Tanzania. Amin's brutal regime lasted eight years, in which time he and his thugs embarked on an orgy of bloodshed in which some 300,000 Ugandans were shot, tortured and battered to death.

But when Idi Amin was overthrown by the Tanzanian army in 1979 and Milton Obote was returned to power the following year, Uganda's troubles were far from over. Seeking revenge on Amin's Kakwa tribe and others, Obote's forces laid waste the land, murdered untold thousands of people and drove upwards of half a million people into Zaire and Sudan as refugees. Then, in what must rank as one of the worst atrocities in history, his army, trying to exterminate guerrillas led by Yoweri Musaveni, slaughtered between 300,000 and 500,000 people, before being eventually defeated by Musaveni's National Resistance Army in 1985.

Musaveni took over the presidency of Uganda the following year and he has been credited with restoring relative stability and economic prosperity to Uganda following those years of civil war and repression under Milton Obote and Idi Amin.

His National Resistance Movement (NRM) ran Uganda as a one-party state until a referendum brought back multi-party politics in 2005. In 2006 and 2011, he won fresh terms in office in presidential elections and again in February, 2011 and 2016, having amended the constitution in 2006 to remove the previous limit on the number of terms a president could serve.

He is now reportedly grooming his son Muhoozi Kainerugaba to *succeed him, having recently promoted him to the rank of Major General in the Ugandan Army.*

Shorty and I reached Nimule, on the Sudan border, the day after leaving Kampala only to find no full time customs or immigration officials at all...for either country, established in Nimule. A white police officer, who acted in an ad hoc immigration capacity on the Ugandan side, told us that the nearest Sudanese immigration officials were at Juba, some 200 kilometres further north into Sudanese territory.

'I don't know what the situation is up there,' he said. 'The whole thing has been pretty chaotic in this part of the world during the past year. There's been some sort of an uprising there, but, although the Government seems to be back in control now, nobody's very sure what's going on. Nothing seems to have filtered down to here. I don't even know if you'll be allowed to travel.'

'Are the river boats running from Juba?' I asked.

'I think they are, because there is road traffic coming through here that is taking stuff up to Juba...wheat and grains, that sort of thing and they're coming back for more, so I presume the river traffic is also functioning. The only thing I can say is to go up and find out. But don't be surprised if they won't let you travel.'

The fact that there were occasional trucks making the journey through to Juba made our task of getting there considerably easier. In fact the truck on which we'd travelled most of the way from Kampala to Nimule had been going through to Juba, but we had left it at Nimule to try to find out more about the immigration requirements. Now, after waiting only a few hours, we found ourselves on the back of another truck, travelling towards Juba, where Noel and I had landed in the RAF Valetta, some ten months previously.

From Juba we knew that the only possible method of surface transportation northward was by riverboat to Kosti, a ten-day trip through the swamps and papyrus reeds that cover thousands of square kilometres of the southern Sudan. There are no roads, just the meandering Nile river that snakes its way through endless near figure-of-eights, covering probably three or four times the distance between Juba and Kosti as the crow flies. But at the time of our arrival in Juba, we knew little of what lay ahead.

SUDAN

The actual township of Juba, which Noel and I had not seen on our transit south, having only spent time at the airstrip, was a shabby, muddy river trading town...to put it kindly, with a population of about

25,000. It was the southern terminus for the river boats and barges that plied back and forth between there and the ports down the river to Kosti. It was however, also becoming something of a road traffic hub, with roads leading off to Uganda, Kenya and the Congo.

It would have been impossible to predict, certainly for two young backpackers like Shorty and I, that Juba would, in the years ahead...a very long way ahead, 55 years actually...that Juba, with a population approaching half a million, would become the capital of a new nation, the Republic of South *Sudan, which, as a result of a referendum in 2011, gained its independence from Sudan.*

As the main town of Southern Sudan, Juba had, even from 1955...the time of the main territory's move to independence, become the spearhead of southern resistance to what was felt to be northern and Arab, or Muslim domination of the country. The southern troops in Juba had mutinied in late 1955, just before Sudan's break from Britain and Egypt.

After a six-month state of emergency, the authority of the central government in Khartoum over the southern provinces had been reestablished, but resistance to leadership from the north bubbled away beneath the surface.

Following Sudan's first independent elections in 1958, the continued neglect of the south by the central government as far as education, infrastructure and health facilities, led to uprisings, revolt and a low-level civil war between the north and south which continued until 1972. An agreement in March of that year, granting regional autonomy to the South, supposedly put an end to the fifteen year rebellion, but it surfaced again in the 1980's with a vengeance, continuing a conflict in which an estimated 2.5 million people have died in the region from either fighting or starvation. At the turn of the century, more than a million were facing famine.

By 2011, the Government in Khartoum had come to realise that independence for the South was inevitable and the referendum which brought independence also saw veteran politician Salva Kiir Mayardit, a member of the Dinka tribe, assume the role of the country's first president. However a power struggle then broke out in 2013 between Kiir and his deputy, Nuer tribesman, Reik Machar. Fighting followed between their supporters, sparking another civil war in which some 300,000 people have died and some half a million fled to neighbouring countries, including Reik Machar. Numerous ceasefires were negotiated and Machar returned in 2016 to assume the role of Vice President, only to flee once more when fighting broke out again.

Back in 1956, arriving only a few months after Sudan's (Northern Sudan's) independence in 1956, Shorty and I were, in retrospect, lucky to have gotten as far as Juba. The Sudanese immigration officer, when we finally located him, was shocked to learn that we had no special permits to be in the southern Sudan. He was a tall, heavily built black man with three horizontal scars on each cheek and a frown on his face. Not an auspicious start, I thought. But at least he spoke reasonable English.

'You have your visas for the Sudan, though?' he asked.

The temperature was oppressive and humid. We were all sweating... we perhaps a little more than he, through apprehension.

'No. We haven't been able to find anywhere in East Africa to get them...'

'What? No visas? And what about tickets... you have tickets?'

'No. We're sorry...but there are no Sudanese consulates in East Africa. Its been impossible to get any information and...'

'You must have a visa. You should have a permit to even be here. I should arrest you. This is impossible. You must return to Uganda.'

'Oh please,' Shorty said. 'Can't we get a permit... and a visa here?'

'No. Its against the regulations. You should not be here without a permit. It has been very dangerous to be here for the past six months. It has been totally closed to foreigners. And anyway, you need money to...'

'But we have money...' I said. '...enough to get us through the Sudan and...'

'...and we have more money waiting for us in Cairo,' Shorty lied.

'If we could just pay for our tickets on the boat...' I went on, '...then we will take the train from Khartoum to Wadi Halfa. Then we would be able to get through to Cairo. Please can't you help us? Can't we get a visa here?'

We continued in this vein for at least ten minutes, I think because we detected from the beginning that, although he may have looked intimidating, he was basically friendly and did not really want to send us back to Uganda. So we persevered, pulling out all the stops.

'We're from Australia and South Africa...' I said. '...and we've come all this way to learn about your country. If we turn back, we'll never be able to see it. This is a once in a lifetime trip for us. Okay, so we haven't got as much money as the rich tourists, but we can get by with what we've got. We travel with the local people, eat what they eat, sleep where they sleep...that's how we get to know it properly. Please don't turn us back now.'

He had gradually been softening, his arguments becoming less assertive, until finally he acquiesced.

'Listen to me. I will talk to the captain of the boat. If you can pay him and he will take you, I will stamp your passports with permission to enter the Sudan. Three weeks...that's all. You can have a temporary permit valid for three weeks. In that time, you must obtain your visas for Egypt...in Khartoum and be out of the Sudan...okay?'

'Okay,' we both said in unison, breathing big sighs of relief.

There was a slight hiccup when he spoke to the captain of the vessel, and the captain informed him that first and second-class passengers had to book and pay in advance and that he could not accept such passengers without tickets that had already been purchased.

But when we told the captain that we did not want first or second-class fares (a dubious privilege anyway), but would travel third-class on the deck of one of the barges being towed and pushed by the river-boat, along with the locals and their cattle and livestock, the problem disappeared and the formality was waived. We could pay the captain direct for third class passages, the equivalent of £2-10-0 each, for the whole trip.

Our accommodation would now be the best we could do for ourselves on what was, to put it mildly, a stinking, crowded barge... one of eight, that were tied by wire hawsers to the front, back and sides of the steamer. For food, we also had to provide for ourselves for the ten day journey. Luckily we had plenty of time, as the vessel wasn't due to sail until the following morning, to stock up a good supply of tinned food, which we thought would probably be the safest food to eat.

The river at Juba was probably half-a-kilometre wide, a great muddy expanse of water flowing through flat countryside lined on both sides by dense dense bush and scrub country. Great floating islands of reeds and grass, some of them even sporting small shrubs and trees, would float by, eventually to be trapped in the vast swampy labyrinth of the Sudd that lay ahead of us on our departure from Juba.

Each of the barges attached to the boat was simply a large metal rectangle with a flat deck open on all sides and a corrugated iron roof erected on metal supports over the entire area. Beneath the deck were holds which were filled with cargo that included rice, millet and other grains and general cargo destined eventually for the capital, Khartoum. The barge we selected to travel on was at the front and on the right. Our living space on it was minimal and confined to an area not much larger than that covered by our groundsheets and sleeping bags.

Around us, probably a hundred of our fellow third class passengers were also doing the best they could for themselves in trying to make space to live, eat and sleep for the next ten days or so. And this scene was duplicated on all of the other barges. They were an amazing mix of near naked tribespeople, others wearing western type clothes such as shirts and trousers or dresses, and Arabs in long white djalabeas and turbans. Many of them had brought along chickens, ducks and even turkeys in cages which they were taking either for sale, or for their own use at their destination. But, as we were to discover, a significant number of these birds would be slaughtered for the cook pot on the way. Goats and sheep were also tied up in several places near us on the barge and quite a few of them would also not finish the journey for the same reason.

The smell from all of these animals defecating and urinating, plus the strong body odour from the scores of people around us...and ourselves, of course, as we couldn't wash properly for ten days, was sufficiently powerful on occasions to make you gag. But I guess being in the midst of it for long enough, we started to get used to it.

Not long after our departure from Juba we were treated to a demonstration of an extraordinary maritime manoeuvre which was to become a regular feature of the first three or four days of our journey through the Sudd. But to describe it, it is necessary to visualise the huge amalgamation of barges of which our floating menagerie was comprised.

Picture a dirty white riverboat, about thirty, or forty meters long, two decks of cabins opening on to railed companionways which extended around the ship on both levels, with an open deck and the bridge above them on the roof. Tied on either side of the vessel were two of the big barges, equal in length to the riverboat. With three more barges tied on behind and three more on the front, we made up a nine-part monster of a vessel, with the power and control mechanism in the middle. But the control...or steering capabilities of such an unwieldy craft were minimal.

We approached the first of perhaps a hundred hairpin bends in the meandering course of the river as it started to wind its way through and across hundreds of kilometres of swampy lowlands and bush country. How to get around the bend? The Captain simply drove the whole collection of barges...at almost full (of course not very high) speed into a selected point on the muddy banks of the inner corner of the hairpin bend. Loud shrieks of wire hawsers being stretched to their limit rent the air as they were tensed and pulled tight when one part of the linked structure (the front three barges) stopped dead on the mud bank and the river began pushing the rest of the body of the vessel around to face the other direction. The front three barges soon broke free from the mudbank and the whole lot drifted backwards into the hairpin. But as soon as we passed the bend, we would be facing the right direction to continue forwards down the river. The captain then gave the vessel full power again and off we went, only to repeat the process a kilometre or so further on... and so on and so on... for three days and nights.

After the first couple of days we had become used to the endless screaming sounds of the wire hawsers being pulled and stretched to the limit as we crashed into and ricocheted off the riverbanks. And then, almost without noticing, our strange agglomeration of barges slid into new territory where we were no longer treated to an endless cacophony of rending metal and where we found ourselves gliding smoothly over long stretches of the river where the course, though narrow, was reasonably straight.

This was that part of the Bhar El Jebel, (the Arabic name for the region) which is also known as the 'Sudd', the largest swamp in the world where, ironically, the going became somewhat easier as a result of regular traffic by large river craft like ours. Without it, the open water we now plied would soon have been swallowed up in the marshes, reeds and floating islands of this immense swamp, where the White Nile spreads itself out over 130,000 square kilometres of territory and where it loses half of its water in evaporation and ground seepage and yet still leaves the enormous volume of water that flows through eventually to Egypt and the Mediterranean.

From the level of the deck of our barge, all that could be seen of the 'Sudd', on either side of the channel were walls of green papyrus reeds that grew, tightly packed, to a height of about three or four meters. From time to time Shorty and I would climb up and sit on the roof of the barge, where we could not only see over the top of the papyrus reeds, but also pick up what little breeze there was. From this vantage point we were presented with what appeared to be a solid green carpet stretching to a flat horizon all around us. No sight of human habitation anywhere.

And yet, amazingly, there were humans in there. Perhaps three or four times during the course of a day, we would pass a lone native paddling a dugout canoe, or an individual standing on a small mudbank...usually on one leg like a stork, with the other crooked, so the foot rested above the knee of the upright leg, while he leant on a spear and watched us glide by. They were all very tall, slim and totally naked. These, we learnt, were members of the Dinka and Nuer tribes, who inhabit the territory along both banks of the river, in much of the Sudd and southern Sudan. How they came to be where they were, or found a way to live in this immense and inhospitable, marshy land was difficult to comprehend.

And it was dangerous! Hardly an hour would pass that we didn't see crocodiles basking on a mudbank, or the tell tale V-shaped wake of a croc's snout as it swum in open water or by the river bank.

It is these Nuer and Dinka tribespeople, as well as the Nuba, from a little further north, who were soon to be threatened with famine, as a result of the emerging civil war between north and south. More than a million were expected to be starving because they have been prevented by the conflict from planting their crops.

That was in 1956. But things haven't changed much as far as the direness of the overall situation in the new South Sudan. The war with the north may have been settled, and there's not the same threat of widespread starvation, but the Nuer and the Dinka people in the south are continuing their own conflict. As outlined a few pages ago, with South Sudan's split from the main country, the chaotic disputes between the two Nilotic tribes has kept the country in crisis after crisis and a repeat of previous horrific massacres is possible at any time.

The Dinka and the Nuer are *similar in terms of language, culture and livelihoods, with the Dinka being in the majority in the north of the new country and the Nuer in the south. During the dry season, different sections of the Dinka and Nuer have had to migrate in search for wetter places, often on land claimed by other tribes. These initially basic issues, have become dramatically escalated by the decades-long conflict with the north that saw the introduction of huge quantities of arms into the region as well as the growth of private armies and competition between tribal war lords.*

There is no realistic long term resolution to the situation in sight.

Apart from an elderly American missionary and his wife, who were travelling first class on the steamer and with whom we could have little contact, we were the only white people on board. So we had no real conversation outside ourselves. We played cards and read and watched the activities of our fellow passengers who, like us, were crammed into uncomfortably small spaces.

The heat was oppressive and we were, day and night, in a continual bath of perspiration that was alleviated briefly most afternoons by torrential downpours of rain. Shorty and I became objects of great amusement when we started the practice of standing out in our swimming costumes whenever it rained. There was a small part of the barge at one end which was not covered by the roof. There the rain fell directly onto the deck leaving a space which was naturally not occupied by any of the other passengers. When the afternoon thunderheads built up and eventually let loose their load of water, Shorty and I would stand in our swimmers in the warm rain washing ourselves with soap... to the accompaniment of gales of laughter from our fellow travellers.

Preparing meals for the hundreds of people on board the barges was a continual and barely believable process. It was performed mainly by the women in each family or group of passengers... although the men generally slaughtered the larger animals. All day long and half the night the screeching of poultry mingled with the baying of lambs and goats as, one by one, they fulfilled their unfortunate destiny. Uncooked meat was hung from the metal ribs under the roof, sometimes for days, before the flies were brushed off and it was cooked and eaten. We were often offered pieces of meat or chicken to cook and eat ourselves, but we always declined politely, with thanks, and stuck to our own relatively straightforward regimen of tinned food.

We had a small camp cooker on which we boiled all our drinking water or made tea or coffee. We also had water purifying tablets if necessary. Most of our meals were made by simply opening cans of tinned meat or sardines or spaghetti, or some other canned food. We had tinned cheese, powdered milk and sometimes fresh vegetables like tomatoes, which we could buy...along with more tinned food, at Arab stores in the occasional small villages we would stop at, every couple of days, along the way.

Gradually the landscape was changing. We were out of the great swampland of the Sudd and the vegetation on either side of the river was becoming increasingly sparse. Within thirty-six hours we had passed into country that was so different to that of the previous week, it was difficult to imagine the two regions existing side-by-side. Now it was arid and rocky territory, with a line of barren hills on the horizon that ran down towards the river ahead of us. The temperature stayed high, but the air was now dry and when the wind blew, it whipped up great whorls of dust in the landscape on either side.

It was in this sort of territory that we stopped one day at a small river town some fifty or sixty kilometres to the west of Malakal, which was approximately two thirds of the way through our journey between Juba and Kosti. And, although I don't recall the name of the town...I think it was Tonga, I'll never forget our first sight of Nuba tribesmen when we went ashore there. This part of Sudan, though to Western eyes relatively uninviting, is occupied by a mix of Arab traders and a Sudanese tribe called the Nuba. The Nuba are agriculturalists, but also keep cattle, sheep, goats and donkeys and consequently are considered to be amongst the wealthiest tribes in Sudan. Like the Nuer and Dinka tribes further south, they are tall, thin and statuesque, with skin so black it seems almost midnight blue. And totally naked.

Even in the towns, where Arab men and women and Europeans

like ourselves, might be walking around, the Nuba make no concessions. They are one of the few tribes in the world who, from the time of their birth to the day they die, never wear a stitch of clothing... at least as far as the men are concerned. The women do condescend to drape a small piece of cloth over their shoulders when they come into a town, but nothing else. And when they are in their own homes or villages, they too wear nothing.

These were the people who were featured in the remarkable and fascinating books by the German photographer Leni Reifenstahl called 'The Last of the Nuba' (1973), and 'The People of Kau' (1978).

From our point of view, it was an extraordinary...if not amazing experience to see three or four of these totally naked men strolling though the town with their long spears held in their hands, stopping to look at items and foodstuff for sale at the Arab market stalls. Then later, as our boat completed the process of loading and unloading cargo, they would stand on the river bank, amongst the crowds of other locals, watching as we pulled out into the stream, with a couple of loud blasts on the horn, to continue on our way north.

Malakal, a relatively well-developed town of about 15,000 people at that time, was our next stop, later the same day. The town sits on the right bank of the river just past the confluence of the Nile, with the Sobat River. We stayed only about two hours to offload some cargo before moving on.

From Malakal there remained a further 500 kilometres of river before we would have to leave our barge at Kosti...not that we wouldn't be pleased to do so. The boat was now travelling at a pace...if you can call six to seven kilometres and hour 'a pace', on broad, open stretches of water through low, flat desert country and we could sense the end of our barge journey coming up. There were a few more stops along the way at small isolated river settlements like Kaka and Aworo Kit, but we cruised straight past some of the other towns which we were told were connected by road to Kosti, Wad Medani and Khartoum to the north and were therefore not so dependent on passing river traffic.

Nuba tribesman: They are one of the few tribes…who never wear a stitch of clothing.

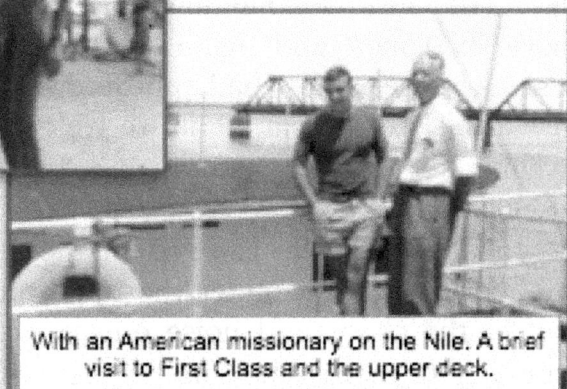

With an American missionary on the Nile. A brief visit to First Class and the upper deck.

'…off the train and into the dusty streets of Khartoum.'

'…we left the Nile to rattle out into the wastes of the Nubian Desert.'

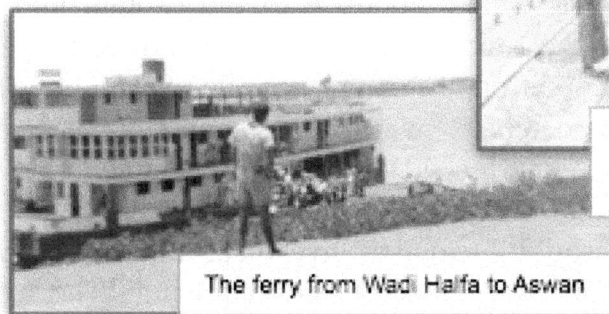

The ferry from Wadi Halfa to Aswan

It was during these last few days between Malakal and Kosti, that we were invited to visit the First Class sections of the boat. The American missionary, whose name we learned was Harlan Jones, had caught sight of us many times on the barge and we had exchanged waves. We had finally met and talked for a while when we had all been ashore in Tonga and again in Malakal. After a request from the missionary, the captain had approved us visiting him and his wife on the upper deck of the boat while we were in port, but not while we were travelling, presumably so as not to offend the other third class passengers.

In any event we revelled in the relative cleanliness, space and temporary peace and quiet the opportunity presented, as a welcome relief to the chaos and noise on our barge. The filth and mess that accumulated there, and on the other barges...from the cattle and livestock and from the cooking and other activities of all the people on board during the course of the voyage, had become indescribable. At the time it was nightmare and now I look back on it in some amazement that we did it at all. Shorty and I knew that we and the missionary and his wife, had been the first white people to have travelled in Southern Sudan since the recent revolt. But we also learnt from the captain of the vessel as we finally disembarked in Kosti, that, as far as he knew, we were the first white people to have ever made the journey as third class passengers.

Kosti was still some 400 kilometres from the capital, Khartoum but, as there was a rail link between the two, via Wad Medani, it was apparently much faster and easier for both people and cargo to cover the distance by train. So, on June 4, 1956, after just on ten days on the boat, we packed up our rucksacks, waved goodbye to the captain and our floating home to head for the train station, expecting...in retrospect I don't know why, something better. But there, for the overnight trip to Khartoum, travelling third class, we found basically the same horrendous conditions we'd experienced on board the river steamer.

Hundreds of Arabs and Sudanese tribesmen, their wives, children, baggage...and of course, the inescapable livestock, including goats, chickens and ducks, crammed the carriages to overflowing. The spaces between the seats, the aisles...every available space, was piled high.

People lay down to sleep on their belongings in the aisles. The conductor, when he came through to check tickets, had to clamber over people and livestock to traverse the length of the carriage. All this in temperatures of over forty degrees celsius. The only way to escape the intensely hot and oppressive atmosphere in the carriages was to leave our packs in the care of an Arab man and his wife, who had two small children and clamber up onto the roof of our carriage, to join those 'in the know'. There we found ourselves among scores of other Sudanese who were spread out along the whole length of the train, sitting on the roof, where there was at least a breeze blowing in our faces as we rattled across the scorching desert and into the gathering dusk.

'Christ its hot,' Shorty said as we struggled off the train and out from the station the following morning into the dusty and bustling streets of Khartoum. The temperature, on a big thermometer in the station...even at 10.00 am, read 110 degrees fahrenheit, or 43 degrees celsius.

'Yeah, but at least its dry,' I said. 'If it was humid we'd be passing out.'

We had no real desire to stick around and enjoy the cultural highlights of Khartoum, so we planned to get out and on our way as soon as possible. But this was not going to be simple, as we had quite a bit to organize in the way of visas and train and boat tickets on to Egypt. Nevertheless we decided that, before getting into that or anything else, we were going to have a swim. Not in the opulent and luxurious swimming pool at the Country Club that Noel and I had experienced on our way down with the RAF a year previously, but in the river.

One might have thought that we should have had seen enough of the Nile over the past ten days, but this was something different. For it is at Khartoum that the White Nile...the river we'd been travelling and which comes from the Lake Albert and Lake Victoria, is joined by the Blue Nile, which descends from Lake Tana, 1,500 kilometres to the south east, in Ethiopia. And we'd been told by a young German we'd met at the station that in Khartoum '...you must swim in the waters of the Blue Nile.' Checking our rucksacks at the station, we set out with costumes and a towel for a small park, not far from the city centre, which overlooks the junction where the Blue Nile flows in to join the

White.

'Wow...look at the difference in the water,' Shorty exclaimed as we stood on the bank. The two rivers were sharply delineated in colour as they met...the White Nile, grey-brown and muddy and unsafe to swim in or drink and...the Blue Nile a fresh, reasonably clear blue-grey colour, with relatively little sediment, supposedly clear of crocodiles and disease for swimming purposes and apparently much better as drinking water...although we didn't put that aspect to the test.

In July, the Blue Nile, swollen by heavy rains in the Ethiopian highlands, is so full that here, at the joining, it holds the White Nile back as it rushes by. Now, as we watched it, the two rivers ran side by side northward from Khartoum for several kilometres before merging their colours into one.For centuries no-one in the ancient world could understand why, in mid-summer when other rivers were drying up, the Nile should be the only one in flood. The mystery has long since been answered, but even now, in the modern world, the Nile 'miracle' is still the only thing that sustains life in the Sudan and Egypt. Without the White and the Blue Nile Rivers, both countries would die.

Our brief swim in the Blue Nile, attracted a small crowd of curious onlookers and provided them with a certain amount of amusement and entertainment as we got out the soap and had a good wash up while standing in the shallows in our swimming costumes. But once we'd dried and dressed, we set about the more serious business of sorting out our Egyptian visas and our train and boat tickets.

We had arrived in the capital on a Sunday, but fortunately, being a Muslim city, Sundays in Khartoum are 'business as usual', so the three main places we had to deal with...the Egyptian Consulate, the train station and the Nile Steam Navigation Company were all open.

Unfortunately though, they were all in different parts of town, so we had to walk, or take buses to get from one to the other. Starting back at the station, we enquired about third class tickets for the train trip from Khartoum to Wadi Halfa, a six hundred kilometre journey across the Nubian desert. Tickets were two pounds each, but, we were told, there were only three trains a week...on Mondays, Wednesdays and Fridays. The next one was due to leave the following morning.

We debated whether or not we should buy the tickets before we had the visas for Egypt and decided to try for the visas first. Our first setback, at the Egyptian Consulate, was discovering that we needed two photographs for each application. This was unexpected. Neither of us had any passport-size photos.

'But I came through Egypt last year,' I said to the official, 'I didn't need any photographs for an Egyptian visa then.' I noticed the scars on his face. He must be Sudanese, I thought...not Egyptian.

'Where did you apply?'

'Umm... in Libya. In Tripoli.'

'I see. Well...maybe its different there. It was different here a year ago. But that was before independence,' he smiled. 'Then we... ah, that is, the Sudan was under British and Egyptian rule. From January this year the Sudan has been an independent nation. The regulations both here and in Egypt have changed.' The huge scars on his cheeks creased slightly with a smile.

We had long since ceased to be amazed by the sight of these dramatic facial scars which are a feature of a large percentage of black Sudanese people...male and female. The wounds are imposed in childhood, when they are ceremonially slashed three times on each cheek and the cuts left open to heal slowly, so that the scars will all be wide as well as long. In the Sudan these scars are considered a sign of beauty in women and strength in men.

'Is there a photographer near here,' Shorty asked.

'Yes...not far. I will give you directions. But our office closes in half an hour... at one o'clock.'

We both moaned.

The man smiled. 'We will be open again at five o'clock for one hour. If you have you photographs, I think it can be arranged.'

We found the photographer in a dingy little store in a nearby back alley. He took some photographs of Shorty and I, but as it would take him time to develop the film and make the prints and he was also closing for several hours anyway for the afternoon siesta, he told us we would not be able to pick them up until the evening.

'We must have them before five o'clock,' I said to him. 'We need them for our Egyptian visas.'

He hummed and hahed for a few minutes and then said he could probably do it, but that it would cost fifty percent extra. We complained a bit more, but then agreed.

'Now lets try and find the place to get the boat tickets,' I said.

'But it'll be closed too. Everybody's closing for a siesta.'

'You never know... it might stay open a little longer than the consulate. At least we'll know exactly where it is and how to get there... and what time it opens and closes. What else have we got to do?'

'We could go back for another swim.'

Traipsing around Khartoum in the heat of the mid-day sun is not recommended, for anyone. It was an intense, overpowering heat... around 46 or 47 degrees celsius, that forced us to seek shade at every opportunity, as well as something to drink. Fortunately at almost every corner there was a stall with someone selling 'Limoon'. I'm not sure if that's how its spelt, but that's how it sounds. Long glasses of iced lemon drink, scooped out of a container cooled by floating blocks of ice. Beautiful and very cheap. Where they got the ice from though, was anybody's question... and a bit of worry. But when you're really thirsty, its amazing how quickly your best intentions, such as only drinking boiled water or name-brand bottled soft drinks, go out the window.

As luck would have it, the offices of the Nile Steamship Navigation Company were still open...until 2.00 pm, so we were able to buy our third class tickets for the 300 kilometre ferry journey from Wadi Halfa, where our train journey would terminate on the Egyptian border, to Aswan. Then finally, back at the railway station, we bought the train tickets for the following day's trip from Khartoum to Wadi Halfa.

Our forays across Khartoum had at least showed us a bit more of the place than the Country Club and our rather unfavourable first impressions of the town from near the station. We had seen several broad tree-lined avenues and some magnificent old colonial buildings. However, being a Muslim country, the streets of Khartoum were filled... 90 percent, with men. There were very few women to be seen... and those that were out and about were almost always in purdah, that is, covered from head to foot, with a veil over their face. The men, whether black Sudanese, or lighter-skinned Arabs or Egyptians, wore long white djalabeas and, more often than not, a white turban tied loosely around their head.

Originally Khartoum was an army camp, set up by conquering Egyptians in 1821. It grew, over the years, into a garrisoned army town, administered in the 1880's by Egypt, but as Egypt was in turn effectively ruled then by Britain, the Sudan had a British Governor General, Major General Sir Charles Gordon. In 1882 he and his garrison were massacred, and the town destroyed by an army of revolutionary Mahdists...Muslim fundamentalists embarked on a holy war. Britain's General Kitchener reconquered Khartoum and the Sudan for Britain in 1898. He began the reconstruction of Khartoum and the Sudan was ruled from then on, firstly by Britain and then jointly by Egypt and Britain. In 1953 the Egyptian government signed an agreement with Great Britain, granting self-government for Sudan within three years. And as outlined earlier, the country was declared an independent republic on January 1st 1956, just months before our visit.

Liberal democracy in the Sudan was short-lived however. Within two years, the Commander in Chief of the Sudanese Army, General Ibrahimn Abbud, carried out a bloodless coup, dissolved all political parties and temporarily suspended newspapers. This and other moves set the scene for decades of authoritarian rule by military officers, like Colonel Gaafar Mohamed el-Numeiri, who seized power in 1969 and held it until he too was deposed in a bloodless coup in 1985, by another military officer, Abdulrahman Siwai Al-Dhab.

Continuing the pattern, another military junta staged a coup in 1989 and its leader, Omer Hassan Al-Bashir soon declared himself President. He carried out purges and executions in the army, continued the ban on political parties as well as independent newspapers, imprisoned leading politicians and journalists and introduced Sharia law in Sudan.

Under the law, stoning to death, flogging and crucifixion still remain judicial punishments.

Additionally, under Bashir, Sudan increasingly embraced Islamic fundamentalism and, for a period, invited Osama Bin Laden to base his operations in the country, a move which prompted the U.S. to list Sudan as a State Sponsor of Terrorism.

In 2003 rebel groups in Sudan's western region of Darfur took up arms, accusing Bashir of oppressing non-arab Sudanese in favour of Muslim/Arab citizens. This precipitated a civil war in Darfur and in the subsequent genocide that followed an estimated 300,000 people were killed; many raped and tortured, prompting the International court of Justice to declare Sudan's President Bashir guilty of war crimes and to issue a warrant for his arrest.

Meanwhile, back in an earlier age, and having organized our tickets, it only remained for Shorty and I to pick up our photographs and visas later in the evening, so we decided to have our own siesta for the next couple of hours. We set off for the Grand Hotel...I think it was the Grand, or the Ambassador Hotel...anyway, one of the best in town. There, having bought an English newspaper from the concierge (a four day-old copy of the London Daily Telegraph), we sat under a fan on the verandah and ordered two limoons. They were three times the price of the same thing from the stalls in the road, but at least we had a slightly cooler place to sit out of the heat for the rest of the afternoon.

Having picked up our photographs just before five, we were at the door of the Egyptian Consulate when it opened, with our visa applications, photographs and passports at the ready. We were told, to our relief, that we could get them back again within half an hour. With that successfully accomplished, we now had all the necessaries for the next stage of our journey.

Now there was the question of where to sleep. It wasn't that we hadn't been thinking about it, or working it out...we had. In fact we had located the equivalent of a small, pension not far from the railway station where we could stay very cheaply (for about 50 piastres) for the night. But we'd been thinking about some advice we'd had from the young German we'd met at the station earlier that day. In addition to telling us about swimming in the Blue Nile, he had also given us some important information about the train trip northward.

'Its supposed to leave at 7.15 am, but they open the gates to the platform around 5.00 am... and there's usually a crowd waiting.'

For third class passengers, like us, with no reserved seating, it was obviously going to be a bun fight... 'first in best-dressed'.

'I reckon we should sleep at the station...by the gate,' I'd said to Shorty, while we were trying to decide whether to stay in the little pension or not. And he had agreed.

In the evening, with our bags still in the 'Left Luggage' department at the station, we had a meal of falafal, humus and vegetables at a small, café and then walked to the Grand Hotel, where once again we settled in on the verandah for a cool drink...this time a beer each. The Sudanese often refer to beer as 'boosa'...and it is apparently from them that we get the word 'booze'.

I remember sitting there, reading another newspaper and watching the thermometer on the wall at the end of the verandah drop imperceptibly as the evening progressed. By nine o'clock it had fallen considerably...to a mere 102 degrees fahrenheit (39 celsius). We wanted to see it drop below 100 fahrenheit before we left to set ourselves up for the night at the station, but the needle seemed to stick at 101 for ages, so we left at ten. Maybe it never got below 100!

At four thirty the following morning we were well awake. Sleeping by the gate to the platform was hardly an original idea. Shorty and I were only two of probably eighty to a hundred people with exactly the same thought. And now the numbers were rising rapidly. At least we had a reasonably good spot with only about a dozen people between us and the gate and scores of others behind us. We'd all managed to spread out on the ground...us on our ground sheets and sleeping bags, to find a little sleep during the night. But now we had to have our wits about us. Everybody was on their toes, ready for what was going to be a mad rush for seats on the train. The train itself had been shunted into the platform during the night and seemed ready, waiting for the onslaught.

'Third class carriages are at the front, right at the far end of the platform' a Sudanese man in the crowd had told us. 'Second and First class are at the rear...close to this end.'

This meant we'd have to run basically the whole length of the platform to get to the third class carriages...with everybody else going for it also.

I guess there are a few disadvantages to being twenty years old... like not having much money, or knowledge of some of the finer things of life, but at least, generally speaking, one was fit and could run along station platforms, even carrying a heavy rucksack, a hell of lot faster than a bunch of older people wearing long robes and struggling with piles of awkward suitcases and large calico bags slung over their shoulders. Plus children, chickens and goats. So when the gates were finally opened at five, Shorty and I streaked off down the platform, passing those who went through the gate ahead of us, to be first on board the first available third class carriage...diving straight inside to occupy two window seats opposite each other on the eastern side of the train. We figured, that although the whole train had pretty serious looking shutters for its windows, that the heat in the afternoon...on the western side of the carriage, would be greater.

Smart thinking, but in the event there was hardly any difference. The whole train was like an oven and only the dry wind, hot as it was, sweeping through the carriage, gave any relief. As in the train journey from Kosti to Khartoum, this one was also filled to overflowing, so, although we had managed to be first on board and to grab what seemed to be good seats, whatever advantage that may have given us, was soon eroded as people continued piling into the carriage occupying every available niche, sitting and lying almost on top of us.

The section of track between Khartoum and Wadi Halfa was built in 1898 by the British and Egyptian armies under the command of General Kitchener, when he was moving south on Khartoum to avenge the death of General Gordon. For about half the distance, as you head north, it follows the path of the Nile, which is not navigable because of a number of cataracts. Then it branches off, heading North West, in basically a straight line across 350 kilometres of the Nubian Desert... one of the most barren and inhospitable pieces of terrain imaginable.

During the first part of the journey, travelling to the east of the Nile, the landscape, though flat and desert-like beyond the river, is at least varied by the towns and settlements along the way. The river itself, edged by date palms and at least some greenery, where irrigation supports crops...particularly cotton, is clearly the source of all life.

But from Abu Hamad where, after travelling for almost thirty six hours, we left the Nile to rattle out into the wastes of the Nubian Desert, the land is so totally barren, dead and desolate that you wonder how anyone could survive out there. And if they could, why? Yet there were people living out there...or rather, existing. At two or three places along the way, the train would stop to take on water. Water? In the desert? Apparently there are several subterranean water tables that can be tapped by deep bores and at these places where the water comes up and the trains stop, people eke a sorry living selling tea and curios to the passengers on the trains. Not more than twenty people in each place, living in earthen huts, with not a trace of greenery, in the way of shrubs or trees around... just a vast flat landscape of sand.

Stopping at these places, Shorty and I would leave the train to have a cup of the hot, syrupy-sweet Sudanese tea and then drench ourselves, at the big train faucet, in the water coming up from below the sands. Back on the train, the cooling effect of our wet clothes in the hot wind was fantastic. It was like wearing an air conditioner.

The whole journey from Khartoum to Wadi Halfa, a distance of about 950 kilometres is supposed to take about 30 hours...that is averaging around 30 kilometres an hour, but it almost never does it on time. I made the same trip again, with my family, twenty years later and it took four days. On this occasion, to the credit of the Sudanese Railways, the trip was just two hours late, arriving in Wadi Halfa at about 2.00 pm on Tuesday...to be told that the Ferry for Aswan would be leaving at 4.00 pm.

000000

EGYPT

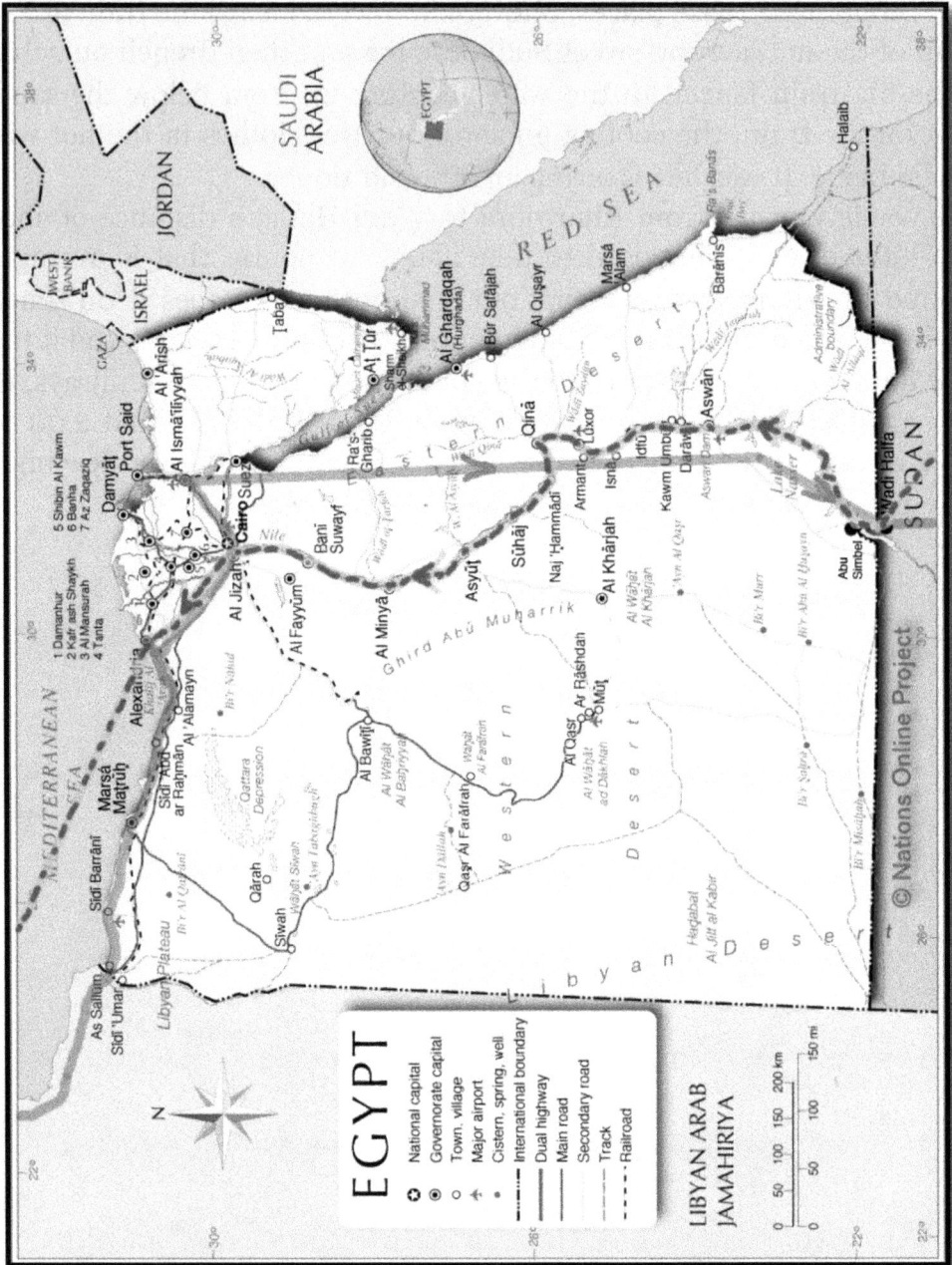

'THERE WERE STRONG ANTI-BRITISH FEELINGS'

Over three thousand years ago... around 1250 BC... the great Egyptian pharaoh, the Sun King, Rameses II, decided to construct yet another monument to himself, as well as one to his wife Nerfetari. There are statues and monuments testifying to the fame and might of Rameses II all over Egypt, but this one is something different. At the time of Rameses reign, Egypt's rule extended well down into what is now Sudan, and preceding warrior kings, from as far back as 1500 BC had constructed a chain of forts along the Nile in Upper Egypt and the Sudan that extended south as far as the fourth cataract on the Nile...that is about 180 kilometres from the tiny present day town of Abu Hamad, which we'd passed through on the train from Khartoum, before crossing the Nubian Desert.

The huge temples that Rameses ordered built were to be carved in the solid sandstone cliff face on the western bank of the Nile about thirty kilometres below present day Wadi Halfa. Its not known exactly how long the labours of thousands of craftsmen and slaves went on before the temples were finished, but the results were the most stunning and spectacular examples of ancient Egyptian art.

We had sailed from Wadi Halfa on time, and as we approached the temple site, at Abu Simbel, the vast size of the monument was apparent even from a distance. As we drew closer, Shorty and I stood at the railing of the third class barge in awe...lost for words. The main temple, dedicated to the sun gods Amon-Re and Re-Horakhte, was faced with four colossal seated statues of Rameses, each more than 20 meters high, two on either side of the entrance to the temple. The second from the left had unfortunately lost its head at some point in the dim past. The smaller temple, just to the north, was dedicated to Queen Nefertari for the worship of the goddess Hathor and adorned with ten-meter statues of the King and Queen.

We were pulling in to a pier to pick up some passengers and a small amount of cargo...crates of empty bottles, from the little settlement near the temples that had developed over the years to provide some services for tourists coming to the site. We were told that the boat would be docked for fifteen minutes...no more.

Shorty and I dashed off the boat and ran towards the temple, somewhat above and to the right of the landing. We paid a man standing at a gate (he was probably just a local merchant) a small fee and walked quickly up to the great statues. There was no way we could see it all and, in fact I had to force myself to slow down and try to think about it all in a more sane manner. Just standing at the base of those immense sculptures and trying to imagine the scene three thousand two hundred years ago...both during construction and after it was all finished, was an incredible experience. The two statues on our left, as we faced the entrance, bore graffiti that had been inscribed there by Greek mercenaries employed in Egypt during the sixth century BC, some six hundred years after the temples had been built. The graffiti has apparently provided researchers with importance evidence of the early history of our alphabet.

Behind the huge open doorway, which is between the second and third statues, is a great hall and fifteen other chambers, filled with stone carvings and murals, extending back sixty meters into the solid rock.

Rameses had the temple built in such a way that each year, on October 20th, the day of his accession to the throne, the first rays of the morning sun penetrate the entire length of the inner chambers and illuminate another statue of himself seated between the two sun gods.

After only a few frustrating minutes, desperately wanting to stay longer inside the great chambers, Shorty and I left to make our way back to the ferry. As we pulled away from the landing and headed out into the stream, I remember thinking 'I'm going to have to come back here some day to see it all properly'.

Little did I know that exactly twenty years would pass before I would return to Abu Simbel. Nor could I have possibly believed that the temples I had just seen, the entire structure...statues, chambers, everything...thousands of tonnes of rock, would have been cut out of the hillside and lifted sixty meters higher up the cliff face and rebuilt exactly as it had been before.

When Rameses' architects designed the great monuments at Abu Simbel, they could hardly have predicted that 3,000 years later a great dam would be built across the Nile at Aswan, some 250 kilometres to the north and that the rising waters of the lake forming behind the dam would ultimately engulf the mighty temples and submerge them forever.

Nor could they possibly expect, or even believe it possible, that a massive international engineering project would be put in operation to save the temples. A project that would use millions of dollars from public subscriptions around the world...a world that the great Rameses and his architects never even knew existed. The project would literally cut the temples out of the solid rock, piece by piece, and lift them to safer ground sixty meters higher and two hundred meters further back.

The United Nations appeal for funds was launched in 1960 and the salvage job was begun in 1964 and completed in 1967. The two temples were painstakingly cut into 1,050 pieces, some of them weighing over thirty tonnes, moved by truck and crane to their new position and reassembled with reinforced concrete backing. The original cliff face, into which they were cut, was rebuilt around them, with no block was more than 2.5 millimetres out of alignment from its original position. It took the equivalent of 4,000 man-years of work!

In their new position the temples also face precisely the same direction as they did, when they were built over 3,000 years ago. So each year at Abu Simbel, as the sun rises on October 20th, its rays are still able to shine deep into the rear chamber of Rameses temple, to illuminate the face of the King.

Of course, all this... that is, the salvage operation, was ten years in the future, and when we arrived in Aswan the following morning, we had no thoughts of the threat to the temples or the great project that lay ahead. There was already a dam at Aswan...a relatively low one that created a small lake extending back from Aswan only a few kilometres. There was certainly talk of a bigger dam...the Aswan High Dam, that was supposedly going to be financed by the United States and Britain. B u t there were lots of problems...mainly political. Considerable friction was building between Egypt and the West. Although we couldn't have known it, the Arab-Israeli War and Britain and France's disastrous raid on the Suez Canal zone were only four months away. Egypt, under the rule of General Gamal Abdel Nasser, had, earlier in the year, been declared a socialist Arab state with a one-party political system, with Islam as the official religion. For the past year it had also been leaning increasingly towards the the Eastern Bloc and the Soviet Union for support, both military and financial.

Taking stock of our own situation in Aswan, we too were in need of financial...but fortunately not military, support. Not that General Nasser could have cared.

We had left Jodie and Elaine in Kampala with roughly £20 each. Now we found we had less than £10 between us.

'I'm down to £4-10-0, plus a few piastres,' I said gloomily, looking through my wallet.

'I've got a fiver...and about 30 piastres,' Shorty mumbled. 'Jeez... we've spent thirty quid between us in just three weeks.

It was true that we had paid for two ferry trips covering 1,600 kilometres and two train rides covering 1,100 kilometres, visas for the Sudan and Egypt, had passport photographs taken, as well as food for both of us for three weeks, but it still seemed to us that the money had just disappeared. In any event...it was pretty clear that getting to Europe, and England, would take quite a bit of doing with just £10 between us!

'We're going to have to head straight through from Aswan to Cairo as fast as possible.' I said. 'Maybe to Alexandria would be better. Perhaps we could get a boat there.'

'To where?'

'Anywhere in Europe. Even to Greece would be okay, but if we could get to Italy or France, we'd be right. Even without any money, we could still make it through to England. My parents are there now. I'm sure they could help us out. But if we run out of money here, we're in trouble.'

There were trains running regularly on the 1,000-kilometre line between Aswan and Cairo but, even though it would be the fastest method of travel, there was no way we could afford to travel by train, so we planned to hitch.

As there had been no Egyptian immigration and customs post at Wadi Halfa, we had to go through the formalities at

Aswan, actually at the nearby river port of Shallal. They were relatively straightforward, however, and once through, we prepared to get under way. Aswan had much to offer in the way of sight-seeing and monuments from ancient Egypt, including the magnificent temple of Philae, which was also destined to be submerged by the rising waters behind the proposed high dam, but Shorty and I had moved into fast forward mode now and we decided to push straight on.

We both agreed though that, on our way north, we should try to spend at least a short time at Luxor and Karnak, to see the great ruins there. So, after covering the two hundred or so kilometres between Aswan and Luxor during the afternoon, in three long hitches, we alighted in the early evening in the town of Luxor. We were able to find the youth hostel relatively easily and settled in there for the night... planning to see as much as we could of ancient Luxor and Karnak the following day and then continue on our way by mid-afternoon. A crazy situation to be in when there were such wonders to see. We knew it would be impossible to give it all the time it deserved, but we were feeling the pressure of time versus money...a bit like an hour-glass with our money running out...and we recognised the harsh facts of having to keep moving.

In ancient times, some three-and-a-half thousand years ago, Karnak and the temples in what is now present-day Luxor were all linked, part of the same great complex of temples and monuments and houses and other buildings that comprised the great city of Thebes. The name Luxor is relatively recent, deriving from the Arabic: 'Al-Uqsur', which simply means 'the temples'. Although there are magnificent statues, obelisks, wall carvings and colonnaded courtyards in one part of the ruins, that is set right in the middle of the present-day town, surrounded by modern buildings and hotels at one end and a shanty town at the other, Karnak, a couple of kilometres away, is vastly more impressive.

The two temple complexes were linked in those distant days by an incredible road of white marble that ran beside the river. The entire distance was lined, on both sides, with sphinxes carved in marble... about three thousand of them! Nearly all of them have been lost, crushed or covered up by successive generations which built the town of Luxor. Only a few remain.

The actual temple at Karnak is such a fantastic, awe-inspiring place that it almost defies description. Built over a period of more than a thousand years, it was the focal point of all life in ancient Thebes, from around 1800 BC to about 600 BC. The main entrance to the temple complex is magnificent...a double row of ram-headed sphinxes, each protectively holding a statue of Rameses II between its paws, led us through a giant gateway between two massive pylons into the Great Court. Beyond lay literally hectares of wonderful and gigantic temples that had been built by pharaoh after pharaoh, down through the centuries, to honour the Sun God... each one trying to outdo his predecessor in the glory and grandeur of his contribution.

The Hypostyle (many pillars) Hall, is probably the most incredible sight in Karnak. Covering some five thousand square meters, at one stage it had a roof of solid stone two thirds of a meter thick! It remains one of the most massive of human creations...the epitome of what ancient Egypt's power and wealth could produce.

To support the roof, there are...still standing...134 of the original columns in sixteen rows. The main columns are 21 meters high, with capitals at their tops so large they could each hold a hundred standing men.

Throughout the complex there are huge stone statues of gods and kings, immense smooth obelisks, walls carved and inscribed with the history of the times, depicting the exploits of generations of pharaohs.

'We could spend days here,' Shorty said as we left Karnak to return to the hostel to pick up our packs and get on our way. 'We haven't even touched the surface.'

On the other side of the river, the great Valley of the Kings, the burial place of Pharaohs for centuries...the magnificent tombs of Tutankhamen, Seti I, Thutmose III, Amenhotep II, Queen Hatchepsut, and the all powerful Rameses II, lay basking in the overpowering heat of the afternoon...all there for us to visit. But, as with Abu Simbel, it would be a further twenty years before I and my family would return to Egypt to visit the wild, rocky and desolate Valley of the Kings and to see Luxor and Karnak properly.

Cairo, in our present frame of mind, held little for us. Arriving there at the end of the following day after leaving Luxor, we stayed in the youth hostel on El Ibrahimy Street, planning only to visit the Museum during the following morning and the Pyramids, on our way out of town heading towards Alexandria. I had thought of returning to see Yahya at the bakery, but I knew we wouldn't be able to just breeze in for a night and say we were heading off the next day. Apart from the fact that it would have been rude to have done so, I could see the whole thing would have grown into a stay of quite a few days...which we didn't want. So we didn't contact either him or his cousin, Jusuf, the magistrate. We were telescoping everything down to get ourselves through and out of Egypt as soon as possible, yet, at the same time, still trying to see one or two of the major attractions.

But there was another element that mitigated against us staying longer. The political climate in Egypt, as far as its relations with the West had changed significantly since I'd passed through with Noel and when we had stayed in Cairo the previous year. There were strong anti-British feelings in the air. Posters plastered in the streets were clearly of an anti-British and anti-American nature. Most of them were posters for the Presidential elections due to be held momentarily. Only one candidate was standing...the current president, General Gamal Abdel Nasser. Although we couldn't read the Arabic wording, we could see the pictures of Nasser and the denigrating cartoon depictions of John Bull and Uncle Sam left us in no doubt that speaking English could have its disadvantages in Cairo at this time. If the occasion arose, we would try, as quickly as possible, to disabuse people of the idea that we were English.

'Australia.... South Africa...' we'd tap ourselves on the chest. 'Not English...' and shake our heads.

We did spend a good part of the day in Cairo at the Museum, before taking a bus, in the late afternoon, to Giza and the pyramids. Leaving our packs in a small café, we walked to the pyramids and began a trek around the base of the Khufu pyramid. It had only been a year since Noel and I had done the same thing with Nick Parkinson, but some things remain as stunning and amazing to behold, no matter how many times you see them. I suppose the fact that the Pyramids at Giza are the only one of the so-called seven great wonders of the ancient world which is still standing...says it all.

The sun went down...a big red ball on the desert skyline to the west...and in the gathering dusk we made our way back to the main road and past the Mena House Hotel and towards the little café where we had left our packs.

I pointed to the hotel, 'Noel and I had drinks on the verandah there, with the bloke from the Australian Embassy,' I said. 'He shouted the drinks too.'

'Jeez, I wish we had him here now,' Shorty muttered.

We returned to the café and ate a cheap meal of eggs, hummus, aubergines, and tea, for about fifty piastres.

'You know, We should be able to camp out somewhere around here,' Shorty dunked his bread into his tea. 'What about the grounds of the hotel...they seem to have a big lawn there.'

I can't remember the exact layout of the area around the pyramids by the Mena House, or how we found a place to sleep. I recall a small side road, turning at right angles to the main road and what was probably a perimeter wall, or hedge around the hotel. Also a few three or four-storey tenement buildings, other houses and lights further along the road on the opposite side, where we could see some people standing around talking...but, as there was no-one close by, we quickly scrambled over the wall and onto a grassy lawn. Ducking down behind the wall, where we were immediately hidden from any passers-by, we simply laid out our ground sheets and sleeping bags to settle down for a night's sleep.

We could hear the passing traffic, as well as music from nearby cafés, radios playing and the voices of passing people. We lay there in the still warm evening air, gazing up into a clear and brilliant, star-filled sky, watching the moon rise and, as we drifted off to sleep, I found myself thinking about those massive monuments just across the main road, about the thousands of people who built them and about the hundreds of thousands of times the moon has risen over them since then. And of the millions of people, over the years, who might have sat out here watching the same moon rise over the pyramids...perhaps thinking similar thoughts about these massive monuments, pondering the imponderable, wondering about the nature of the cosmos and why we're all here.

There is virtually nothing on the 200-kilometre desert road between Giza and Alexandria...except desert. Noel and I had travelled the same road the previous year on our way from El Alamein down to Cairo, missing Alexandria on the way. Now the opportunity was there to visit the city, but with our finances in such a parlous state, almost down to zero, Shorty and I found ourselves thinking about nothing more than how we were going to get out of Alexandria...before we even got there.

We were lucky to find cheap and clean accommodation in a small hostel not far from the centre of Alexandria, walking distance from the city's Western Harbour, the main port area. It was here that cargo ships from all over the world were docked and where we intended to concentrate our efforts on finding a vessel heading to virtually anywhere in Europe.

It was early afternoon by the time we had settled in, got ourselves a map and asked advice about port activities from the people at the youth hostel. We were about to set off to make some sort of a recce of the port and the boats there, when we were interrupted.

'You guys have come up from East Africa...through Sudan?'

The question came from one of two blond young men in shorts and sandals,whom we'd seen sitting in the courtyard of the hostel, when we arrived. The accent sounded German, but they turned out to be Austrian.

'We heard from the manager that you have come up through Sudan,' the second one explained. 'We are hoping to go down that way... towards East Africa.' He smiled. 'How is it down there?'

Shorty and I both looked at each other... and also smiled.'

'Well...ah.. that's a long story,' Shorty replied. 'How long have you got?'

They both looked a bit puzzled...and we both laughed. 'No, don't worry,' I said. 'Its just that we've had a hell of time getting through... but you may find it easier. The main thing is...everything depends on how much money you've got, because you basically have to show them that you have enough money to pay your way all the way through. Not only through the Sudan, but probably through East Africa as well. We didn't come through East Africa...except for a few days in Uganda, we came up through the Congo.'

They sat down beside us and started plying us with more questions about ferry boats and trains. We stayed and talked to them for more than an hour as they pored over their map of Africa and wrote notes. We went over the route north through the Sudan that we had followed and told them where to go in Cairo and in Khartoum to get the various train and boat tickets and visas that they would need. It seemed that, as they had considerably more money than either Noel and I had on the way south, or Shorty and I had on the way back up, that they might not run into quite the same problems we had.

While looking at the map with them, I also did a little calculating...about the trip that Noel and I had made heading south through Africa, compared to the northward one Shorty and I had just completed. In the whole of the distance from Durban to Alexandria... some 10,000 kilometres...only about ten percent of the journey, about 1,000 kilometres, was on the same route that Noel and I covered the previous year.

By mid-afternoon we had satisfied most of the Austrian boys' queries and were back on track, heading out into the city and the port to try to find a ship on which we could ship out. The Port of Alexandria has long been Egypt's major port, exporting all of the country's cotton, as well as traditional items such as fruits, vegetables and perfumes. Oil and natural gas are now exported, but back in 1956, Egypt's offshore deposits had not been discovered. Nevertheless the port, a vast network of breakwaters, quays and wharves, was full of ships flying foreign flags.

'We've got to be able to find something amongst this lot,' Shorty said as we entered the offices of the Port Authority.

'Yeah, but they're not all going where we want them to go. And even if they are, they may not necessarily want to take us.'

In the Port Authority building we were eventually able to locate a list of incoming and outgoing vessels that was posted on one wall, which was fortunately in English, as well as Arabic, and when we had learnt to interpret it properly, gave us information about which ships might be worthwhile approaching.

'Its amazing, out of all those ships out there, only four going anywhere in Europe.' Shorty sounded dejected. 'Plenty for the States, or South America... or Asia.'

'But there's more coming in tomorrow... and the day after,' I said. '...and anyway, maybe one of these four will be okay.'

Only one of the four was destined for northern Europe... to Hamburg. Two of the others were for ports in the Mediterranean... Marseilles and Trieste...the other for Lisbon.

Showing my seaman's papers for the voyage I had made on the Danish ship, the Tekla Torm from Genoa to Casablanca, we were able to obtain permits to enter the port seeking work on board the various ships. But, after two hours spent on and off the four candidate vessels, we drew a blank. No luck on any of them. So we returned to the youth hostel in the early evening to prepare one of our standard el cheapo, culinary triumphs of bread, cheese, sardines and tomatoes.

As none of the newly arriving vessels that we hoped to try were due in port until at least later the next day, we decided to at least try to see a little of Alexandria itself. So the following morning we set off for a walk around the central business area of the town, and a visit to the Graeco-Roman Museum, which includes a huge collection of ancient carvings and other artifacts, most of which come from findings within the city.

Looking at Alexandria then (in 1956) it was difficult to imagine how it was once the greatest city in the ancient world. Apart from the collections in the museum, and a few remaining classical monuments, like the 27-meter tall marble column known as Pompey's Pillar and the remarkable catacombs dating from the

2nd century BC, there is little of the great Greek city that remains. A Roman theatre was uncovered near the central railway station in 1959, three years after our visit, but there was no clue to its existence when we were there. In fact we probably walked right over the top of it.

Founded in 332 BC by Alexander the Great, Alexandria remained the capital of Egypt for almost a thousand years. The city's great pride and one of the Seven Wonders of the Ancient World, was the huge lighthouse, the Pharos of Alexandria, which stood at the eastern extremity of the island of Pharos...now joined to the mainland by a short isthmus dividing the two ports...the Inner Harbour and Eastern Harbour. Reputed to have been more than 135 meters high, it was still standing in the twelfth century AD. But by 1477 it had been torn down by the ruling Sultan Qa'it Bay to build a fort.

During its heyday, Alexandria was a major centre for Greek scholarship and science. Scholars such as Euclid, Archimedes, Plotinus the philosopher and Ptolemy and Eritosthenes, the geographers, studied at the city's great research institute known as the Mouseion. Cleopatra courted first Julius Caesar, then Mark Antony in Alexandria. Christ's disciple St. Mark is said to have made his first convert to Christianity in Alexandria.

The coming of Christianity eventually led to the decline of Greek and eventually Roman culture in Alexandria and then, in the seventh century, the city fell first to the Persians then to the Arabs. Under Muslim rule all traces of the Graeco Roman city disappeared. It prospered for a while as a centre for the burgeoning East-West spice trade but was soon eclipsed politically by the emergence of the new capital, Cairo. By 1798, when the French army, under Napoleon, invaded Egypt, the great city of Alexandria had declined to just a fishing village.

However, the cotton boom in the nineteenth century and the opening of the Suez Canal set Alexandria off on another cycle of rapid growth. This continued, under direct British rule for forty years from 1882...then under indirect rule and patronage until 1952, when the monarchy under King Farouk was ousted in a bloodless military coup by a group of young Army officers led by

Nasser, who was at that stage a Colonel. Nasser assumed a background role while an older general, Mahommad Neguib, took on what turned out to be a figure-head position as President. In 1952 Neguib was deposed and Nasser emerged as the country's Prime Minister, eventually taking over the Presidency, in the elections that occurred as Shorty and I left Cairo.

General Nasser, as the world now knows, was destined to dramatically change Egypt's relations with the West. And Shorty and I just happened to be in Egypt at a fairly crucial period in those changing times. Nasser had openly courted the Soviet Union and, in the Cold War climate of the day, seemed to be deliberately fostering strong anti-British and anti-American feelings amongst the populace. Feelings that were growing stronger all the time...although fortunately, it seemed to us to be more focussed in Cairo than in Alexandria.

The election of Nasser coincided with the official departure of the last British servicemen from Egyptian soil (British army and air force personnel had continued to be based in Egypt ever since World War II, ostensibly for the defence of the Suez Canal). This was the occasion for a wave of anti-British demonstrations in Cairo, to be followed a week later by a huge parade of Egypt's new Russian-supplied military hardware, including tanks, mobile rocket launchers and aircraft.

'The sooner we're out of here the better,' I said to Shorty as we made our second foray into the docks to try and find a ship out. We'd seen the newspaper banners of the demonstrations in Cairo and talked to other Europeans in the Youth Hostel, who'd been reading foreign language press reports also. Admittedly Cairo was where most of the noise was being made, but who could tell when Alexandria might pick up on it too.

To make matters worse, our money was fast disappearing. We figured it would last us three more days and then... and then? We had just sufficient to pay our board at the hostel and buy bread and sardines and maybe a tomato or two... for three more days. We had to get a ship.

No luck. There were two ships going to northern Europe... a Swedish vessel and a British one.   But neither were prepared to take us on board.

'You must be a member of a British union,' we were told on board the British ship. 'Sorry matey...you've got to have a British seamen's ticket before we can take you on.'

'Is that the same with all British ships,' I asked.

'Yep.'

The Swedish one was something similar, although we didn't have to be union members. We did have to have a Swedish Seaman's ticket though. A bit Catch-22-ish. It was marginally better than the British situation however, as apparently it didn't apply to all Swedish ships... there were a few that might take us on.

Another day (the second of our last three) ticked by. Nothing doing. Plenty of ships there...even ones that would take us on, but they were going to the wrong places.

'Maybe we should just take what we can get...just to get out of here,' Shorty said. 'And then work something else from wherever we get to...like Rio or somewhere.'

'Well...that's what it'll come to, I guess. We won't have any option after tomorrow.'

We were both trying to fight off a huge depression as we trudged back from the Port at the end of our fourth day in Alexandria.

'It has been worse than this,' I said to Shorty. 'When Noel and I were in Casablanca...we had absolutely no money and I had no passport. But, we can always get a feed down here from the ships. We won't starve. And at least you've got twenty quid waiting for you in London.'

'Yeah, but what about now? What about the hostel? How are we going to stay there if we can't pay them?'

'Okay... that's another question. We'll face it when it happens.'

But Lady Luck must have been smiling on us. For, on the last day...our fifth in Alexandria, June 12th, when all we could squeeze from both our pockets was one piaster, which I think was worth about the equivalent of five cents...we found a ship.

The Italian motor vessel Meligunis, out of Messina, was sailing for Tunis and Dublin on the following day, with a cargo of Egyptian onions.

The captain, Commandante Mauro Maugere, a slim, dark moustachioed man of about forty, said he would take us on as deckhands.

Once again, I had shown him the certificate I had received from the '*Tekla Torm*' in Casablanca and mentioned a Finnish timber ship I had worked on briefly in the Baltic and the North Sea at the end of 1954.

'Hava you been helmsman?' he asked.

'Ahh... well, yes,' I fibbed, thinking quickly that a positive response was required. 'But, ah...not really on a full-time basis. Just once or twice.'

'Uh huh,' he nodded. 'Okay... your passaportes are good?'

'Yes. Yes,' we both replied... our spirits rising.

'You will need certificate for immigration here...to leave Egypt.' He turned and spoke to another officer in Italian, then back to us. 'You go with this man...give him passaporte details. We sail tomorrow morning, ten o'clock. You coming here tonight...six o'clock.'

Armed with a typed certificate offering both Shorty and I employment on the M/N Meligunis, we returned exhilarated to the youth hostel, to pick up our packs, say our goodbyes to the people we'd met there and to make our way, in the late afternoon, to the Customs and Immigration office at the port.

Passing through the formalities there without problems, we climbed the gangplank on the Meligunis with a huge sense of relief and satisfaction. We had traversed the whole length of Africa from South to North... and now...although we had no more money, at least we would have food and accommodation...and more importantly, we were moving on.

oooooo

MEDITERRANEAN / IRELAND / UK
Aboard the M/V Meligunis

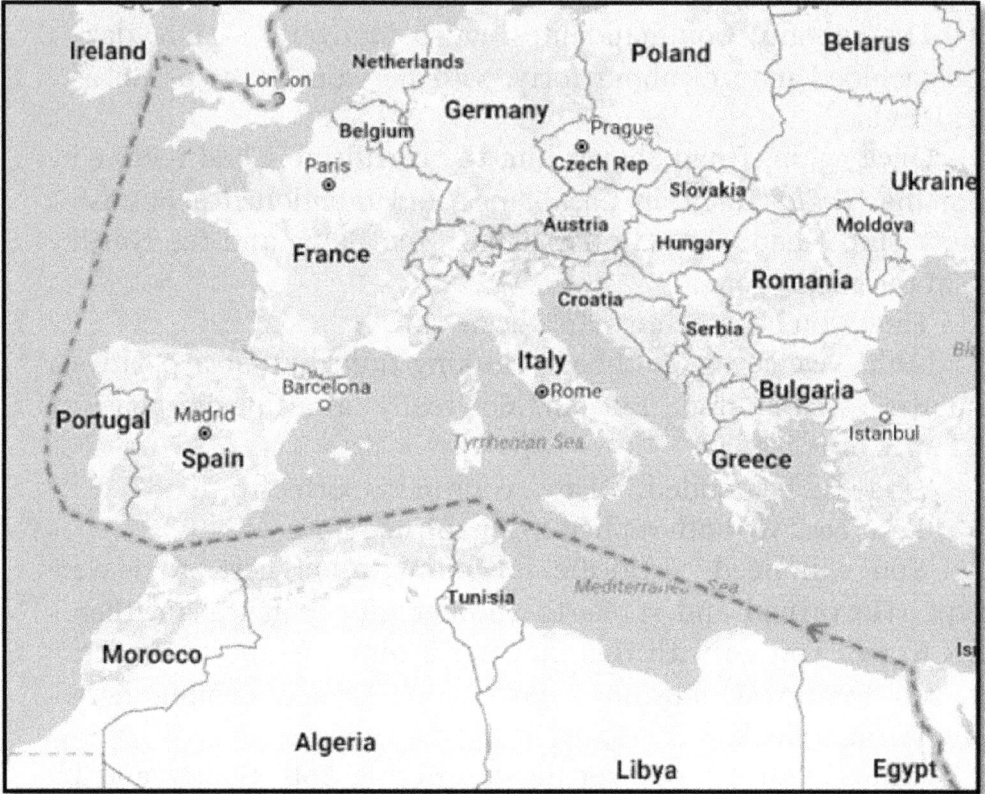

24

OUT OF AFRICA

As cargo ships go, the Meligunis was relatively small...about three or four thousand tones and by no means a state-of-the-art vessel. But Shorty and I were so pleased to have been signed on, and to be sailing off on our way to Europe, that it could have been a lifeboat with an outboard motor and we'd still have been happy.

We'd been taken on as deckhands for no pay...just food, board and passage. We were assigned all the normal tasks that deckhands do, cleaning decks and companionways, chipping rust, painting, tidying up, greasing machinery...virtually anything the bosun told us to do. He was a stocky little guy called Giussepi Corelli from Brindisi, who had been around the world several times on other Italian ships and spoke passable English. We got on well together and he seemed reasonably pleased with the way we worked.

I think basically it was because we obviously enjoyed what we were doing. The weather was great...hot, sunny days, a cool breeze blowing off the sea, working hard, getting covered in grease and rust, then a good shower and clean up in the evening. Then a couple of Nastro Azurro beers, followed by pasta, salads and red wine for dinner. No complaints. Plus the fact that we were out of Africa and on our way to Europe. What more could anybody ask?

On about the third night out from Alexandria, my response to the Captain's question in port about whether I'd ever been a helmsman came back to haunt me. Well, not exactly haunt, but certainly to put me on edge and introduce a sudden sense of apprehension which wasn't there before.

'Captain say for you go to bridge,' the bosun said to me shortly after we'd finished dinner.

'The...er...the bridge? The captain wants me on the bridge?' I said. 'What for? Why?'

'You steera d' boat.'

'Me? Steer the boat? Aahh... yes... umm...okay. Aahh...when?'

'Now. You go now.'

Shorty smiled at me and simply said, 'Good Luck'.

Good luck!!? Why the hell I should have been chosen to work at the helm, when there were other Italian seamen to choose from, almost certainly with far more experience than I, I'll never know. I mean, don't people have to have certificates and diplomas before they can take over the helm of a three thousand tonne ship sailing in the Mediterranean? I didn't know. But there I was, fronting up to the bridge in the darkness, my heart beating quite a bit faster than normal, thinking...how am I going to do this? And what the hell do I have to do anyway?

The lights from the compass, the radar and several other instruments dimly lit the faces of the Captain, the First Officer and another seaman at the wheel, who were standing on the bridge talking. Ahead, through the windows on the bridge, the sea and the night sky were as one...dense and black, with no delineation between the horizon and the sky.

The Captain and the First Officer turned towards me and nodded, then motioned me to come in. The seaman at the helm simply smiled and walked away, leaving me the wheel!

If my heart rate had been a few beats up as I approached the bridge, it now went into overdrive. I felt a sudden wave of panic sweep over me. I probably flushed, or went deathly pale, I don't know...and fortunately, in the darkness on the bridge they couldn't have seen it anyway. But somehow I managed to step casually into the position behind the wheel and put my hands on it. I turned towards the Skipper and the First Officer with what must have been a sick, helpless smile... again, fortunately, the darkness was my friend.

'I... umm...' I began.

'The course is here...' the First Officer spoke in English and pointed to a small blackboard by some other instruments in front of me. '297° ' was all that was written there in chalk.

'297 degrees,' I said. 'Keep it at that?'

'Yes.'

Nothing more was said. The First Officer continued talking to the Captain...and they just left me to it. But, Holy Mackerel! How the hell was I going to....? I looked down at the small round glass dome of the compass in front of me. The illuminated figures marking off degrees around the circumference were magnified for about three or four degrees on either side of the centre line, which was supposed to be where the course we were following should show up. But when I looked it said 300°.

Should I turn to port, or starboard to correct it? (at least I knew about port and starboard). It took me a few seconds to work it out, because the way the compass display was set up was confusing. It looked as if I should turn to starboard (right)... when I actually had to turn to the left (port). While I was desperately figuring, with the two men chatting away behind me, I kept the wheel rock steady. In those few seconds.. the reading on the compass had changed to 302°.

I started to turn the wheel to the left. The compass didn't change. I turned a bit more. It still didn't move. I turned some more. The compass was moving now... 300°, okay. 297°. Good. Start to bring the wheel back a bit to the right now...but, oh oh. The compass now read 294°. Jesus. Now 290°, Oh God! I turned the wheel further to the right, and perhaps a bit faster. Still it kept going to port. 287°. Then it steadied and began to move back... 291°, Aha. 297° Uh huh. 301°. No! Start turning back to port again. But the compass still kept turning the wrong way 305°, 307°. Steady... then back again.

Now I noticed the silence behind me. It was patently obvious to the Captain and the First Officer that I was making a mess of it. The First Officer stepped up beside me. His English was perfect... and fortunately his manner was sympathetic.

'You're over-correcting,' he said. 'The ship takes a while to respond. You really only have to make minor adjustments... not big movements of the wheel.'

'Uh huh...okay. Thanks,' I nodded, turning to him. 'The ..ah, ship I was on before...it was smaller. It seemed to turn faster.'

'Okay,' he smiled. 'Just relax. Take it easy.'

And that was that. For the rest of the journey...another two weeks, I spent four hours at the wheel, every second night. A piece of cake! Although, it had to be admitted that most of the time I was at the helm in wide empty stretches of ocean, with not much traffic. When there were the lights of other ships on the horizon, or heading our way, I made sure to give them as wide a berth as possible without steering too much off course.

But my efforts on that first night did not go unnoticed.

'We could tell when you took the wheel,' Shorty laughed the following morning. 'We were standing outside the galley at the stern, and we could see the ships wake. It was a straight line. Then it suddenly went into a series of 'S' bends', weaving all over the place.'

'Oh, well...' I said, with a slightly self-assured air, '...I was just settling in. Getting the feel of it. It takes time, you know. Every boat's different.'

'Really?' Shorty laughed. 'Do tell.'

We reached Tunis six days after leaving Alexandria, on the morning of June 19th, 1956, having passed just north of Malta on the previous day. On checking back in my old British passport, I calculated that Shorty and I had arrived in Tunis exactly a year to the day since Noel and I had passed through there on our way across North Africa.

I told Shorty about the expedition Noel and I had made with the French student teachers into the red light district of Tunis and about our meeting with the Polish girl who had been so helpful to us both.

'We've got to go again!' he said enthusiastically. 'Do you think you could find it?'

'No way. We were wandering through back streets for ages...and we had the French guys with us. They knew their way around. We'd get lost, for sure.'

'No, no...we'd be okay. I'm sure. We've got to give it a try.'

As it happened, the opportunity for a second sortie into the seamy side of Tunis never arose. We had docked in Tunis simply for taking on some cargo and once the job was complete...by about seven in the evening, we were on our way again. We'd had no opportunity to do much more than go ashore and walk around the dock area to stretch our legs. In any event, the crucial deciding factor, even if we had been staying longer, was money. We couldn't have gone out on the town, because we had none.

The days slipped by. Perfect weather. At times we could see a distant line on the horizon to our left which was the coast of North

A Deckhand on board the Meligunis

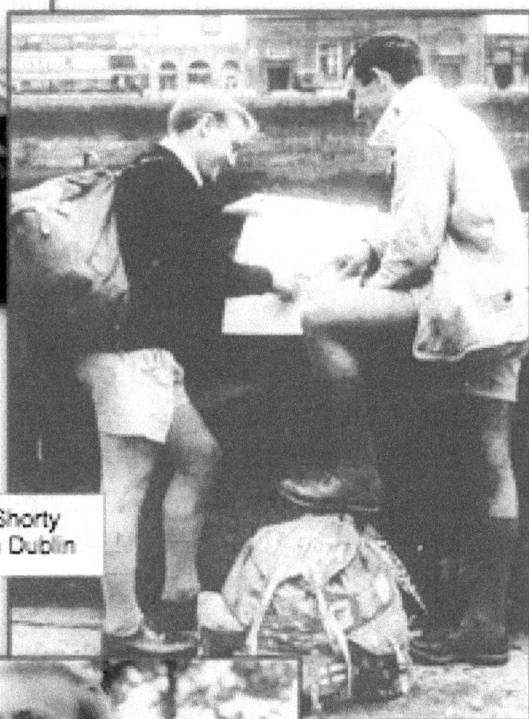

Press photos of Shorty and I on arrival in Dublin

Africa, then as we approached the Straits of Gibraltar, we could see the southern coast of Spain. Once through the Straits, however, we didn't see land again, except for brief and distant glimpses of Cape St. Vincent in southern Portugal and Cape Finistere at the north western tip of Spain, until we came to Dublin.

In the Atlantic, the weather deteriorated somewhat, although not so much as to make things nasty. I recall doing my shift at the wheel on a couple of the nights sailing north across the Bay of Biscay, about three hundred kilometres out in the Atlantic, with sheets of rain pouring down and being able to see no further towards the bow of the ship than the derrick above the forward hold. On those occasions, at least one person...the First or Second Officer, or the Captain, would be checking the radar very frequently.

Though not raining, the weather was decidedly cool when we arrived in Dublin on June 29th, but both Shorty and I felt elated at having made it at last to Europe. Packing our gear up, we extricated from the bottom of our packs, for the first time, jackets and sweaters which had been of no use to us for months. We definitely needed them in Dublin, even though it was supposed to be summer already.

I think Captain Maugere must have felt a little embarrassed to send us off the ship with absolutely no money, even though that was the basis of our employment from the beginning. Just before we left, he told the Second Officer to give us £5 sterling between the two of us.

We both thanked him and shook hands with the crew, who had been good friends to us over the past two weeks, and then headed off down the gangplank into Dublin port.

The city of Dublin is in a beautiful setting, at the head of an attractive bay and straddling the river Liffey, which flows down through the surrounding hills to the shores of the Irish Sea. The city itself is relatively small...only six or seven kilometres in any direction to its boundaries, although the suburbs stretch well off into the hills. Its a low-built, steepled city of red brick and grey stone, centred on ancient Dublin Castle, one of the few buildings that date prior to the seventeenth century. There are also green parks, shade trees and attractive front gardens that make the city eminently liveable.

It was during this period of the mid-1950's that the government in Dublin launched a series of new schemes that were designed to bring

Ireland into the mainstream of the 20th century. Detailed five-year plans for economic development were drawn up, policies were adopted to encourage investment in new industries...particularly from foreign sources and a heavy investment program for the tourist industry was put in train. Naturally, these events were not apparent to us during our brief stay, but anyone who has visited Dublin recently can attest to the fact that somebody must have got it right, because the city has flowered into a truly international capital.

Before making our way to England, Shorty and I had decided to try to sell our story to a newspaper. Not a full feature article...just a news story. We thought we might be able to get an extra five or ten pounds to help us along, for a bit of a story about our travels through Africa as well as a couple of our pictures that we'd taken on the way. So, after looking up the address in a phone book, we made straight for the offices of the Irish Times.

'We don't usually pay for news stories,' we were told by a journalist who'd been called to the front desk in the entrance to the office. 'But your story sounds interesting. I'll just check with my editor to see if we might be able to arrange something.'

The end result was that they took us out to stand by one of the bridges over the River Liffey to take some photographs and then did a little write-up on us in the Times, as well as finding five pounds from petty cash to pay us. It doesn't sound much, but in those days there were plenty of people being paid only five pounds a week as a salary. Working in London the year before, I had only been earning seven pounds a week...and this was Ireland. So five pounds seemed pretty good to us.

Now we had ten pounds between us. Enough, we felt, to get us to London, via the ferry to Holyhead, from where we could hitch the rest of the way.

London was still the goal...and we weren't there yet, so virtually all of our thoughts were still focused on simply getting there. Up until now, what would happen after London had hardly entered our heads. But suddenly, after leaving the ship in Dublin, these thoughts started to creep in. It seemed pretty sure that in whatever travels we embarked on after London, Shorty and I might have different agendas.

'What are we going to do when we get to London?' Shorty said at one point as we sat on the ferry to Holyhead. 'I mean, I know you're planning to head back to Australia. But do you want to work in London before that, or go straight to Norway?'

I had spoken a lot about Lise and that I wanted to get to Norway to see her before I left Europe for Australia. Also I felt that there was a better chance of picking up work on a ship in Norway than in Britain. But, of course, I recognized these were *my* plans. They wouldn't necessarily fit in with what Shorty might want to do.

'There's the old flat in South Ken that Noel and I shared with the North Bondi boys...some of them are still there. We could doss down with them for a while, for sure. But staying and working in London? I don't know. I sort of feel, if I do that, I'll get... well, you know... trapped there.'

'Trapped? It'd be great to work in London.'

'Yes, yes. I know what you mean. It was great when Noel and I worked there before. We had a terrific time...and you'd love it. But its different for me. Now I've got to get going...got to get back to Melbourne for the Olympics.'

'Yeah, but you could save money in England...probably just as much as you could in Norway.'

'I don't know about that. I doubt it...although, its true Noel and I never earned much when we were working in the forest in Norway, or in the paper factory at Lillehammer. But anyway, I want to see Lise... that's for sure and I'm certain it'll be easier to get a job on boat there. The British unions would kill any chances I've got here.'

Shorty nodded. He looked a bit dejected.

'Anyway, you'd really like Norway,' I said. 'You can get jobs there just as easily as in England. You might as well come over there.'

'Yeah, but I want to see a bit of England and...and the rest of the Continent.'

He was right, of course. 'Yeah, I guess so...' I said. '...and you'd be crazy not to do it, while you're here. But you've been talking...several times on the road, about coming out to Oz.'

'Yeah...and I want to. I want to get out there and get into some of that surf you're always raving on about. But...but right now, it seems ridiculous to be just arriving in Europe and then planning on heading straight off.'

'For you, maybe... but not for me. Because I've already done a lot of the things in Europe that you're wanting to do now. But you're right. It'd be crazy for you to head off now. I guess, in the next week or so, we've just got to work out exactly what we each want to do...'

'Well, at least I've got that bit of extra money in London,' Shorty said. '...or at least I hope I have.'

The apartment on the first floor at 16b Creswell Gardens, just off Old Brompton Road, in South Kensington was the flat that Noel and I had shared with four other Australians and one South African eighteen months previously. There were now two new occupants (Australians of course... and young blokes like us) to fill the vacancies left by Noel and my departure. But there was always room for a couple of extras to doss down on one of the couches, or on a Japanese futon and our friends in the flat had told Shorty and I, when we arrived in London that we were welcome to move in to the Creswell Gardens flat whenever we liked.

Not that I intended, or wanted this to be a long term situation. Creswell Gardens was to be only a very temporary stopover. I wanted to get going. Shorty had picked up the draft for twenty pounds he had prudently sent on to the Midlands Bank in London and thankfully my parents had insisted on giving me a similar amount, although, there wasn't really much insisting involved. I knew that, with care, it should last me for several weeks, but staying in London would eat it up more quickly than being on the road, or in Norway. So, from my point of view, now was the time to move on.

But Shorty had the London bug. He wanted to run around and see everything; to go to the Houses of Parliament, Westminster Abbey, the Tower of London, Piccadilly Circus, the Horse Guards, Buckingham Palace...and so on. I did some of them with him...others, he took off to see by himself. This was all done in a matter of a few days. It was still less than a week since we had arrived from Dublin. Nevertheless, I was beginning to get itchy...needing to make a move. I said as much to Shorty.

'Look, I know there's lots of things you want to do in London, so, its probably better that you stay here at the flat and get a job and so on... and I take off for Norway. I'm thinking of leaving this weekend.

'What about my birthday?'

I'd forgotten that Shorty's twentieth birthday was coming up in a few days time. 'Oh...yeah, its on Thursday isn't it?'

'Friday. But I want to go out on the town...and do something... you know... something different.'

'Okay, that's fine. We will. But I just wanted to say...that I'm heading for Norway on the weekend.'

'Uh huh... well, I've been thinking. I'm still thinking...but I'll probably come with you.'

To be honest, I wasn't exactly overjoyed at the prospect of Shorty coming along to Norway with me. I wanted time to be with Lise on my own and Shorty would tend to make the whole thing more difficult and complicated. But....

'Lets go to Soho...that's where all the action is, isn't it?'

Shorty was already pretty drunk...all three of us were in fact. Ray, the other South African staying in the flat at Creswell Gardens...who'd been there when Noel and I had lived there before, and whom we'd always called the Babbling Brook, because he was a pretty good cook... had come out with Shorty and I on his birthday to have a few drinks in the Drayton Arms pub in South Kensington.

'What about the party?' I said. 'They're going to have the party back at the flat later on.'

"Yeah... but that's not for a while... not till eight or nine o'clock, is it? We can have some fun between now and then.'

We staggered down the escalators at South Ken station onto the tube to Piccadilly Circus. It was about six o'clock in the evening. The tube was crowded, not with people heading home from work...but people heading into the centre of London for entertainment, to Piccadilly, to the movies and theatres at Leicester Square, the restaurants and nightclubs.

Shorty wanted to go to a nightclub...or a strip club in Soho for his birthday.

I was drunk, but not quite that drunk. 'It'll cost a bloody fortune to go into one of those clubs,' I said. 'They're real clip joints. Apart from the cover charge, you'll have to buy the girls expensive whiskey, which is only cold tea...and....'

We were walking past a series of strip joints in one of the back streets. Shorty was ogling the semi-naked girls on the posters outside the clubs...as the men standing at the doors tried to hustle us in.

And then... 'Hi guys. Whatcha doin? Like a little fun this evening?'

A tall good-looking blonde, with a short skirt (not a mini. This was eight or nine years before minis came in) and a low-cut top, spoke to us as we rounded the corner from Windmill into Brewer Street. She had an American accent.

'You from the States?' I asked.

Nope... Canada.'

Shorty wobbled slightly as he stopped and blinked. It took him a second or two to take her in and to realise what she was on about. His eyes focused and he smiled.

'You been here long?

'Oh... about six months. Now... how about it, are you guys interested in some fun?'

'Fun?' I said. 'Maybe. Shorty here...its his birthday. How much is the fun?'

Big white teeth flashed in a disarming smile. 'That depends on what you want.'

'What's available?' Shorty asked.

'Well, basically its... pussy on wheels, short time, all night, or a dirty month.'

It was obviously a little patter she had, because it came so easily. We laughed. 'Could you run through that again?' Shorty asked.

She did.

'How much is a dirty month,' I asked.

'Too much for you guys... I can tell.'

'What about all night?'

'A hundred pounds.'

'A hundred quid! Jesus Christ!' Ray exclaimed.

'Its worth it if you've got the money,' she said.

'And a short time? How much is that?' Shorty asked.

'Twenty quid.'

'And how long is that? How long is a short time?'

'Just until you come. But its in a bed...I have a room. Its comfortable.'

'uh huh... and pussy on wheels. What's that... and how much is it?'

She smiled again. 'That's the economy option. We drive around in the back of a cab. We do it on the back seat...until you come. That's a fiver...plus the cab fare, of course.'

'Holy cow. What about the driver?'

'He doesn't look. He's paid not to look.'

'That's the go Shorty! Pussy on wheels. The economy option. I'll put in a couple of quid... a birthday present.'

'And I'll put in a couple too,' said the Babbling Brook.

'So its only going to cost you a quid. Beauty!'

Shorty hesitated only a moment, then grinned broadly. 'Okay. Pussy on wheels. Lets go.'

She took Shorty by the hand and they walked half a block, with Ray and I following, to the next corner and a cab rank, where they slipped into the back of a vehicle and, after a brief conversation with the driver, drove off into the crowded traffic of the Soho night.

Ray and I simply stood at the corner waiting, chatting and laughing about what Shorty might be doing at any particular moment on his trip around Soho.

'...like what happens when you stop at a traffic light, or a pedestrian crossing, with all the people passing by?' Ray said. 'It'd put you off.'

People passing us in the street were eyeing us with bemused and puzzled stares as we split our sides laughing. A couple of tough looking characters gave us a nasty look, as if perhaps we were laughing at them.

Shorty was only gone about fifteen minutes, before the cab pulled up again by the kerb and let him and the girl out. She smiled at us and walked back towards her place on the corner. 'See ya guys,' she called, 'Any time you like. I'm always here.'

'So, how was it? What was it like?' Ray and I both threw questions at Shorty.

'It was great. We just cruised around the back streets. The driver must do it all the time. He must know the streets with not much traffic. We stopped for a couple of minutes in one laneway, where there was nobody around, but then a car came up behind us and we had to keep moving.'

'And she was good?'

'Great man. She was great.'

oooooo

25

I COULD MARRY LISE

For some reason I thought we might be able to find a cheap passage to Norway from the fishing port of Grimsby at the mouth of the River Humber. I can't remember where the idea came from, but I know Shorty and I spent a fruitless afternoon there, on our second day out from London, scouring the waterfront trying to find a fishing boat... anything really... that might be heading for Norway. We had said goodbye to my parents and to our friends at the flat in South Ken and set off about mid-day on the Saturday following Shorty's birthday bash. We hitched up as far as Lincoln, where we stayed in the youth hostel, with hopes of being on some sort of vessel from Grimsby to Norway the the following day. I guess we thought our experience with the Meligunis in Alexandria could be repeated in England. Fat chance.

Moving north, through Kingston upon Hull, late in the afternoon of Sunday, we reached York, where again, the local youth hostel provided convenient and cheap accommodation. The following morning we were on our way to Newcastle and Tynemouth, to start the search for a cheap passage again. No luck. It seemed there was no way we could avoid paying the standard ferry fare to Bergen of £7-10-0 each. We were stuck with it. It was a big hole out of what money we had. But at least it put us, overnight, on the west coast of Norway, only a day's hitching from Oslo.

The road from Bergen to Oslo, a trip of about 450 kilometres, traverses some spectacular countryside. From Bergen, it heads straight up into the mountains, presenting, almost immediately, magnificent views of the fjords, broken bays and endless islands to the south, before crossing some rugged mountain terrain and coming down into the steeply-walled Hardangerfjord. We travelled along the northern slopes of the deep fjord on the back of a truck. But the weather was brilliant and warm, so we were perfectly happy and comfortable there. Fortunately too, the driver included us in the ferry fare he paid when we came to Kvandal, the point at which we crossed Hardangerfjord.

From the other side, at a small town called Kinsarvik, we were climbing again, now up to a high, barren plateau, then down to green forests, grassy fields and brightly painted farmhouses, with fair-haired, sun-tanned children running around. The scent of the pines, as the truck sped on through the countryside and forests, brought the time I'd spent in Norway two years previously, well before meeting Lise, flooding back to me.

As mentioned in Chapter 16, Noel and I had spent six weeks working as lumberjacks in the forest near Hakadal, a tiny settlement to the north of Oslo. We were working on a contract basis for a small local logging concern and the owner provided us with accommodation in a log cabin by a fresh mountain stream. High up on the side of the mountain on the opposite side of the stream, he showed us hundreds of trees that had been marked for felling. All we had to do was chop them down and trim the branches off. He would pay us so much per tree.

I don't remember how much we received for each tree, but I do know that it was so little, we could only just afford to buy food...even though we were working so hard that we'd stagger down the mountain every day absolutely exhausted. But we loved it.

We'd also make occasional forays down to the Youth Hostel in Oslo on the weekends, to see what international talent was presenting there. And more than once we managed to convince two or three girls to come up and stay in our little log cabin... to cook for us (and provide some extra-curricular comforts in the evenings) while we went off to work each day in the forest.

But then the snow came...meters of it, covering our work, so it couldn't be checked and paid for and also making it all but impossible for us to get at the marked trees to cut them down. So, reluctantly, we had to leave.

We hitched to Lillehammer, the small mountain resort town, some 200 kilometres north of Oslo, (*the site of the 1994 Winter Olympics*) and we found work there in the paper factory as labourers. As related earlier, this preceded my winter trip to Finland and Noel & I eventually making our separate ways to London at the end of 1954.

    The various lifts Shorty and I managed to find on the road to Oslo, after getting off the ferry in Bergen left us still some 150 kilometres short of Oslo on our first night in Norway. We stayed overnight in the small, but excellent little youth hostel at Nesbyen, then took off for Oslo in the morning. However, despite the fact that it was mid-summer and there was plenty of holiday traffic on the roads, we didn't seem to have much luck and the remaining distance in to Oslo took us most of the day. It was about five in the evening when we finally arrived, but the sun was still high. Being so far north...on about the same latitude as the Shetland Islands, the Norwegian capital has daylight from about 4.00 in the morning until ten or eleven at night, in midsummer. We stayed in the same big, modern youth hostel at Haraldsheim which Noel and I had frequented when we'd been working in the forest... and the girls were just as beautiful.

But this time I had a different agenda. Soon, I hoped, I would be meeting up with Lise again. I had written from London telling her I was coming to Oslo, but I hadn't said exactly when. Now Shorty and I were here and...well, I wanted to do it properly. I wanted to see her on my own first. But there were things that Shorty and I needed to do before I could meet up with Lise. We had decided once again to try and sell our story to a newspaper, in order to get a little extra cash, if possible, so a visit to the Oslo newspaper 'Aftenposten' was planned for first thing in the morning.

As it had been with the Irish Times, there was a little reluctance on their part, at first, to pay us for a news story, but once the editor recognized that we were fairly legitimate and that the story had some merit, they decided to do it. They ran a small article about our African experiences with a photograph of Shorty and I taken in their offices. we were paid 50 kroner (about £2-10-0) each for the story and they paid me an extra fifty kroner for some of my photographs which they didn't use. But we were happy. It gave us a little extra cash, which was always needed.

'I'm going to try to meet up with Lise this afternoon,' I said to

Shorty as we left the Aftenposten offices. 'I don't know if she's going to be at home or even if she's in Oslo right now, but I'll try to ring her parents home to find out.'

'Okay...well, if you do contact her, you won't want me around. I'll just take a look around town and meet you back at the hostel later.'

'Yeah... okay. You'll get to meet her, later. Its just that I'd like to see her on my own first.'

'No problem. I understand. Just go ahead and organize it.'

As Lise had never actually given me a telephone number for her parents' home on Maridalsvein, where she lived. I had to ask someone to help me use a telephone directory to find the number. But it proved a relatively simple matter and before long I was speaking to Lise.

Although it was well over a year since I'd seen her and we'd only known each other during a brief period of two or three weeks hitch-hiking together in Southern France, Italy and Austria, I had thought of Lise more and missed her more than any other girl I'd ever met...even long-term girlfriends I'd had back home before leaving Australia. I'd never met a girl with such a wonderful, sunny disposition and happy personality and with such a great sense of humour before. And she was beautiful. She was slim, but well-built, with a great body and, like most Norwegians she had blue eyes and blond hair. It was long and wavy, but when we'd been travelling together in France and Italy she'd usually worn it tied back in a bun, or up on top of her head, for convenience... only letting it down, around my shoulders at night, when we were making a place to sleep in some barn, or under a hedge along the road.

Many times, over the months in Africa, even during the periods when I'd had other girls on the beach in Durban and elsewhere, I had found myself thinking about Lise. Was it love? I mean real love? I kept asking myself and wondering why she had become important to me. Why had I given Norway and seeing Lise again such a high priority... even above the fixation I had of heading back to Australia for the Olympics?

And now, after all this time, what would she be like? Maybe she'd be different? Maybe she'd have another boyfriend? Would she feel the same about me? I found I was quite nervous about seeing her. I was nineteen and she was eighteen when we'd met. Now I was nearly twenty-one and she was twenty. Time to marry? I found it hard to believe that I could even think about it...marriage had always been so far outside my general plans. I was far too young. So much more to do and see before settling down with the responsibilities of children. And yet... and yet, if I didn't give it some thought, I felt I could lose her.

Amazing how all these thoughts race through your mind as you're preparing to see someone you care for... love... someone you haven't seen for a long time. I was a basket case by the time I rang the front door bell of her parents' apartment.

'Hello Lise,' I said as she opened the door.

She looked stunning. A light summer dress and sandals. Her hair up in a roll on her head... a great smile.

She came through the doorway and kissed me, before saying anything else. And then 'Yan... Yan...' was all she said. She spoke perfect English, but always pronounced my name as if it were the European version of Ian or Iain...that is, Jan.

I returned her kiss and we stood for a moment or two, looking at each other. 'You look wonderful,' I said.

'And so do you. Come inside. Come and meet my mother. My father is still at work.'

It was quite a large, comfortable apartment... well furnished and decorated tastefully. Her mother was sitting in a lounge chair in the sitting room. She got up, smiling, to shake my hand.

'Hello, Yan. Ve have heard so much about you from Lise. It is good now to see you at last.' She laughed. Her words had that beautiful sing-song lilt that Norwegian...and of course, other Scandinavian languages, seem to have, and which comes through even when they are speaking English. She would have been in her mid-forties and, although her hair was greying slightly, her high cheekbones and clear complexion spoke of a beauty that had faded only imperceptibly.

We sat and talked initially about some of my travels in Africa, then about the time when Lise and I had met in Cannes and what she had been doing since then.

'Oh, just study, study, study all the time, Lise laughed. 'I am so glad to be finished now for the summer.'

'But you like what you're doing, don't you?' I asked. 'I mean its interesting, isn't it?'

'Oh yes, I am doing European history and economics. I like the history... but the economics drives me crazy.'

'I will make coffee,' Mrs. Bjerke said, getting up from her chair. ' Do you like coffee Yan?'

'Yes... please. That would be fine.' I replied as Lise's mother disappeared into the kitchen.

'Where are you staying now?' Lise took my hand in hers.

'At the youth hostel, but...but Shorty, that's the guy I've been travelling with on the way up through Africa...he's still with me. I'm not sure what he's planning to do. I think he wants to either go a bit further north in Norway, or just head across into Sweden, and down through Denmark to Germany. He hasn't made up his mind yet. You could meet him tomorrow...perhaps we could have a coffee in town?'

'Yes... yes.' Lise nodded. 'And I'll get Bibbi to come also.'

Bibbi was the name Noel had given to Åse Hønefoss, Lise's girlfriend, when we had all met at the youth hostel in Cannes. Lise's proper first name was Bjørg.... Bjørg Elisabet Bjerke. She preferred to be called Lise and Åse preferred to be called Bibbi, so that's the way it was.

'Are you still wanting to go back to Australia soon?'

'Yes,' I nodded...and then shook my head slowly. 'Its difficult. I would love to stay here...I mean, stay longer, so that I could spend more time with you. But...well, I've had this plan in my mind for ages...I've written to you about it...about getting back to Australia to work at the Olympic Games. I don't know if it will happen, but I've got to try it.'

Lise said nothing for a moment...then, 'So when will you leave from here? How will you travel?'

'I'm going to try to get a boat...a ship from here. It'll probably take time. Who knows, I might not even be able to get one going to Australia, or Singapore perhaps... anywhere in the Far East would do. And I'll need to get a job here in the meantime.

Again she paused, without saying anything...looking slightly glum. Then a big smile spread across her face. 'So...' She slapped her hand on the coffee table in front of us. '...if our time is short, we have to make the best use of it. Before you take any job... or even look for one... we are going... you and I, are going... camping out on an island in Oslo Fjord. I've been thinking about it since you wrote from England. I have asked my brother to lend me his tent. We can go out there any time. It is so beautiful. I know many places for camping. We can stay there for a few days and just swim and lie in the sun and...' she lowered her voice and laughed softly. '...and make love all day.'

Offers like that are hard to refuse...not that the thought even crossed my mind. But I couldn't help feeling bad about Shorty. It seemed as if I was going to end up leaving him out on a limb, while I sailed off into the fjords with Lise.

Fortunately it didn't turn out like that, although I'm sure if Lise hadn't been in the picture, Shorty would not have taken off from Norway as soon as he did.

'I've been thinking about things this afternoon, while you've been seeing Lise,' Shorty said to me that evening, when I returned to the youth hostel. 'I'm going to make for Sweden the day after tomorrow... and head down the west coast and across to Copenhagen. There's no use me sticking around much longer. We've done our big trip...and now we've got different paths to follow. I can't follow yours, because there's other things I want to do. And you can't come along with me, for the same reason.'

Looking back on it, as I have many times over the years, there was a certain poignancy about that moment that wasn't apparent at the time. These things never seem to be clear until long after. But, here was that point in time...the moment when two people who have been together as good mates for many months, done some rough travelling together and had some tough times...were to part company, never to see each other again. We didn't know it at the time, of course, but more than sixty years have passed and I have never seen or heard of Shorty over all those years...except for an article about him I saw in the surfing magazine Tracks in the late 1990's.

Surprisingly I was mentioned in the interview Tracks had done with Shorty in South Africa...and there was a photograph of he and I with our rucksacks on our backs from that time. Shorty was apparently running a company called The Surf Travel Company, out of Durban... taking international surfers to some of the best out-of-the-way surfing spots in South Africa. But what had happened in his life in all those years in between? I had no idea.

Who knows, maybe we'll meet up again sometime, on the beach

there and I'll find out.

But, back in Oslo in 1956, I remember feeling a mixture of both guilt and relief. Guilt because of leaving him to head off on his own. But, I kept telling myself, he's an adult. He's independent, I don't have to feel responsible. The relief I felt was that Shorty had made the decision to go, before I'd told him I was planning on going camping with Lise. Anyway, at least he'd have a chance to meet her, before he took off.

'Lise wants to meet up with you tomorrow. Her girlfriend, Bibbi... she travelled with Noel and I and Lise last year. She's coming along tomorrow too, to have some coffee in town. You'll meet her.'

'What's she like?'

'Sensational. Really beautiful.' But then I suddenly thought, what if Shorty takes a shine to Bibbi when he meets her... he might want to stay longer. 'Well, you know...sort of beautiful, umm...fairly good looking anyway.' I said.

Shorty certainly agreed that Bibbi was beautiful when we all met in a little café not far from the Town Hall plaza the following morning. Both Lise and Bibbi looked stunning, in summer dresses and high heels. Bibbi could have been Lise's sister. They were about the same size, both blonde and blue-eyed, although Bibbi's hair was a little more wavy, and she had slightly larger cheekbones, which, if anything, emphasised her Scandinavian origin. I found myself thinking, what are a couple of incredible-looking birds like these doing with two guys like Shorty and I, who've hardly got two pennies to rub together. They could have anybody they wanted. But I suppose that's the way the world runs...there's no accounting for taste and of course...pheremones.

As it happened, I needn't have worried about Shorty taking to Bibbi, or vice-versa. She wasn't going to be in Oslo anyway.

'I am going with my family to a hut in the Jotunheimen Mountains tomorrow,' she told us at one stage.

'Jotunheimen...where's that?' Shorty asked.

'Oh... about two hundred kilometres to the north. We go there every summer. It is very beautiful.'

'What a shame,' Shorty looked dejected. 'Can't you stay in Oslo longer?'

'Oh no. We want to get away from the city as soon as possible. I look forward to this in the summer.'

Bibbi, of course asked about Noel, and I told her about our last meeting in Luanshya and as much as I could about his planned movements. Noel had written reasonably regularly to Bibbi from Africa, as I had to Lise, and suggested to her that she come out to Australia. Apparently both Lise and Bibbi had discussed it seriously...and it was still on the agenda with them.

The girls shouted Shorty and I to lunch and we all went out to Frogner Park to wander amongst the amazing sculptures there for a couple of hours in the warmth of the summer afternoon. Then Bibbi had to go and Lise went off to pick up the tent which we planned to use camping in Oslo Fjord.

'I must go to my brother's place to pick up the tent,' she said. 'We can go out to the fjord tomorrow. Will you be ready?'

'Of course,' I laughed. 'We can go now, if you like.'

Shorty and I said goodbye to each other after breakfast at the youth hostel the following morning, Saturday 21st July. He had decided not to head further north in Norway, because of his limited money supply.

'I know I could stay and work here...to save a bit more cash,' he said. 'But, I think if I'm going to look around for a job, I'll probably do it in London. I like it there. In the meantime, I might as well make the most of what I've got left and see a bit of northern Europe, on the way back to London. Anyway, you're going off camping with Lise, so I might as well take off too.'

I nodded a trifle guiltily, saying nothing for a moment or two...and then, 'Anyway, Copenhagen is great. There's a terrific youth hostel there too.'

'Yeah... well, that's what I'm going to do. Head off to Sweden... down the west coast towards Denmark. Maybe I'll find something else to do in Sweden, if it turns up.'

'You never know,' I smiled...and told him about an experience, two years previously, when I had been hitching up the west coast of Sweden in freezing rain.

'I was dropped off in this little village and I stood in the rain on the outskirts waiting for a lift for about half an hour before going back into town to get a cup of coffee. I saw a sign saying 'Varma bad' ...that means 'hot baths'. I can't remember how much it was going to cost, but I was nearly broke, so it must have been cheap and anyway, I was frozen stiff, so I went inside and paid my money...and there's this young bird there who leads me into a room with an oversized, bathtub in it.'

'Jesus,' Shorty gaped.

'Just a regular shaped bathtub, full of hot water. She tells me to take my clothes off and get into the bath.'

'Holy mackerel! What did she look like?'

'Great. She was about thirty, I suppose. She was pretty tall...and thin, with dark hair. I was eighteen... nearly nineteen and I thought, I guess this is pretty standard stuff...the way they do things in Sweden. So I took all my clothes off'

'What happened then? Was she still there?'

'Yep. She closed the door and picked up a cloth...and told me to get into the bath.'

'Oh my god!'

'So I lay down in the bath and she just knelt down beside it and started going all over me with the cloth and some soap.'

'Yeah... and then..?' Shorty's eyes were wide with amazement.

'Well, I started to get a bit worked up. Then she says, stand up. She spoke pretty good English. So I stood up and she went to the cabinet and got out a stiff scrubbing brush and started working all down my back and the back of my legs with this scrubbing brush. Then she says, turn around, and... well, of course, there I was with a big hard on. There was nothing I could do about it.'

'What did she do?'

'She just smiled and scrubbed all around it. I was waiting for her to grab it, but she didn't. I made a move to sort of touch her hair and bend towards her, but she just smiled and shook her head... and waived her hand a bit, as if to say... 'that's not allowed'... and that was it. She finished off washing me in the bathtub again, then dried me down... then left me to get dressed.'

'Christ! Where is this place?'

'I think they're all like that. I mean the small towns in Sweden. They all have bath houses like that. Although I don't know if they do it in the summer. Probably cold baths.'

So at least Shorty left Oslo for the west coast of Sweden with his spirits high and a sense of great anticipation of possible delights to come.

Oslo Fjord in July is a little paradise. Pine covered islands in the midst of a beautiful inland waterway stretching south some sixty kilometres to the Skaggerak and the North Sea. I don't remember the name of the little island that Lise took us to, but it was one of several on a ferry run from Oslo that took little more than half an hour before we hopped ashore and made off towards one end of the island to find a camping spot. The island was long and narrow, no more than a kilometre or two in length, and less than half that in width.

'There's a little place near the bottom of the island where not many people go,' Lise said as we walked. 'Most of the other campers go to the north, because the camping places are easier to get to. This way is a bit more difficult. We have to climb over some rocks and through some thick shrubs, but it is very nice... and there is a beautiful spot for swimming too.'

Whatever she said was okay by me and wherever she led me was fine too. Looking at her, as she strode ahead on the narrow path, in her little hiking shorts, brought back wonderful memories of the weeks we'd spent on the road together in Italy and Austria two years previously. My mind was whirling with thoughts of the times and places we'd made love...and now I could hardly wait to hold her in my arms again. And I knew she felt the same.

We both had our rucksacks which we'd stocked up with supplies of fruit and vegetables and tinned food, that we could cook on a little primus stove. There was also a small store near the ferry landing, where other provisions could be bought later if we needed them.

We had been climbing slowly on a path which led now into a small pine forest. Shortly Lise turned off to the left and clambered up over some rocks, with me close behind. Coming out of the trees, we were presented with a beautiful view of the waters of the fjord to the east, as well as several other nearby islands.

'Its not far from here,' she said, beginning to climb down the rocks towards the water.

The descent, not more than twenty or thirty meters, led us into some thick bush, including blackberries, which we had to skirt around, but within minutes we were down onto a piece of flat grassy terrain, about ten meters square, amidst tall pines, that ran right down to a rocky shoreline and the clear blue waters of the fjord.

'There's a little spring back there...' she pointed to some fern-covered rocks, back in amongst the trees. 'We can get water there, but we've always boiled it first.'

'Fantastic,' I said as we took off our packs and laid our supplies on the ground. 'How did you find this place?'

'We found it once many years ago when Bibbi and I were camping out on this island with the Girl Guides. We weren't camped here. We were up at the other end of the island, but we all came down here on a trek one day and found it. Bibbi and I and other friends have been back here several times.'

'With other guys... I'll bet?' I smiled.

'Maybe,' she laughed, moving towards me and putting her arms around me. 'There's nothing wrong with that, is there?'

'No,' I said, bending over to kiss her. Suddenly we were struggling with each other, tearing at buttons and zippers, throwing our clothes on the ground until we were both naked, rolling on the grass and pine needles, entwined in each others' arms.

'How will you get your ship from here?' Lise asked later. 'It will be difficult, I think. There cannot be very many ships going from Norway to Australia.'

We were lying, in the early evening, on a ground sheet outside our tent. We had swum and sunbaked for almost an hour before setting up the tent and preparing things for an evening meal. Then we'd lain on our backs to talk and watch the sun drop between the pines.

'No. It's going to be a problem, I think. And I'll have to find a job in the meantime. I'm going to do that as soon as we go back from here.'

'Where will you stay? You can stay with me... at home.'

'Where? In your room?'

'Yes. It will be no problem. My parents would not mind.'

'No. I couldn't do that...I haven't even met your father yet. I can stay at the Youth Hostel. But I can only stay there for three nights at a time. There is another one in Oslo though, so I should be able to move from one to the other.'

We spoke for a time about all these problems... accommodation, a job and a ship home. They were of course all my problems, not hers, but Lise naturally felt concerned about them.

'And when you get back to Australia...to the Olympic Games, what do you want to do then, after that?' She rolled her head onto my shoulder and cuddled in to me.

'I don't know. Noel and I have talked about going to America... The States. Travelling around there and working a bit, then going right down through South America.'

'Bibbi and I have been talking about going to The States also.'

'To do what?'

'Same as you. Work and look around... travel.'

'When?'

'Next year... 1957.'

'Great! We could meet up there. Travel around... maybe even go to South America together.'

We swam and lay in the sun and made love for three days at our hideaway spot on the little island and only saw half a dozen people...on land...during the whole time. Plenty of small boats and yachts came by, mostly at a distance, but, because of the difficulty of access, only occasional walkers, plus another couple looking for a camping site, came by our own camp. We wore no clothes for the whole period we were there... but there's nothing unusual about that in Scandinavia... and the few passers by we did see would have probably been more surprised if we'd been clothed.

This rediscovery of Lise was something of a turning point for me. I began to feel that I loved her in a way I had had never experienced before. In all of my dealings with girls and women...even the serious girlfriends I'd had prior to leaving Australia two years previously, at the age of eighteen, the question of marriage had been something so remote as to not even be thought of, let alone considered in any rational way. Now I found myself actually thinking that I could marry Lise. That we could share a life together.

I didn't actually say it to her...that would have been too much. But just thinking of marriage was fairly outrageous for me. After all, I was only twenty, and hadn't I often said to Noel... with him taking the same view...that 'no woman is going to get me until I'm at least 28 or 30 years old.' There was too much to do...too much to see, before something like that happened. Marriage, I thought, was settling down and having children.   But was it really? Is it necessarily like that?...I started thinking. With somebody like Lise, who loved travelling, liked camping, didn't mind sleeping under a hedge or in a barn, maybe marriage could be different.

Not that I wanted to spend our lives sleeping under hedges...it was the principle of the thing, the fact that she wasn't fazed by something like that and took pleasure in the excitement of new adventures. Maybe twenty wasn't too early.   And somehow I felt that she had the same feelings. She never mentioned marriage either, but I knew she loved me...at least she said as much. But marriage never came into it...only the idea that we should meet again for more adventures, after I had returned to Australia.

'Jeg ha reste in Norge, tre maneder i nitten femti fire. Jeg jobbet i skogen, i Hakadal, og pa en papir-fabrikk i Lillehammer. Jeg likte godt i Norge for mur.

Anders Bjerke sat back in his chair nodding appreciatively and chuckling. 'Good. Very good. After only three months here, you speak Norwegian well.'

Lise's father, was a solid, good-looking man in his late forties. He was blond and balding and wore rimless glasses which, had it not been for an impish smile and infectious laugh, would have made him appear rather stern and serious.

We were eating dinner at Lise's place after returning that afternoon from the fjord. We had been talking about my previous experiences in Norway, as a lumberjack and working in the paper factory in Lillehammer, during which I had tried to remember some of the Norwegian I had learnt.

I don't remember what he did for a living, some sort of administrative work in an office, to which he commuted on a nine-to-five basis every day, but whenever I was at their apartment, Lise's father came across as a bright, intelligent and basically happy man... as was his wife.

They asked many questions about Australia. I think I was the first

Australian they'd ever met, so there were endless questions about kangaroos and koalas... even the platypus.

'I had an uncle... no, a grand...how do you say...great uncle who once worked on a whaling station in Western Australia,' Anders said.
'I know it, because my father told me. But I never met my grand uncle... we only heard that he had worked there. We never knew anything about it...or about Australia. But, of course we have seen pictures in books. I think it is a beautiful country.'

'Yes,' I said.

We talked too of my plans to try to find work in Oslo, as well as a ship going to Australia, on both of which subjects Mr. and Mrs. Bjerke were encouraging, but unable to be of any real help.

I slept that night at their apartment...with Lise, in her bedroom. We were both, after all, almost twenty-one and, although at that age, in the company of parents, it is natural to still feel the vestiges of childhood attitudes, Mr. and Mrs. Bjerke made it clear that they considered it perfectly acceptable that I should sleep with Lise.

But some relics of childhood feelings must have remained, as we both experienced a little of the forbidden fruit syndrome...making love so close to her parents' room. We whispered and laughed softly for half the night as we rolled about in Lise's bed.

Within three days I had found a job... as a luggage porter at Fornebu airport with SAS... Scandinavian Airlines System. The fact that I spoke a little Norwegian and understood a bit more, had helped, but was not essential. I can't remember why I should have applied to SAS, or who if anyone had suggested it to me. The tip had probably come from one of the other young people staying at the big Youth Hostel at Haraldsheim, to which I returned after leaving Lise on the morning after we'd come back from the fjord. There were scores of young backpackers...German, Dutch, French, Italian, English, American and other Australians passing through the hostel all the time. Most were just travelling and enjoying the summer vacation, but others, like myself, were also looking for some short-term employment to bolster their finances.

Anyway, I was told on a Friday afternoon that I could report to the airport on Monday morning ready for work at 7.00 am, when I should also collect my uniform. Once I got into the job, I found it to be pretty basic stuff...quite hard work, in that there never seemed to be much down time, but reasonably enjoyable. With a team of other guys, I would drive little electric trolleys around the airport, picking up luggage to load into the holds of departing planes...as well as offloading them from arriving aircraft and taking them into the collection halls. Of course all of the aircraft were propeller driven. Commercial jet aircraft were still a thing of the future. So we were trundling around loading and unloading aircraft like, Lockheed Constellations, Douglas DC-4s and DC-6s an occasional Boeing Stratocruiser, which were flown by Pan Am and BOAC and the one which attracted most interest... the new Vickers Viscount, the world's first commercial turbo-prop plane, which was operated by BEA, British European Airways. BOAC were also operating the Comet, the first commercial jet aircraft, at the time, but it was not flying in to Oslo.

During the three days I had been looking for a job, I had also taken time out to visit the Port of Oslo, to see how things operated there and to check out the program for incoming and outgoing vessels over the next few weeks. As I understood the register, there seemed to be three vessels that would be arriving in and departing from Oslo over the next month that listed Australian ports as a destination. One leaving on the 11th of August, another around the 15th, and the third on the 29th or 30th.

But,I was concerned that, unless I was taken on one of these vessels, I might not make it back to Australia in time for the Olympics and, as I said in a letter to my parents from Oslo, 'I hope one of them comes off because I'd like to start work on a newspaper before the games start in November. The trip (on a cargo vessel) normally takes six weeks or two months, but with what's happening in Egypt, and possibly having to go around the Cape, it may take longer.'

The Egyptian situation...that is, the crisis precipitated by General Nasser, was spiralling rapidly downwards towards some sort of confrontation. Things had worsened considerably in the few weeks since Shorty and I had left Egypt. And just a week previously... while Shorty and I and Lise and Bibbi had been having coffee near the Town Hall plaza, the U.S. Secretary of State and the British Foreign Secretary had announced that both their countries were withdrawing their promised financial support for Egypt's construction of the Aswan High Dam.

In retaliation...on the day before I got the job with SAS... President Nasser defiantly declared martial law in the canal zone and seized control of the Suez Canal Company, telling his people that tolls collected from ships passing through the canal would pay for the dam within five years.

The British government, enraged by the nationalization, and the French, angered by Egyptian aid to the revolution in Algeria, plotted with Israel...which was already hostile towards Egypt because of its blockage of the Gulf of Aquaba to Israeli vessels and its open threats of war against Israel...to develop their own military solution to the problem.

But all this was still to come. And, although there were headlines in the newspapers, Egypt now seemed somewhat remote to me and I simply felt lucky that Shorty and I had got out when we did. In the meantime I had to persevere in trying as hard as I could to get a job on one of those ships. At this stage, however, they weren't even in port and the only response I could get to my queries, at the offices of the companies that represented the vessels, was basically that: '...it is entirely a matter for the captain of the ship whether you can be taken on as crew. He is the only one to make the decision.'

Having at least worked out the shipping options and also found a job, I now began to pursue another small, but as it turned out, not unimportant, mission... to do some groundwork on a possible job back in Australia at the Olympic Games.

Keith Byron, the press photographer with the American wire service, United Press, who had shared the flat with Noel and I in London...and whom Shorty and I had seen again while we were there before heading off to Norway, had given us some contacts in the UP office in Oslo. It was Keith, you may recall, who'd first put the germ of an idea in my head, that I could perhaps become a 'photo-journalist'. He had just been posted to the UP Bureau in Beunos Aires and was due to leave the week after Shorty and I arrived in London. I had asked Keith, while we were there, for the address and names of people working for UP in Sydney, which was the main office in Australia, but also in Oslo. This was not intended to help in trying for a job with UP in Norway, but simply to make a contact...to ask for information, some sort of guidelines that might help me go for a job when I got back home to Australia. I could easily have taken a similar approach with the office in London, but somehow it seemed more formidable there. A huge office, scores of people...whereas, here in Oslo, it should, I thought, be a relatively small operation... easier to approach.

I went into the office in Oslo and met a young American journalist who'd been based there for 18 months. There was nothing he could do for me as far as employment was concerned, but, after a little research he undertook on my behalf, he did give me some more details about UP people who I might be able to contact in Melbourne during the Olympic Games.

'Apparently they're shifting almost the whole operation down to Melbourne from Sydney from about two weeks before the games, until after they finish...so you should be able to make contact with them there, instead of in Sydney,' he told me. 'The people to see are either Bob Miller, the Australian Bureau Chief, he's an American, or the Sydney Manager, Eric Riel.'

Keith Byron had already given me Bob Miller's name, so I noted Eric Riel as another, or alternate one to contact when I eventually got back to Melbourne.

There would, of course, be scores of other Australian and international news and media organizations at the games, which I could try for employment...but I felt encouraged to have a starting point with at least a couple of names.

As I was now working at the airport, my time with Lise was cut down. At first I thought we would have plenty of time to see each other on weekends. But the SAS job didn't quite work out like that. I was on shift work, which could be changed quite suddenly from day work to night and from weekdays to weekends. Nevertheless we still found plenty of time to be with each other, as I would have time off during the day to fit in with night shifts, and weekdays off to compensate for any weekend work. This was complicated by the fact that the Oslo Youth Hostel's rule of allowing no more than three consecutive days accommodation had me leap-frogging back and forth from the Harladsheim hostel to Oslo Hostel No. 2 and back again. I can't remember what else that hostel was called, but that's the way it shows up on the stamps in my old Youth Hostel card.

The accommodation scene was also not very helpful to Lise and I as far as making love was concerned. We arranged, on several occasions to meet at her parents place, when she knew that her mother would be out of the house during the day, and we managed on a few other occasions, when we were out at night...perhaps after going to the movies, or having a cheap meal in town, to find a secluded place in a park where we could make love. But in general, we were handicapped in the way so many young people are, in having nowhere to go where they can be completely alone.

However, we did have time to do interesting things together. We went back out to Frogner Park to see more of Vigeland's incredible statues. Said to have been the most prolific sculptor of all time, Vigeland spent most of his lifetime in the creation of his major work in Frogner Park. It consists of more than 200 individual sculptural projects, including an entrance, a bridge, a fountain, a circular staircase, a mosaic labyrinth, all of which are covered with carved human figures. A central monolith, weighing some 270 tonnes, is carved with 121 human figures. It is surrounded by 36 groupings of statues covering various periods in the cycle of life... birth, childhood, adolescence, maturity, old age and death.

We went also to the Viking Ship Museum and the Kontiki Museum to see the actual balsa raft on which Thor Heyerdahl sailed across the Pacific, the huge ski jump at Holmenkollen, looking strangely awkward in mid-summer without any snow and the nearby Ski Museum. I remember too, sitting with Lise, in a small outdoor café in the centre of town, where a car, which was first prize in a lottery, had been placed on platform nearby.

The car was the new Citroen DS, also called the 'Goddess' ...considered then to be the world's most revolutionary vehicle.

'Lets get a ticket,' I said. 'If we win... I'll come back after the Olympics, and we can drive it around Europe.'

'And then sell it and go to America,' Lise laughed.

During my occasional weekdays off, I made a point of revisiting the shipping companies which would have vessels bound for Australia in port over the next few weeks. The company with one leaving on the 11th of August, a Danish company...I can't remember the name, looked hopeful, as did the Norwegian ship the 'Themis', a Wilhelmsen Lines vessel, which was presently loading cargo in Finland and due to come in to Oslo and sail again by the 14th.

'I still can't guarantee you anything as far as work is concerned,' the local manager told me for the third time, but I will put in a good word for you with the Captain, when the ship arrives.'

I had pulled out all stops in my visits to the Wilhelmsen Line offices and fortunately, from an enquiry over the counter on my first visit, I had been referred to the office manager...even though they kept stressing that the Captain made the final decision.

I smiled a lot and made much of the fact that I was an Australian trying to get home for the Olympic Games. I pointed out I had seaman's papers, having worked on other ships: Finnish, Danish and Italian... and that I was prepared to work for just my passage...no money.

'I'll be saving you a lot of money,' I smiled. 'And I work hard.'

The manager had laughed. 'Okay, okay...I'll do my best.'

And evidently he had, because, on the day after the Themis docked in Oslo, I was told in the Wilhelmsen Line offices that I had the job. I could sail on the Themis on Monday, August 13...in four days time. For a brief moment I was stunned...then elated. I then set about spending as much of those last few days in Oslo with Lise.

It was an incredibly emotional period. I knew that I loved her more than any other girl or woman I'd ever met. I knew that I wanted to live with her, travel with her, marry her...and eventually have children. Then, why was I leaving her? Why was I driven to follow this course of going back to Australia to the Olympic Games?... It wasn't as if I was an athlete and my country needed me. I didn't really know if I'd even be able to get to see any of the Games. I was on a course that had been set almost as soon as I had left Australia...a course that had become stuck in my mind, so that now I couldn't see any other way.

'Maybe I could come to Australia, instead of going to The States,' Lise said on the wharf, just before I sailed. 'We could be together there and work for a while, before we went to travel in America.'

'Yes. Yes. Great. It would be terrific, if you could do that. You'd like Australia. We could travel there too.'

'I love you, Yan. I want to be with you.' She came towards me.

'Oh God...' I held her tight. 'I don't want to leave you either Lise. I don't know why I'm doing this. I just feel as though I have to. I... I...'

'Its alright,' she patted my back. 'Its alright. I understand. I do understand...that its important for you. I will come to Australia to be with you next year... as soon as I finish at University.'

'When?'

'In June.'

'Wonderful! Great!'

A call from the ships deck for me to come on board.

I kissed her and held her tightly in my arms, fighting back tears, loving her, not wanting to leave her. Choked up and hardly able to talk, I went to gangplank.

'G...goodbye Lise. I... I love you.'

As the ship pulled out into the roads of Oslo harbour, I saw her standing on the wharf, amongst the few other family members of the crew. She stood there, her light summer dress and blonde hair whipped by the afternoon breeze, waving to me for a long time, until the ship changed course to make its way down the fjord and I lost sight of her as the wharf was obscured from view. Lise.

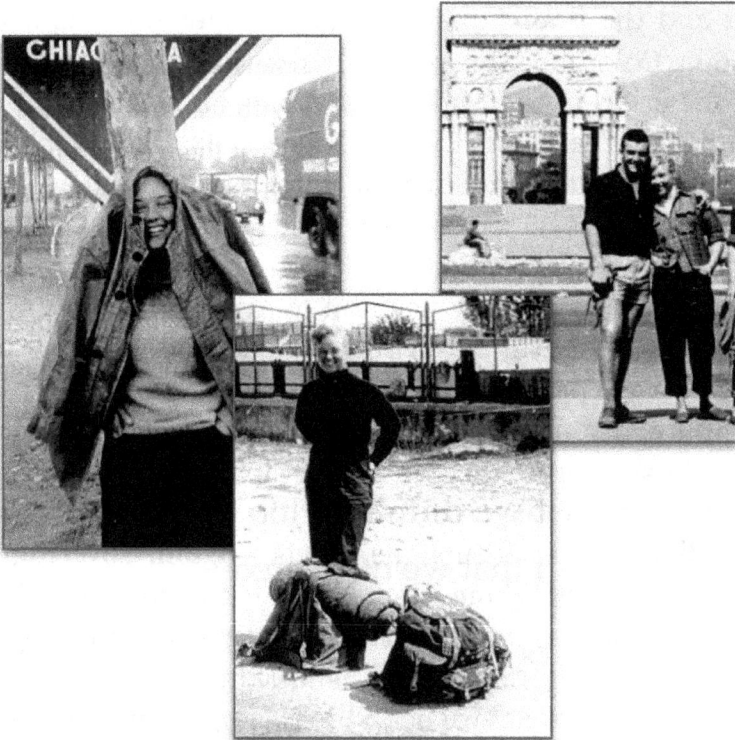

Lise

ooooo

26

MAGPIES WARBLING IN THE TREES

The MV Themis was somewhat larger than the Meligunis... around 10,000 tonnes. I think. There was no consignment of any significance that she was delivering from Norway to Australia, but, according to the schedule, she planned to pick up cargo during the next week or so at Hamburg, Bremmen, Rotterdam, Antwerp and Lisbon, sailing then for Port Said and the Suez Canal. Barring problems there, she would call then at Aden, Colombo, Singapore, Brisbane and Sydney.

But the crisis in the Middle East had not been off the front pages, or the radio for the whole period I'd been in Oslo. What was Britain going to do? Would Israel play a part? Nobody knew. Certainly the people at Wilhelmsen Lines had no way of knowing...at least one wouldn't have thought so, nor did they give any hint of any contingency plans. Not that I was in any position to know what they were thinking anyway, although it was often the subject of discussion amongst the crew as the voyage progressed.

Hamburg, Bremmen, Rotterdam, Antwerp came and went in a blur. Big, busy ports...cargoes being loaded non-stop. Uncovering hatches... folding the big steel roofs of the hatches back to one side by crane. Loading cargo, closing the hatches again, covering them with hefty tarpaulins and locking them down with great steel bars. Hauling ropes, cleaning decks, chipping rust, painting, until finally we were on our way to Lisbon. Somehow, shuttling between those northern European ports, I felt as if we hadn't left. Norway and Oslo were still just a few hundred kilometres to the north. But now, as we pulled out of the port of Antwerp and sailed down the Westerschelde out into the North Sea, turning towards the English Channel, I felt that we were at last on our way.

I had written to Lise from Hamburg and Rotterdam and there was a letter waiting for me from her when the ship's agent came aboard at Lisbon, where the Themis docked four days after leaving Antwerp.

'I so wish that I was coming with you,' she wrote. 'I miss you already. I want to come to Australia. I will come to Australia...next year.'

I felt good that she planned to come to Australia. Whatever happened to me in the meantime, as far as working at the Games, would be over and done with by the New Year and something else would have happened...life would be continuing on a new path. What it would be was anybody's guess. But the idea of having Lise in Australia by the middle of the year...about nine months down the track, was good. It would mean adjusting the original rough plans Noel and I had worked out for travelling through the Americas' together, but so what?

I liked being on the road with Noel. He was one of the best of travelling companions. But I'd been travelling without him for almost a year now, so my future travels didn't necessarily have to be with Noel. Lise and I would make a good team. I knew it.

We spent only one night in Lisbon, having taken on most of our cargo of Portuguese wine and large quantities of cork during the first day.

I went ashore with a few of the crew members for some Sagres beer in a small taberna near the port, but I returned to the ship for the evening meal, not having sufficient money, or the desire for some of the hell-raising they were intent on for the rest of the evening. There'd probably be other opportunities later in the voyage anyway, I thought. Wrong.

As soon as the loading was finished during the following morning, we were under way...out from Lisbon, southwest, into the Atlantic. We were due, on our original schedule, to turn eastward into the Mediterranean after about 120 kilometres and, after passing the Straits of Gibraltar, make straight for Port Said, at the other end of the Med...although some of the crew said we would also call at Naples.

None of that happened. We just kept heading southwest, further into the Atlantic, all day. It didn't take long for the word to get around. The crew talked of nothing else. Many were disappointed. Others were quite happy with the decision. We were not going through the Mediterranean...or Suez. Obviously the orders had come through from

Wilhelmsen's head office to the agent in Lisbon.

The crisis over the canal was continuing to build. England and France were concerned that Nasser could, at will, close the canal and cut off oil shipments from the Persian Gulf to Western Europe. Diplomatic efforts had failed to make any headway and Britain, France and Israel would shortly attack Egypt in order to secure the zone. At this time, of course, their preparations were secret. Wilhelmsen's decision to avoid the canal had simply been a prudent one.

The Captain was now directed to take the ship direct to Fremantle, in Western Australia, with a brief bunkering stop scheduled in Dakar, French West Africa, in seven days time, at the end of the month.

In my last letter to Lise I had told her that I would be able to get mail from the ship's agent in Port Said. Now, according to the First Officer, any mail sent there would be sent on to Fremantle.

'When will we be there?' I asked.

'Around the 21st, or 22nd of September, I think. It depends on the weather.'

'Almost a month?'

'Yes... I guess that's right,' he nodded casually. 'Almost a month.'

'Do we call anywhere else?'

'Dakar...to take on fuel. But that will only be a few hours. There is a chance we can call at Capetown, if we can get a cargo there. But at this stage it seems unlikely.'

A month at sea. I didn't have much in the way of books with me. There were one or two Readers Digest condensed books in English on board, which I would probably get around to, if things got really desperate. But, for the moment, I was reading a book that I had picked up in an English language bookstore in Oslo...a book that I found quite inspirational, in that it told of an adventure in South America that had similarities to my own experiences in Africa, with Noel and Shorty. The Book Club edition I had, had been printed one year previously, in 1955. It was by a young English traveller called Sebastian Snow, who in 1951 had made a lone journey, at the age of twenty one, from the headwaters of the Amazon, to Iquitos, some 1,600 kilometres, down river. It was called simply 'My Amazon Adventure.'

Finishing the book a couple of days after leaving Lisbon, I resolved to try to do something about putting my African experiences down on paper.   I had plenty of notes and diary entries, but nothing in any narrative form. With almost a month of days and nights at sea looming ahead, I felt it presented a good opportunity for me to try to tell something of the story of my 'African Adventures' with Noel and Shorty.

I arranged to borrow a typewriter from the Purser's office and set it up in my small cabin. Despite the course I had taken in South Africa... I found my typing   was very rusty and my ability to touch type had deteriorated considerably, with no practice for six or seven months. But as the days progressed, I would sit, after dinner, for two or three hours at the typewriter, tap-tapping away and gradually it all started to come back.

Dakar, near Cape Verde, on the western-most tip of Africa, in what is now Senegal, is better known to modern-day television viewers as the final destination of the incredible desert motor race... the Paris to Dakar Rally. In those days the rally did not exist and Dakar was simply the capital of French West Africa, a vast territory covering an area of 4.5 million square kilometres...equal in size to virtually all of Europe and with a population somewhere around twenty five million people.

Now, the population would be approaching 120 million for the same territory, which has long since been split into eight different countries. Beginning in 1958, French West Africa rapidly separated into what are now the independent territories of Mauritania, Senegal, Guinea, The Ivory Coast, Mali, Niger, Benin and Burkina Faso, two of which are now amongst the poorest nations in the world.

Viewed from the sea, Dakar is...or was then, particularly attractive, as virtually all of the buildings were painted white, in what was quite a tropical setting, with offshore islands and dramatic cliffs with a corniche road on the coast adjacent to the town. We had no chance, however, to explore Dakar, as the fuelling procedures lasted only five hours and there was no shore leave for the crew.

We left Dakar, on the afternoon of the same day we arrived... the 31st of August and did not see another ship, or any sign of land, save the distant lights of Capetown on the night of September 9th, until we sighted the west coast of Australia, late in the morning of September

21st.

The three-week voyage from Dakar could not have been better. My recollections are of brilliant, sunny days, calm seas, working... mainly on deck, in just a pair of jeans or shorts and work boots, chipping rust and painting, as well as doing other odd jobs at the bosun's direction. Also...getting a good suntan, eating good food and typing away in the evening on my African tome. The timing of the voyage from Europe to Australia had worked well. I completed typing the outline of my story, up to the point where I arrived in Western Australia...on the night before we arrived there.

As it happened, as explained in the 'Notes On The Text' section, those fifty pages that I typed never saw the light of day...for over forty years. I pulled them out of a bundle of old papers in the late-1990's and took them, with some other old reference material, to Greece and started to work on it all again.

Anyway...back on board the Themis, as we approached the West Australian shoreline that beautiful, sunny morning, I remember being very moved at the sight of my homeland. I stood at the bow of the ship, alone, gazing towards the low line of cliffs and sand hills forming that part of the West Australian coast that could be seen taking shape on the distant horizon. I thought of the Dutch explorers who first sailed up the coast, back in the 1600's, knowing nothing of the vast continent that stretched another five thousand kilometres to the east.

Five thousand kilometres!...a pretty formidable distance, but I felt I could hitch it in a reasonable time. The ship would apparently remain berthed in Fremantle for several days, before sailing for Adelaide and Melbourne, so I felt I could make faster time hitch-hiking across than waiting for the ship to take me.

I had practically no money though...roughly thirty shillings. Unlike the skipper of the Italian vessel Shorty and I had sailed on, who had some sympathy for us and gave us five pounds between the two of us, to the Captain of the Themis, a contract to work for your passage, was apparently just that...and no more. To be honest though, I don't think it had anything to do with the Captain. The question was probably never raised with him. I had mentioned... diplomatically, to the purser that I could do with a little financial assistance.

'I know there is nothing owing to me,' I said. 'But I have practically no money. Anything would help.'

'I'll see what I can do,' he told me. 'I'll talk to the First Officer.'

But nothing came of it. I'm sure it never got to the First Officer, let alone the Captain.

I worked on the ship for the rest of that day, after we had berthed in Fremantle Harbour, had a good evening meal and slept on board that night, ready for an early start the following morning. Knowing I wouldn't have much to spend on food, I stuffed myself with a huge breakfast of eggs and bacon and lots of bread and coffee... as well as taking some bread and cheese in my pack, before saying my goodbyes to the friends I'd made on board. Then, slinging my rucksack on my back, I went down the gangplank on to the wharf and, although I didn't do what the Pope usually does... kiss the ground, I almost felt like doing it. I then made my way to the Customs and Immigration office and after the brief formalities, headed out of the port and into Fremantle.

It took me quite some time to get from Fremantle across the metropolitan area of Perth. I had determined to hitch the whole way... not being prepared, or in a position to pay fares on buses or trains. So, I took a route around to the south of Perth, through Melville and Kensington and it was not until after midday that I reached Midlands on the eastern perimeter of Perth, at the beginning of the Great Eastern Highway. It appeared to be heading East, but it didn't seem to be much of a highway...and it certainly wasn't Great.

Anyway, I wasn't worried. I was immensely happy to be back in Australia and on my way to Melbourne. Just hearing Australian accents and the sounds of magpies warbling in the trees, on a couple of occasions when I was stalled for a while in the suburbs, were enough to keep me smiling to myself, in contemplation of a bright future, as I waited. In addition, I felt the amazing intensity of the light...it just seemed much brighter and stronger than in Europe and the great feeling of space; the knowledge that the road I was heading down would keep rolling on and on for thousands of kilometres.

Although I only had a pound to my name now (I'd spent ten shillings on a film), I felt that with luck I could make it string out to Adelaide, where my elderly great aunt, Elsie had offered to put me up for a day or so. I had written to her from Dakar and a reply had been waiting for me in Fremantle...along with other letters from Lise and from my parents. (Its interesting, in these days of cheap and easy telephoning, faxes and email, to realise that in those days communications between people over long distances worked very well... it was just that the whole process was much slower.)

At the end of that first day, after passing an hour or so on the outskirts of Northam, I had only reached the small town of Cunderdin, about 160 kilometres from Perth. I hoped that the pace would improve the next day, or I'd be in trouble. I camped out in the bush, outside of Cunderdin...just in my sleeping bag, on a ground sheet and was up early in the morning, to pick up a good ride to Merredin, about a hundred kilometres to the East. The temperature was cool...being winter time, but the whole area, which is one of Western Australia's richest wheat producing regions, was crying out for water. They had seen no rain for months and everything was as dry as dust. Reaching Coolgardie by the end of the day, I felt a little better about the distance covered...over four hundred kilometres.

At Coolgardie the Great Eastern Highway continues on towards the big mining town of Kalgoorlie, some forty kilometres to the east. But if you want to keep going towards eastern Australia by car, you have to skip Kalgoorlie and turn southward from Coolgardie to follow the Eyre Highway, which leads, within a hundred kilometres or so, to the great open plains of the Nullabor.

Coolgardie then was basically a tourist-oriented town, featuring deserted reminders of the rip-roaring days of its gold-mining past, before the turn of the century and before the gold ran out and the miners shifted to work the more productive Golden Mile of Kalgoorlie. But had the gold really all run out? I recalled the news story of how, only five years earlier, in 1951, the Eldorado nugget, a 2,000 ounce... or 55 kilogram... chunk of gold had been found just outside of Coolgardie. Camping that night, on the outskirts of the town, I couldn't resist the temptation to kick over a few rocks and brush the leaves aside around my little camp area. You never know.

Waking the next morning in the midst of what seemed to be a dust storm, I managed to eat some bread and cheese, trying unsuccessfully to shield the food from the wind, only to find every bite containing minute particles of grit.

Taking up a position by the side of the road, I waited perhaps an hour before picking up a lift heading south towards the big dry salt lakes Lefroy and Cowan, to reach Norseman, some 200 kilometres on, after a dusty trip in high winds. The road from Coolgardie to Norseman had been an unsealed, dirt road. It would be like that for the next 2,000 kilometres to Adelaide.

Norseman stood virtually on the edge of the Nullabor Plains, with practically nothing beyond it, as far as regular habitation was concerned, for over a thousand kilometres. Only the odd water tank and petrol dump had been established across the Nullabor at intervals, for emergencies. I'd been dropped off at a fork in the road, just outside Norseman, to the north of the town, where a signpost said: Adelaide: 1000 + miles. (I can't remember the exact distance, other than the fact that it was more than a thousand miles).

I sat on my pack, in the shade of a stringy bark tree, by the side of the road and waited...and waited...and waited. Nothing came by heading east. Well, a few vehicles did, but they were only going to outlying homesteads, not far from Norseman. I could see that I might have a long wait in front of me. Looking at the map, it was clear though, that whatever non-local car did come past would almost certainly be going the whole distance across the Nullabor to South Australia. There was nothing much else in between. My fears of a protracted stay on the road there...slowly starving to death, were heightened after a brief conversation with two other young guys, carrying bed-roll swags, who appeared on the road, walking back towards me from the east. They had been obscured from my vision by a slight bend in the road. As they strolled up, they both smiled.

'G'day. Headin' for Adelaide?' one of them said.

'Trying to,' I replied. 'Not much traffic though. I've been here since about ten o'clock this morning.'

He laughed. 'Don't want to depress you, but you might as well settle in. We've been here for a week.'

'A week!' I exclaimed. 'Holy cow! ... waiting to get to Adelaide?'

'Yep. We've been sitting just down the road.'

'And nothing has come.'

'Couple of cars. But they couldn't take us...or didn't want to. One truck, but he just kept going.'

'Have you been out here all day... every day?'

'Yeah... well, most of the time. We've been back into the pub a few times to have a beer or two. That's where we're going now.'

'What about at night?'

'Nah. We've been staying at the pub. We come out during the morning and early afternoons. That's when most of the traffic seems to be...what traffic there is. Its either coming through from Kalgoorlie, or Perth.'

'Mmm,' I muttered. 'Doesn't sound too promising.'

'Not so far. Good luck anyway....' They continued walking back towards Norseman.

'Thanks.'

'They say there's jobs going in the meat works at Kalgoorlie,' one of them shouted...and they both laughed. A friendly laugh, rather than derisive. After all...they were in the same boat.

I sat reading for another two hours, during which time not a single vehicle passed. The sun was low in the sky and I had already looked around to pick out a spot to spend the night, when suddenly a utility truck coming from the direction of Kalgoorlie turned down the road and stopped beside me.

'How far ya goin?' He pushed a battered, sweat-stained Akubra back on his head.

'Well... Adelaide actually, but anywhere down the road will...'

'I'm goin as far as Balladonia homestead,' he drawled. 'Its about 200 kilometres down the track. If you want to come that far with me, you're welcome.'

'Yeah...yeah. Great...' I said, picking up my pack and tossing it in the back of the ute next to a pile of rabbit skins, some cartons and other supplies. 'Ahh... is there anything there... at Balladonia?'

'Bugger all really. Its not much more than an old ruin.'

He'd started the car and we were on our way, before I'd even thought about the decision I'd made. I hadn't even looked at the map to see where he was talking about. It might not even be on the Eyre Highway.

I opened my map, as we trundled along and found it. A tiny dot saying Balladonia HS where the dirt road, running south east in a perfectly straight line for just on a hundred kilometres, suddenly joins the overland telegraph line running almost due east towards South Australia. At that point there's a forty-five degree bend in the road and it continues running beside the telegraph line for another perfectly straight stretch of about a hundred and sixty kilometres, before there's another bend in the road. Balladonia Homestead... or the ruins of it, sits right on that first bend.

'Umm... when you say there's bugger all there...its not a homestead any more?'

'Hell no. It used to be a homestead once... God knows when, but then the postal department used it as a station on the trans-Australia telegraph line around the turn of the century. It was occupied then... and probably for a good while afterwards... I don't know.'

'And....ahh, does anyone live there now?'

'Not permanently. There's water and a petrol dump there. There's a couple of people...a bloke and his bird, who've been out there for a while. They sell the petrol and a few other things. Can't see what they do it for. Its a bastard of a place for my money.'

'What are you going there for?'

'Rabbits. I trap 'em. Thousands of the bastards out there. I've got traps all over the place. I just skinned this lot...' he jerked his thumb towards the back of the truck, '...this afternoon. I wanted to get out to Balladonia before dark, but I'm not going to bloody well make it... time ran out on me. Anyway, we'll be there tonight.'

'How long will you stay out there?'

'Coupla days. I sorta do a circuit. I got two or three other places.'

'There's a bounty on them is there?'

'Yep. You can make pretty good money on it too. Just gotta know the right spots.'

We barrelled on, with a great cloud of dust billowing up behind us and the sun sinking red behind it. We passed through some low, rolling, but arid country shown on the map as the Dundas Hills. They were hardly hills, but I suppose they had to be viewed in comparison to the rest of the territory that surrounded them, which was dead flat, open and empty. Particularly as we turned slightly south east, passing another spot on the map called Newman Rock, a large rock pile to the left of the road, which now stretched out before us in the gathering gloom, in an absolutely straight line, for almost a hundred kilometres.

Finally, about eight-thirty in the evening we arrived at Balladonia...what there was of it. A more desolate and lonely place would be hard to imagine. It had once been a large, stone house, but now only a few rooms remained usable, while the rest were crumbling and empty. In the darkness it seemed completely deserted...except for a chink of light from a kerosene lantern I perceived in one window.

'I'm going to drop you here, mate,' the trapper said. 'I've got a campsite about seven or eight k's out from here. I wanna start there first thing in the mornin. So if you see Bernie...he's the guy that's living here... tell him I'll be back tomorrow for some petrol.'

I hauled my pack out from the back of the ute and shook his hand. 'Thanks a lot,'

'Good on yer mate...   Good luck with the hitchin. You might get one tomorrow. If not I'll probably see ya back here.' He shifted the car into gear and drove off on a track that led around the back of the house and off into the darkness of the countryside. A blind in the window of the house was pulled back slightly as someone looked out... then released. But no one came to the door.

I stood in the yard listening to the sound of the car dwindling away to nothing...until there was just silence. Should I go and knock on the door? No real reason to...I thought. I've got some water, got bread, cheese, some dried fruit...and, of course sardines. Okay, until tomorrow at least. After that, maybe they've got something there to sell.

In the meantime... just in case a truck or something might come by during the night, I decided to sleep by the roadside at the entrance to the property. There was a low stone wall running beside the road, with an opening for the driveway into the yard. I spread out my groundsheet and sleeping bag next to the wall and crept into it fully clothed. The temperature was dropping and I was already feeling chilly.

On the Nullabor in winter, although there might be clear and sunny days...once the sun sets, whatever warmth there might have been in the earth seems to leave it as fast as possible. I had my socks on as well as jeans, a woolen shirt and sweater, inside my sleeping bag and I was still freezing cold during the night. I woke from a fitful sleep, as the sun was rising, to find the outer layers of the bag sopping wet from a heavy dew that had fallen during the night. I got up, spread the sleeping bag over the rock wall to dry and then began walking up and down the road continuously, as well as jogging occasionally, to get the blood circulating in my limbs and to try to warm up a bit.

In the light of day I was able to take in the surroundings more clearly. The terrain, in all directions, was flat and empty, with what little vegetation there was consisting of low gorse or shrubs. The yard of Balladonia homestead had a few larger shrubs and two or three small trees near a shed that was some distance from the main house. Somebody had clearly done a relatively recent repair job on at least one part of the roof of the main building. New corrugated iron sheeting covered one end of the house and a verandah over the front door. But the rear two thirds of the building had no roof at all. Wrecked vehicles and other nondescript mechanical junk littered various parts of the yard on either side of the house.

I made myself something to eat...including a cup of tea on my little primus stove, which made me feel much better, then settled down to wait. As the sun rose higher and the temperature climbed slowly, it became comfortable enough to sit down against my pack and read, without feeling cold. There was some movement in and around the buildings behind me. I saw a man come out of the house and do some work in the shed, then a woman, who emptied some garbage in a 44-gallon drum, and went back inside. I waved from my position by the entrance to the yard and then, out of politeness, strolled over the say hello to the man.

It wasn't a very productive conversation.

'Good morning,' I said as I walked up to him.

'Uh huh,' he nodded.

'It was a cold night last night.'

'Uh Huh.'

'Does it get much colder than that? I thought I'd freeze.'

A pause. 'Wouldn't know.'

I too paused. 'I'm making for Adelaide. You been getting much traffic through?'

'Nope.'

'Is it mainly trucks... or cars? Ah... the... er traffic that you do get.'

He'd been bending over, working on the inner tube of a car tire. He looked up at me as if I was stupid. 'Not much of either mate.'

I stood for a few moments, thinking what an arsehole he was... and that he and this place deserved each other.

'Oh...the bloke who gave me the lift out here...the rabbit trapper, said to tell you he'd be back through here this afternoon.'

'Uh huh,' he muttered, still looking down.

I turned and walked away without saying any more. I didn't care if I never saw him again...although I didn't relish the thought, if no vehicles came, of having to go back to him or his woman to ask if they had any food to sell. I began to think, that it would be better for me to go back to Norseman with the rabbit trapper and start from there again.

Fortunately I didn't have to make the decision. Around the middle of the day a Volkswagen van, fitted out as a camper, came trundling down the road from the direction of Norseman and pulled in to the yard to top up with petrol.

There were two men and two women in the vehicle and they were travelling all the way through to Adelaide. After a brief conversation, they agreed to take me along with them.

'There's room in the back...no problem,' the driver of the van smiled. He was tall and thin and looked to be in his late forties. He pointed to the big roof rack on top. 'We've got a tent and we're camping out every night. But you look as though you're prepared for camping too.'

'Sure am,' I replied. 'I can sleep out. Just so long as I can travel along with you during the day, I'll be more than happy.'

The other three passengers were members of the same family. The man's wife, their daughter...aged about thirty and her grandfather (the father of either the tall man or his wife... I'm not sure which) who appeared to be in his mid to late seventies, but hale and hearty and of good spirit and humour.

It was with a great sense of relief that I set off with my new companions from Balladonia. The thought of being stuck there for several more days, with unfriendly people in the house, was not appealing. Now, with the assurance that I could reach Adelaide with one long lift, I felt on top of the world.

The Nullabor plain, once you get down to the serious business of rolling across it, is a pretty impressive place. A vast, basically flat plateau, some 260,000 square kilometres in area, covered in low scrub, saltbush and grass. Although technically its not a desert, for all intents and purposes it could be, as the only water available is from big corrugated iron tanks spaced about 80 kilometres apart along the road, which collect water from occasional rainfalls and the run off from heavy dews. The Nullabor was once a sea bed and has no surface streams. It is, however, honeycombed with large systems of subterranean caverns, several of which have been found to contain aboriginal art as ancient as that in some of the French and Spanish paleolithic caves.

I'm not sure when the caves were actually discovered, or even if they are or were accessible, but at the time of our crossing in 1956, neither I nor my travelling companions knew about them, so we just drove on.

Some 500 kilometres after leaving Balladonia, we made our closest approach to the coastline of the Great Australian Bite at the deserted telegraph station of Eucla. Eucla is the classic stopping off place for all trans-Nullabor travellers because it is so surreal. Here the deserted old sandstone buildings have been all but engulfed by enormous shifting sand dunes. We stopped and walked around the lonely outpost in the glaring heat of the day, wondering about the people who had lived and worked in the isolated little office when the telegraph line across the continent was first opened. It was abandoned early in the century, when newer technologies no longer required a repeater station there at Eucla.

A further 250 kilometres or so took us past White Wells homestead, also long since abandoned with nothing to see, but of some interest on the map because it was at the Head of the Bite... where the Great Australian Bite extends the furthest north into the continent. From this point it was also only about 150 kilometres north to Maralinga, the area of South Australian desert which the Australian government had allocated to Britain for testing its atomic weapons.

Britain had tested its first atom bomb on the Monte Bello Islands, a small group of deserted rocky islets, just off the north west Australian coast, in 1952...with no reaction from the Australian public. In May 1956, they tested a second weapon at Monte Bello and in September of the same year...the month I was hitching across the Nullabor, they began testing nuclear weapons at Maralinga, in a program that saw almost twenty British nuclear weapons detonated there during the 1950's.

Some twenty-two years later, in 1978, amid growing concern that Australia had been deceived as to the extent of the potential dangers of the testing, Australia asked Britain to remove almost 500 grams of deadly plutonium from the site. Six years after that, in 1984, the South Australian premier John Bannon presented tribal elders from the Maralinga region with title to some 76,000 square kilometres of land that had been appropriated from them 30 years previously, for the weapons tests.

Overall, it took us four days of fairly relaxed driving to reach Adelaide. Stopping frequently during the day, and camping out at night, we'd crossed the Nullabor proper in two days, the Eyre Peninsula on our third day, stopping somewhere between Iron Knob and Port Pirie for the night and then driven down through Port Augusta to Adelaide on the final day.

Thanking my new-found benefactors profusely, I said goodbye to them and the VW van in Port Adelaide, to make my way to Henley Beach, where my Great Aunt Else had a small house two streets back from the beach.

Else was what they called a maiden aunt...in other words, she'd never married. According to my parents, she'd had a long-running affair with a sea captain, in the early part of the century, but he had disappeared...or died, or something, after which the right fellow never came along. Else...who was my mother's father's sister, was in her early seventies at this time, having retired several years earlier after a lifetime of working for the Adelaide Advertiser. I'm not sure what her job was at the end of her career, but I know my parents always spoke proudly of the fact that Aunt Else had worked very closely for a long time with one of the icons of early twentieth century Australia, Daisy Bates, during the time she also worked at the Adelaide Advertiser.

Else was over the moon at my arrival. It had been almost five years since I had seen her. I had spent two years of my secondary schooling in Adelaide, when the family had been living there, in 1950 and 1951 and, as we had lived at Grange, which was relatively close to Henley Beach, where I would often swim, I saw Aunt Else quite frequently then. She was effusive in her admiration of the travelling I had done...to the point of my own embarrassment.

'Oh, you have had such wonderful adventures,' she would say. 'And you have been so brave to have been in such dangerous places.'

'They weren't really dangerous places, Auntie, and I certainly didn't have to be brave to go there. Anybody could go there...to Africa and do the same things we did, right now.'

'Oh...tush, you're just being modest. You should be on the radio...they should be writing about you in the paper. I'm going to telephone someone I know at the Advertiser.'

'No, you don't have to do that. Its not necessary.' Unlike the previous occasions when Shorty and I had sought out newspapers to whom we could sell our story, now that I was back in Australia, I felt a little reluctant to do the same thing. Also, the financial imperative had diminished somewhat as, on my arrival at my aunt's place I was given a letter containing a bank draft for fifty pounds that had been sent from London by my parents.

Nevertheless Aunt Else did contact The Advertiser which wrote a small blurb about the home town boy who had 'Hitch-hiked over two continents, worked as Norwegian lumberjack, been stranded in Casablanca, forced to run from an outdoor bed by a prowling lion in Kenya and worked in the Rhodesian copper mines.'

That little write up in the newspaper and meeting up with my Great Aunt were two of the more pleasant aspects of returning to Adelaide. But I had a sad and distressing task to fulfil while staying with Aunt Else.

One of my closest friends, when I was at school at St. Peters College in Adelaide, was a guy called Richard South... everybody called him Dick. He was actually two years older than me but, because he lived nearby at Henley Beach and we were in the same swimming club and used to go to Friday night dances together to get onto the talent from Woodlands and MLC Girls schools, Dick and I became good friends. In fact, he was instrumental in me losing my virginity, in that he told Cynthia Rawling, one of his several girl friends at dancing class one Friday night, in front of me and to my huge embarrassment, that 'Iain has never been all the way with a girl.'

'Really?' Cynthia smiled. 'Perhaps I could do something about that.'

'Yeah!' Dick had laughed enthusiastically. 'Why don't you go home with Iain tonight.'

Cynthia and I had walked down King William road, from the St. Peter's Cathedral hall in North Adelaide, where the dancing class was held, into town to catch the Henley Beach tram. But on the way we made a diversion down into Elder Park, where, by the banks of the River Torrens, in the darkness underneath a large tree, Cynthia had shown me what its all about.

Later, on the tram, Dick had asked how things had gone and Cynthia had smiled and nodded. This had set Dick off...laughing and kidding me loudly about losing my 'cherry'. I was even more embarrassed than before, but Cynthia seemed to take it all with a little smile, not saying anything. She had been sixteen at the time. I was only fourteen.

Anyway, now I was almost twenty one and Dick, at twenty three, was dying...of cancer. A malignant melanoma. He was very blond and had pale skin with quite a number of moles. During his National Service in the Navy, he'd had one of these moles on the side of his chest cut off. Unfortunately it had been a melanoma and not all of it had been removed. It had spread, over a period of two years, to the point where he was now riddled with cancer and had only a month... or less...to live.

I had been unaware of all this until I tried to make contact with him from my Aunt's place and spoke to his parents. They had said that Dick was seeing nobody any more, but that they were sure he would like to see me. He said he would and I arranged to visit him on the afternoon of the third day after my arrival in Adelaide.

He was lying, very pale and thin on a couch in a sunny room at the front of the house, with a light blanket over him. He held a hot water bottle to his stomach.

I searched for words. 'Does that help a bit?...the hot water bottle?'

'Yeah,' he sighed. 'I'm taking all sorts of pain-killers too... morphine, that sort of stuff. But this just makes me feel a bit more comfortable.'

We talked for quite a while about some of the things I'd been doing and seeing in Europe and Africa over the past couple of years. But, though he seemed to take pleasure in hearing of my adventures, I found myself feeling awkward and guilty that I should have had such a fantastic couple of years, while he had been sliding down a long path towards an early death. I found myself playing down some of the things that had happened, not wanting him to feel cheated by life.

I stayed with him for about an hour, at which point his mother came in and said, 'Dick has to have some medication now. I think he also needs some sleep. He gets very tired lately.'

I had explained that I was heading for Melbourne as soon as possible, in the hope of getting a job at the Olympic Games.

'Will you be coming back this way again?' Dick asked.

'After Christmas,' I lied. 'I'm er, coming with a friend from Melbourne. We're going to ...ah... to do some camping on the Eyre Peninsula. I ahh... I could call in and see you then, if its okay.'

'Sure... sure,' Dick said softly. 'I'll see you then.'

And that was it. I shook his hand and walked out of the room. I Said goodbye to his mother, who was in tears...and never saw Dick again. He was dead within three weeks.

I reached Melbourne in two days of good hitching, after saying goodbye to Aunt Else and leaving Adelaide early on October 3rd. Crossing the Mount Lofty Ranges, behind Adelaide, I found the town of Murray Bridge...less than a hundred kilometres away, completely flooded. Days of torrential rain along the New South Wales, Victorian border had swollen the Murray River, so that by the time it reached Murray Bridge, only thirty kilometres from its mouth, the the Murray River had burst its banks and the town was half under water. Skirting around it, I continued down the Dukes Highway through Bordertown, Nhill, Horsham and Ballarat, coming in to Melbourne through Sunshine in the west, on a Thursday evening.

I had reached the goal... well, 95% of the goal that had sat so fixedly in my mind all the while I had been travelling with Noel and with Shorty in Africa. Now all that remained was to get a job at the Olympic Games, which were now only fifty days away.

oooooo

27

THERE MAY BE SOMETHING YOU CAN HELP US WITH

Writing about this now, just before turning eighty-one, I find it pretty amazing that, at the age of twenty one, I should have just assumed, for many months in advance, that I would be able to come back to Australia and, without any real qualifications, step into a job at the Olympic Games. On giving it a little more thought, however, one realises that one of the many deficits in getting older is the tendency to become more cautious about things, to trim back your goals and to think...oh, I wouldn't be able to do that...so there's no use trying. And so you don't try something that might very well have worked out. Of course, there are also times when there are benefits in caution, whether you're young or old, but looking back on it...this wasn't one of them.

I can't help thinking how fortunate I was to be simply filled with a sort of blind optimism, because as things turned out, I did manage to get a job that enabled me to work in the main stadium and at the Olympic pool for the duration of the games. As a consequence, I was able to see virtually all of the track and field and swimming events, but more importantly...to be set on the path towards a career as a journalist.

But first...on my arrival in Melbourne, I made for my grand parents' home in East Malvern. They had moved to Melbourne a few years previously, when my Grandfather (my mother's father), Arthur Adams, had retired from his job as Chief of the Hansard Staff, at Parliament House in Canberra, where he had worked for many years and was known simply as A.P. Having been a journalist and parliamentary reporter for so long, he was understandably enthusiastic about my ambitions to find a journalistic job for the Games...but not particularly optimistic.

'You know, newspapers and press organizations...they generally only take people on who are qualified in some way. With newspapers, you have to go through a long process...many people start just as copy boys. Eventually you can become a graded journalist...you know, C grade, B grade, A grade that sort of thing. But it takes time. And right now, you don't have any real experience.'

'I know that, Papa. I may not have journalistic experience, but I have...well...now, some experience of the world and how things work. And I'm going to try to come in... sort of...sideways. I'm not going to try the newspapers first off. I'm going to go to the wire services... one of the American ones...U.P., United Press...first.'

Although I planned to begin by calling on the people at United Press, I knew there would be plenty of other foreign news services represented in Australia, if not on a permanent basis, then at least for the duration of the games....which I could also try. These were the British news service Reuters; the American wire service The Associated Press (AP); their Australian affiliate, Australian Associated Press (AAP); the American International News Service (INS); and Agence France Presse (AFP). In addition, of course there were scores of other Australian and foreign newspapers that would be represented at the games.

I rang the Sydney number for United Press and discovered that the staff who were coming to Melbourne for the games were not there yet, but were in the process of making the move south in order to start setting up the bureau, well in advance of the Games. The office would occupy several rooms in the Melbourne Cricket Ground itself which was to be the main stadium for the games. I spoke to Eric Riel, the Manager of the Sydney Bureau.

I'd intended, when I rang, only to find out exactly when they'd be in Melbourne and the telephone numbers of the bureau in the stadium, so that I could either just turn up on them, or telephone and come straight in. But he caught me a little on the hop.

'What's it about? Can I help you now, in any way?' he said.

'Well...not right now. Its just that, well...I'd like to come and meet you briefly when you get down here,'

'About what?'

'About a job...about working for United Press during the Games. I'm a photo-journalist (said without a moment's hesitation... and with plenty of conviction)...I've been working in Europe and Africa for the past couple of years and only just returned to Australia last week. I'd like to talk to you about doing some work for U.P.'

'Uh huh. Well, I'm not sure that we're going to have anything to offer you. We've got a lot of guys coming out from the States...as well as from Britain, South America and Asia. There's probably not a lot of room for...'

'Don't make your mind up now...one way or the other,' I said. 'Just give me a few minutes, when you've got the time... after you've settled in down here. I just want to show you some of my work and tell you a bit about myself. Twenty minutes... that's all.'

'Okay,' he said. 'We can do that. Who knows, there's so much stuff we've got to do down there, there may be something you can help us with. Give me a call in Melbourne around the 5th...the 5th of November, that's a Monday.'

I put the phone down, let out a huge whoop and practically did back flips down the hall of my grandparent's house.

'He's going to see me!' I yelled. '...there may be something you can help us with... he said. Wow. That's it!'

'When does he want to see you?' my grandfather asked.

'The 5th of November... that's in about three weeks'.

'And what did he say you could do. What sort of work?'

'Nothing. He didn't say anything about what I could do. He just said there might be something I could do to help them. I mean, really I don't care what I have to do. Anything would be great...working for United Press during the Olympic Games will be...'

'They might have you sweeping the floors, cleaning up the office.'

'That'll be okay too. Anything to start off with. I'm sure I'll be able to get something else going once I get in there.'

During the intervening period before I could meet with Eric Riel, there were several things I wanted to do. One of them was to visit the Melbourne Herald to see if they were interested in a story along the lines of the ones shorty and I had had published in Ireland and Norway...not for money this time, but purely for the publicity. I felt that a little press coverage might be of some help in the interview with United Press, or any other media organization I might be seeing.

The Herald ran a two column story with a big photograph of me with a beard and my pack on my back, under the heading 'World Hiker', with an abbreviated story of some of my African travels with Noel and Shorty. I clipped it and put it aside for later.

I also began to look up some of my own friends in Melbourne... but more importantly, on the 17th of October, I went down to the Port of Melbourne to meet the Arcadia... on which Noel was arriving from Cape Town.

'You know, Bryce and I should have left with you and Shorty, when you came through Luanshya,' Noel said as we sat over a couple of beers in a nearby pub after he'd come ashore. 'We only stayed another six weeks after you, before we took off and headed north also.'

'What made you change your mind?'

'Well, a couple of things began happening there...like strikes and small riots, in a couple of the Copperbelt towns...blacks protesting wages and so on. We talked it over and thought that it was about as good a time as any to say goodbye to Rhodesia.'

'So where did you go?'

'Well,' he laughed. '...we also went up through the Congo, although I don't think we followed exactly the same route you and Shorty took.' He outlined their route which seemed to overlap ours in several parts...and also crossed from the northern Congo into Uganda.

'From Uganda we went into Kenya and spent quite a bit of time in the game reserves. We went back to Amboseli, but also to Masai Mara and Tsavo, where we took some great shots...then down to Malindi on the coast. Its a real paradise. Great diving and spear fishing. From there we went to Mombasa and eventually got a Union Castle ship down to Lourenço Marques, and then overland back to Johannesburg.'

'Thats the reverse of the way Shorty and I had come.'

'Yeah. Then Bryce stayed in Jo'burg... and I think he's gone on to London. I went on down to Durban to check out the surf. I met up with Chookie and Bobby Burdon there and a few of the other guys who knew you and Shorty on the beach.

'So how long did all this take... ?'

'Well, it was September when I left Malindi... and I stayed in Durban until I went down to Capetown to catch the ship home...two weeks ago.'

I told Noel about my hopes of getting a job with U.P. for the games. He too was keen to get some sort of job going, but there was the possibility that the company he had worked for before leaving Australia would re-employ him, so he wanted to check that out first. We also had plans to attend the World Surfing Championships, which were to be held in Australia for the first time, early in the New Year...1957. The championships were of particular significance to Noel and I, as they were to be staged at Torquay, a beach about 100 kilometres to the south of Melbourne, that was one of our old stamping grounds and the site of our old Surf Club.

A few days after Noel's return I celebrated my 21st birthday. Well, it wasn't really much of a celebration. My grandparents had bought a small birthday cake which they presented me that evening at dinner... and which we ate over the next few days. But there was no party. Not that I wanted, or even expected any festivities. I didn't. The last couple of birthdays had come and gone without any hullabaloo...in fact I recall spending my nineteenth birthday on my own, while hitch-hiking in Norway, sleeping in a barn and vomiting all night, as a result of some sort of food poisoning... so this one was pretty good by comparison.

The Games were due to start on November 22..a Monday and would run through until the Closing Ceremony on Saturday, December 8. Normally, of course, the Olympics are held during July or August, in the northern summer. As this was the first time they had been held in the southern hemisphere, it was naturally also the first time the summer games would be held during a northern winter. This initially provoked some protest from northern nations to the effect that their athletes would be disadvantaged...in their training schedules, which would normally bring them to their peak during the northern summer. By the time the games were starting in Melbourne, they would be off their best performances, it was claimed. When it was pointed out that athletes from southern countries had operated under this very same disadvantage for every previous Olympic Games, the protests died away.

In the month prior to the Games, Melbourne and its two million inhabitants were gearing themselves up for the biggest event of their lives. The city had embarked on a beautification program... in which trains, trams and buses, parks and city streets were all cleaned up and given face-lifts, or paint jobs. City buildings were brightened... and work on the 880 buildings in the huge new Olympic Village in the north-eastern suburb of Heidelberg was all but complete. And, of probably greater importance, the State's archaic liquor licensing laws were given a comprehensive workover, in order to avoid international ridicule during the Games. Prior to 1956, Melbourne and all of the State of Victoria, were subject to the notorious six o'clock closing laws, that required all pubs to close at 6.00 pm every evening.

They were Victorian laws in more ways than one and, from a sociological viewpoint, disastrous. Workers, whether white or blue collar, would finish work in the late afternoon and head for the nearest pub to have a few drinks. At around ten minutes before the closing time at six, the barman or barmaid would call, 'last drinks please', and people would invariably order three or four drinks each. The bar would stop serving drinks at 6.00 pm sharp and customers would have to finish their lined-up drinks by 6.15 pm. The result was that people would pour out of the hotel bars three parts sloshed, to stagger home to their wives and families well and truly drunk.

Licensed restaurants, which generally meant up-market restaurants, could serve alcohol with a meal, but there were no small cafés or restaurants where one could simply buy a drink. Fortunately the prospect of derisive criticism from tens of thousands of international visitors for the Games, hastened the demise of the outdated laws.

But there were other, more dramatic international developments that would come into play in the lead up to and during the Games themselves.

Momentous changes were under way in Eastern Europe that would come to a head in the few weeks prior to the games. During the previous year, 1955, Nikita Khruschev had cemented his grip on power in the Soviet Union and had begun to institute more relaxed policies as far as Russia's relations with the communist countries of Eastern Europe. Just a few months previously, in June 1956, in order to demonstrate that Stalin's repressive policies were a thing of the past, Khruschev signed an agreement with Jugoslavia, in effect confirming Jugoslavia's separate path to socialism.

'Socialist development can be different in different countries,' he had said. This statement alone represented an enormous change in policy for the Soviet Union. Also, in an historic address to the Communist Party Congress in Moscow, he severely criticized Stalin and his past excesses...accusing him of the genocide of his own people in the massive and brutal programs of forced collectivization of agriculture, in which an estimated ten million peasants died, in the late 1920's and early 1930's.

The combination of these events and statements by Khruschev opened the floodgates of pent-up criticism and resentment in Eastern Europe against local Stalin-type leaders. The rising tide of unrest and discontent, led by a coalition of workers, intellectuals and students, broke out into active fighting in the streets of Budapest and several other Hungarian cities in the last week of October, 1956...less than a month before the games. As it happened, the Hungarian Olympic team had left Hungary a week or so previously for a round of pre-Games competitions and training in Western Europe...and so were cut off from events in their homeland, a situation which was to have dramatic repercussions in Melbourne.

Coinciding with these sensational events in Hungary, ten Israeli brigades suddenly invaded Egypt on October 29th, advancing rapidly across the Sinai Peninsula towards the Suez Canal, routing the Egyptian forces as they went. England and France, following plans they had secretly developed with Israel, demanded that both Israeli and Egyptian forces withdraw from the Canal Zone, declaring at the same time that they would intervene to enforce a cease-fire called for by the United Nations.

British and French aircraft bombed Port Said on October 31st and, in a combination of parachute and sea-born landings on November 5 and 6, took Port Said and Port Fuad, to begin the occupation of the Canal Zone, while the Israelis consolidated their hold on the Sinai Peninsula.

At the same time, the first phase of the Hungarian Revolution, as it was being called, was over...with what was seen as a victory for the rebels. Imre Nagy, a moderate and independently minded politician, and a long-time supporter of peasants' welfare, became Premier of Hungary. He agreed, in response to popular demand, to establish a multi-party system and call elections. On November 1st, to the anger and outrage of the Soviet Union, he declared Hungary to be a neutral country and appealed for aid and support from the United Nations.

Had the appeal come at any other time, the response from the U.N. might have been different. But with the drama of the Arab/Israeli war occupying it, coupled with British and French preoccupation in Egypt, and U.S. anger at the unilateral moves by France and Britain, the United Nations procrastinated and delayed support for the Nagy government in Hungary. Taking advantage of this lack of response, Khruschev ordered Soviet troops and tanks into Hungary on November 4th, to overthrow the Nagy regime and begin a massive and brutal repression of the revolution in which thousands of people, including Nagy himself, would die.

With these events unfolding in Europe and the Middle East, all of Melbourne...as well as Australia and the world, had been watching with baited breath. What would President Dwight Eisenhower and his Secretary of State, John Foster Dulles do about Britain and France's military intervention in Egypt? Both were reportedly furious over the affair. Would the United States step in to aid the embryonic democracy in Hungary and defy the Soviet Union? Would the world be plunged into World War III? But more important than that...to me at least... was the question: would the Games be cancelled?

The atmosphere in Melbourne was electric. There had been isolated calls for the Games to be cancelled and at least five nations pulled out during those hectic three weeks before they eventually got underway.

Sunday, November 4th, 1956: Soviet troops Invade Hungary.

Monday, November 5th, 1956 (dawn): British and French troops invade Egypt.

Monday, November 5th (11.00 am) Iain's interview with Eric Riel of United Press.

....I mean, lets get all this into the right perspective!

'So what do you think you can do for us?' Eric Riel was sitting behind a makeshift desk in what seemed like a concrete bunker in the bowels of the Melbourne Cricket Ground...the soon to be Olympic Stadium. The place looked as if a bomb had hit it. Workmen were installing cabinets, desks and electronic equipment, as well as several teleprinter machines along one wall.

Riel was tall, dark haired and good-looking, in a film-star sort of way. In fact, the easiest way to describe him to a film-goer might be to say that he looked and sounded like Ephram Zimbalist Junior. Of course you have to be of a certain age to know who Ephram Zimbalist Junior is, or was. And if you've never seen 77 Sunset Strip, then there's not much point. Anyway, he spoke in a deep voice, with an American accent, although he wasn't American.

As I learned later, he was born in Tientsin, China in 1922 and was fluent in English, French, German, Russian and Mandarin. He joined UP in Shanghai in 1948 in the last days of the Chinese Civil War and was transferred to Sydney at that time. In any event, he had a pleasant and friendly, though somewhat serious demeanour.

'What can I do for you?...well, that's a little difficult for me to say,' I replied, '...when I don't know how your operation is going to work and what sort of things you are going to want to get done. But I'm willing to....'

'So what sort of work have you been doing?'

'I've been travelling a lot...I think I mentioned to you that I'd spent a year or so in Africa... ahh...' (pushing a couple of newspaper cuttings onto his desk) '...these are a couple of press clippings about that aspect of it...and I've been working...um...mainly on a free-lance basis for...well, a couple of small newspapers in Rhodesia...The Daily News in Ndola and the Lusaka Times. And also... ah...the Natal Mercury, in Durban. I did some photographic work for them.' (Lies, lies, lies, but... I thought... its going to be difficult for him to check up on any of them. And in the meantime...)

'Hmm. Freelance work?...reporting? writing?'

'Uh huh, that's right.' I was starting to get a little worried. I wasn't going to be able to follow this too far. He could trip me up at any moment. I could sense that he really didn't believe that I had much...if any...journalistic experience. He'd only have to start asking specifics and I'd be done. But, I began to feel as if he almost didn't care.

'Okay,' he sighed, '...maybe all this isn't too important for what we might be wanting you to do...'

My heart took a little jump. At least they needed something done.

'When can you start?'

'Whenever you like...today. Right now.'

'Good. Okay, come with me. I'll show you how this place is going to work and we'll try and figure out some things for you to do.'

He led me into a large room, which, for want of a better word, was going to be the nerve centre of the United Press operations during the Games. It was about ten metres square with a large table in the centre. There were three or four small rooms off to the sides.

'A lot of this won't concern you...but we like everybody to know who's who and what's happening, so there's a minimum of foulups when things start to get hectic.'

I nodded confidently.

'We're going to have a number of journalists who'll be reporting from the stadium here, as well as from the different venues for our various international services...in different languages: English, Spanish, Japanese, for example. The main one...or rather, the biggest one, is our English language service, based in New York. Everything from here has to go to New York first, before its disseminated to the rest of the world on our wire service. So all the reports and stories from the various sites will come in here first...to this table.' He gestured to the big, rectangular wooden table in the centre of the main room. 'this is where everything will be checked and edited, before going straight to the teleprinter operators, who'll be sitting at those machines along the wall there... Spanish and Japanese operators will be on other machines in the rooms to the side.'

We walked into the other rooms, where more electricians were busily running wiring along walls and connecting up several other teleprinter machines.

'These machines will have Spanish language operators and they'll be connected directly to Madrid...but also, for our South American service, direct to Buenos Aires. The Japanese ones, in the other room have a direct line to Tokyo.

'What about French and German services?' I asked.

'Its all a matter of coverage. UP has English language services into Paris and Bonn, but, Agence France Presse and the German service more or less have the business sewn up in their own languages.'

He turned and half sat on the edge of a desk. 'But all that is not so important from your point of view at the moment. You'll start to pick up on that sort of thing after a while. For the time being the most important thing for you to get into your head, if you're going to work for us, is that time means everything. Time. A few minutes can make all the difference between whether a newspaper will use our story or our competitor's. There are hundreds...no, thousands of newspapers around the world who take our service, but there's a great many of them that also take competitive services...like Associated Press, Reuters, International News Service, Agence France Presse. We're all competing. And if the first Bulletin on a story comes through on our machine, the chances are the editor will follow up, by using the UP story as it keeps coming through, even though a competitor may be sending their version through only a few minutes later.'

I nodded again. It was all fascinating stuff, but I still couldn't see where I was going to fit in.

'Now...' he looked to one side and briefly worked his bottom lip with the fingers of his left hand... thinking. 'We think we've got all of the events in the main stadium, the swimming and the majority of other venues covered...not perfectly, but as best we can. What we don't have any coverage of...and where we think you could fit in, is out at the Olympic Village. We need someone to keep an eye on what's happening out there. The teams will all be arriving over the next week or so. I think you could be of real help to us, by just being out there the whole time, scouting around, keeping your ear to the ground, picking up on little stories that emerge out there, rather than at the actual events.'

'Great!' I felt elated that, at last he'd spelt out a job description for me. 'I'll take my camera along and shoot anything that looks worthwhile.'

'Uh huh. Good idea. I'm not sure that there'll be a great demand for photo coverage from the village. We'll have processing and wire photo facilities ready by the time the Games begin, but its just as well to be prepared, so...yeah, take your camera out there.'

He slid off the table. 'So lets go and get you signed up and accredited.' He smiled... 'Good to have you aboard.'

ooooooo

28

MY FIRST SCOOP

I generally think of this as my first job as a journalist, although I have to admit, in the strictest sense of the word, I wasn't actually writing anything that was ending up in print. I would patrol the Olympic Village, go frequently to the Village Press Centre, pick up the handouts, talk to people, ask questions, follow up on little leads about various athletes, telephone several times a day to Eric with what I thought might be news-worthy tidbits and then report in personally at the end of the day, to the bureau in the main stadium.

I remember, for example, witnessing the arrival of some of the Russian team members at the village and being astonished to see the centrepiece of their basketball team...a nine-foot (2.76 meter)-tall giant... as he clambered out of the bus. (In the end he couldn't stop the U.S. from winning Gold in the basketball)

The Japanese team arrived and brought several of their own cars with them... attracting some attention in the press. They were Toyota Toyopet Crown deluxe models of which the Melbourne Herald said:

'Japanese cars are something of a curiosity in Melbourne...' the article went on to describe some of the cars' features and interior fittings. It explained that the vehicles had come in with the Japanese team, but considered it likely that 'some will to be imported for sale in Australia before long.'

As the days went by and the village started to fill up, the whole atmosphere began to become more and more dynamic and stimulating. The Village itself was quite incredible and arguably the best facility, up until that time, at any Olympics. It consisted of almost 900 houses and town houses that would later be taken over by the Victorian Housing Commission and either leased or sold to the general public. During the Games, the Village provided some 6,000 beds, as well as some 20,000 meals a day for athletes and officials.

I was generally out in the Village to cover the arrival of most of the teams...particularly the more important ones, like the Soviet Union, The United States, Germany, Britain, France, Japan etc. And for each team arrival there was always a flag-raising ceremony, attended by the whole team for that particular country, as well as a number of Australian and International Olympic officials. For most of the ceremonies, my report to Eric Riel on the phone was fairly standard and probably rated no space whatsoever on the UP wire. You could have had the same few paragraphs with just the nationality changed:

'The Star-spangled Banner rang out over Melbourne's Olympic Village today as a welcoming band played the U.S. national anthem and the Stars and Stripes were raised, in what American athletes are hoping will be just the first of many airings for "Old Glory". About 200 of the 440 total U.S. competitors lined up at the flag-raising ceremony to hear a brief welcoming speech by...etc. etc.'

Pretty straightforward stuff. In fact, to be truthful, most of the other journalists, had become bored after the first few ceremonies and didn't bother turning up for every ceremony. After all, they were all basically the same routine. But there was one of the flag-raising ceremonies to come that turned out to be anything but routine. One which...it could be argued, changed the course of my life.

As I've mentioned, the Hungarian Olympic team had left Hungary just prior to the Revolution and, like most of the Communist teams...whether from the Soviet Union, Eastern Europe, or China... it had been set up with several political minders on board. These minders, who in some cases doubled as coaches, but often had no other obvious task, were, in effect, political commissars who came along simply to ensure that were no embarrassing deviations from the Party line, no public exhibition of dissatisfaction with Communist rule at home and, most importantly, no defections. And they had plenty of power and leverage, in that the majority of athletes had left families and loved ones back in their homeland.

But, during the period after the Hungarian team had left Hungary, the Revolution had turned everything upside down. Many of the old Communist Party Officials back home had been thrown out, a new democratic government had come in. In other words, the power base of the political minders on the team had simply fallen apart. Suddenly they had no base at all...their authority was nil. At least for the period of time before Soviet troops eventually crushed the revolution.

While making its way to Australia, the team was apparently in turmoil. There were fights between team members and officials of opposing political views. There were defections even before the team arrived in Australia and it was complicated by the fact that it arrived in two parts...sixty on Saturday, November 10 and a further ninety or so on the following Monday. The first contingent was greeted by hundreds of local Hungarian Australians, wearing black armbands, and holding Hungarian flags draped in black crepe in protest to the Soviet invasion of their country.

Enormous tensions were apparently developing within the team, but for a time they managed to maintain an impression of unity and of being no different from any of the other teams. But their flag-raising ceremony at the Village was to burst the whole thing wide open.

Having been present at most of the other ceremonies, I turned up for this one twenty minutes or so in advance, somehow expecting it to be different, or newsworthy in some way, but not knowing how.

What later emerged was that the leader of the Hungarian team, who was with the second contingent, which had not yet arrived in Melbourne, had sent a message from Darwin to the Australian organizing officials saying that they did not wish the current Hungarian flag to be raised in the village. This was a red, white and green horizontally striped flag which carried a communist emblem, in the centre. A different flag, with the crest of a 19th century Hungarian patriot, Louis Kossuth, should be raised.

Australian officials had evidently obtained one of these flags from the local Hungarian community and were on their way to the welcoming ceremony, when the whole procedure was dramatically short-circuited.

There were other journalists there... more than the usual number, but not enough to give the impression that something out of the ordinary might be going to happen. As it turned out, they were all newspaper journalists. For some reason there was nobody there from any of the other wire services...at least none of the English language services.

A few minutes before the officials had arrived for the ceremony, a group of Hungarian team members, along with twenty or so local Hungarians, began assembling at the base of the flagpole and suddenly, with great flourish and animation, took a Hungarian communist flag and, with a knife, slashed the emblem...which consisted of a hammer, an ear of wheat and a red star... from the centre of the flag, leaving a gaping hole.

Amazed, I had stepped quickly forward and begun taking photographs.

They then hauled it up the flag pole to exultant cheering and slogan shouting in Hungarian and English:

'Down with the Communist flag! Long live free Hungary!'

People were yelling. Other Hungarian team members, presumably communist officials, were altercating with those team members and locals who had hauled the flag up. Then the Australian officials arrived with their flag. More vigorous and loud discussions.

Chaos reigned for several minutes. For a short while the Australian officials seemed stunned and unsure of what to do. I continued taking photographs for only a minute or so, debating whether I should go and try to talk to some of the athletes and officials. Then I thought of Eric Riel's words, '... a few minutes can make all the difference...' and I rushed to a telephone.

I breathlessly told him what had happened.

'Okay, okay. Great,' he said. 'Now, just calm down and tell me, from the beginning, everything that went on.'

Taking it all down in shorthand, he stopped me only a couple of times to ask things like what sort of uniforms were they wearing, what colour, how many were there, etc. When I had told him everything, I said, 'Do you want me to go back and start getting quotes from them? I've got lots of photographs too.'

'Photographs?'

'Yep... of everything.'

'Great! Great. Okay... look... go back there and see if you can get a few quotes, but don't spend more than five minutes or so at it. Just a couple of names of the main people...and then get a cab as quickly as you can back to the bureau here with that film. We'll get it processed and on the wire as soon as possible.'

Back at the ceremony, the holed communist flag was hauled down and the Free Hungary flag, which carried a long diagonal black stripe of mourning across it, was eventually hoisted up the flagpole to replace the damaged one and things began to calm down.

As things turned out, that little story…simple and complete in itself though it was, was, I suppose, my first scoop. With no other wire service at the scene, Eric had got the story off to New York within minutes, from where it was on the outward wire to the rest of the world, a few minutes later. It turned up on the teleprinters of Melbourne and other Australian newspapers, who subscribed to U.P., in some cases well before their own journalists had filed the story.

My roll of film was processed and the photographs put on the wire well ahead of any of the pictures of the other photographers at the scene.

'We like what you did out there,' Eric said a couple of days later. 'You did a good job…worked quickly. That's what we need.'

I had come into the bureau at the end of another day to report the various happenings at the Village. Everything was comparatively quiet now and I felt pretty sure nothing quite like the Hungarian flag-raising was likely to happen again. But one could never be sure and, with the Opening Ceremony and the beginning of the Games getting nearer, Eric wanted me to keep as close an eye on events at the Village as I had for the past two weeks.

'But when the Games start,' he said, 'We've got a new job for you. At least…we'll see how it works out. Anyway, come and meet a couple of the other people who'll be running the show here.'

I knew these would be the U.P. staffers who'd been due to arrive from New York. The bureau itself had changed considerably over the week or so since I'd first seen it. Everything was in working order now. The teleprinters were up and running, with several of them manned by operators both male and female. There were filing cabinets and desks covered with paper. The big table in the centre of the main room also had sheets of paper over one end of it… as well as a large, but half-empty bottle of scotch whisky at the other end. A slim, grey-haired man with small rimless glasses, who looked to be in his fifties, drained a cut-crystal glass of its contents and put it down empty beside the bottle. Pale-skinned, he wore a white business shirt, open at the collar, with his tie loosened slightly. He wore coloured braces a-la-Larry King... predating Larry's style by about forty years.

'Hi, you must be 'Eye-an' (Americans can never pronounce Iain or Ian). 'Sure like what you did the other day. Keep it up.' He clamped a half-smoked cigar back in his mouth.

'This is Leo...Leo Petersen,' Eric introduced me and I shook Leo's hand. 'Leo is one of our Vice Presidents, from New York...as well as Editor-in-Chief, in charge of all our Olympic coverage. Everything that comes in passes over this table, before it goes on the wire and either Leo, or Bob Miller...sometimes myself, will check it out and edit it, if necessary, first.'

I wondered about the bottle of scotch...whether that would remain a fixture on the table throughout the games.

'Hi Iain, I'm Bob...Bob Miller.' A smiling, dark-haired man, sporting a colourful Hawaiian shirt, had come over to the table. He was about 1.7 meters tall, also with glasses and probably in his mid-forties. 'I've just come down from Sydney. How're you getting on? Eric tells me you're goin' great guns.'

'Well, I hope so. I'm really enjoying it anyway.'

'Good... good. I'm sure there's going to be plenty for you to do.'

'Bob's the Australian Bureau Chief in Sydney,' Eric explained. I would later learn that Miller had been a celebrated war correspondent during World War II, in Europe, the Middle East and Asia, as well as in Korea during the Korean War.

'Where's Oscar?' Eric asked.

'He's out in town at the moment,' Miller replied. 'He'll be back soon.'

'That's Oscar Fraley,' Eric said to me '...he's our senior sports writer. You'll meet him a little later. He's going to be doing a lot of the stuff here in the Main Stadium...all the Athletics. They'll be running for eight days, from the day after the opening, until the 1st of December. I want you to meet him because I think you'll be able to work in here... that is, out in the stadium, with him. Anyway, he'll be able to tell you more about what he wants when you meet him.'

'So, you won't want me working out in the Village once the Games start?' I'd been prepared, from the beginning, for the possibility of my role being confined to the Olympic Village, although the prospect didn't appeal to me very much. It was clear that, once the Games got underway, it'd be much more interesting in here.

'No. I'm sure there'll be more productive work for you in here. You can switch from the Village to here on the Thursday...the Opening Ceremony. '

'Great. That's fine by me.'

My memory of Oscar Fraley's statistics, such as height and build are a bit hazy, but I recall him being probably in his early forties. He had sandy hair...was reasonably good-looking, with more of a suntan than Leo, but with a similar propensity for scotch and cigars... and cigarettes. I was impressed by him. He was a hot-shot journalist, who, when under pressure, worked in the most convincing and professional way. During the two and a half weeks of the Games, I only saw him and the rest of the UP team during working hours. I was much too junior and insignificant an employee to have anything to do with their social life, which I'm sure was pretty hectic. But my recollections of him and Leo Petersen were of the classic mould of hard-drinking, hard-playing, but also hard-working journalists who really delivered the goods.

There was no indication at that stage, that Oscar Fraley was destined for fame and fortune from the sales of his first book...a book he was presumably writing at that time, or at least a bit before, as it was published in 1957. That book, plus sales of film and TV rights, plus royalties from the long-running TV series that came from it, would make him a multi-millionaire. The book, and the 'sixties television series and a more recent film, were called The Untouchables...the story of the racket-busting Chicago cop, Elliot Ness. He went on to write and publish more than thirty books.

The Opening Ceremony was the only event of Day One of the Olympics; Thursday November 22.

There was not much for me to do on that opening day, except watch the proceedings. Oscar and Eric had written various prepared stories that were ready to go with the ceremony. So, as the day's events were all planned and known to the media in advance, unless something dramatic and unexpected happened, the stories could almost stand as they were, without much changing.

I knew, however, that things would be very different from the following day and I was excited about my new role. The way U.P. had arranged their set up in the stadium, Oscar Fraley would be up in the stands with his binoculars, a schedule of events and a telephone headset and microphone which stayed open and connected to the bunker down below. He wasn't connected to Leo or Eric, but to a typist, who sat at a regular typewriter. Watching the various athletic events occurring at any one time in the stadium, Oscar would dictate stories down the phone to the typist in paragraphs of not more than three or four lines at a time. The typist would rip out the page, after those three or four lines, almost toss it over his or her shoulder to a waiting hand, which would poste-haste lay it in front of Leo Petersen. Leo would scan it quickly, scribble some changes...or, as was often the case with Oscar's copy, just leave it as it was and hand it to another minion who would place it in front of a teleprinter operator, who was linked directly to New York...and it would be there in seconds. A similar routine was being followed, with different reporters and editors, for the Spanish and Japanese services.

All this was pretty impressive to a novice like myself, but what I found quite incredible was the way Oscar dictated his stuff. He could dictate a story, without writing it down beforehand, in exactly the way a newspaper would end up printing it. The first short 'grabby' paragraph containing the important and relevant information, plus a bit of colour, followed by successive paragraphs which filled out the details of the event, other competitors, past records broken etc. along with more colour. And he'd move from event to event, sometimes having to come back to pick up where he'd left off from an event which had been running for some time...such as the long jump or high jump, while other track events were being held at the same time.

Where I fitted in was simply to provide the quotes. Under normal circumstances...that is without me, or someone else there to provide them, Oscar would have no way of incorporating the quotes of the medal winners into his stories. My job was to watch and wait for each event to be finalized and then to attend the press conference for every medal winner and make notes of their comments, with particular emphasis on the words of the Gold Medal winners. I would then rush up to Oscar's position in the stands, tell him what was said, listen in awe as he translated them into his journalese, over the phone to a typist below, then rush off to another press conference... and so on.

In between, of course, I had an unbeatable view of the Athletics, plus the amazing experience of seeing and listening to the medal winners at close quarters. With my press accreditation, I could go virtually anywhere...even onto the field on occasions, to specific media locations. And I was getting paid for it! Sometimes I had to pinch myself to believe it was all happening.

Track and Field at the 1956 Olympics turned out to be an American walkover. The U.S. cleaned up fifteen gold medals out of twenty four events in the men's competition, with not a single gold for Australia. The women's' events were different however, with Australia winning four gold medals out of nine track and field contests...the U.S. taking only one, in the high jump. The bright little 18-year-old blonde, Betty Cuthbert won Gold in both the 100 and 200 meters...both of which events had been captured by another great Australian sprinter, Marjorie Jackson, at the 1952 Helsinki Games. Shirley Strickland won her second Olympic gold for the eighty meter hurdles and Australian women took out the four by 100-meter relay.

I have to admit though, that from my point of view, I was too busy to get caught up in any really nationalistic fervour during the eight days of track and field events. I was mainly running around getting whatever quotes and any other information I could glean on the (mainly American) gold medal winners.

Of course, apart from the international tension created by the Anglo-French invasion of Egypt and the Soviet invasion of Hungary, which were still filling the newspapers' front pages, there was the hostility that had been growing steadily during the 'fifties between the Soviet Union and the United States, in what was now being termed the Cold War. At that time it was little more than six years old.

The power of East Germany as a sporting nation was yet to emerge, as both East and West German athletes competed (uneasily) in one team until the 1968 games in Mexico City. So the battle for medals in Melbourne turned into a U.S. versus Soviet Union competition. The Games were unfortunately reinforcing a relatively new concept that winning at the Olympics was of profound ideological importance in the overall struggle between East and West.

During the last four afternoons of the Track and Field events in the

Main Stadium, the swimming events were starting up at the nearby Olympic Park pool. These were largely elimination heats, but, as there were no night events at the Main Stadium, I was able to go over to the pool in the evenings with Oscar and Eric to get the feel of how the swimming events would be held. Once the Track and Field finished, we would be focussing most of our attention here at the pool. Once again, Oscar would be hooked up with a telephone headset so he could deliver his spiel down the line to the bunker in the main stadium, where Leo would be waiting, with his bottle of scotch at his side, to check and edit whatever came through. As for me...I was to do basically the same as I did for the athletic events, chase up quotes from the Gold Medal winners.

The pool itself was quite something... with huge glass windows at either end and seating for some 5,500 people. And now...it was my turn to experience a bit of nationalistic fervour, if not quite hysteria. Because, as the swimming got under way it was clear that Australia was going to clean up...winning five of the seven gold medals for men and three of the six for women.

Looking at the men's swimming events in the Olympics now...and those that were held in 1956, its amazing to me that, by comparison, there were so few then. For example, there was no 200-meter freestyle race...no 100-meter butterfly, or breast-stroke events, nor was there a 200-meter backstroke event. And there were no 200 or 400-meter individual medley races, or 4 x 100-meter freestyle and medley relay events.

The same was true of the women's swimming races, with virtually the same races missing from their 1956 line up as in the men's events... except that, oddly, the women had a 4 x 100-meter freestyle relay, while the men did not.

None of this was an issue at the time, however...certainly not with me. I revelled in the fact that I could not only watch Australian swimmers keep winning gold, but could be at the press conferences to hear, first hand, what they had to say. To begin with, when I went into my first press conference, back in the athletics stadium, to hear Bobby Morrow talk about his 100-meter and 200-meter wins, all I did was listen to what the other journalists asked. I would busily write the answers down on my little note pad and scuttle up to give them to Oscar, but as the games progressed and I'd been to most of the press conferences...there were often questions that I'd like to have heard answered that nobody had asked...so, from the back of the room, I started asking them.

I remember feeling a bit nervous and thinking of myself as a something of a ring-in amongst these other obviously professional journalists, but the feeling quickly wore off when I started to think, I've got as much right as they have to ask questions. I'm just doing my job. Not that anybody said anything to me that was critical or questioning. It was simply a small personal hurdle I overcame...a little milestone.

Anyway, the swimming was fantastic. The incredible Murray Rose...only 17 years old at the time, taking both the 400-meter and 1500-meter gold medals and breaking, in training swims just before the Games, the eighteen-minute barrier for the 1500-meters for the first time. Then repeating it in the heats... and again in the final. I remember the huge wave of applause...a prolonged, standing ovation that engulfed the swimming stadium, when his time of 17 minutes, 58.9 seconds came up on the board. Strange to think of that now, in the light of subsequent swimmers who have successively broken the 17 minute, 16 minute and 15 minute barriers, bringing the record down to (at the time of writing) around 14 minutes 30 seconds.

Then there were Australia's two great champion women swimmers Dawn Frazer...the first woman to break the 60 second barrier for the 100 meters freestyle, taking gold for the event in world record time, with Lorraine Crapp second. And then Lorraine Crapp winning the 400-meters, with Dawn Frazer second. Both the men's and women's' freestyle relay teams also won gold. In fact, Australia won every freestyle event, both male and female, at the 1956 Olympics.

If it had all stopped there...if Eric Riel had said, 'Thanks very much Iain, you've done a great job, but we can handle it from here on...' and he'd paid me off, I could hardly have complained. I'd had an unbelievable time, seen thrilling and extraordinary events at close quarters and more importantly, started to gain something of an understanding of how the media works. Fortunately he didn't and there was still one more remarkable experience to come in the swimming stadium... the finals of the Water Polo.

It was almost as if fate had dictated it. With preposterous irony, the elimination process had narrowed it down to Hungary and the Soviet Union to play in the semi-final for the Olympic Silver medal Medal. With scenes of bloodshed in the streets of Budapest and Soviet tanks crushing all independence in Hungary, filling the newspapers for the past weeks, any Olympic spirit that might have been there before, went out the window for this match. The feelings of acrimony, loathing and contempt that now existed between the two teams was unmistakable as they took to the water.

It was as fierce and violent as a water polo match could be. There were plenty of penalties...but, the referee was at something of a disadvantage in dealing with a contest of this nature. Water polo being what it is, there are things that can go on beneath the water, that are not visible to the referee and, in unattributable comments reported after the match, it would seem that the Hungarians had determined to attack the Russians in every way possible.

Apparently they grabbed at their opponents' testicles, causing agonising pain. Punches were thrown by both sides. Blood was flowing from cuts on several of the players. The match was called off at half-time. But the game had to go to someone. So, with Hungary leading 2-0, they went through to the final, to play Jugoslavia the following day... and won.

The semi-final had hardly been won with sportsmanlike tactics, but the Hungarians felt... and said as much, that there had been little evidence of sportsmanship in the way the Soviets had crushed their homeland in the preceding weeks.

Fortunately the closing ceremony of the Melbourne Games did something to regain the higher principles of the Olympics after such a bitter grudge match towards the end of the Games had highlighted enmity and animosity between teams. At the suggestion of a young Australian Chinese man, John Wing, for the first time all the athletes of the various national teams entered the stadium all together, not as teams...symbolising friendship and the brotherhood of nations, rather than autonomy and separateness.

I watched much of the closing ceremony from the stands with

Oscar and Eric. As with the opening ceremony, most of the story work had been preplanned and pre-written by Oscar, Eric, Bob Miller and Leo Petersen. I was already redundant...as far as the Games were concerned. But just two days previously, at the time I'd been thinking that... if it all stopped now, I'd still be happy, Eric had walked up to me in the swimming stadium.

'I've been talking it over with Bob. We're very happy with the way you've worked here and we'd like you to come up and work with us in Sydney, when the Games are over.'

'With United Press, in Sydney?'

He smiled... 'Yep. How do you feel about that?'

'Great. Just great.'

So now, the games were over. My goal of returning to Australia and working at the Olympics...a goal that had been set so long ago, had been reached and fulfilled. The long-term obsession that had dictated most of my actions over the past eighteen months, had been satisfied. A job with United Press. Good...good. A step forward. Where it would lead I had no idea. But, as John Lennon said, quite a few years later, 'Life is what happens to you when you're busy making other plans'. And my next few years fell very definitely into that category... life being totally different from my plans.

oooooo

WHAT NOW?

(A SORT OF EPILOGUE)

Of course it depends on whether we're talking about the 'now' at the end of the journeys just related, or the 'now' of the present day... 2016, as I'm putting the last touches and updates to this little story, sixty years after it all happened.

The second option is a pretty easy one, because at 81, lets face it, I'm on the way out. Nothing dramatic... but, at this stage it could be bye-byes at virtually any time and to be honest, that's the way I want to go. So, for the moment, we're talking about the 'now' of December 1956.

To a certain extent, there's also an element of philosophy that comes into it at this stage, because, on reading it all through, in the process of bringing the story all together, I came realise that the story is really about a coming of age...or a right of passage, if you like, of three young men, including myself, as they moved into adulthood.

I think it also illustrates, perhaps only in the broader sense, the sort of message I have tried to pass on to my children and grand-children...the crucial concept of choices. That the choices one makes now and, actually, at any stage in life, can dramatically influence and alter the path your life will follow.

I'm not sure if I was fully aware of this overarching concept of life, when I was at the stage described at the end of the book narrative, because from then on things got well and truly off track for a while.

My broad plans then had been to work with UP, but leave Australia again to travel, within a year or so, to the United States, to meet up there with Lise. Or alternatively to meet up with her in Australia and move on from there.

But, within little more than six months of starting with UP in Sydney, I would be working as a labourer, pouring concrete on Townsville airport, then carving faces in coconuts for a living in Northern Queensland. Before the year was out I would be unexpectedly married and, early in the next year, the father of a son. In the four years that followed, I found work as a car washer, airline traffic officer and camera salesman...and gained an officer's commission in the New South Wales Scottish Regiment.

I travelled, in 1962, to Singapore and on to Saigon...well before the Vietnam War, then to Hong Kong where, I would at last find my way back onto the path of being a journalist. For three years there, after being joined by my family, I slipped into the the role of producer and presenter of a nightly current affairs radio program on the English Service of Radio Hong Kong. There I would meet and interview such people as Richard Nixon, the Beatles, Marlon Brando, William Holden, Judy Garland, Louis Armstrong and Dave Brubeck, amongst a host of others. But at the same time I became involved in a prolonged love affair leading to a traumatic and distressing marriage breakup and divorce...and departure for the United States and Canada.

From Canada, while working as a reporter on a nightly current affairs program, I travelled to the Dominican Republic on assignment to find myself caught up, on one occasion, in a revolutionary fire-fight in which five people died around us.

Based in New York for eighteen months, I studied film and TV production, as well as working, on a free-lance basis, for the BBC and the Australian Broadcasting Commission (ABC).

Back in Australia, in 1967, by this time with a daughter and another son, I joined a nightly television program, *This Day Tonight*, to work as a reporter. In the early 1970s, based in Singapore, I worked as a foreign correspondent for the ABC, covering the Viet Nam War and the Indo-Pakistan War, as well as seemingly endless other events in Asia. A three-year stint in Sydney followed, hosting...first a nightly radio program and then the ABC TV program I had previously worked on as a reporter.

In 1976, twenty years after the African journeys described above, I left Australia, with my wife Trish and two children, to travel to South Africa on an assignment for the ABC. The planned series of four TV programs, which I researched there over several weeks, fell through because of the huge anti-apartheid riots that year, which broke out in Soweto Township, outside of Johannesburg...riots that were subsequently brutally suppressed by the Government. However, this disruption to our plans led us, as a family, to set off from Capetown, heading for Cairo, with plans to replicate much of the journeys...and to cover a good deal of the ground I had been over with Noel and Shorty in 1955 and 1956. That journey, using only public transport and even, on several occasions, hitch-hiking, led to a book, jointly-authored with Trish: *Africa Overland* and a successful adventure novel I wrote, set in South Africa: *The Azanian Assignment.*

Two more major journeys with our children followed, in 1978 from Canada, overland to Tierra Del Fuego at the tip of South America...and then, in 1980, across the South Pacific, in small boats, from Chile to Australia, via Easter Island, Polynesia, the Cook Islands, Samoa, Tonga, Fiji and Vanuatu. And two more jointly written books came from these journeys: *South America Overland* and *Across the South Pacific.*

In Australia again, I returned to work for three years with the ABC, once more as a reporter... on a TV science program, *Towards 2000.* This led to participation in the founding, in 1985 and part-ownership of an independently produced commercial TV science program called *Beyond 2000,* which ran for ten years until 1995, eventually airing in over 100 countries.

In the years since then, Trish and I have travelled extensively in China, as well as East and Central Asia, worked as volunteers for an Australian aid agency in Hanoi, with the English service of The Voice of Viet Nam Radio, built a road and drainage system to three remote villages in northern Laos, as well as a primary school for one of the villages. We are currently investigating the possibilities of helping villagers in the same district set up several efficient pig-farming arrangements as cash crop ventures for their communities.

But all that is another story.

The people who gave me that first job and with whom I worked at the '56 Games, Eric Riel, Oscar Fraley, Bob Miller and Leo Petersen are understandably all dead...of heart attacks or strokes or cancer. Its sixty years ago and they were in their 'forties or more at the time.

But, more importantly...

WHAT'S HAPPENED TO:

Noel,

Noel is still around. He's 82 at the moment and hanging in there. A few problems...a pacemaker, prostate...but nothing really serious affecting him at the moment. He has lived virtually his whole life in the United States.

Since our travels in Africa together, there was a brief period back in Australia, during 1957, after the Olympic Games, when he and I shared an apartment in Sydney. He was working as a photographer with the Sydney Morning Herald, while I was working with United Press. But as he had a good deal more money than I, saved up from his work on the mines, so he decided to take off, early in that year, with a couple of other surfers from Sydney, for the U.S.

He had a successful life in the States on the sales side in big American corporations, like IBM and Xerox, as well as in his own company. He has travelled widely over the years, in Europe and Asia and returned to Australia frequently...but never to live.

He lives on Puget Sound, south of Seattle with his third wife, Judy. He has two children, from his first marriage and four grand-children.

Bryce,

Bryce died in Canberra in 2012 of cancer at the age of 79. The reader may recall his comments to Noel and I (chapter 15) about spending the first third of his life making money, the second third travelling and having a family and the last third writing...writing books.

The real life fractions might not have been so clearly defined as he described them as a young man, but in general, that's what happened with his life.

After coming to Australia in pursuit of a talented young woman called Benita, whom he met in London, he built an extremely successful career in advertising, both as an executive in well-known companies and in one of his own.

He started writing...or at least published his first book, *The Power of One* in 1989. It has sold more than 8 million copies, has been translated into 18 languages and been made into a movie. It was the first of 21 successful novels for Bryce. He had three sons from his first marriage and lived with his second wife, Christine, until his death.

His tombstone, in the small cemetery near the rural village of Hall, about thirty kilometres from Canberra, simply reads:

In Memory of
Bryce Courtenay
1934 to 2012
Writer and Story-Teller
'This is what happened'
'You done good'

The quotes are the first words of *The Power of One* and the last words of his final novel, *Jack of Diamonds*.

Shorty

Shorty died of prostate cancer in South Africa, in November, 2009, aged 73, at Humansdorp Hospital. Humansdorp is not far inland from the international surfing mecca, Jeffreys Bay, or J-Bay as its known to surfers, on the coast of the Eastern Cape Province, where Shorty had become one of South Africa's surfing legends.

In 1957, after we had parted ways in Norway, Shorty worked in London briefly and then, in 1959, introduced surfing to the English Channel Island of Jersey. He was a founder of the Jersey Surfboard Club that year and returned to the island in 1999 to celebrate the club's fortieth anniversary.

After his return to South Africa from Europe, he succumbed to a few conventions...taking a job as an appliance rep and marrying a dancer, Rose, with whom he raised three children.

But, he was one of a few of the early surf pioneers, who finally turned their backs on business suits and city life and moved off in search of the perfect wave. In the late 1980s, with his children grown, he packed up everything and moved with his wife to J-Bay to 'live the dream' and, as he said, 'surf one of the fastest right-hand breaks in the world'.

He took a job managing the Salt Rock Lodge Guest House there, in return for a roof over his head. He earned additional income by forming a company that took foreigners to remote and little-known surfing breaks and, in the last few years, since his wife Rose died, and as his own health declined, he lived on a government pension.

But as one of his oldest friends said, 'Shorty lived the life many people want to live, but are afraid to',

On November 28, 2009, close to a hundred surfers paddled their boards out beyond the break at J-Bay and scattered Shorty's ashes in the surf.

Lise

For me this is the saddest part to write...not because of Lise's death. She may well be still alive. The sad part is that I don't know... and I have found it virtually impossible to find out.

I did learn, in 1973, when I visited her home with my wife and our own two young children, then 5 and 6 years old, that Lise was married and living...I think it was in Sandefjord, a town to the south of Oslo.

There was a sense of slight unease on her mother's part, I think, about me returning some 17 years after my relationship with her daughter, to do what...renew the relationship? That wasn't the reason. It was simply something friendly and loving to do. Anyway, the message was there that her mother was reluctant to pass on additional information, so that's how it was left.

And so the years went by.

Now, I am 81 and Lise would be at least 80, if she were alive. and here I am, unexpectedly moved by deep and uncontrollable emotions about a lost love and lives that have been lived separately, with no knowledge, one of the other.

Not that I really wish things had worked out that Lise and I should have followed through on the plans we made as 20-year-olds. Trish is the love of my life and has been for the fifty-plus years we've been together. She is all of the things that Lise was to me back in the mid-1950s ...and much, much more.

But, I have tried through various genealogy websites and sites for Norwegian Births, Deaths and Marriages, as well as Census information, to track down Lise...without success. The process has been complicated by the fact that I haven't known her married name and Norwegian privacy laws which prevent publication of information about births and marriages after certain dates in the 1930s. Death information is available up to the present, but Lise does not get a mention in those lists.

So why should I have suddenly been so upset and distressed by something that has not affected my emotions so deeply for all these decades? I have to admit...its this book! Writing up all these stories of the past and the overwhelming feelings of nostalgia that they bring to the surface have had a profound effect on my feelings about life and death.

I have to say, though, that its only these last bits of catch-up material and the introspection they bring on that have had this effect. The overall impact of the book on me, as I've worked through the old original material, has been one of real joy and...wonder at the experiences and adventures Noel and I and Shorty went through in those far off days. But, more than anything, I've felt a sense of immense gratitude and great privilege at having had the opportunities to live them.

ooooo

Read about other titles by
Iain Finlay:
The Azanian Assignment
Savage Jungle

By Iain Finlay and Trish Clark:
*Africa Overland
*South America Overland
*Across the South Pacific
Good Morning Hanoi
The Silk Train

Titles marked with an asterisk were originally
published under Trish's previous name,
Trish Sheppard.

More details below
Also visit
<highadventureproductions.com>

THE AZANIAN ASSIGNMENT

Iain Finlay

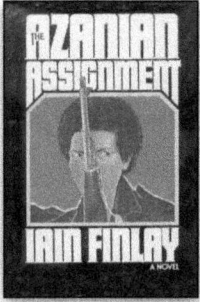

Banned in South Africa on its first release in 1978, this fast-paced, fictional drama stands the test of time as an engrossing thriller set against real-life situations in eastern and southern Africa at the time. Set in Apartheid-era South Africa, in what was then a few years in the future (1981), this is a political intrigue adventure novel, which predicts the downfall of the apartheid system, albeit more than a decade earlier than when it actually occurred and more violently than the real event.

The mysterious hi-jacking in Johannesburg of a plane reportedly carrying a secret gold shipment to Europe, sees Tony Bartlett, the East African correspondent for a London newspaper, flying south to a small town in Tanzania where the hijacked plane is reported to have landed. Escaping a murder attempt on the TanZam Railway, and directed by his editor to continue following up the story in South Africa, Tony finds himself simultaneously swept into the opposing worlds of the country's right-wing extremists and the underground revolutionary movement of the Azanian People's Army.

Nelson Mandela is still in prison on Robben Island, but elaborate plans are underway to release him and other leaders of the African National Congress (ANC). The apartheid regime faces military and diplomatic pressure from all sides, both within the country, from neighbouring African states, and the major powers.

Meeting and moving among real politicians and diplomats of the time. as well as running afoul of BOSS, the dreaded Bureau Of State Security, Tony becomes intimately involved with Ingrid, a beautful, but dangerous Afrikaaner political extremist. The connection leads him to uncover a vast conspiracy that will drastically affect the country's future, whichever side wins the looming battle.

(Available from Amazon...a New edition in 2017)

447

SAVAGE JUNGLE

Iain Finlay

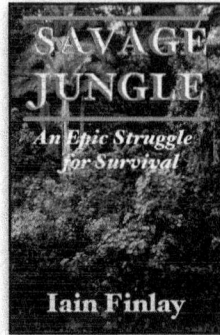

This is a story of courage and endurance...

...and of one man's grim determination to survive against all the odds. Arthur Shephard had just turned twenty-four when his depleted battalion was placed in the path of the Japanese Army, as it drove down through Malaya in January 1942.

Incredibly, the Australian force stopped the Japanese in their tracks, in one of the great battles of the Malayan campaign. But the Japanese were only temporarily halted.

Arthur's survival in the jungle for three-and-a-half years...nevert captured by the Japanese... constantly on the run, fighting battles, ot only with the eenemy, but against starvation and a succession of deadly diseases , which claimed his companions one by one, is one of the most amazing stories to come out of World War II.

This is the story of Arthur Shephard's survival, as told from his diaries and from recordings made with him before his death in 1984. So it is a true story, a slice of history. It is also an incredible adventure through dark and dangerous times.

"Arthur Shephard epitomised the Australian 'digger' of past legendary status and set the standard for subsequent generations - he should never be forgotten. Lest we forget".

Brian Vickery OAM
Lieutenant Colonel (Retired)

(Available now from amazon.com eBook + Kindle versions available 2017)

TRAVELING WITH CHILDREN:

THREE BOOKS

By

IAIN FINLAY & TRISH CLARK

THREE INCREDIBLE ADVENTURES

Africa Overland
South America Overland
Across The South Pacific

You'd love to travel to remote and exotic places but...you have kids. So? Why let that stop you? You're worried about their education...think you should wait. Don't!

Iain and Trish didn't. They made three big journeys through some of the toughest territories in Africa, North and South America and the South Pacific with their two young children. Using public transport; buses, trains, trucks, trading vessels, sometimes hitching, each of them shouldering their own backpack, they spent months at a time on the road.

Spread over a period of just on four years, during the 1970's, their travels took them first from Capetown to Cairo. Eighteen months later they journeyed overland from Canada to Tierra del Fuego, at the bottom tip of South America and within another year and a half, they island hopped across the South Pacific from Chile to Australia.

Not only did they survive to write the books, which also look at the history, politics and way of life of the countries through which they traveled, but, with the passing of the years they have come to realise how much their travel adventures truly sealed an on-going adult friendship with their children.

Africa Overland is the first in the series. The following hard copy illustrated titles will be available during 2017/2018. Digital eBook versions available shortly after.)

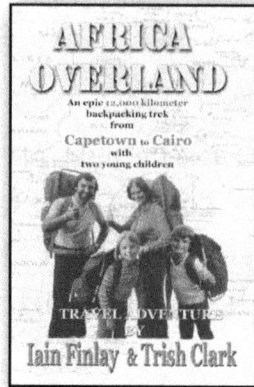

AFRICA OVERLAND

Iain Finlay & Trish Clark

Capetown to Cairo! A magical phrase...the journey of a lifetime.Around 12,000 kilometres, nine countries, four months on the road with nothing booked or arranged in advance. With their two children; a son aged eight and daughter nine, carrying their own back-packs and often sleeping in rough circumstances (like in the back of a truck laden with copper ingots), Iain, Trish and the kids get to see: Kruger National Park, Victoria Falls and travel on the TanZam railway. They experience the vast herds of game in Serengeti, Lake Manyara, Ngorongoro Crater and Amboseli, go to the source of the Blue Nile in Ethiopia, travel on 'Kitchener's Railway' across the Nubian Desert from Khartoum to Wadi Halfa, Aswan and the great temples of the Nile Valley... all the way down to Cairo and the Pyramids.

(Original 1977 edition available from Amazon

New edition + eBook version available late 2017)

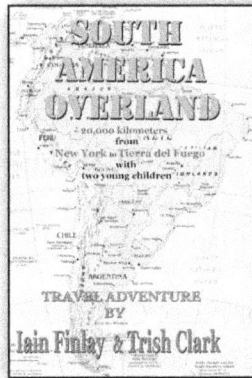

SOUTH AMERICA OVERLAND

Iain Finlay & Trish Clark

This amazing journey includes much more than just South America. It starts in Canada as Iain, Trish, their ten-year-old son and daughter, aged eleven, set out in a blizzard that covers most of the US, to deliver a car cross-country to San Diego. Then they travel by train and bus through Mexico, Belize, Guatamala, El Salvador, Honduras, Nicaragua and Costa Rica to Panama. Along the way they visit the great Aztec and Mayan temples of Tenochtitlan, Palenque, Tikal and many others.

Then on to Ecuador and Peru, where they puzzle over the mysterious lines in the Nazca Desert and visit the fabled Lost City of the Incas at Machu Picchu. Across the Andes, on the Amazon headwaters, at Pucallpa and down-river, they find barges, ferryboats and a trading boat for a 3,000-kilometer, month-long journey down the Amazon to Iquitos and Manaus.

On through the Matto Grosso to Bazilia, Rio and Sao Paulo, Iguasu Falls, Montevideo and Buenos Aires, before hitching for much of the way south through Patagonia to the amazing glaciers of southern Argentina, the Magellan Straits and Tierra del Fuego. Here they reach the southernmost city in the world, Ushuaia, Six months, 17 countries, 23,000 kilometres:

(Original 1980 edition available from Amazon

New edition + eBook version available early 2018)

ACROSS THE SOUTH PACIFIC

Iain Finlay & Trish Clark

Leaving Santiago, Chile after a frightening night of earth tremors, Iain, Trish and their two children, now 12 and 13 years old, fly to Easter Island, where, using their own tents, they camp out in remote corners of the island as they explore the huge, enigmatic stone monoliths. From there, its Tahiti and the stunning beauty of Bora Bora, Morea and the unbelievable Tuamotu atolls.   In the Cook Islands they board a copra trading vessel for a journey through the island chain; Aitutaki, Rakahanga and Manihiki. When it breaks down, mid-ocean, they go overboard with the crew to swim in water 3,000 metres deep. American and Western Samoa are next, in the midst of a typhoon. Then the pleasures and beauty of Tonga, the Fiji Islands, Vanuatu and New Caledonia, before finally returning to their home in Australia. The message about travelling with your kids is: do it before their teens. By then its too late. Iain & Trish only just made it.

(Original 1981 edition available from Amazon
New edition + eBook version available mid 2018)

GOOD MORNING HANOI

Iain Finlay & Trish Clark

When Iain Finlay and Trish Clark arrive in Hanoi on an 18-month work assignment for the English language service of the communist government-run radio network, they can hardly foresee the intense and exceptional experiences that await them. Coming to Vietnam for an Australian aid agency, their intended role is to coach and instruct, or at least to share their knowledge, with a small group of young reporters. But they find that they learn more than they teach.

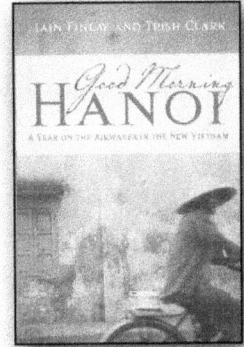

As friendships with their colleagues grow, Iain and Trish are involved in developing and presenting a daily radio program - the first run by Westerners on a regular basis - and they become immersed in the stimulating life of one of Asia's most enchanting cities. In the process, they gain fascinating insights into Vietnamese society and culture, as well as a greater understanding and respect for the new Vietnam.

Good Morning Hanoi also illuminates the lives of a group of people dwelling in crowded conditions around a small courtyard in central Hanoi where Iain and Trish find a house to rent, and who become like an extended family living in the heart of the city.

In Good Morning Hanoi, Iain and Trish, two of the founders and producers of the international television program Beyond 2000, return to a country from which they had reported during the Vietnam War. They find an extraordinarily friendly people whose resilience and irrepressible good nature enable them to put the past behind them and move into the future with confidence.

(Illustrated hard copy version available now from <www.amazon.com> Kindle + eBook versions in 2017)

THE SILK TRAIN

Iain Finlay & Trish Clark

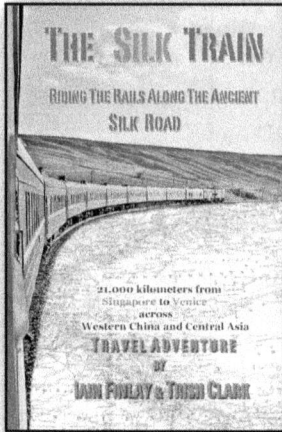

The Silk Train is travel adventure with a geo-political backbone. Veteran journalists Iain Finlay and Trish Clark set out to travel 21,000 kilometres from Singapore to Venice, by hopping on and off trains up through South East Asia, across China, Central Asia, the Caucasus, Turkey and the Balkans. Much of their route covers territory along which the ancient Silk Road trails wound their way over the past two thousand years. They planned to use rail lines that form part of an embryonic, UN-backed Trans-Asian Railway network, that will eventually create unbroken freight and passenger corridors all the way from China's far-eastern seaboard, to Europe.

While visiting some of the great historic sites of China and Central Asia, among them: Xi'an, Dunhaung, Samarkand and Bukhara, they also become aware of the changing dynamics of Big-Power politics across the vast Central Asian steppes, once the stamping grounds of Genghis Khan and Tamerlane, which now include the newly independent countries of Kazakhstan, Kyrgyzstan and Uzbekistan. They very quickly realise that, by far the most important items of trade along the modern equivalents of the Silk Road, are now oil and natural gas. Oil is the new silk. It is the new trans-national currency of the Silk Road, with China and its voracious, seemingly insatiable appetite for energy, emerging as the most significant factor in the political and economic arena of Central and South East Asia.

Further west, Russia's increased pressure on the Caucasus, particularly Georgia, is just another indication of how vital the world's dwindling energy resources are and will remain for most of the twenty-first century. By journey's end, in Venice, they realise they have travelled a very different Silk Road than that of Marco Polo.

(Illustrated hard copy version available now from:<www.amazon.com>
Kindle + eBook versions in 2017)

Highadventurepublishing.com
and
Highadventureproductions.com
are part of
High Adventure Productions
PO Box 111
Tumbulgum, NSW 2490
email: iaintrish@mac.com
AUSTRALIA

455

www.ingramcontent.com/pod-product-compliance
Lightning Source LLC
Chambersburg PA
CBHW080548090426
42735CB00016B/3181